THE AMERICAN ALPINE JOURNAL

1983

THE AMERICAN ALPINE CLUB
NEW YORK

THE AMERICAN ALPINE JOURNAL

VOLUME 25   •   ISSUE 57   •   1983

C O N T E N T S

COVER PHOTO: Mount Everest Group from Pumori.
Photo by Ned Gillette

ISSN 0065-6925
ISBN 0-930410-21-1

Manufactured in the United States of America

*Articles and notes submitted for publication
and other communications relating to*

THE AMERICAN ALPINE JOURNAL
should be sent to

THE AMERICAN ALPINE CLUB
113 EAST 90th STREET
NEW YORK, NEW YORK 10028 USA

Once Around Everest

NED GILLETTE

EVEREST, the "third pole", is still the ultimate lodestone for most mountaineers. While climbers are seeking new ways to gain the summit, Jan Reynolds and I decided to put a different twist into our expedition to the world's highest peak. We tackled it horizontally instead of vertically, thus becoming the first to circle Everest. The Mount Everest Grand Circle Expedition was a new way of looking at an old subject. It was the Camel Expedition of 1981/1982.

Traditionally, mountaineering teams are tied to one Base Camp. But we were free, like mountain gypsies, to rummage through the most magnificent terrain on earth, always on the go at elevations above 17,000 feet. And we had the chance to immerse ourselves in two exotic cultures—Tibet and Nepal.

Our trip was broken into two halves: the first in Nepal during the winter, the second in Tibet in the spring. The reason for this is that the border is closed, and Everest stands astride the two countries. Our orbit, put together like two halves of a clamshell, took four months and covered 300 miles (including the approaches to and exits from Everest). Jim Bridwell, Steve McKinney, Craig Calonica and Rick Barker supplied expertise during different segments.

As a classy way to touch the border and begin the Nepal leg, we climbed Pumori, a 23,442-foot pyramid just west of Everest. In the Himalayan winter, jet stream winds descend onto the tops of the highest peaks. "To survive in winter in the prevailing conditions above 8,000 meters is a hazardous game, to climb in them nobly treads the borderline between will-power and insanity." (*Mountain, #72*). Considering ourselves more adventurous than insane, the reasonable height of Pumori well suited us. The ascent, led by Bridwell, followed a new line to 22,000 feet. It was moderate but sustained in difficulty, with steps up to 80°, and was located several hundred meters to the right of the major icefall on the east face. The original ascent route was then followed from the northeast ridge to the summit.

We failed on the first attempt at the northeast ridge. We thought we were in a race with the coming winter storm season which ordinarily hits at Christmas, so dashed up the route with little acclimatization and minimal food. One camp was established at 21,000 feet. The mountain was in perfect condition—hard snow, accepting ice, and bare rock. Although the price for climbing in the winter is cold and wind, there are compensations. Little of the year's precipitation arrives, lessening avalanche danger substantially.

Photo by Ned Gillette

**At 20,900 feet on PUMORI.
Changtse and the West Ridge of
Everest in the background.**

It was difficult to discover from "authorities", whether local or foreign, if this winter was a benign oddball. Polish and British Everest expeditions experienced devastating conditions in the winters of 1979-80 and 1980-81. The fact is that the winter of 1981-82 saw no major storms from mid-November to January 23. Virtually every day was climable at elevations below 7,300 meters. Above, we could only guess. For a month we watched Everest across the Khumbu from Pumori. Although it was often crowned with severe lenticular clouds, there appeared to be enough reasonable days for the summit, even well into January. The conclusion must be that a *good* winter presents viable climbing.

Meanwhile, back at Base Camp, Christmas was a bit sullen. We had let Pumori go without a good fight. Our second assault of seven days, featuring smarter and tougher climbers, saw Camp II placed on the northeast ridge at 22,000 feet, and the summit reached on January 6, 1982 by Bridwell, Reynolds and myself. To the north, Tibet looked like a defoliated Nevada. High winds and extreme cold dictated a rather brief sojourn. Custom one-piece climbing suits designed by The North Face and made of Goretex and Thinsulate worked nicely. This was the first major winter ascent by Americans in the Himalaya.

Thirty hours after the mountain was cleared, the lower route was swept by a colossal avalanche of collapsed ice séracs. The ensuing silence was broken by Jim's gentle summary, "Well, that's luck."

At this point most expeditions head home, but we now climbed over three passes of nearly 20,000 feet (Mingbo La, West Col, Sherpani Col) to swing around to Makalu on the east side of Everest and finish the first half circle. Miraculously, the weather still held. Original plans had called for skiing this section, but no new snow had fallen for the past two months and glacier surfaces were rock hard. We simply strapped on crampons and tramped across.

At Makalu our luck deserted us. The weather broke. Hopes of relief evaporated when our hard-working Sherpas failed to meet us. Civilization stood five storm-riddled days to the south, and the trek out, without food, added another episode to the high-altitude crash diet plan. Logical a path may be when laid out from lowland to mountain, but this sensibility escapes the traveller that first chooses to follow it in reverse. Clues were submerged in deep snow, calling for clever sleuthing. Neanderthal camping was the order of the hour as we elected to sleep in caves under giant boulders in order to build fires.

In April and May we were back at the circumnavigation (fondly referred to as the circumskition). Negotiations with the Chinese Mountaineering Association were remarkably easier than during our foray to China in the summer of 1980. Then it took nine days in three separate cities; this time, one-half day in Beijing. (Incidentally, indulging in benign political skullduggery, we purposely neglected to tell either Nepal or China about the entire circle until after completion of the expedition. They both were most delighted in the concept.)

Exploits in Tibet were fascinating rather than dangerous. Culturally, the treasures of this forbidden kingdom were finally opening to foreigners, even though there have been great changes since the Chinese occupation of 1950.

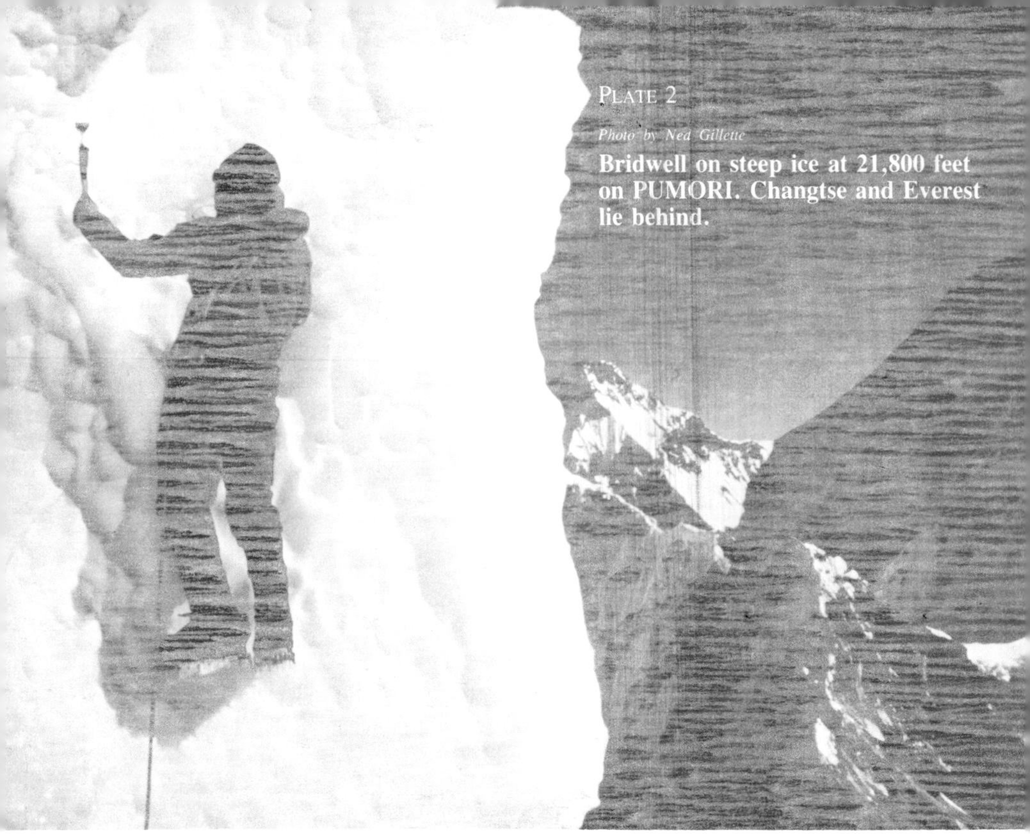

PLATE 2

Photo by Ned Gillette

Bridwell on steep ice at 21,800 feet on PUMORI. Changtse and Everest lie behind.

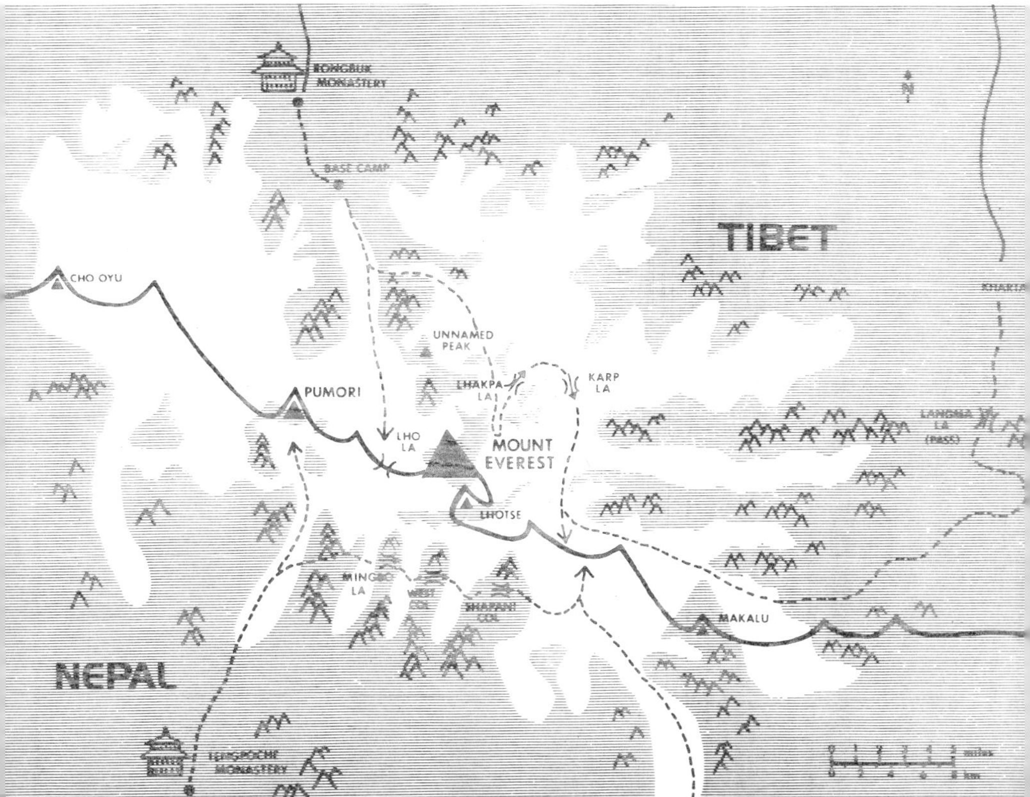

RONGBUK MONASTERY

BASE CAMP

TIBET

CHO OYU

KHARTA

UNNAMED PEAK

PUMORI

LHAKPA LA

KARP LA

LANGMA LA (PASS)

LHO LA

MOUNT EVEREST

LHOTSE

MINGBO LA

WEST COL

SHARPU COL

MAKALU

NEPAL

TENGBOCHE MONASTERY

miles

km

To a large extent the old Buddhist civilization is disappearing before our very eyes. But there are oases. For instance, Lhasa's Jo-Khang temple, some 1300 years old, has been reopened to pilgrims. Inside, it was overpowering. We were immersed in fumes of butter candles and endless deep chanting. Here was the essence of Tibetan Buddhism, which is a combination of their ancient belief in shamanism and blood sacrifice, Tantric magic and sexual rites, and the attainment of Nirvana through the help of enlightened Buddhas. The air was loaded with religious fervor, and we left exhausted.

Historically, our mountaineering route around the northern flank of Everest had much in common with the original 1921 British reconnaissance. That expedition searched for the most practical route up the Tibetan side of Everest. We would travel much of the same terrain.

This connection with the past was made all the more dramatic when members of Chris Bonington's team (in to climb the east-northeast ridge) discovered inscribed stones near the Rongbuk Base Camp. They were pieces of a memorial erected nearly 60 years ago, and since destroyed by Tibetans. It commemorated those who died on the first three British Everest expeditions of 1921, 1922 and 1924—and especially the tragic climb of 1924 when Mallory and Irving vanished with no trace.

Not all whose footsteps we echoed were afforded the luxuries of vast support teams. Facing the necessity of surveying north of the subcontinent, the British ingeniously trained Indians of the intellectual class to penetrate and map closed lands. These Pundits, disguised as pilgrims, counted measured paces with the aid of rosaries numbering only an even 100 beads and stored statistics on scraps of paper concealed in prayer wheels. On foot, alone, with little money and facing great danger of arrest and execution, their journeys covered thousands of miles and lasted up to four years. Pundit Hari Ram, coded #9 or MH, completed a half circumambulation of Everest in 1871 by travelling from Darjeeling to Kathmandu in a wide arc north through Tibet.

Mr. Ram most certainly did not stray into Tibet's glacier terrain, so leaving a pioneering ski effort to us. (C.M.A. wrote in response to our request to ski-trek: "According to material we get, the ice-skating or skiing cannot be conducted at the Rongbuk Glacier. Please consider your itinerary.") Confident, we stayed our course, and on May 2 skied at a leisurely pace up to the Lho La and the border, to the west of Everest. Looking across at nearby Pumori and down into Nepal meant the circle was finally closing. Our shouted toasts of "vodka, vodka," went unanswered from the Russian Base Camp 2000 feet below. With scant trace of any Shangri-La powder, we negotiated a squibbled descent on cross country skis.

Now we swung around to the east of Everest by trekking up the East Rongbuk Glacier (climbing a lovely unnamed, unclimbed peak along the way, then finding more skiing in the upper basin), then over the Lhakpa La and Karp La, and into the unsurpassed pristine beauty of the Kangshung Glacier valley. We had seen Everest from all sides, and turned for home with a deep and intimate affection—a reverence—for the highest mountain.

Photo by Ned Gillette

Descending from PUMORI. The Khumbu Icefall is below.

The simple fact that we felt compelled to concoct such an extraordinary approach to Everest is in itself a comment on adventure in the 1980s. You can no longer be the first to climb the highest peaks or the first to explore blank spots on the map. Unsanforized, our planet looks appallingly small in comparison to our view of it at the turn of the century when it lay unwashed of a good deal of human accomplishment. Then explorers, heroically self-sufficient, still faced the terror of the unknown.

In an increasingly shrinking and competitive world, style is the essential ingredient of adventuring: taking new approaches to old subjects. There is still plenty left to do; we just have to use our imagination more since the old frontiers gave out.

Lindbergh started us off on this new adventurism in 1927 by dropping in on Paris. Plenty of people had crossed the Atlantic, but none with such dramatic boldness. Alone, yet married to modern mechanical genius, he forever reduced the world to comprehensible, conquerable proportions.

Today, mankind can jump into its machines and charge through the densest jungle or dive the deepest ocean. The systems of society distance self-sufficiency. But there is still a yearning to leave our signature upon a deed by our own skill, persistence and strength. We already know that we can fly over it or wheel through it, given a big enough support team.

The realities of the 1980s, in which there remain no true geographical explorations as once known, demand that adventure be contrived and maybe a bit strange if one is to leave new footsteps. The rules of the game are chosen by the players. It is by these rules of relative self-sufficiency that validity is acknowledged, brilliance praised. To be worthy, a challenge is often set back in time, excluding the use of mechanical assistance to better square the odds. But the final mark of success is returning better friends, as we did on the Mount Everest Grand Circle.

Summary of Statistics:

AREA: Nepal and Tibet around Mount Everest.

FIRST WINTER ASCENT: Pumori, 7145 meters, 23,442 feet, via new route, East Face to Northeast Ridge, January 6, 1982 (Bridwell, Gillette, Reynolds).

CIRCUMAMBULATION OF MOUNT EVEREST: Nepalese Section, December 1981 and January 1982; Tibetan Section April and May 1982.

PERSONNEL: Ned Gillette, Jan Reynolds, James Bridwell, Stephen McKinney, Craig Colonica, Richard Barker.

The Great Couloir on Everest

JAMES WICKWIRE

WITH THE DECISION of the People's Republic of China in 1979 to open its autonomous regions, including Tibet, to non-Chinese mountaineers, new opportunities to climb Mount Everest were presented. A few months later, Chris Kerrebrock, a strong, young climber from New York City, initiated an Everest application with the Chinese Mountaineering Association. Lou Whittaker became the leader of a small nucleus of Rainier guides that included Kerrebrock, Phil Ershler, Marty Hoey, Eric Simonson and George Dunn.

When Whittaker and the others received word from the CMA that permission for a post-monsoon 1982 attempt had been granted, I was asked to join this elated group of Pacific Northwest climbers. Later, other Rainier guides were added: Dan Boyd, Larry Nielson, Joe Horiskey, Tracy Roberts and Gary Isaacs. Ed Hixson, the U.S. Nordic cross-country ski team physician, was selected as the expedition's doctor. Dave Mahre, with whom I climbed extensively in the 1960s, at 54 became our oldest member. Nawang Gombu, the first person to have climbed Everest twice, came from Darjeeling. Finally, Dick Bass, a ski-resort developer, and Frank Wells, a motion-picture executive, joined the team.

As a tune-up for the challenge of an unclimbed route on the North Face of Everest, Kerrebrock and I decided to go to McKinley in the spring of 1981. Our objective was a new route up the mammoth Wickersham Wall, climbed only twice previously. Before we could reach the base of the Wickersham, however, disaster struck. Pulling a heavily loaded sled between us, Chris Kerrebrock suddenly plummeted into a hidden crevasse. We were too close together for me to brake the fall, and the sled and I fell in with Chris. He was wedged tightly in an 18-inch-wide slit between the glassy walls of ice. Despite a broken left shoulder, I managed to inch my way up 30 feet to the surface and out of the crevasse. I was safe but, after several hours of effort on Jümars in the crevasse, I was unable to free Chris from his icy trap. He died of hypothermia about nine hours after the accident.

In a state of considerable anguish and guilt, I spent two weeks alone on the Peters Glacier before Doug Geeting made an unprecedented landing on the

PLATE 4

Photo by James Wickwire

**MOUNT EVEREST from the north.
Camp IV = 23,700 feet; Camp V
= 25,000 feet; Camp VI = 26,500
feet. X = Accident at 26,200 feet.
HP = High Point at 27,500 feet**

upper glacier to retrieve me. Avalanches, storms, extremely little food, my shoulder injury, and exposure to other crevasses as I worked my way back up the glacier all combined to make this the most trying ordeal of over twenty years of active climbing.

For weeks afterward, I was tormented by questions about whether to climb again. During this time, Everest receded into the background. Gradually, though, the desire to climb returned, and with it, the ambition to tackle Everest. On a trip to Beijing that fall to negotiate the protocol agreement with the CMA, I told Lou Whittaker that I would go. We were successful in persuading the Chinese to allow us to come in the pre-monsoon season, a time we believed would provide more optimum conditions on the route.

We left Seattle on March 9 with great expectations. With Steve Marts' inclusion as cinematographer, there were 17 of us. We would have preferred a smaller team, but as we planned to do all of our own load carrying from Base Camp to the mountain, we felt the larger numbers were justified.

As the key element of our intended route, we chose the most striking feature on Everest's North Face—the Great Couloir or Norton Couloir as it is sometimes called. At the very head of the Central Rongbuk Glacier, we would climb in an arc ascending from near the slopes below the North Col, up across the broad 40° to 45° face to the base of the Great Couloir at 25,000 feet. Once in the couloir, we would climb to its head, onto the Yellow Band, through a still higher Gray Band, then to the summit. Our intended route and that of Reinhold Messner on his phenomenal solo climb of Everest from the north in 1980 would most likely coincide above 27,000 feet. A significant difference, however, was that Messner on his monsoon-season ascent had been able to climb on a mantle of snow covering the rock bands and filling the small gullies of the upper face. We expected more difficult climbing due to the lack of snow.

Lhasa was disappointing. Over thirty years of Chinese occupation and control had removed much of the mystery and romance of this remote Tibetan capital. Nonetheless, interspersed between conditioning hikes up the hillside behind our government-operated rest house, we were fascinated by the fabled Potala Palace, home of ten Dalai Lamas, and the Jokhang Temple where Tibetans came in great numbers to pray. The small, cast-iron bed of the 14th Dalai Lama in the Potala was still made, presumably to await his return.

In what has become in two short years a standard approach to Everest from the Tibetan side, we journeyed to near the base of the mountain in a combined fleet of jeeps, trucks and, for part of the way, a minibus. Despite having flown directly to Lhasa at 12,300 feet, we soon adjusted to the increasing altitude without the usual assortment of headaches and minor altitude sickness. A severe sinus condition plagued me, aggravated as the result of the dusty three-day ride across the Tibetan plateau. It was not until we reached 17,000 feet that I could breathe normally.

At the road's end, on a gravel bed overlying the Rongbuk Glacier, we caught up with Chris Bonington's Everest expedition. Although only six in number, Bonington's team planned to tackle the difficult northeast ridge rising above the Rapiu La. At 27,510 feet, this ridge terminated in the Northeast Shoulder still some 1700 yards and 1500 vertical feet from the summit. Using alpine-style tactics, Bonington, Peter Boardman, Joe Tasker and Dick Renshaw, with two companions in support, were taking on a very big project. Stimulated by our supply of hot buttered rum, the two expeditions enjoyed a festive evening together before we separated.

The weather remained clear and cold for most of the first month following our arrival at Base Camp (16,900 feet) on March 21. While our three CMA personnel took up residence there, the five tons of gear we brought were carried by yaks to an Advanced Base Camp (18,400 feet), about six miles from the mountain. We spent three weeks carrying loads up the debris-strewn glacier to Camp I (18,800 feet) and Camp II (20,300 feet), at the foot of the massive north face. Rest days were few and far between, and we all felt like pack animals before we had completed this laborious process.

On April 8 the real climbing began. Rather than taking a direct route up the face with an unacceptable level of avalanche hazard from a large ice cliff at 24,000 feet, we opted for a less direct approach that took us up alongside an icefall beneath the steep flanks of Changtse, Everest's close neighbor to the north. Slightly above 22,000 feet, we established Camp III on the north face proper. The campsite was at the base of a sérac that offered protection from snow avalanches off the face above.

A weather pattern of high winds and daily snowstorms slowed progress. But after four consecutive days of effort, on April 18 Ershler, Hoey, Boyd and I succeeded in establishing a route to Camp IV (23,700 feet). An unlikely-appearing snow mushroom was the only feasible campsite. Hours of shoveling produced two small platforms that barely accommodated our two tents. Above, the slope eased somewhat. Bypassing the prominent ice cliff in mid-face, we pushed the route on May 1 to a rocky moat at the base of the Great Couloir (25,000 feet). Camp VI was the most sheltered; an overhanging rock wall formed a natural roof.

Several attempts were made to establish Camp VI high in the Great Couloir. A lead pair of Dunn and Simonson covered most of the distance; Ershler and Boyd, hampered by the latter's temporary intestinal sickness, went a bit higher but still had not located a campsite. Finally, on May 15, Hoey, Nielson and I, who formed the first summit team, along with Mahre who was in support, made the climb up the hard snow and occasional patch of ice in the couloir.

While Nielson and Mahre searched for a campsite at 26,300 feet, Hoey and I waited 200 feet below in the couloir on the only rock of any size. At 5:30 P.M., as I started to carry a section of rope to the lead pair, Hoey fell suddenly and without warning from the fixed rope. I yelled "Grab the rope!" Sliding head-first, she rolled to her side and made a valiant try, but was not able to grasp the fixed rope. She was visible only for the first few hundred feet of the fall, disappearing into the mist and cloud that clung to the face. I was certain

PLATE 6

Dan Boyd at 24,000 feet on EVEREST. The Central Rongbuk Glacier lies below.

PLATE 5

Marty Hoey at 24,000 feet on EVEREST. The First and Second Steps are seen at the upper right.

she had fallen 6000 feet down the entire face. In utter disbelief, I looked at the anchor. Marty's waist harness and Jümar were still attached to the fixed rope. Somehow, the buckle had suddenly unfastened when she leaned back on her Jümar. Without her ice-axe, imbedded in the hard snow at the anchor, she never had a chance to arrest the slip.

Without establishing Camp VI, the three of us somberly descended to the next camp below. Our hopes for an immediate try on the summit were shattered. The next morning Mahre and I descended to Camp II where we were tearfully reunited with our teammates. Earlier, Lou Whittaker had led a search party to the base of the face, but could find no trace of Marty. She had disappeared into the bowels of the enormous bergschrund there.

Nielson, who stayed at Camp V, was joined by Dunn and Simonson a day later. Together, on May 17, they climbed the Great Couloir and established Camp VI in an open crevasse at 26,500 feet. The next day, without the benefit of supplementary oxygen (although one bottle per summit climber had been carried there), the threesome climbed to near the head of the couloir. Nielson decided to make a solo attempt on the summit; Simonson, whose knee had been struck by a falling rock the day before, and Dunn opted to return to Camp VI.

Not following Messner's route that took a higher exit from the Great Couloir, Nielson climbed a narrow, twisting gully to reach the Yellow Band. Continuing to 27,500 feet, he was confronted with a difficult, unprotected move and wisely decided to retreat. Later, as Nielson descended toward Camp III, he realized he had frostbitten his hands and feet. Dr. Hixson later diagnosed moderately severe frostbite and there ensued an evacuation of Nielson from the mountain.

We had time for one more attempt to reach the summit. On May 24, however, at 24,500 feet Mahre, Dunn and I turned back in the grip of the first serious monsoon storm that dumped a load of unsafe snow on the face. The expedition was over.

The accident that took Marty Hoey's life was not the only tragedy on the mountain. On May 17 Peter Boardman and Joe Tasker were last seen climbing above 26,000 feet on their bold route. They never emerged from behind a rock tower on the ridge crest, and after days of anxious waiting and searching, Bonington was forced to conclude that they had most likely fallen down the Kangshung Face. Two of the best Himalayan climbers thus were lost in an accident eerily reminiscent of the Mallory-Irvine disappearance 58 years before.

We did not succeed in reaching the summit of Everest. But we pioneered a new route high on the North Face. Of perhaps greater importance, we were a completely united team. We managed to avoid the personality clashes that have troubled so many recent large Himalayan expeditions. Most of us left Everest with the desire to return—as climbers do when success has been just beyond their reach.

Summary of Statistics:

AREA: Tibet

ATTEMPTED ASCENT: Mount Everest via the North Face to c. 8380 meters, c. 27,500 feet, March to May, 1982.

PERSONNEL: Louis Whittaker, leader, James Wickwire, Philip Ershler, Marty Hoey, Eric Simonson, George Dunn, Edward G. Hixson, M.D., Dan Boyd, Dave Mahre, Larry Nielson, Joe Horiskey, Gary Isaacs, Tracy Roberts, Nawang Gombu, Richard Bass, Frank Wells and Steve Marts.

Cholatse

GALEN A. ROWELL

IN APRIL 1982 while the first Russian expedition was climbing Mount Everest from Nepal with a cast of nearly a thousand climbers and porters, five of us attempted Cholatse, the last named, unclimbed peak in the Everest region. We felt almost smugly certain of success. Our team was strong and our motives were fitting and proper. We had avoided preclimb publicity, funded cash costs entirely out of members' pockets, planned not to use Sherpas above Base Camp, and brought the latest equipment, courtesy of several manufacturers. The mountain—however hard it might prove to be—was only 21,130 feet. Furthermore, all five members had previously seen Cholatse and believed it could be rushed up and down in two to three days with good weather.

We were unanimous in our underestimation of the mountain. The white coating that appeared to be snow on our chosen southwest arête turned out to be brittle ice for thousands of feet. To complicate matters, unseasonal premonsoon storms brought wind and snow every afternoon.

Before the climb I led a two-week photography trek in the same region for Mountain Travel, passing countless yak caravans loaded with bright-colored duffels, trekkers in even more vivid hues, and Sherpas decked out in boots, jackets, and specialty items that were only just hitting the shelves in stores in the United States. It was hard to keep in mind that thirty-two years earlier no Westerner had ever visited the Khumbu homeland of the Sherpas. In that short span, the Khumbu had become the Mecca of the Himalaya, visited by far more people than any other region so close to a great peak. More than 8000 trekkers and climbers from every major nation were to come in 1982, mostly bound for Everest Base Camp. The finely shaped lower peaks—Ama Dablam, Thamserku, Kantega—were climbed legally or illegally by the middle sixties. Why Cholatse had gone untouched was something of a mystery. It was a bit too hard to climb illegally without attracting attention, but no one knew for certain why it had been kept off the permitted list.

Cholatse, sometimes spelled Tsolatse or given the Tibetan name, Jobo Lhaptshan, became the "last virgin of the Khumbu" not by way of virtue, but by paternal restrictions of the Ministry of Tourism begun when the mountains of Nepal first opened in 1950. Cholatse's continued closure was more a quirk of Asian bureaucracy than a clear rationale. It was not worth a large peak fee, and it was hidden up the Gokyo Valley, lacking the obvious appeal of mountains closer to the classic route to Everest Base Camp. Another consideration was that some Sherpas considered Cholatse a very sacred mountain, one of five goddesses surrounding Everest. Others said the peak had no special significance. The Rimpoche of Thyangboche Monastery told me simply, "All mountains are sacred."

Four years earlier, Al Read, director of Mountain Travel Nepal, asked me to join his prospective Cholatse climb. He kept after the government until they finally gave him a permit late in 1981. As late as six weeks before departure, the expedition had no funding, no equipment, and just two certain climbers: Peter Hackett and me. Read had a busy trekking season, and he decided to "godfather" the expedition rather than actively climb himself. He had also invited Bill O'Connor, a British mountaineer with considerable Himalayan experience, but was unsure if Bill was coming until he arrived in Nepal for the expedition. Peter and I decided on a minimum of four climbers for an alpine-style bid on what appeared to be a safe but steep ridge. We invited Vern Clevenger and John Roskelley to round out the team.

We met in Kathmandu and sent our gear ahead on porters, saving some of the cost of flying it to Lukla. The others took off on a two-week acclimatizing trek together while I was with my photography trek. On the morning of April 15 I left that group in a village not far from Lukla, from where they would fly home, and took off toward Cholatse with one strong porter. We covered five normal trekking days in one, reaching a point half an hour below Base Camp at dusk in clouds so thick that we couldn't find our way up the remaining trailless hill. The next morning I arrived to spot the other four heading out of Base Camp for the peak. I stayed back to rest while they spent the day establishing a route through a long icefall to a col at 18,600 feet where an advanced camp could be placed. Fixed line was placed on the final 600-foot headwall to help haul loads on the final bid. They returned to Base Camp late in the day.

For the next four days it stormed; not all the time but just enough to quell our enthusiasm. The morning of April 20 was clear. We regained the col with food for two more days, and fixed three ropes on the hard ice above. In the afternoon it snowed yet again.

The next morning was clear, but Hackett was too sick to climb. A world expert in mountain medicine, he was quite sure that his ailment was short-lived and not due to altitude. We faced a triangle of awful decisions: wait a day or two and not have enough food to attempt the climb; leave a sick man alone, a man whose desire for Cholatse and efforts on behalf of the expedition exceeded any of our own; or make multiple trips through the icefall, which, due to hanging glaciers above, Hackett felt was as dangerous as the Khumbu Icefall on Everest. We trusted his judgment. Just six months before he had gone through that icefall on his way to the top of Everest.

After considerable discussion Hackett volunteered to stay at the col camp until we returned from the attempt. To fail so indignantly on a lower peak after

success so recently on Everest was hard to swallow. He said goodbye, then crawled into his bag as we jümared slowly up the ropes above the col.

Hackett's wasn't the only failure. On previous light expeditions where we had brought our own time-worn gear, I had rarely witnessed an equipment failure. That day Vern's crampons sheared a front screw. A new superwide strap tore off my crampon at the rivet. John's "Lifetime" ice tool broke off clean at the adze. By noon my digital watch was in pieces, and I had hacked big chunks of foam out of the new Alveolite inners of my plastic boots to try to make them fit something other than a ballet dancer's heel. To top things off we came to the only feasible campsite far too early in the day. At just 19,000 feet it seemed far too low for a round-trip to the top the next day.

In the afternoon Clevenger and O'Connor cut a tent platform out of hard ice while Roskelley and I fixed our four climbing ropes on the steep ridge above. On the last lead I stopped to place two ice screws for protection across a traverse of an 80° bulge. After Roskelley followed, he said, "Any one of us can climb anything on this mountain, but we're going to have to get up this fast, or we're not going to make it. I'm the fastest, and I can lead most of this without protection if it's okay with everybody."

It was. One day's food remained after two days of climbing. We were up at 3:30 A.M., the tents were left in place, and Roskelley led off. Pitch after pitch of steep ice went by without the placing of a single point of protection. "Ready?" Roskelley would say with two ice tools stuck in the wall. I would pay out rope continuously for ten minutes as he climbed with thirty pounds on his back until the rope ran out. Then he would place ice screws for a belay, and I would follow. Clevenger and O'Connor would follow later, pulling out the ropes and screws for use above.

Fifteen rope-lengths of steep ice—2,250 feet—brought us to the summit plateau by noon. We cached some gear and headed on with O'Connor in the lead. When a massive crevasse blocked the route, Roskelley did an end-run up yet another ice pitch. There we found not the summit, but a hidden 300-foot ice headwall. After twelve long hours of climbing, Roskelley and Clevenger reached the top in a full blizzard with their hair on end from electricity in the air. O'Connor and I joined them minutes later, and we all beat a hasty retreat.

It was too late to attempt a descent to the high camp, so we stomped out a platform at the top of the ridge and camped without a tent or bivvy sacks in a mild snowstorm. Lightning flashed in the southern sky over India as we heated water for one freeze-dried dinner between us. The others were testing Quallofil bags that would hold their loft when wet. Mine had torn a seam before the climb, so I had brought a down bag instead. Knowing that it would collapse like a wet sock as soon as my body heat melted the falling snow, I wore boots, overboots, and one-piece Gore-tex/Sontique climbing suit to bed.

In the morning the temperature was −19°C., my bag felt like a giant Coke bottle, but I was warm inside my waterproof garments, as were the others in their fluffy bags. As the first light hit Makalu, Everest, and Ama Dablam, we packed up to begin twenty frightening diagonal rappels back down the ridge,

PLATE 7

CHOLATSE.

which overhung to the south most of the way down. Our loads grew lighter as we consumed almost all of our ice hardware for anchors every 150 feet.

At the col Peter greeted us, recovered from a short bout with the flu, but still a bit weak. He joined us, and we continued our descent toward Base Camp. Just below the glacier we were met by a welcoming committee that included Al Read, his family, several friends, and our Sherpas. A "Welcome Home Cholatse Expedition" sign graced an arch of willow branches over a gate in the stone yak corral at the entrance to camp. The Sherpas were preparing a victory dinner and baking a cake for us.

A more idyllic return from a climb is hard to imagine. We were far off any trekking route, camped in a meadow eye-to-eye with peaks on the other side of the Gokyo Valley, sharing our joy with a few friends.

The next morning I walked over the hill to watch the clouds. Below me two figures were sitting by a rock—our Sherpas watching the same movements of land and sky. On the next hill were three more figures; local herdsmen also just looking at the scene. Each group was separate, yet motivated by similar emotions. None of us would have come here and shared this experience without our particular ulterior motives. Our Sherpas were hired hands on an expedition, the herdsmen were tending family yaks, and our objective was to climb a mountain. Trekkers on a trail might have snapped a picture or two, but invariably they would have kept on walking instead of sitting down to silently soak in the world around them.

I saw how little the essential values of the Khumbu have changed with the recent onslaught of tourists. We were able to share the essence of these mountains with those who lived in them, just as the first Khumbu travelers had done thirty years before.

One of the reasons Sherpas integrate so well with Westerners is that unlike hill farmers or merchants, they have no single life purpose. They herd, they farm, they trade, they work for trekkers and climbers. Remove the specifics of Third World life from their scenario, and they have it made even by our highest jet-set standards.

A typical Sherpa family lives on an acre of land in a town within sight of the mountains. Their children walk to school with no fear of trouble on the way or in class. They raise their own livestock, grow their own vegetables. For part of the year the husband travels, making a better salary than in town. He brings things back from exotic places and tells exciting stories around the fireplace. While he was gone his wife managed the land, the animals, and represented the family in frequent community affairs. Together they travel to other villages and visit their summer home in a high meadow.

An hour below our Cholatse Base Camp was a cluster of fields and stone buildings that comprise the summer settlement of Na. Called *yersas*, these Sherpa summer homes are set in high-altitude pastures where yaks and goats graze during the warmest parts of the year. In one building I had tea with Sonam Dorje, eighteen-year-old son of a Sherpa from Phortse who had been on eleven Everest expeditions. All the Na yersas were owned by Phortse

PLATE 8

Photo by Galen Rowell

John Roskelley leading at 19,500 feet on CHOLATSE.

families. Sonam had worked on several Mountain Travel treks, but he told me he would not be doing such work for two more years. "I'll be staying here from March to August. Sometimes my father comes; sometimes I'm alone. When one of my four brothers is old enough to stay here, I'll go back to work as a trekking Sherpa."

With his previous earnings from trekking he could have easily bought a transistor radio, like many of the lowland Nepalese who now violate the quiet air space of their villages. Instead, Sonam bought a pressure cooker to save precious fuel cooking potatoes and vegetables at his 14,500-foot summer home. On the wall he has hung art paper with Tibetan characters which he learned to draw at school. Next to his work hang a Marlboro ad and a *Time* cover.

The juxtaposition is not as disturbing as it seems. On another family's wall I spotted a picture from *Time* of the musician, Rostropovich, and his wife. I learned that the family had put it up simply because it captured an expression of love between husband and wife. They had no idea who the people were.

After a rest day, several of us decided to extend our trek home by crossing the Cho La, a 17,800-foot pass connecting the Gokyo Valley with Pheriche on the Everest trekking route. Our intent was simply to see more of the region around the peak we had climbed, but in a larger sense our urge to circle around a mountain meaningful to us was exactly what reverent Tibetan Buddhists do with landmarks that have special meanings in their lives.

How different our Khumbu experience was from that of the Russians on Everest. Their memories would be weighted toward months in a sterile world, while only four days of our month were actually on the heights. Those four intense days, however, had paid us top dividends for an extremely low investment. By cutting corners in every way, our month's lightweight expedition and trek with a Sherpa crew and government-required liaison officer (kept warm and content in a Namche Bazar guesthouse at our expense) ended up costing less than half the tariff of most commercial Khumbu treks. The entire expedition except for Peter reached the summit of an unclimbed peak, and more importantly, returned healthy and happy—the true bottom line of a successful expedition.

Summary of Statistics:

AREA: Khumbu Region, Nepal

FIRST ASCENT: Cholatse (Jobo Lhaptshan). 21,130 feet, via the southwest arête, summit reached on April 22, 1982 (Clevenger, O'Connor, Roskelley, Rowell).

PERSONNEL: Vern Clevenger, Peter Hackett, Bill O'Connor, Al Read, John Roskelley, Galen Rowell

Everest's Northeast Ridge

CHRISTIAN BONINGTON

HE EXPEDITION was one of the most arduous any of us had ever been on. Our small team was tackling the long, unclimbed northeast ridge of Everest without oxygen and with its main difficulties situated near its end between 26,000 feet and 27,500 feet, where the ridge was joined by the north ridge, the route taken by the pre-World War II expeditions and the successful Chinese expeditions of 1960 and 1975.

The climbing team consisted of Peter Boardman, Dick Renshaw, Joe Tasker and myself, supported by Charles Clarke, who was expedition doctor, and Adrian Gordon, neither of whom planned to go beyond Advance Base.

Base Camp was reached on March 16 after a three-day drive from Lhasa with halts at the towns of Xigaze and Xegur. The team was accompanied by a group of ten trekkers led by David Newbigging, chairman of Jardine Matheson of Hong Kong who sponsored the expedition. Base Camp was situated at 17,000 feet, near the foot of the Rongbuk Glacier and a few hundred yards above the site of the pre-war British camps. We spent the first week acclimatising and exploring the route up the Rongbuk Glacier, which the trekking party was able to share in, some of them reaching 20,000 feet.

Advance Base was established on April 4 at 21,000 feet, after a three-day trek with 13 yaks carrying the loads up the rock-covered moraines that lead to the head of the East Rongbuk Glacier. There were two more ferries by the yaks of all the food and gear needed by the expedition, while the climbing team started work on the northeast ridge. It was still bitterly cold with constant high winds sweeping down the glacier.

The team was, in effect, employing siege tactics but using a minimal quantity of fixed rope and digging snow holes for all the lower camps. This approach had the advantage of reducing the weight of gear to be ferried up the ridge and also ensured that our camps were secure, since tents would have been at great risk in the high winds. Using snow holes also had the advantage that the four members of the team were always together which made discussion of plans and ideas very much easier.

Our first snow cave was established on April 10 at 22,500 feet, just below the crest of the ridge. We then pushed the route across steep snow slopes to reach the site of our second snow cave at 23,800 feet on April 12 and began digging out a cave but almost immediately hit rock. Fortunately it was very

PLATE 9

Photo by Adrian Gordon

The Northeast Ridge of EVEREST from the north. Three snow caves and Second Pinnacle are marked.

crumbly and we were able to dig the rock away, but as a result it took around fourteen hours of work spread over several days to dig out a snow hole big enough for four.

We went down for a rest at Advance Base on April 14, returning to the ridge on the 18th and moving into our second snow cave on the 20th. While we did this Adrian and Charlie were supervising the yak herders who were ferrying our gear up from Base Camp. Above the second snow cave, the ridge steepened into two steps, which we climbed on the 21st and 22nd respectively. The first was up a steep snow gully and the second on broken rock. These were the first stretches where fixed ropes were placed. We then dropped back to Advance Base on the 23rd, but this time descended to Base Camp for a few days rest, having found that it was impossible to recover fully at 21,000 feet.

We returned to Advance Base on April 29, making the journey in a day. While Charlie and Adrian made an attempt on Point 6919 on the eastern side of the upper Rongbuk Glacier, the rest of us returned to the ridge, reaching the second snow cave on May 1. The following day, Pete and Dick moved up to the top of the snow shoulder at 25,700 feet to camp there for the night, whilst Joe and I carried food and gas cylinders up to their high point and returned to the second snow cave. We moved up with our personal gear the following day, while Pete and Dick dug out a snow cave just below the crest of the ridge on its southeastern side.

Several hundred yards of gently ascending ridge led to the foot of the first pinnacle. This was where the main difficulties of the climb started, at a height of 26,250 feet, higher than all but fourteen mountains in the world. The ridge now narrowed into a knife-edged crest of snow, barred by a series of rocky pinnacles. This section was just under half a mile in length, with a height gain of nearly 1300 feet before it was joined by the original Chinese route which took the north ridge leading up from the North Col. We knew that this part of the ridge, before it joined the old route, would probably give us some of the most difficult climbing ever attempted at that altitude. Once we had climbed this section, however, we would be on known ground which would be technically easy compared to the unclimbed stretch before us.

On May 4 Pete and I started climbing the first pinnacle, Pete making a very bold lead up ice and broken rock that provided no secure cracks for piton anchors. As a result, I had to join two ropes together to let him make a run-out of around 250 feet. He was going so strongly I was very happy to let him stay in the lead, and that day he pushed out another 300 feet of rope to reach a notch in the ridge giving a view of the eastern side of the ridge.

The following day, Dick and Joe went out in front, Dick leading a pitch which was by far the most difficult so far, on steep and very insubstantial snow. At the end of this difficult stretch of climbing at a height of around 26,700 feet, he experienced a strange tingling down one side of his body. He therefore returned to the snow cave, while Pete belayed Joe for another pitch leading up towards the top of the pinnacle. That day they reached a height of around 26,900 feet.

We were all worried about Dick's symptoms and now, after four nights at nearly 26,000 feet, we were extremely tired. We decided to descend to Base Camp for another rest, where Charles diagnosed that Dick had had a mild stroke and recommended that he should return to sea level as soon as possible. He accompanied Dick as far as Chengdu.

Back at Base Camp I also came to the conclusion that I had gone as far as I was able, particularly as I was so much slower than Pete or Joe and might well hold them up in a bid for the summit, which we hoped to make on our return to the mountain. In addition, we had always hoped to reach the North Col, establish a dump of food there and mark the route back down, so that this could be used as a line of descent once the unclimbed section of the northeast ridge had been negotiated. We had not had the time nor the energy to do this, but it now seemed a useful function for Adrian and me to perform while Pete and Joe tried to complete the ridge and go for the summit.

Pete, Joe, Adrian and I returned to Advance Base on May 13 and on the 15th, Pete and Joe went straight up to the second snow cave in six hours, a sign of how well they had recovered from the previous sortie on the ridge. They reached the third snow cave the following day. They were well set up, with a good stock of food and fuel and about 800 feet of rope for fixing at the high point.

Meanwhile Adrian and I tried to reach the col, but the route was more complex and difficult than we had anticipated and by six o'clock on the evening of the 16th, we were still about 300 feet below the North Col, our way barred by a broad crevasse below a sérac wall. It was here that we had our last radio contact with Pete and Joe. We agreed that there should be two radio calls the next day, one at three in the afternoon and the next at six. Pete, who took the call, sounded full of optimism and said that he and Joe were both going well. Adrian and I then returned to Advance Base, planning to have a rest the following day, before trying to complete the route to the North Col.

Throughout the 17th we were able to watch the progress of Pete and Joe through our powerful telescope. They had obviously made a very early start, probably at dawn, for they were at the previous high point by nine in the morning, but then their progress slowed and it took them the rest of the day to run out around four rope-lengths on new ground, most of it on the northwest side between the rock and the crest of snow, in clear view from Advance Base. They climbed late into the evening, reaching the foot of the second pinnacle, where they disappeared round the corner onto the snow on the eastern side of the ridge. We assumed that they were having difficulty in finding suitable snow for a tent platform or snow cave. They had not answered our radio calls at either three o'clock or at six, and we assumed that either they had been too engrossed in the climbing or that perhaps their walkie-talkie had developed a fault.

On the morning of the 18th, Adrian and I set out for the North Col carrying our personal gear. Throughout the day we searched the crest of the east-northeast ridge concentrating on the area where we knew they had to come back into view since the way on the other side of the ridge was barred by steep rock.

PLATE 10

Photo by Christian Bonington

Kangchung Face of EVEREST with Northeast Ridge at right.

The view from the slopes of the North Col was particularly good since it looked directly onto this part of the ridge.

That day we only reached our previous high point, camping on the edge of the crevasse and completing the route to the North Col on the morning of the 19th. We continued to examine the crest of the ridge throughout that day and the next through our binoculars, getting increasingly worried when they failed to come into sight. We knew that they could not reach the upper slopes of the north ridge without coming into view.

In view of the very short distance that they would have had to cover on the other side of the ridge before being forced back into view on our side, there seemed only one explanation for their disappearance—that they had both had a fall, perhaps as a result of a snow slip, on the Kangshung side.

By this time Charlie had returned to Advance Base making the journey back from Chengdu, at near sea level, to 21,000 feet in only five days and we decided that it was essential to make a search to try to see what might have happened. Neither Charlie nor Adrian had the mountaineering ability or experience to venture with me onto the ridge itself, and anyway, unless we had been able to reach the high point we would not have been able to see anything. On the other hand, there seemed an outside chance that they might have descended to the Kangshung valley on the other side of the ridge, and by getting to its head we should at least have seen that side of the ridge. We decided therefore that Charlie and I should travel round to the Kangshung Glacier while Adrian held a grim and solitary vigil at our Advance Base in the remote hope that they might still come down the ridge.

Charlie and I returned to Base Camp on May 22, drove by truck to the village of Kharta on the eastern side of the mountain and then made a forty-mile trek over the Langma La Pass and up the Kangshung Glacier, until, from its head we could examine the entire huge face. There was no sign of them, but we could see that if they had fallen down it, they could not possibly have survived.

And yet we still did not give up hope. As we drove back to Base Camp, I almost convinced myself that I had completely misinterpreted the situation, that Pete and Joe would be there, laughing at our panicked response to their disappearance, insisting on going back for another go. But they were not at Base Camp. Adrian, who had stayed at our Advance Base until the 28th, had seen nothing. We had to accept that they were dead. Charlie carved a plaque in their memory on a stone chosen from near the site of the memorial to Mallory and Irvine and we mounted it on a cairn on a small knoll above Base Camp.

We had been so close to success, had worked harder, and had been more stretched both physically and mentally than we had ever been before. But there was extraordinarily little discussion about plans, for it was as if, through the many climbs we had done together, that we all knew and agreed instinctively what should be done at each stage of our climb. We were totally united in what we were doing, and until the tragedy it was the happiest expedition any of us had been on.

PLATE 11

Photo by Christian Bonington

Boardman, Tasker and Renshaw on Everest's Northeast Ridge. Note climbers on First Pinnacle at 26,500 feet.

Pete and Joe are an immense loss to the entire mountain world and to an even wider field. Not only were they outstanding mountaineers, they were also fine creative writers and warmly compassionate people, who had already achieved an extraordinary amount for their years, and yet had such a huge potential for development before them.

Summary of Statistics:

AREA: Tibetan side of Mount Everest.

ATTEMPTED ASCENT: Mount Everest via the Northeast Ridge to about 27,000 feet, where Boardman and Tasker were last seen.

PERSONNEL: Christian Bonington, leader; Peter Boardman, Dr. Charles Clarke, Adrian Gordon, Richard Renshaw, Joseph Tasker.

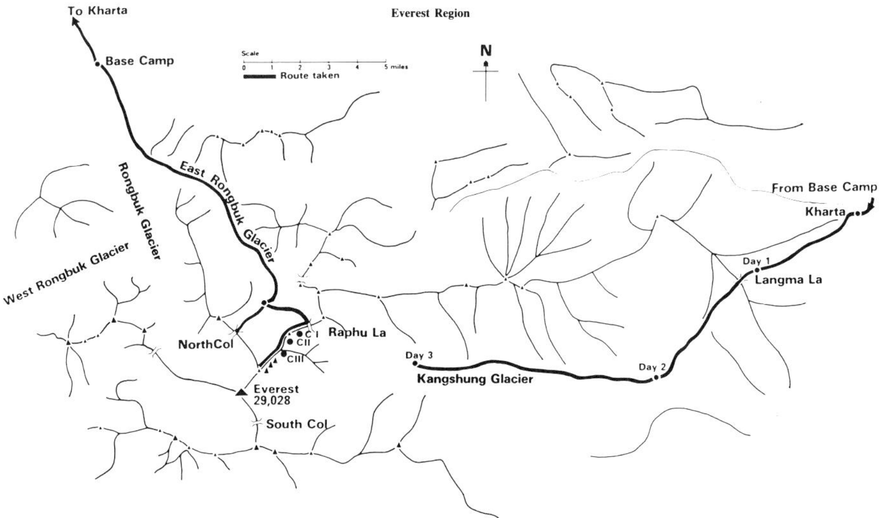

South Ridge of Ama Dablam

SUE GILLER

"WHEN WOMEN are on a mountain, it always snows." This was not the weather forecast we had hoped to hear. With Camp III still not reached, and with the afternoon weather becoming worse and worse with each passing day, we did not want to clear the mountain because of a storm. Still, perhaps Sherpa wisdom did not apply to foreigners. All we could do was hope for the best.

A year earlier I had a phone call from Annie Whitehouse. In 1978 Annie had obtained a permit to climb the south ridge of Ama Dablam in the spring of 1982, but having just enlisted in the Air Force, she felt she could not continue working on the expedition. Would I take over the permit and organize the trip? It took only a brief moment for me to answer "yes."

Over the ensuing year, events progressed like clockwork. I soon had a climbing team of eight, all competent mountaineers with experience climbing all over the world, plus a great Base Camp manager, Tanyalee Erwin, who had gained experience in the "Nepali way" on a previous expedition to Nepal. Four members I knew from a trip to Dhaulagiri in 1980. Shari Kearney, Lucy Smith, Heidi Lüdi and Susan Havens had experience in working with the Nepali government and a knowledge of the thousands of details of putting together a Himalayan expedition. Also joining us were Anne Macquarie who had just returned from Pakistan, Jini Griffith who had climbed in the Pamirs, and Stacy Allison, the "baby" of the expedition at 24 years, who had just finished an alpine ascent of the Cassin Ridge. All were competent technical climbers, at home on ice and rock.

Working hard over the summer and winter of 1981, we put together the necessary equipment, obtained sponsorship from several companies and sold T-shirts to help raise the needed cash. By early March we were packed and ready. On March 6, we left reality and time-travelled back to the magical kingdom of Nepal. Our great adventure had begun.

We spent a busy week in Kathmandu meeting our Sherpa staff, purchasing last-minute food and equipment, and packing for the trek to Base Camp. Because of problems with Royal Nepal Airlines, we had to trek in for twelve days from Lamusangu rather than fly to Lukla. From the midlands of Nepal, we crossed numerous drainages to reach the Dudh Kosi which we then followed upstream to Namche Bazar. There was not a flat stretch on the entire

A climber returns to Camp II on
AMA DABLAM.

trek. We were in shape! Upon reaching Namche Bazar, we had walked 150 miles and gained over 40,000 feet and lost 30,000 feet of elevation.

For the four days from Namche to Base Camp below the south ridge of Ama Dablam, we exchanged lowland porters for yaks. The sound of yak bells often helped us to find our way through the afternoon fog to the campsite.

Base Camp at 16,100 feet was reached on April 3. Used by the local Sherpas as a summer yak-pasturing camp, our next month's home came complete with several ready-made buildings, requiring only a tarp for the roof, and a sandy beach beside a small pond for sunbathing. Excited to begin the climb, we spent hours the first day gazing up at the mountain which towered above us, begging to be climbed.

We began work immediately. The route to Camp I at 18,700 feet was marked on April 4 by Lucy and Stacy. Past expeditions had scattered so many cairns around the boulders that we often got confused as to which way to go. How strange to need trail signs pointing the proper way on a Himalayan mountain open to climbing for only three years!

Camp I was in the middle of a steep talus field at the beginning of the technical climbing. We found already built tent platforms, which made for level if lumpy sleeping. This camp was protected from most of the winds but was often in the fog and snow during the afternoon snow showers. The goraks were in attendance daily and I sometimes felt they were watching over these strangers who periodically came to feed them exotic tidbits.

We spent several days carrying supplies to stock Camp I before Jini, Lucy and Anne moved up to occupy the camp and work on the route to Camp II. It took them three days to fix the ridge, using about 2000 feet of line. Each evening the progress report via radio brought excited comment on the pleasures of the climbing. Following a narrow ridge of excellent granite, the route snaked around the gendarmes, sometimes on the left side of the ridge, sometimes on the right and occasionally along the top. There was never a dull moment with tremendous exposure and spectacular views of the mountains around us.

We placed Camp II above the Yellow Tower, a 100-foot 5.8 vertical headwall. My favorite camp, this was a split-level series of small ledges with tent platforms already made, as was a trash heap from previous expeditions. Set right on the ridge top, this site offered a magnificent panorama, with the summit temptingly close above us. We found several unopened cans, some without labels, left by an earlier Spanish expedition. We would often treat ourselves to a "surprise" with dinner by opening an unknown can. We dined on Spanish fish, beans, baby eels, and in celebration of the summit, we scored a can of escargot in tomato sauce. These treats helped a little to alleviate our disappointment at the quantities of trash around the tent sites.

On April 11, Susan, Shari and Stacy moved up to occupy Camp II. Daily afternoon snow showers began, causing problems on the rock traverses and hampering the leading. Although we had planned to spend two or three days to reach Camp III, the altitude slowed us down. After an initial rock section of 5.8 difficulty (the First Step), most of the climbing was on ice (40°-70°) or

snow. We found water-ice on the slabs above the First Step, along with so many old fixed lines that they created a hazard, entangling our crampons. We removed over two packs full of line to clear the way. We then traversed under the Second Step and gained the Mushroom Ridge which connects the top of the Second Step with the upper snowfields. A short ice pitch out of a crevasse gained Camp III at 20,800 feet.

On April 18, Susan, Shari, Lucy and Stacy left Camp II to establish Camp III. It took them two days to reach the camp as they were fixing most of the Mushroom Ridge as they went. Camp III was on top of a hanging glacier, below the summit snowfields. Situated on a large flat shoulder of snow, it was easily the most comfortable tenting of all the camps, but quite cold and windy.

It was while the team was working its way along the Mushroom Ridge that I received the Sherpa-style weather forecast. With success so close, I felt increasingly anxious that the weather would finally turn truly bad and I would have to call everyone down to sit out a storm, or worse yet, that we would be pinned down and use up our dwindling supplies. So, praying that the weather would hold for a few more days, we carried on.

After a rest day at Camp III on the 19th, with more afternoon snow, the first team left for the summit at six A.M. on the 20th. It was a crystal clear day with a steady wind from the north. The rest of us in support at Camp II watched the climbers as they worked their way up the snowfields. Small black ants on an immense sugar lump, they moved agonizingly slowly. They reached the summit at 3:30 P.M. and disappeared from our view onto the broad top. At four o'clock they reappeared and began rappelling the route, soon to disappear again into an afternoon storm. I retired to my tent, the radio left on for their call when they reached camp. As the snow pelted the tent, I alternated between elation at their success and anxiety. Eight P.M.—no call. Nine P.M.—no call. At 9:20 finally, Shari came on: they were safely down! Such a relief! Now, if only the weather would hold two more days and give the rest of us a chance at the summit!

The next day Anne, Jini, Heidi and I moved up to Camp III while the others went down to Camp II for a deserved rest. We had a completely clear day and our hopes rose. On April 22, we left camp at five A.M. Knowing how long it had taken the first team, we left as early as possible to use all available light. We slowly worked our way up the snowfields climbing on good consolidated snow of moderate steepness, gratefully using any steps left by the first team. Although we consciously tried to hurry, often climbing simultaneously, time seemed to ebb away. We were all dismayed to see our clear morning dissolve into fog at ten o'clock. So much for a view! As we finally reached the summit at 1:30, it immediately began to snow heavily. But we didn't care, elated at our success. After a few minutes on the summit we descended, reaching camp at seven o'clock.

We spent the next five days clearing the mountain. As though to show us how benevolent it had been, the weather socked in on the 23rd and 24th, snowing and blowing heavily. We were happy to have the fixed lines to help us down to the lower camps. Because of the snow, we were unable to clear our lines above the First Step, but below that we removed all our ropes and many others left by earlier trips. By April 27, everyone and everything was down to Base Camp.

Ama Dablam has been called "the most beautiful mountain in the world", and to the Sherpas, it is itself a god. Viewed from Pangboche, its ridges sweep gracefully upwards, drawing the eye to its symmetrical pinnacle of a summit. A mountaineer's mountain, it inspires a desire to climb it in all who see it. We were grateful for the opportunity to dance attendance upon its majestic flanks and briefly to share the view from its summit with the mountain gods. A nearly perfect climb on the nearly perfect mountain.

Summary of Statistics:

AREA: Khumbu Himal, Nepal.

ASCENT: Ama Dablam, 6856 meters, 22,495 feet, via South Ridge, April 20, 1982 (Havens, Kearney, Smith, Allison); April 22, 1982 (Giller, Macquarie, Griffith, Lüdi).

PERSONNEL: Susan Giller, *leader,* Stacy Allison, Jini Griffith, Susan Havens, Heidi Lüdi, Shari Kearney, Anne Macquarie, Lucy Smith, Tanyalee Erwin, *Base Camp Manager.*

Shishapangma's Southwest Face

Douglas Scott, *Alpine Climbing Group*

HISHAPANGMA LIES a hundred miles west-northwest of Everest to the north of Nepal and wholly in Tibet. The Tibetan name means "The Crest above the Grassy Plain." The Sanskrit name, Gosainthan, means "Home of God." Its height has been given as 8013 meters or 26,291 feet, although recently the Survey of India has called it 8046 meters or 26,398 feet. If the latter figure is accepted, Shishapangma is the world's thirteenth highest peak. It had been climbed before. The first ascent was made in 1964 by the Chinese, who had 195 members working on the northern side. In 1980 Tibet was opened to foreigners. In 1980 and 1981 Shishapangma was climbed four more times from the north by the Chinese route or variations of it.

The vast south side, the Nyanang Phu Glacier and the Phu Chu valley had never been visited except by local yak men part way. Thus the southwest face, the main objective of our expedition, was unknown except for photographs taken from the air or from peaks in Nepal, fifteen miles away. We hoped to climb the face without a reconnaissance and in alpine style.

Nick Prescott sought permission for Shishapangma. He wrote the Chinese Mountaineering Association in the summer of 1979, was "invited to apply" at Easter of 1980 and received permission in the summer. His original team backed out and he handed the expedition over to me in March of 1981, though he continued to do nearly all the difficult administrative work. Our final team comprised Roger Baxter-Jones, Alex MacIntyre, Elaine Brook, Paul Braithwaite, Nick Prescott and me. Elaine and Nick would climb during the acclimatization period. Then Elaine would make contact with local Tibetans and Nick would be in support of the rest of us on Shishapangma's southwest face.

Climbing in China is about five times as expensive as climbing a comparable peak in Nepal. Consequently we travelled light and declined to have an expedition cook and mail runners. All in all, this was a very spartan trip.

We arrived in Beijing on April 4 and arranged our onward schedule with the Chinese Mountaineering Association. Wu Ming, our interpreter, joined the expedition there. We flew to Chengdu on April 8 and to Lhasa on the 9th. There we were joined by our liaison officer, Pemba. After visiting the old town of Lhasa, on the 10th we travelled by lorry to the roadhead at Nyalam, arriving

PLATE 13

Photo by Douglas Scott

SHISHAPANGMA's Southwest Face
Bivouacs are marked. Descent to
right.

PLATE 14

Photo by Douglas Scott

**Alex MacIntyre on
SHISHAPANGMA's Southwest Face.**

on the 14th after visiting Shigatse and Shekar. Although we enjoyed the drive across the vast Tibetan plateau, we saw ruined monasteries dynamited by Red Guards during the Cultural Revolution. We established Advanced Base Camp on May 3, just south of the unclimbed peak of Nyanang Ri (7071 meters, 23,200 feet).

The acclimatization period was from May 4 to 25. Braithwaite was ill with an old chest complaint and remained in camp with Prescott, who was suffering from diarrhoea and poor acclimatization. With three bivouacs, from May 4 to 7 we climbed up the south ridge of Nyanang Ri and across leftwards on ice and snow below the summit to the northeast ridge. We did not go to the top. Elaine got to 19,000 feet and retired as she was unable to acclimatize in the short period available. Braithwaite sadly left for home on May 13 rather than risk permanent injury. Elaine Brook left for Lhasa on May 15, having many adventures and staying with various Tibetan families en route.

The remaining four of us established Castle Camp at 19,000 feet, three miles northwest of Advanced Base. We headed first for Pungpa Ri, which is really a shoulder of Shishapangma about a mile away and separated from its parent by a 24,000-foot saddle. Baxter-Jones, MacIntyre and I set off from Castle Camp at 10:30 A.M. on May 17 and climbed a 45° couloir to bivouac below a col at 22,000 feet. The next day we climbed the south ridge (UIAA Grade IV) in a strong wind to a bivouac 500 feet below the summit. On May 19 we went to the top of Pungpa Ri (7445 meters, 24,425 feet) and descended by the same route, arriving at Castle Camp at eight P.M., a very long day. We had now accomplished our acclimatization and knew of at least one way down from Shishapangma, although so far we had not seen the way up in detail. Whilst we were on this route, Prescott had reconnoitered a minor peak at the southern end of the Shishapangma ridge, which he subsequently climbed part way up.

On May 25 Baxter-Jones, MacIntyre, Prescott and I left Castle Camp and traversed for two miles across glaciers and under dangerous séracs to the base of the southeast face. We then climbed for a thousand feet on easy rock and snow to find a perfect bivouac site in a little rock basin on a buttress jutting out from the face. Prescott went down from there to remain at Castle Camp in support. On the 25th we climbed mostly unroped, taking a line that slopes up from right to left to just southeast of the summit. MacIntyre and Baxter-Jones took a line up 50° ice and snow and I went up a rock rib before the three of us joined to climb the last 1500 feet (with some Grade V sections) of mixed ground to bivouac at 23,000 feet in the obvious "pea-pod" snow couloir. On the 27th we climbed up this unroped to bivouac at 25,000 feet. We continued unroped up the couloir on May 28 to the southeast ridge, which we followed for 500 feet to get to the summit at two P.M. We went to the higher east summit, which is about 80 feet higher than the west summit some 300 yards away. MacIntyre and I went across toward the west summit but stopped short of the top because of dangerous cornices.

That afternoon we descended the southeast ridge to bivouac at 24,900 feet. On May 29 we descended further to the saddle at 24,000 feet. Then after climbing down another 400 feet roped, we went down 45° to 55° snow ice unroped except for two rappels to the glacier and around to Castle Camp at seven P.M.

Although the climb was somewhat easier than expected and not as long—about 8500 vertical feet—it proved to be one of the most satisfying we have done in the Himalaya, a classic line up varied terrain on a major isolated and unexplored face.

Summary of Statistics:

AREA: Tibetan Himalaya.

ASCENTS: Pungpa Ri, 7445 meters (24,425 feet), first ascent, via South Ridge, May 19, 1982 (Baxter-Jones, MacIntyre, Scott).

Shishapangma, 8013 or 8046 meters (26,291 or 26,398 feet), new route, the Southwest Face and traverse down the Southeast Ridge, May 27, 1982 (Baxter-Jones, MacIntyre, Scott).

PERSONNEL: Roger Baxter-Jones, Alexander MacIntyre, Elaine Brook, Paul (Tut) Braithwaite, Nicholas Prescott, Douglas Scott.

Gongga Shan—
Minya Konka Revisited

Douglas Kelley *and* Joseph E. Murphy

O N OCTOBER 3, 1982 Dana Coffield and Douglas Kelley reached the summit of Gongga Shan, a 24,891-foot peak in western Sichuan province of the People's Republic of China. Fifty years earlier two other Americans, Richard Burdsall and Terris Moore made the first ascent of the mountain, then called Minya Konka. In the intervening years savage weather and avalanche combined to defeat six of nine expeditions to the peak, and more lives were lost attempting the mountain than had made it to the summit.

The 1932 expedition was a remarkable achievement. It sailed from Boston at the height of the depression, spent two months at sea, and docked at Shanghai as the Japanese began shelling the city. There the expedition split; four members continued, travelling fifteen hundred miles up the Yangtse river to find a mountain whose height and location were unknown. Theodore Roosevelt's sons had seen the mountain from considerable distance while searching for pandas and reported that it was higher than Everest. Moore's party found the peak, surveyed it, and after 27 days reached the summit by the northwest ridge. For a quarter century thereafter, Minya Konka remained the highest summit reached by Americans.

In 1957 the Chinese in launching their first major mountaineering expedition selected Minya Konka, which they renamed Gongga Shan. Gongga was the logical choice because it is one of China's four sacred mountains and the highest peak in China proper. They picked the northwest ridge as their route. It was a massive effort with twenty-one Chinese climbers, an equal number of scientists, and a large support group. The team made the attempt under the leadership of Shi Zhan Chun who later led the successful Chinese Everest expedition. Thirteen climbers were caught in an avalanche on the snow chute below Camp I. Many were injured, but only one perished. Six members of the team reached the top and of these three died while descending the summit ridge.

When the Chinese opened eight peaks to foreigners in 1980, the first expeditions[1] allowed to return to Gongga were American. One American

---

[1] See *A.A.J.*, 1981, pages 309 to 315.

PLATE 15

Photo by Douglas A. Kelly

GONGGA SHAN from Tsumei La on the west. The Northwest Ridge on the left skyline. The ridge was reached via farthest left spur.

expedition attempted a new route up the south face. The team was led by Andy Harvard and included Henry Barber, Lou Reichardt, and Jed Williamson. The other expedition sought to repeat the northwest ridge. Four members, Yvon Chouinard, Rick Ridgeway, Kim Schmitz and ABC cameraman Jonathan Wright were caught in an avalanche just above Camp I and swept down fifteen hundred feet. Wright died in the fall and was buried on the mountain.

In 1981 a Swiss expedition was to attempt the peak from the southeast, via the Hailoko Glacier, and a Japanese expedition tried the northeast ridge.[2] The Swiss were turned by bad weather to other peaks. One Japanese fell when 100 meters from the summit. The other seven in the summit party retreated, but they too pitched down the north face and were killed.

In the Spring of 1982, Japanese, Swiss and Canadian expeditions[3] attempted the peak. The Canadians tried the original route, but were turned back at Camp I by an accident and unfortunate weather. The Japanese approached the mountain from the east, placed two men within 300 meters of the summit, but then retreated in the face of storms. After one member perished from exposure, the other staggered into Base Camp and discovered that his teammates had abandoned him. He survived a nineteen-day ordeal but later lost his fingers and feet from frostbite. Three Swiss climbers attained the summit, reaching the northwest ridge from the east, but one slipped descending the summit ridge and died. The experience of the prior expeditions caused us to approach our preparations with great caution.

Our expedition was initiated by Ned Andrews and Doug Kelley who had met in Peru on separate expeditions in 1979. In 1980 we applied for permission to attempt the mountain by the northwest ridge and were granted a permit for the fall of 1982. Joe Murphy flew to Beijing in February 1981 to complete the arrangements and sign the protocol. The party consisted of seven Americans: Joe Murphy, *leader*, Ned Andrews, *deputy leader*, Sharon Caulfield, Dana Coffield, Barbara Kelley, Doug Kelley, and Michael Lehner, and two Chinese, Mr. Wong, liaison officer, and Mr. Liu, interpreter.

On the advice of the Chinese we planned a two-month expedition to allow sufficient time for the attempt. We knew that the Canadians had but two good days in eighteen in the spring of 1982. The Swiss, a year earlier, had seen but four fair days in fifty. The Swiss geologist Imhof had predicted bad weather in September and early October. We knew that our prospects would depend on favorable weather.

We arrived in Beijing on September 3, reached Chendu 1200 miles to the southwest by train on the 9th after a stop in Xian to see the archaeological site, and made the end of the road at Liu Baxiang by minibus on the 13th. From here horses carried our equipment, but to minimize expenses we planned not to use porters. After crossing a 15,200-foot pass, the Tsemei La, we arrived at the

---

[2] See *A.A.J.*, 1982, pages 383 to 385.
[3] See "Climbs and Expeditions" section of this *Journal*.

Photo by Dana Coffield

Looking back at the "HUMP" on GONGGA SHAN.

PLATE 17

Photo by Douglas A. Kelly

Coffield on Gongga Shan's North Face at 21,500 feet. Camp IV was placed in upper right of photo.

Gongga Gompa Lamasery at 12,600 feet on September 16 where we established Base Camp. We were still in the grip of the monsoon which had brought daily rain since the first of September. On arrival at the lamasery Michael Lehner became violently ill with dysentery.

On September 17 we began carrying loads to Advanced Base Camp located at 14,500 feet, five miles away in a meadow just below the northwest ridge. The route descended 300 feet from the lamasery to the Little Gomba River valley and then followed the river to the meadow. The carry was long and arduous because it involved crossing the river several times. Over the next three days we carried thirteen loads to Advanced Base. Because of the difficulty that past parties had in establishing Camp I and uncertain weather, we felt it important to commence exploration of the route to Camp I as soon as possible. At a team meeting on the 18th Murphy designated Coffield and D. Kelley as the lead team, and himself and Lehner as the second team.

Kelley and Coffield moved to Advanced Base Camp on September 19 and immediately began exploring the route to Camp I. Although not technically difficult, the route from Advanced Base to the ridge was objectively the most dangerous area on the mountain. All the previously reported avalanches had occurred in the afternoon. Kelley and Coffield decided that they would only travel on the snow from dawn to 9:30 A.M., the time the morning sun hit the slope. The traditional route followed a snowfield to the right of a rock pyramid. The Canadians got mired down when they tried to avoid the snow and stay on the rock. We found a couloir between the two which, despite continuing rockfall, remained free of avalanche danger except while climbing the rock band and traversing the lower part of the snowfield on the way to the couloir. We relied primarily on that route thereafter. On the afternoon of the 23rd, Coffield and Kelley moved to a temporary camp at 16,200 feet, just below the rock band to avoid the tiresome three-A.M. starts. They arrived just in time to watch an avalanche sweep over their previous day's route across the rock band. It was an ominous sign. The following day they moved to Camp I at 18,000 feet.

Camp II was established on the ridge at 19,800 feet on September 26. Kelley and Coffield were confined to the snow cave they had dug in an indentation in the ridge line for the next three days by 60 to 80 m.p.h. winds which blew northwest along the ridge. Murphy and Lehner broke through to Camp II on the 29th and spent a night in a tent next to the snow cave. The winds were so high they blew Murphy's pack off the ridge, and so Murphy and Lehner returned to Advanced Base Camp to obtain replacement equipment for the former and additional high-altitude provisions.

On September 30 Coffield and Kelley proceeded up the broad, gentle ridge against high winds in low visibility carrying provisions to Camp III. The camp was placed at 20,800 feet to the north of a three hundred-foot bulge in the ridge called the "Hump". The Hump was the major technical obstacle of the climb, extremely steep on the west, nearly as steep and avalanche prone on the east. It would have to be renegotiated on the descent from the summit ridge.

They spent a sleepless night on October 1, holding the tent down in gale-force winds. A foot of snow fell during the night, but the next morning was clear and windless. Coffield led around the east side of the Hump but retreated because the slope was avalanche prone. They then found a crevasse which sloped diagonally upward for two-and-a-half pitches to the crest of the Hump. From that point they descended three hundred feet to the narrow, corniced ridge between the Hump and the main summit ridge. They continued up the ridge onto the east face, against high winds, and pitched Camp IV in a diagonal crevasse at 22,000 feet. The campsite gave protection from avalanches but was difficult to find on the descent.

On October 3 Coffield and Kelley left for the summit at seven A.M. on a bright, clear, almost windless day. They ascended the ridge on firm snow until blocked by weirdly shaped snow gendarmes a thousand feet below the summit. They traversed east across snow-encrusted rock in deterioriating weather. Beyond the maze of snow formations, they front-pointed 150 feet to the northeast face which led to the summit. They attained the summit at 4:30 P.M. in low visibility and began the descent at five P.M. They arrived at Camp IV after several hours in darkness, in a driving snowstorm, replete with thunder and lightning.

The next day they retraced their steps to Camp II. The reascent of the Hump was treacherous due to a foot of new snow and whiteout conditions. Michael Lehner greeted them at Camp II where he had spent two nights waiting for them in a bivouac sack after carrying a load of provisions from Camp I. Gongga was not to release them easily and they received yet another night of snow. After another agonizing decision about avalanche conditions between Camp II and Camp I, the three returned to Advanced Base without mishap on October 5.

In the following week we climbed two additional peaks northwest of Advanced Base. On October 6 Andrews and Caulfield attempted Nochma but were turned back by adverse weather. Andrews and Murphy made the first ascent of Nochma (18,790 feet) by the southeast ridge on October 8, and two days later Coffield, D. Kelley, B. Kelley and Lehner made the second ascent. On October 12 Coffield and Lehner made the first ascent of Gomba (18,840 feet) by the south ridge; Andrews and Murphy made the second ascent on October 13.

Summary of Statistics:

AREA: Sichuan Province, People's Republic of China.

ASCENTS: Gongga Shan (Minya Konka), 7587 meters, 24,891 feet, fourth ascent, via Northwest Ridge, October 3, 1982 (Coffield, D. Kelley).

Nochma, 5727 meters, 18,790 feet, First ascent, via Southeast Ridge, October 8, 1982 (Andrews, Murphy); October 10, 1982 (Coffield, B. Kelley, D. Kelley, Lehner).

Gomba, 5755 meters, 18,840 feet, first ascent, via South Ridge, October 12, 1982 (Coffield, Lehner); October 13, 1982 (Andrews, Murphy).

PERSONNEL: Joseph E. Murphy, *leader,* Edmund D. Andrews, Dana Coffield, Sharon Caulfield, Barbara Kelley, Douglas A. Kelley, Michael C. Lehner; Mr. Wong, *liaison officer,* Mr. Liu, *interpreter.*

PLATE 18

Photo by Douglas A. Kelley

Northwest Ridge of GONGGA SHAN from the "Hump."

Jiazi

RICHARD M. NOLTING

THE WEST FACE of Jiazi rose into veiw as I made my way across boulders to the edge of the Riuchi Glacier. The face was probably a mile high, broad, craggy and laced with snow-and-ice runnels—an ice-climber's mountain with a lot of routes to choose from. I was awed and stopped to ponder. Doug McCarty and Pat Callis caught up and passed me, mesmerized and babbling about a Callis-McCarty route on the face as if it were a years-old classic. But detailed route-finding could wait. From our brief reconnaissance we three now knew that the west side of Jiazi was where we wanted to be.

Jiazi is part of the Hengduan Shan, a north-south range bordering Tibet on the east but actually in the Sichuan Province of China. Our expedition of eight climbers and three cinematographers had been assembled by Fred Beckey with assistance from Jim Williams and funded by Quaker Oats. We were a diverse bunch coming from Montana, California and Alaska, with little or no "big-time" expedition experience and prone to chronic individualism. This latter trait tended to neutralize group decisions on the mountain. We also frustrated and ultimately amused our friends Messrs. Song and Zhao of the Chinese Mountaineering Association (CMA), who tried to keep us on schedule during our movements through China.

With our Tibetan horse train we had hop-scotched up the Jiazi Longba, first making Base Camp at the British Army Expedition site (A.A.J., 1982, pages 282-3.), and then moving further up to 13,000 feet after Fred Beckey decided this gave us the option to reach Jiazi from the west as well as the north. We had taken advantage of the British experience by coming to this valley and avoiding the east side. Now we were weighing their attempts on the north ridges with what we saw here. After our west-side reconnaissance and another by Beckey and Dave Stutzman* that same day, everyone favored a western approach.

We established Glacier Camp at 16,000 feet near the base of the west face. Once there, we quickly developed a more sober view of the route possibilities. Objective dangers seemed minimal—the face was virtually free of rockfall and

---

*Tragically killed in an avalanche while on ski patrol at Big Sky, Montana, December 24, 1982.

Photo by Richard Nolting

West Face of JIAZI. South Ridge route ascends skyline from South Col on right. West Face route ascends couloirs above climber's head.

hanging ice. However, a steep band of rock, the nemesis of the British expedition, crossed the upper 1000 feet of the mountain and appeared to be a deterrent to good routes on the northerly side of the face. All of us wanted to try the west face, but it seemed too uncertain for a first ascent, and too difficult to film. The south ridge to the right of the face looked more suitable. Moreover, it was not practical or safe for all of us to climb the face by the same route. But Dave Stutzman and Jim Williams were hooked on an elegant line leading directly up to the rock band, where they figured exits left and right surely existed. They proposed that after initially supporting a group effort to the south ridge, they would return to the face for a try.

The south col at 18,000 feet was a deep notch between Jiazi and G-Gongga; it was the first step towards reaching Jiazi's south ridge. On Halloween Doug McCarty and I tried to climb up to the col but barely got a third of the way. With John Markel and Pat Callis adding their efforts, we spent parts of two more days climbing to the col via a gully on the left side. The final leads had stretches of water ice and were somewhat steeper than the usual 45° angle. We fixed about 1500 feet of rope, giving us a veritable trade route from glacier to col. Jim Williams and Dave Stutzman returned from a west-face reconnaissance to help load-carrying to the south ridge.

On November 5, when we moved up the gully to put in Col Camp, the marginal weather finally turned against us. Our pleasure at reaching the col in two and a half hours was squelched by harsh winds and snow that blasted up the gully behind us, and four hours passed before we managed to cut a platform and pitch a tent. Conditions improved for a while the following day, so we made another gear shuttle and Peter Pilafian and Rob Hart came up with a second tent. Biff Bracht had experienced pulmonary edema and was forced to remain at Glacier Camp.

Now the storm took over completely. We six spent the next eight days wondering how long we'd have to hold out. We became convinced that the heart of winter was arriving. Frustrated by a continual bout with bronchitis, Fred Beckey was never able to get as far as the south col. His presence, however, was felt through the medium of our radio as he confirmed or criticized our moves and offered advice.

More favorable weather and dwindling provisions finally forced a move. Pilafian, Hart and McCarty went back down and left Callis, Markel and me with sufficient food for a summit attempt.

Above the col, rather than a south ridge, was a broad snow slope dotted with rock islands, stretching 1500 feet above the col. Though apprehensive about avalanches should there be more storms, we hoped we had time to get up the face. On November 14, our first climbing day since making Col Camp nine days ago, Callis and I bucked strong winds and made it to the lowest rocks, tying off 330 feet of climbing rope before retreating. John Markel joined us next day, and carrying gear and food for five days, we again fought the wind back to the ropes. Gusting wind continued to knock us sideways as we jümared to our high point. We continued up 50° slopes on firm snow, often using running belays to avoid being surprised by the wind. Several hours after dark, we finally sprawled exhausted on a large sloping rock. We used our two small tents as glorified bivy sacks, being unable to carve out more than a two-foot-wide niche in the slope. A cocoon of anchoring ropes and gear enveloped us. The night was magically still and not particularly cold. The next day mild winds and clear sunny skies allowed us enjoyable climbing above our bivouac and in three hours we reached the top of the face. The majestic north face of Gongga Shan had come into view directly south, but the most arresting sight was the sharply plunging northeast ridge of E-Gongga immediately southeast.

Above us and to the west rose the south ridge. We proceeded a short distance along the top of the south face to a bergschrund at the base of the ridge. In a corner of the schrund Pat found a cave with room for both tents and freedom from winds.

Our cave proved so comfortable that we did not start up the south ridge until 10:30 the next morning. With light packs we third-classed on reasonably firm very steep snow and eventually came out on an easy broad ridge 100 yards from the south summit 700 feet above our cave. In case we got no further, Pat filmed John and me walking the last few feet to the high point. We then wandered around taking still shots and studying the north summit. It looked like an easy 500-foot rise to the summit, but the half mile of intervening ridge might be time-consuming. The mind-numbing snow slog we had feared all along finally materialized. Fortunately it only amounted to a 45-minute wade around some cornices, and solid snow and easy slopes took us the rest of the way.

The summit of Jiazi was broad and seemed stable enough despite an abrupt drop on the east. We had noticed a thin corniced pinnacle that appeared on the ridge a quarter mile north. Was it higher? We hoped not, for the ridge narrowed dramatically in that direction. After filling a water cup, we leveled both summit and pinnacle and satisfied ourselves that we were on the highest point. Dave and Jim might soon be contemplating that pinnacle from the other side if they succeeded in climbing the west face.

Perhaps an hour later we headed back south. Down-climbing and several rappels brought us to our cave after dark. A radio call to Glacier Camp informed the others of our success and we celebrated by sleeping late once again. An afternoon start preordained a nighttime descent, but by now this schedule was almost ritual. The tenth rappel down the south face at twilight was on our last ice screw. Would it reach the col? Pat and I strained to keep John in view as he rappelled into darkness. We exulted when he suddenly disappeared over the bergschrund at the bottom. Pat and I then took our turns plunging over the schrund and into the roaring wind of the south col. After a night in the surviving tent at the col, we descended the fixed ropes with as much gear and camera equipment as we could manage.

During the next two days we sat lazily in camp watching Jim Williams and Dave Stutzman, now into the sixth and seventh day of their ascent, climb through the rock band and then finally on November 21 up to the north end of the summit ridge. They had done it! Some 5000 feet of ice-and-snow climbing

Photo by Jim Williams

Stutzman reaching rock band at top of JIAZI's West Face.

and eight bivouacs, together with a long spell of benign weather, had put them on the top of the west face. But now what? A long narrow ridge lay to the south between them and the summit. If they chose to forego that, a northern descent might lead into similar difficulties. Did they still have the equipment to make a safe descent of the face? Time was getting short. The expedition was due to leave Base Camp on the 24th. More importantly, the skies were cloudier each day. The following day, Jim and Dave were out of sight and we began conjecturing about their route down—and when yet another day passed, about other possibilities. On the third day they still had not shown up and we were distinctly worried.

The Tibetan porters had been up each day from Base Camp to check on Pat Callis and me and relay messages since we were out of radio range. Cheerful and gregarious, they loved a cup of tea and a smoke, and our tent was sometimes jammed with as many as eight people during these sessions. On that day, the Tibetans intuitively shared our concern and took turns scanning the mountain with the binoculars. Suddenly at two P.M. two more Tibetans showed up from below, gesticulating wildly as they handed me a note from Fred. Dave and Jim were safe at Base Camp! The collapse of a cornice had stopped them from attempting the summit ridge. After they had lost a pack containing stove and hardware down the east side, they descended the east face after it. The next day they climbed up to the northeast col and continued nonstop through the night down the Tshiburongri Glacier all the way to the Jiazi Longba, arriving dazed and gaunt at Base.

In a happy frenzy we packed up the remnants of Glacier Camp and headed down, accompanied by the singsong chants of the Tibetans and yodels by Pat. The reunion at Base Camp was heady. Everyone was physically together for the first time in a month. The place looked like a Montana dude ranch with dozens of horses and yaks. This was our caravan, ready to carry us down the valley to the other China, leading back to a different world.

Summary of Statistics:

AREA: Hengduan Shan, Sichuan, China.

FIRST ASCENT: Jiazi (Rudshe Konka), 6540 meters, 21,457 feet, via south ridge, summit reached on November 17, 1982 (Callis, Markel, Nolting).

> West Face to the ridge just below the summit, November 14 to 21, 1982 (Stutzman, Williams).

PERSONNEL: Fred Beckey, leader; James Williams, assistant leader; Patrik Callis, Robert Hart, John Markel, Dougal McCarty, Richard Nolting, David Stutzman, climbers; Biff Bracht, Peter Pilafian, Michael Stringer, cinematographers.

High-Altitude Archeology
and Andean Mountain Gods

Johan Reinhard

NTHROPOLOGISTS who climb normally must wait for free time to get into the mountains. Even when we study mountain peoples, such as the Sherpas of Nepal, the research rarely involves climbing unless it is to cross a pass to reach another populated valley. In South America, however, I learned of ruins (predating the Spanish conquest of 1532) on mountain summits, including well-built stone structures up to 22,000 feet. Such heights were not even *reached* again until nearly 400 years later. More than 40 sites had been discovered above 17,000 feet. This was something to attract the attention of any climber/anthropologist and what was to lead to my vacation in South America extending from a few months to three years.

Little has been written about these sites in English, Evelio Echeverría's account being a rare exception.[1] However, in South America some Chilean and Argentine climbers have been investigating them for several years. These climbers are mainly untrained in anthropology; only a few, such as the Chilean Pedro Rosende and the pioneer in the field, the Argentine Antonio Beorchia, have undertaken serious studies. Among professional anthropologists, only the Argentine Juan Schobinger did detailed work on more than a single site, although a few others made valuable contributions to the analysis of materials. Nonetheless, even the most basic questions remained unanswered: Who made them, how far through the Andes were they distributed and, above all, why were they made? It seemed logical that the only way to solve these questions would be to combine an investigation of the high-mountain sites with historical research as to the reasons for mountain worship.

I began in May 1980 by climbing Licancabur (19,421 feet; 5921 meters), a beautiful cone-shaped volcano in northern Chile, with Rolf Pfaffelberger. The ruins on the summit had been partially surveyed by Chilean climbers, and, for those not familiar with the symbolic significance of simple lines of stones,

---

[1] See "The South American Indian as a Pioneer Alpinist" in *Alpine Journal*, vol. 73: pages 81-88, London.

PLATE 21
Photo by Johan Reinhard
The World's Highest Archeological
Site on the Summit of Llullaillaco at
6721 meters or 22,051 feet.

the site is not overly impressive. The crater lake, frozen at that time of year, especially interested me, and I decided to return during the summer months to study the site and lake in more detail. Shortly thereafter, the archaeologist George Serracino and I investigated a rumor of ruins on the summit of Paniri (19,503 feet; 5946 meters), not far to the north. While Serracino searched a lower-lying crater, I climbed to the summit and found, among other things, an intact, circular dwelling and remains of a one-room structure with walls six feet high.

I left Chile with plans to return after receiving financial support in the U.S., but upon entering Peru the bag containing all my notes and slides was stolen. In Arequipa, Peru, I briefly joined Antonio Beorchia and other Argentine climbers to examine the remains of structures on Misti (19,093 feet; 5821 meters), and then returned to Chile to redo my previous research. I repeated the ascent of Licancabur with the archaeologist Ana María Barón, this time making plans of the summit ruins and, with Barón, mapped the large complex of over 150 stuctures at its base (15,200 feet; 4634 meters). This complex was exceptionally well preserved and gave the impression that the Incas, who had constructed them, had only recently left. Afterwards, Serracino and I returned to Paniri and carefully resurveyed the summit ruins. This site, too, proved to be of Inca origin.

In the meantime I had collected historical references to mountain worship, which up to that point hadn't proven very promising. Although high mountains, such as Coropuna, Illimani, Huascarán, Ausangate, and Salcantay, were known to have been worshipped in Inca times, the early Spanish writers rarely explained the exact reasons for this. In September 1980 an unpublished manuscript by the Inca specialist Tom Zuidema came into my hands. He briefly mentioned that mountains were still worshipped in a village not far from San Pedro de Atacama, where I was staying in northern Chile. I went there with Barón, and in the course of this trip I reached the summit of Miscanti (18,440 feet; 5622 meters). I continued alone to climb Chiliques (18,952 feet; 5778 meters) and Lejía (19,001 feet; 5793 meters). Archaeological remains were found on all of these peaks with important ruins on the summit of Chiliques. At its base I also found a complex of Inca ruins (called *tambo*) such as the one at the foot of Licancabur, but previously unknown to archaeologists familiar with the area. While returning from the ascent, I met a herdsman from the village who told me that Chiliques was the most important mountain worshipped in their annual ceremony for rain. The people were unaware of ruins on any of the peaks near their village, yet there exists an exact parallel between the relative importance of the mountains worshipped today and those with archaeological remains on their summits. Later I obtained a detailed account of their annual ceremony. It was this that prompted more intensive work on current-day mountain worship, since the beliefs and ritual clearly dated back at least to the Inca period. A later expedition with Barón and Serracino to the mountain confirmed the Inca origin of the site.

I found archaeological remains on three other peaks in the area above 18,000 feet, and in January 1981 Barón, Serracino and I returned to Licancabur on an expedition sponsored by the University of the North, Antofagasta. While carrying a load to the summit, I located structures at two places high on the mountain and various pieces of wood showing this to be the route used by the Incas. Two days later we ascended to camp on the summit and remained for four days. To see if offerings had been made in the lake, I carried up diving gear (loaned from DIGEDER, Antofagasta) and proceeded to make a very cold dive. At c. 19,200 feet; (5854 meters) this surpassed by c. 4000 feet the next highest known dive. (Unfortunately, a last-minute foul-up prevented the use of compressed air.) The lake is over 200 feet long and proved to be relatively deep—about 15 feet in the center. I found a dark layer, roughly four feet thick, covering the center-bottom and consisting of millions of crustacean larvae— something hardly to be expected at this altitude. Diving into this dark swarm under such unusual circumstances proved to be an unforgettable experience. Like others at altitude, I too have occasionally had the sensation of someone accompanying me who didn't exist. Never before, however, did I have visions of this being a giant squid! I also saw underwater mole-like tunnels through the sand made by something I wasn't able to identify. Although a few pieces of wood were found at about 12 feet, these were apparently thrown in without any purpose in mind and no offerings of any type were seen. We also carefully surveyed all the ruins on the summit and made a few exploratory excavations.

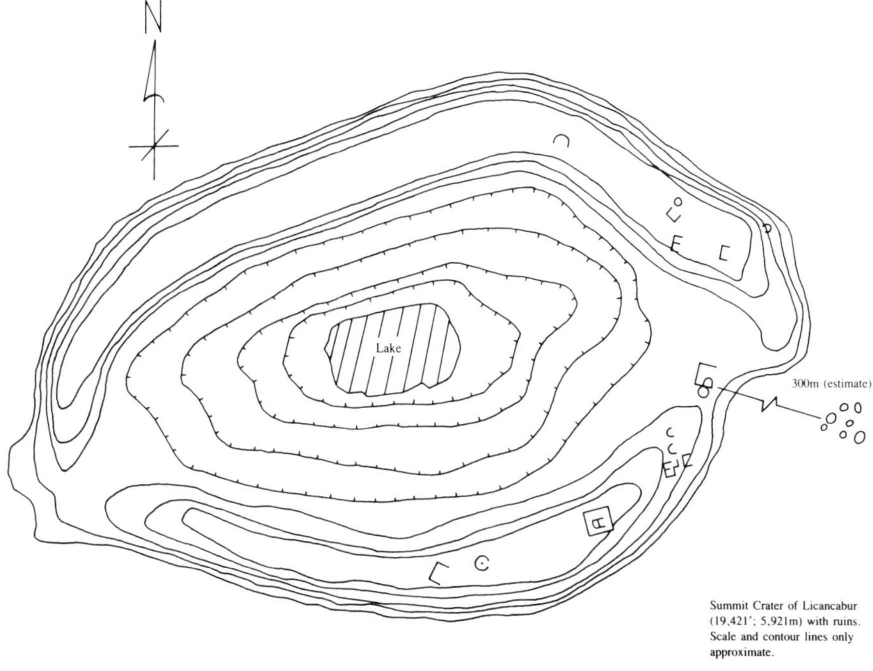

Summit Crater of Licancabur
(19,421'; 5,921m) with ruins.
Scale and contour lines only
approximate.

0   50m

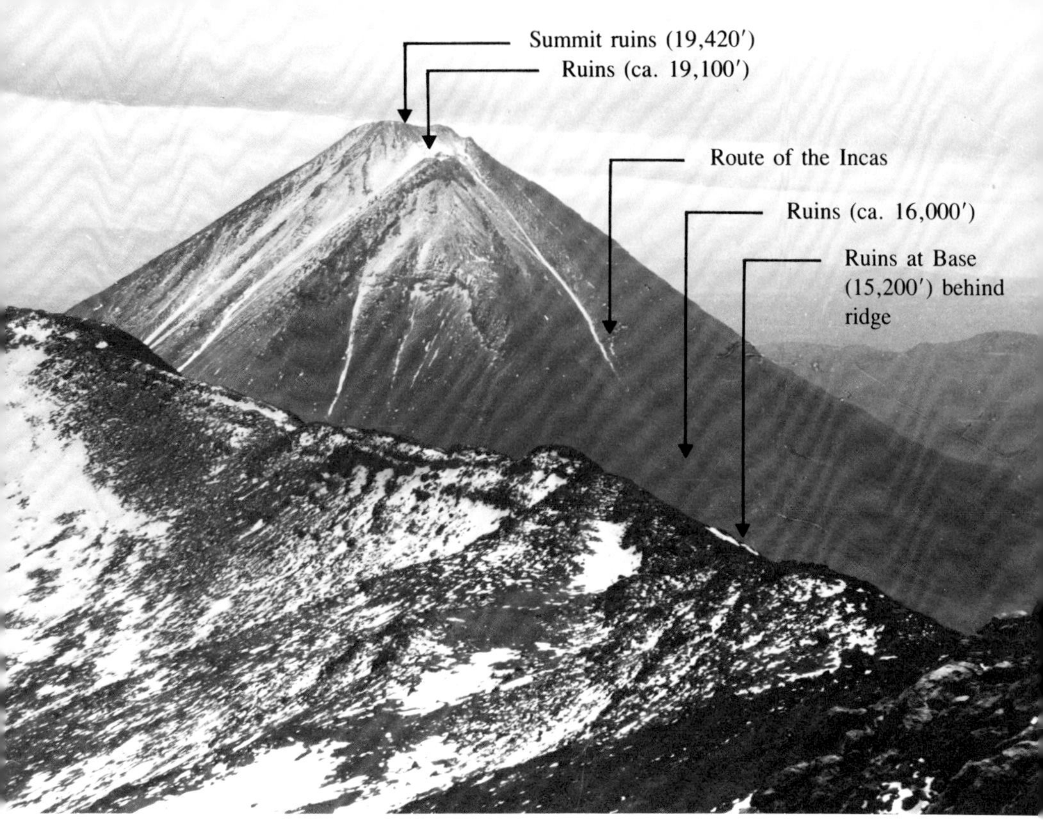

PLATE 23

A 16-foot retaining wall built by Incas to form an artificial platform on Tata Jachura's summit. Small mound of stones on right contains offerings made in recent times.

After Licancabur, I went to Aconcagua. I had heard of guanaco (a wild camelid related to the llama) bones between its two summits which I thought might indicate there were ruins nearby. It seemed unlikely that the guanaco would have gone to nearly 23,000 feet on its own volition. Unfortunately, after searching the summit (and finding no archaeological remains) a storm hit, and I was unable to take the time to search for the bones.

Next I joined Antonio Beorchia for a trip to northwest Argentina where ascents of Cerro Azufre (19,057 feet; 5810 meters) and Quehuar (20,106 feet; 6130 meters) were made. Storms occurred during both summit days on Quehuar, leaving four feet of snow and making work difficult. Antonio had surveyed impressive ruins here with walls six feet high and three feet thick, including a raised platform with steps leading to the top—an incredible feat at 20,106 feet. But now there was little visible beneath the snow, and we could only dig down to the layer of ice in which Antonio had seen the frozen body of an Inca child years before. Treasure hunters had been there before us, however, and, using dynamite, had blasted the "mummy." We picked pieces of cranium and an ear out of a wall that showed it originally had been perfectly preserved. Ironically, the treasure hunters destroyed something more valuable than anything they could have hoped to find.

A similar human sacrifice had taken place on the summit of Cerro El Plomo (17,810 feet; 5430 meters). This frozen Inca body was found in 1954 and is being kept refrigerated in the National Museum of Natural History in Santiago. It still yields valuable information, not only for anthropologists but also for physicians. So well preserved is the body that scientists have even tried to revive worms found in it. It is an example of the sparsity of anthropologists trained in high-altitude archaeology that none had even visited the summit site until 1982. Interestingly, human sacrifices to mountains have taken place in recent times, especially during droughts or when viewed as necessary to appease the deity when a construction work, such as road building, was taking place near it.

Following the Quehuar trip, I joined the archaeologist Julio Sanhueza and photographer Manuel Guzmán to explore the mountains of Tarapacá in far northern Chile, a project made possible by the support of the Professional Institute of Iquique. No high-mountain ruins had been reported from c. 16°26′ to 21°11′S. latitude, and it seemed likely that some would exist in the region, as we knew mountain worship still figured prominently in the beliefs of the people in the more isolated villages there. In the course of a two-week trip, we found ruins on the summits of three peaks, two of which were over 17,000 feet. On the summit of one, Tata Jachura (17,138 feet; 5225 meters), we found a large retaining wall, typically Inca, extending down for 16 feet. A few yards below Wanapa's summit (17,597 feet; 5365 meters) Manuel Guzmán, Raul Contreras and I found a large artificial stone platform, also of likely Inca origin. There may well be structures on the scenic mountain Cabaray (19,221 feet; 5860 meters) as rumors indicate, but it was deep in snow when I climbed it and no ruins were seen. Of particular interest is the fact that offerings are still made

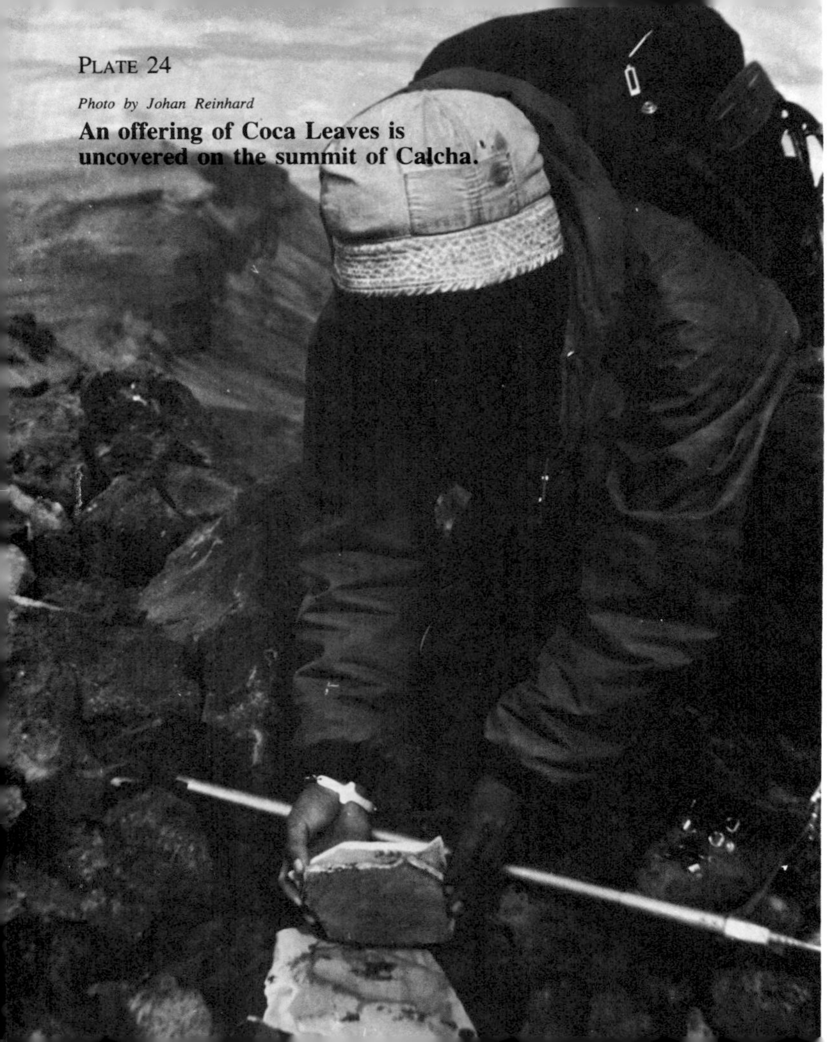

PLATE 24

Photo by Johan Reinhard

An offering of Coca Leaves is uncovered on the summit of Calcha.

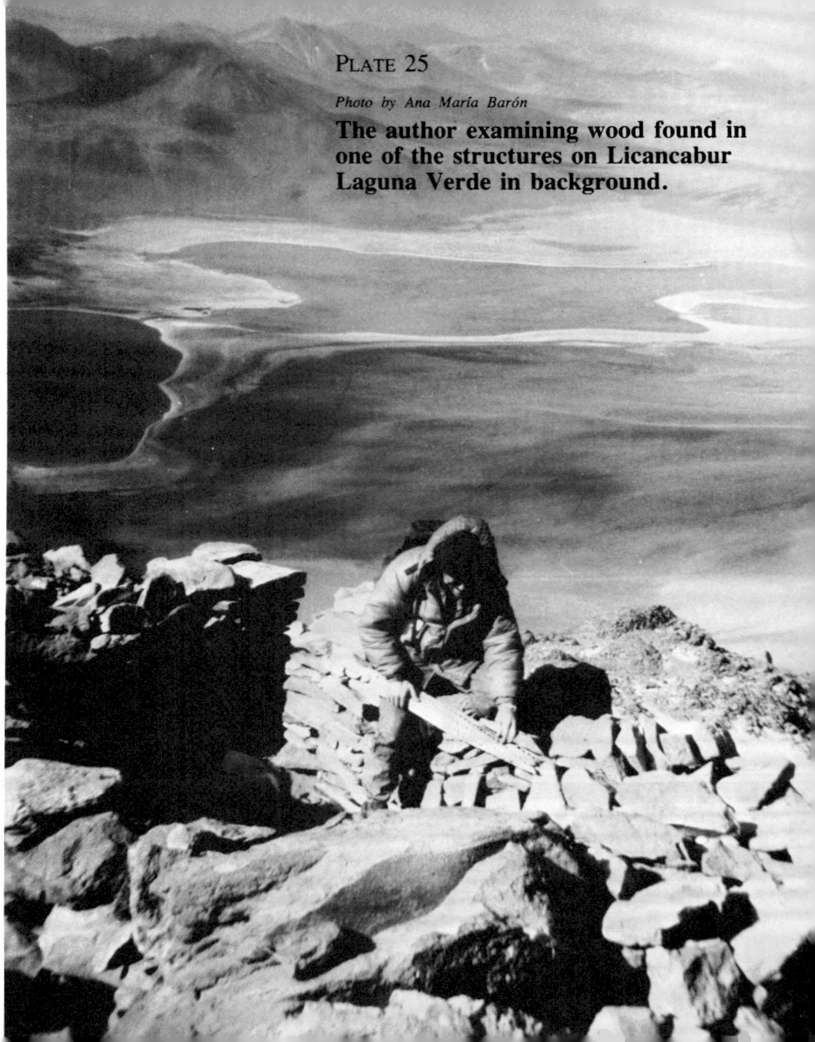

PLATE 25

Photo by Ana María Barón

The author examining wood found in one of the structures on Licancabur Laguna Verde in background.

annually in this area to the mountain gods for basically one reason—water. One peak, 17,663 feet (5385 meters) high, is still being climbed to perform this ritual.

By this time I had collected extensive information from historical sources, studied numerous ethnographic reports of other anthropologists, and had conducted my own research among villagers. I found that mountains were worshipped for a large number of reasons in the Andes. I have used the past tense here, but in fact virtually all these reasons still exist in traditional villages today. Mountain deities were frequently believed to be the original ancestors of peoples. There was a widespread belief that the souls of the dead reside in sacred mountains. (Indeed, still today some people in southern Peru believe Saint Peter is waiting with the key to open the door, not of the gates of Heaven, but of the spirit world within the mountain Coropuna!) Mountain gods were seen as protectors of man, livestock and crops, besides lords of all wildlife. Ritual specialists were selected by them who cured illnesses, foresaw the future, etc., all with the help of the mountain deities. They frequently communicated with them through birds, especially the condor. In the eyes of many Andean villagers today, the most powerful of the mountain gods are either equal to a supreme deity or act as his intermediaries to the people on earth.

But of all the reasons for mountain worship, one stands out—fertility. Mountain deities controlled meteorological phenomena (rain, snow, frost, hail, lightning, etc.) and through them were responsible for the fertility of crops and animals. Agriculture and pastoralism in the Andes is very dependent on cli-

PLATE 26

Photo by Johan Reinhard

The condor is believed the representative of the mountain gods. It plays a role in a festival, fed special food and drink and released.

matic factors: hail can devastate crops, floods or droughts can destroy herds and crops, and so on. The association of mountain gods with water has led to a symbolic connection between lakes, mountains and the ocean, conceived as the mother of all water. For this reason ocean water and seashells figured prominently in mountain worship, and mountains with lakes on them, like Licancabur, were especially sacred.

Mountains were usually worshipped for a combination of reasons. However, it was with regard to fertility that the majority of rituals in the past (and present) were undertaken. As we have seen, people are still ascending summits over 17,000 feet to make offerings for rain. It is much more common, though, for them to make these on the summits of lower hills or from other special places from which the most important peaks can be seen. This worship is normally done in secret or with a Christian veneer, there being no significant change in basic beliefs that have survived for over 500 years.

But what of the origin of the sites? I found in a report of 1570 clear references to the Incas building sites on mountains already worshipped by peoples they conquered, i.e. mountain worship was not something the Incas initiated, but rather was common before their arrival. Nonetheless, the evidence points to the Incas as responsible for the construction of the majority of high-mountain sites. This apparently was done to gain greater control (through building places of worship and making offerings to please the deities) over the elements necessary for the economic welfare of the people. Throughout the Andes the Incas either constructed or expanded irrigation canals, terraces, etc., for the purpose of increasing production which in turn helped support the Inca state and religion. The Incas also took the idols of the people they conquered to hold as hostages in Cuzco. Mountains proved something of a problem for the Incas in this regard, but it seems they solved it with characteristic audacity—they climbed to the summits, thereby coming into a more direct relationship with the mountain gods and usurping local worship. Contrary to the hypothesis of several scholars that high-mountain sites were made for sun worship, there is no solid evidence of this from historical sources. Although sun worship could well have taken place at these sites, the reason they were built clearly related to the importance of the mountains themselves.

If the Incas constructed them, why haven't any high mountain sites been reported further north? Actually, they have been noted by historical sources as existing in Ecuador, and expeditions have noted seeing archaeological remains over 16,000 feet in the central-northern Andes. The reasons they haven't been found much higher probably are due to the low permanent snow cover in the northern area, the lower heights of peaks in northern Peru, less research in these areas, and less interest in the modest ruins on summits even if they were found.

To test this theory I went to the Cordillera Blanca in Peru. I located ruins up to 16,000 feet that were previously noted by the 1932 German expedition on the west side of the Cordillera. I had the good fortune to meet Rob Blatherwick, who knows the mountains of the Cordillera Blanca well, and we

PLATE 27

Photo by Johan Reinhard

The world's highest divable water at 19,200 feet in the summit crater of Licancabur.

PLATE 28

Photo by Ana María Barón

In the crater lake on Licancabur. It was full of plankton, including larvae of millions of crustaceans.

went to the eastern side above the famous archaeological site of Chavin. We found structures at 15,500 feet (4726 meters), while villagers told us that others were on the summits of mountains of similar heights. Not high by southern Andes standards, but in this area they were as high as one could expect due to permanent snow cover at greater elevations. While looking for ruins, we climbed over the snow ridge separating the Huantsán and Carhuascancha river valleys (which involved a harrowing descent through an icefall above Lake Tumarina) and explored the area around Cerro Ango.

Other climbs followed this, including four ascents over 21,000 feet in Argentina that yielded no results beyond proving that not *all* the easy high mountains had been ascended in ancient times. However, a grant from the Explorer's Club and Brush Foundation enabled me to return to Peru in the summer of 1982 and obtain some interesting findings.

In the region of Arequipa, southern Peru, Miguel Zarate and I made several ascents. We first went to Pichu Pichu where ruins had been studied some years before and remains of a human sacrifice had been found at c. 18,368 feet; (5600 meters). We made a more precise plan of the site and located remains of wall sections leading to the second summit.

During an ascent of the eastern summit of Hualca Hualca (c. 19,516 feet; 5950 meters) we found a puma skin at the foot of a prominent boulder at about 19,188 feet; (5850 meters). The skin had been sewn and used as a container for ritual food offerings. We were told by a villager that offerings are still made to Hualca Hualca in an annual ceremony for water.

In collaboration with the National Institute of Culture, Arequipa, we next climbed Huarancante (c. 17,614 feet; 5370 meters). On the summit we saw the remains of charcoal and the river stones reported by Paul Rose and Peter Ross, and also found a spondylus shell and a llama figure carved from spondylus. The spondylus was considered indispensible in ceremonies for obtaining water during Inca times, and the river stones obviously played a role in such rituals. Preoccupied with surveying the site, we let an electrical storm catch us on the mountain and ended up having to bivouac until it cleared. Later we reached a herdsman's hut by moonlight. While surveying remains of a stone platform on the summit of Calcha (17,243 feet; 5257 meters), we once again were caught in an electrical storm. After these experiences, our dedication to science began to wane. However, we eventually did climb two summits in the Chachani Range, finding a large quantity of old wood on the lower one (c. 19,024 feet; 5800 meters). There are the remains of a wall on the main summit (19,867 feet; 6057 meters), but it appears to be of recent origin, and no traces of the Inca site noted nearly 100 years ago were seen.

Later I made a brief visit to the Cordillera Negra in central Peru where Rob Blatherwick and I climbed one of its highest peaks (16,420 feet; 5006 meters) listed as Cerro Rico on most maps. (The highest peak is actually called Almakaka by local inhabitants.) Although we did not find ruins on its summit, we saw remains of an *apacheta* (a stone mound of ritual use) just below it and stone structures at the pass (15,839 feet; 4829 meters). These appeared to be of recent construction, but it is not unlikely that much older structures were built there in the past. We didn't have time to check more carefully because once again we were caught in a snowstorm—something rather rare at noon in a cordillera which didn't come to be called "black" (negra) for nothing.

After the unseasonal blizzards on Aconcagua, Quehuar, El Plomo, Almakaka, Calcha and Huarancate, plus the theft of all my equipment and notes, the diaphragm of a lens sticking open with a loss of 25 rolls of film, and other mishaps I won't bother to recount here, I began to wonder if there wasn't something to the widespread belief of a curse associated with reaching the summits of sacred mountains. Generally, the local inhabitants are afraid of them, and not just due to the physical hazards. In their minds the mountains are inhabited by powerful deities, very much alive, with various servants of the deities and other dangerous spirits wandering the mountain slopes as well. This combination of religious and practical factors leads villagers to doubt that people could reach the summits even if they were fool enough to try. After I told one disbelieving villager I had been on the top of a major mountain in the area, he thanked me for the information and introduced himself as Jesus Christ.

Up to the present time (October 1982) I've made a fair number of ascents searching for ruins, including 36 over 17,000 feet, and have found 17 sites previously unreported in the literature. Several sites about which some information existed were investigated in more detail, and I reached a point where patterns and findings began repeating themselves. It took time to gain an eye for symbolic structures and for tying together various bits of evidence to reconstruct what happened 500 years ago. Of course, this process is still by no means complete. Interesting information was also collected in Peru, Chile and Bolivia indicating that mountain worship played a significant role in even low-lying ceremonial centers of great antiquity, a topic too complex to deal with here.[2] It might be added that many of the beliefs held with regard to high mountains in the Andes also pertain to low ones and are found as far away as the coastal region.

As to sites on high-mountain summits, it seems that the majority of the well-built structures above 18,000 feet were built by the Incas. No high-altitude ruins have been found to definitely predate them, and where positive identification has been made they have proven to be of Inca origin. Virtually all the areas in which they have been located were occupied by the Incas only for a period of about 40-60 years prior to the Spanish conquest. Since the better constructed sites were obviously used over time, there is no doubt that the Incas were regularly undertaking ascents up to 22,000 feet which most of us even today find challenging. These may not be technically difficult, but in terms of altitude, mountaineering sense (e.g. route-finding) and physical stamina they can at least be considered demanding. Imagine these ascents (not to mention the building of stone structures) being made in the 1400s! Overcoming the

---

[2] See my article "The Nazca Lines, Mountains and Fertility," in press, *Boletín de Lima*, Lima, Peru.

psychological barrier— brought on by a fear of mountain deities and evil spirits and a belief of general bad luck befalling climbers of sacred mountains—was itself a considerable accomplishment. One need only recall the superstitions prevalent at the time of the early climbs in the Alps to have some ideas of what the Incas were up against. Although I've seen cairns with prayer flags at 18,000 feet in Dolpo on the Tibetan border, I'm not aware of anywhere else on earth that structures were acutally built at such heights in ancient times.

In order to do this the Incas solved many of the basic problems of high-mountain ascents. We tend to take such solutions for granted today, but in mountaineering terms they represented a great step forward. One of these was the use of a "base camp" with camps at intervals on up the mountain. There are also buildings on the summits that clearly indicate they were used as temporary refuges, most likely for a single night (offerings were normally made at sunrise). They also had lesser structures built at points in visual contact with the base camp, probably used for signalling (albeit perhaps of a religious nature to indicate the sacrifices had begun). They managed to make routes that are not always obvious, but invariably showed mountaineering savvy. Straw was used for bedding and poles utilized to form supports for blankets, a sort of half-tent structure with a stone foundation. Findings indicate wool caps with flaps to cover the ears were used, as were leather sandals or moccasins with wool socks. Although ropes have been found, they were probably used only for carrying loads and not as aids in climbing. There is no indication that any technical aids were utilized, and the wooden pegs that climbers believed of Inca origin (found in place on a mountain in Peru) certainly date to more recent times. Huge piles of wood have been found on the summits and considerable amounts of ashes. In such thin air they may have had to use some flammable substance to help the wood burn, although we also found tinder at some sites. Llamas were used to carry supplies to the base camp (corrals have been found at them) and porters were doubtless employed to help build and supply the camps. At one summit site of 20,739 feet; (6323 meters) walls held in a rock-and-gravel filling to form a platform. This could only have been made with stones brought from 300 feet below. It was estimated that 4000 carries would have been necessary to complete the structure.

From a scientific standpoint research on high-mountain ruins really began only after the discovery of the famous El Plomo mummy in 1954, although occasional reports of such sites had been made since the 1800s.[3] Interest died down somewhat after this until the discovery in 1964 of an Inca body on El Toro at c. 20,664 feet (6,300 meters).[4] This find was also the catalyst for its co-discoverer, Antonio Beorchia, to establish the Center for Archaeological

---

[3] *La Momia del Cerro El Plomo* (1957), ed. by Grete Mostny and published in Santiago, Chile, remains a classic.

[4] This led to two publications that remain essential reading, the special Vol. 21 of *Anales de Arqueología y Etnología* (1966) and *La "Momia" del Cerro El Toro* (1966) ed. by Juan Schobinger, both published in Mendoza, Argentina.

Investigations in High Mountains. In 1973 this extraordinarily dedicated man began editing the first of four volumes on the topic of high-altitude ruins, the latest appearing in 1980. Antonio is now preparing a further volume which will bring together in summary form the essential data relating to all the known sites. The Center also maintains an archive and is the principal place where information on this topic is available to interested scientists. It is hoped that those climbers in possession of information and/or materials relating to high-mountain ruins will inform either the Center or myself. The address of the Center is: Centro de Investigaciones Arqueológicas de Alta Montaña, República del Líbano 2621, Correo de Capitán Lazo, (5423) San Juan, Argentina. In the U.S., I can be contacted at P.O. Box 74, New Lenox, Illinois 60451.[5] Thanks to a grant from the National Geographic Society, I will continue with research on high-mountain ruins through 1983.

The number of high-mountain sites is limited and few of the important ones were investigated prior to being pilfered and, occasionally, destroyed by treasure hunters and mountain climbers in search of souvenirs. Even if only one or two minor items were taken by each climber, a site would rapidly be depleted of finds, and we may never be able to determine who made them or reconstruct what took place there. Simple items, such as potsherds, can be extremely valuable to archaeologists, since they provide clues as to the origin, date of construction and functions of structures. Nothing should be taken from these sites—indeed it is against the law throughout South America to extract archaeological artifacts without prior permission. If there is some compelling reason to do so, a careful plan must be drawn and exact location of the site made known to archaeological authorities. There have been cases of climbers "saving" items and donating them later to museums, but lacking a site plan it has been impossible to analyze them in context. Such information might be more valuable than the finds themselves. We have also found that climbers have used the stones from symbolic structures (simple outlines) to make cairns or even, as on Misti, to spell their club's name! By removing even a few stones, the symbolic form can become unrecognizable. Although often simple in appearance, a careful study of the finds relating to the sites, their orientations, the patterns they form relative to each other, etc., will help us understand the religious beliefs underlying their construction. It would be a tragic loss to man's cultural (and mountaineering) heritage if materials which hold the key to such important ancient beliefs should disappear before they can be studied.

---

[5] For those who would like further details of the research summarized here, I have an article entitled "The Mountains of Power: an Ethnoarchaeological Study of High Mountain Ruins," in press, *Cuadernos de Historia,* Santiago, Chile.

Photo by H. Adams Carter

Rondoy, Mituraju and Jirishanca. Starts of Czechoslovak routes are marked by arrows. Polish route on Jirishanca is marked.

Czechoslovaks in the Cordillera Huayhuash

JAROMÍR STEJSKAL, *Czechoslovakia*

OUR SIX-MAN PARTY from Czechoslovakia visited the Cordillera Huayhuash in June. We established Base Camp on Jahuacocha.

The two youngest climbers, Dušan Becík and Ján Porvazník, chose the most difficult objective. Joined by the Englishman, John Tinker, they attempted to climb the center of Rondoy's west face. After a second bivouac in the first third of the face, on a very difficult traverse, Tinker took a 100-foot leader fall, but was luckily not much hurt. They decided to back off as the difficulties were greater than expected. Long sections of steep bare ice alternated with rotten rock.

They spent four days recovering in Base Camp, sampling pisco and going through "psychotherapy." Finally Dušan and Ján told John Tinker they were sorry to leave him and decided to start up again.

On June 6, early in the morning, the pair set off. On the following day in the afternoon, they reached the previous second bivouac. Nearly the whole next day they traversed below a huge sérac which hung from the upper third of the face. After entering the system of gullies that plunged down from the summit ridge, they had their third bivouac. They pushed forward, hoping to reach the summit the following day, but the snow gullies and ridges seemed endless. Approximately 650 feet below the summit, they had their fourth bivouac. At ten A.M. on June 10, they broke through the summit cornice.

But that was not the end of difficulties, as they faced a dangerous descent down the east ridge. After rappelling 1650 feet, they reached the glacier and by crossing the Paria Col, they returned to Base Camp.

Another two-man party, Slávek Drlík and I, attempted Jirishanca's southwest face. After the first pitches, still full of enthusiasm, we were "cooled down" by a huge, unavoidable bergschrund. After climbing 125 feet of nearly overhanging ice, we waded up 650 feet in the snowfield above. Below the huge ice couloir leading to the summit wall, there was another bergschrund. Getting over this took a lot of time, as a section of completely vertical ice had to be climbed. Overcoming these two obstacles deflated any hopes of a fast climb of

PLATE 31
Southwest Face of MITURAJU.

PLATE 30
Photo by Jaromir Stejskal
West Face of RONDOY.

the face. We decided to retreat, leaving 250 feet of fixed rope hanging over the schrunds.*

Another attempt—with proper respect this time—was made starting on June 11. We got past both the bergschrunds very fast and halfway up the 70° central couloir. On the way up the gully, an avalanche fell from the summit cornices. There was no hiding place, but fortunately we lost no more than a Bluet stove. On the next day we got to right under the summit wall, where we hacked a bivouac platform in the ice.

In the morning, sure of reaching the summit, we started up the rock summit wall in the mixed terrain, without bivouac gear. The difficult terrain—smooth slabs and unpleasant traverses—required a lot of time. It was obvious that we were not going to reach the summit that day and so we returned to the bivouac, leaving the most difficult sections fixed.

During the rappel to the bivouac, the weather deteriorated. All night we kept being buried beneath the snow collecting there from the whole summit wall. Our "great day" finally came, when we managed to find the right groove leading exactly to the summit. At two P.M. we balanced on the unstable cornice, hoping it would not break away. That same day we rappelled to the bivouac and on the following day descended to Base Camp.

Next, Yerupajá's west face was climbed on its left side by Ján Krajčík, Ján Kulhavý and Ján Porvazník.

The third new route was the first ascent of Mituraju, the 5684-meter summit which lies between Rondoy and Jirishanca. On June 21 Dušan Becík and I started up the southwest face, up a 65° gully that led directly to the summit. During the day and a half we were on the climb, the weather conditions were bad. It snowed continuously and small snow slides kept sloughing down the gully. We had to dig through the summit cornice. There was room on top for only one person at a time.

Summary of Statistics:

AREA: Cordillera Huayhuash, Peru.

ASCENTS: Rondoy, 5870 meters, 19,259 feet, new route via West Face, June 6 to 10, 1982 (Becík, Porvazník).

> Jirishanca, 6094 meters, 19,994 feet, new route via Southwest Face, June 11 to 14, 1982 (Drlík, Stejskal).

> Yerupajá, 6517 meters, 21,381 feet, via West Face, June 20 and 21, 1982 (Krajčík, Kulhavý, Porvazník).

---

*To that point the Czechoslovakian climbers followed the route first climbed in 1971 by Dean Caldwell and Jon Bowlin and followed by French climbers in 1981. Those two groups traversed from there upwards to the left to join the Cassin route on the west ridge. The Czechoslovaks continued on directly upwards.—*Editor.*

Mituraju, 5684 meters, 18,648 feet, first ascent via Southwest Face, June 21 to 22, 1982 (Becík, Stejskal).

PERSONNEL: Jaromír Stejskal, leader, Dušan Becík, Slávek Drlík, Ján Krajčík, Ján Kulhavý, Ján Porvazník.

Southwest Face of JIRISHANCA.

Taulliraju's Southwest Face

MICHAEL A. FOWLER, *Alpine Climbing Group*

OUR TEAM WAS composed of Michael B. Morrison, Christopher Watts, Anita McKee, Michael F. O'Brien, Dr. John English, John Zangwill and me. A two-day approach brought us in early May to a perfect Base Camp at 13,125 feet in the impressive Quebrada Santa Cruz, dominated by Taulliraju looming above the Punta Unión Pass.

We decided to attempt Kurikashajana as a convenient medium-altitude training peak. After a bivouac at 16,400 feet, we headed up the unclimbed south ridge. Lack of acclimatization, soft snow and bad weather discouraged us from going beyond the south summit.

After four days we turned to our chief objective, Taulliraju's southwest face. Morrison, Watts and I were to try the east buttress of the face whilst English and Zangwill opted for the west buttress*. The weather was bad and the latter team hardly went beyond the foot of their spur. We managed to climb six pitches on the east buttress after a common start with Nicolas Jaeger's route. (See *A.A.J.*, 1979, page 232.) After a day's climbing in very dubious weather, we had to admit defeat and return to Base Camp.

Unfortunately we had seemed totally incapable of climbing as a rope of three. After much heart searching, only Chris Watts and I returned for a second attempt the next day. Our line was almost entirely to the left of Jaeger's route. Starting at the toe of the spur, we climbed a rock pitch to gain prominent snowy gangways on the south side of the spur. We followed these over several steep sections for a couple of pitches until it was possible to trend leftwards, away from Jaeger's route, to gain the snowy crest of the buttress, where we made out first bivouac. We ascended the very soft snow ridge mainly on the left (west) side until we could traverse left for 60 feet to gain an icy couloir leading up to the end of the snow ridge. Above this, the angle increased and very steep rock grooves, trending slightly right for two pitches, led to an ice patch where we hacked a ledge for our second bivouac. On the third day we continued just to the right of the crest up very steep mixed ground until, after four or five pitches, this line ended in very steep blank granite walls. Further progress without bolts appeared impossible but by following a thin horizontal crack

---

*Climbed by Italians in 1980. See "Climbs and Expeditions" section in this *Journal*.

TAULLIRAJU. Italian route on left, Fowler-Watts route in center, Jaeger route on right.

PLATE 34

Photo by Michael Fowler

**Chris Watts on aid pitch on third
day on TAULLIRAJU.**

leftwards on aid for 30 feet, we crossed a vertical wall to the very crest of the buttress. We were lucky to find a crack left of the crest which gave us an aid pitch to gain the obvious snow band at two-thirds height, where we bivouacked for the third time. The intimidating next band had only one weakness, a prominent 80-foot icicle which gave some exciting climbing leading to the final ice slopes, up which we continued for two pitches for our fourth bivouac. Above this, vertical climbing on extremely rotten ice enabled us to pass a rocky cliff on the left, before traversing right over uniquely Peruvian ice formations to join the southeast ridge just below the summit (5830 meters, 19,128 feet), which we reached at noon on the fifth day, May 26.

Due to our having hardly any equipment left, we were forced to down-climb the top two grade-5 pitches, and then about 20 rappels and one more bivouac on the same site as our second night saw us back on the glacier at the foot of the base.

Meanwhile, the rest of the team, Mike Morrison, Mike O'Brien and Anita McKee, climbed Millishraju II (5500 metres, 18,209 feet) from the northeast on their second attempt on May 22 whilst John English and John Zangwill were defeated by dangerous snow formations on the unclimbed south face of Rinrijirka. McKee, Morrison, O'Brien, Zangwill and English also had the misfortune to be stopped on the ordinary route up Huascarán by a 40-foot vertical ice wall for which they had not brought enough equipment. (This line of ascent is frequently an easy walk.)

Summary of Statistics:

AREA: Cordillera Blanca, Peru.

ASCENTS: Taulliraju, 5830 meters, 19,128 feet, new route on the Southwest Face, May 22 to 26, 1982 (Fowler, Watts).

Millishraju II, 5500 meters, 18,049 feet, from the northeast, May 22, 1982 (Morrison, O'Brien, McKee).

PERSONNEL: Michael B. Morrison, Christopher Watts, Anita McKee, Michael F. O'Brien, Dr. John English, John Zangwill, Michael A. Fowler.

Kichatna Spire's East Face

Scott Woolums

E COULD HEAR THE roar of powder avalanches coming. Seconds later they would hit our porta-ledges, smashing the tent flies against our faces while we waited out a 48-hour storm. The spindrift had already soaked our bags and us in this miserable camp. Bill Denz and I were deep in our own thoughts as the winds buffeted our ledges. Five hundred feet of overhanging granite were below us and 2500 feet still to climb. We read or scribbled our thoughts down. On the second day I had to move, to do something different. In all my clothes and then covered with a Gore-Tex and Thinsulate suit, I crawled out into the wind and spindrift. Belayed by Denz from inside his ledge, I managed almost a full rope-length before retreating freezing to my porta-ledge for a hot drink and another long night.

We had flown to the Shadows Glacier two weeks before in early April and placed Base Camp at the foot of the huge east face of Kichatna Spire. We had chosen this time of the year since in my experience in the Alaska Range April has the best weather. We were the earliest party to try a route in the Cathedral Spires. I had read accounts of waterfalls, wetsuits, rockfall and 30-day storms on the precipitous walls. It was a gamble to be so early, but it paid off. In April there was no water running off the big walls. The snow was so light that we could blow it off the face holds. Temperatures dropped to $-20°$ F but the weather was usually clear during the early spring high-pressure systems.

It was hard to envision this as the wind bit intensely during our first two days on the face. On the first day we had climbed three A4 pitches off the glacier and worked our way up a small prow which led to the major corner and crack system in the center of the face.

Sunshine warmed our ledges on the fourth morning. Both of us were anxious to start grinding away at the pitches above, glad to be moving after being confined for so long.

Finally, on the seventh pitch, at the top of the prow, the angle eased. I was free-climbing in mixed terrain, first 50 feet, then another 60 feet and still no real protection other than a poor small stopper. I climbed another 50 feet and heard Denz yell, "No more rope!" What now? I traversed, hacking out massive quantities of ice, and at last smashed an angle placement into the ice and rock. I tied off 15 feet of haul line and moved up some more to where I could place an A1 Friend. After belaying Denz up and hoisting our two haul bags, we were at our second camp.

For the next couple of days the climbing was vertical with short over-hanging sections. Everything was chocked with ice, forcing us to chip and

PLATE 35

Photo by Ed Cooper

KICHATNA SPIRE from the east.
Woolums-Denz route (April) on
right. Black-Graber-Schunk route
(June) on left.

scrape for each placement, which limited our free-climbing. The routine was the same: fix three leads and then pull camp up. We had strings of hook moves, Friends behind loose flakes or seams into which we bashed small RPs. Fortunately the rock improved with the altitude and the worst, at the start, was behind us.

We placed our third camp almost halfway up, under a huge roof, which from below had looked like the major obstacle. Luckily for me, it was Bill's lead. I belayed from my ledge, enjoying the sunshine while he tackled a 25-foot, upside-down, flaring groove. Just cleaning this pitch was as hard as anything I had led so far!

The next day we started up the overhanging flared chimney above the roof, very strenuous climbing for 200 feet. The weather took a turn for the worse. It was as hard as climbing to stay warm in the hanging belays in the spindrift. I had all my clothing on plus Bill's duvet and my half-bag. Fortunately the powder avalanches hissed by about ten feet out from the belay.

Clearing weather got us started early the next morning and, moving camp up, we attacked progressively easier pitches above. The clear weather brought bitter cold, a trade-off. We climbed almost in a trance, putting pitch after pitch behind us, past our fourth and fifth camps, but still in great weather. We traveled at a snail's pace, having to clear each placement and finding only rare protection in the free-climbing sections. Late on the eighth day, we fixed rope to the bottom of the summit icefields and rappelled back to our porta-ledges.

At first light we could see from the thin, high clouds approaching bad weather. We threw minimal bivouac gear into our packs and kicked off our haul bags, watching them bounce only twice before sliding out onto the glacier nearly 3000 feet below. We were now committed to getting down soon. We had thrown down all our extra food, fuel, ropes, hardware and our porta-ledges. We climbed the fixed ropes to the summit icefield and then fourth-classed up a steep snow-and-ice gully, interspersed with several mixed sections, to the summit. It was odd to be able to see 360° around with no more rock above. The granite spires of the Cathedral Mountains rose out of the huge deep valleys between them. But by now, the storm was moving in fast, with the wind whipping in from the south.

We were committed to traversing the mountain and started down the north ridge, the first-ascent route. After weaving around mixed sections and traversing ice and a corniced part, we began to rappel. The increased wind was blowing our rope horizontal. At each rappel we crossed our fingers, hoping the rope would not hang up on the many perlon-eating flakes. Our prayers didn't help; our rope hung up. Bill jümared up and freed it. After ten rappels, we came to the top of "The Secret Passage," a 1500-foot-long couloir. With perfect snow conditions, it took us an hour to descend to the glacier.

It was a relief to walk on flat terrain again. Bill grabbed the haul bags and I retrieved the snowshoes we had stashed at the foot of the climb for the endless walk back to Base Camp. We collapsed there with no thought for anything but sleep.

We were scheduled to fly out the next day, but instead of the plane, a seven-day storm came, dropping five feet of snow. On the first decent day our pilot, Jim Okonek arrived. As we flew out through the clouds, I felt it had been a dream. Had it actually happened? Then I looked at Bill's big grin. I knew it was very real!

Summary of Statistics:

AREA: Cathedral Spires, Kichatna Mountains, Alaska.

THIRD ASCENT BY A NEW ROUTE: Kichatna Spire, 2748 meters, 8985 feet, via East Face, April 1982 (William Denz, *New Zealander* and Scott Woolums, *American*).

Kichatna Spire: East Face Prow

MICHAEL GRABER

TUCKED AWAY in a corner of the Alaskan Range lies a maze of glaciers and rock known as the Cathedral Spires. Approximately 45 miles southwest of Mount McKinley, the Spires are famous for Yosemite-like walls and terrible weather. Kichatna Spire, the highest peak in the area, towers over its neighbors like a giant, ice-encrusted tombstone in the center of a graveyard. Its honey-colored granite walls drop straight down to glaciers on all sides. So difficult is this peak that after its first ascent in 1966 (*A.A.J.*, 1967, pages 272 to 278), it took 13 years and at least seven failures before it saw a second ascent (*A.A.J.*, 1980, pages 473 to 480).

The east face of Kichatna is one of the largest, continuously steep rock walls in North America. More than a face, it is a series of three vertical to overhanging buttresses stacked side by side. The left buttress is the longest. Nearly 1000 meters from glacier to summit and practically ledgeless, this prow sweeps straight to the summit.

In June 1978, Alan Bartlett, David Black, Alan Long and I flew into the Spires to attempt this face. During the month we spent there, we had several close calls and miserable weather. The sheath on a fixed rope broke and Black slid back down the first pitch until the rope's sheath bunched up and his Jümars locked. Bartlett took a long leader fall and accidently knocked a large block of granite loose. It fell and struck Black, knocking him off the belay stance. At the top of the eighth pitch a storm moved in and, after lying soaked and cold in our hammocks, we rappelled back down the route. The overhanging sections were technical and dangerous. Once back on the glacier, we were still forced to wait out the weather for 17 more days until we could fly out. Needless to say, we weren't anxious to return.

Four years later, however, the memories of our ordeal on Kichatna Spire had faded enough so that Black was able to convince me to return. We had a difficult time finding a third; the wall had a bad reputation. Although George Schunk knew the Spires and had heard the rumors, he accepted almost immediately. I often wondered about my partners; they had subjected themselves to the high-pressure brutalities of medicine and law to the point where even Kichatna Spire seemed like a vacation.

Our strategy this time would be different. We knew that our route had at least one good ledge approximately 500 meters off the glacier. Our plan was to fix the initial 120 meters and then, when the weather appeared stable, climb day-and-night until we reached the ledge. At this point we would have two

PLATE 36

Photo by *Michael Graber*

Schunk at a Porta-ledge Bivouac on East Face of Kichatna Spire.

choices. If the weather was good, continue for the summit. If the weather was bad, face the ugly affair of rappelling back down the route. In any event, we wanted to avoid another bivouac in hammocks during bad weather.

The month before we were ready to leave, we received the disappointing news that the face had been climbed. However, their ascent was not on the line we had attempted, but on the buttress to the right of ours. Their route was a fine one. Yet we felt that the exposure and directness of our route justified a renewed effort. We didn't have the first route on the face but we felt we might have a chance at the best one. The question of disappointment quickly disappeared and we were ready to go.

In mid-June 1982, we found ourselves back on Kichatna Spire, fixing the first two pitches. The climbing seemed to go more smoothly this time—maybe it was the Friends or maybe it was the fact that we had been here before. Late in the second day, Schunk and I rappelled as the first storm moved into the range.

The next three days passed with intense inactivity. During moments of inspiration, Black lectured on mountain medicine, Schunk told us of our rights under search and seizure laws and I addressed ways to improve a parallel turn. For exercise we stepped out into the blizzard to go to the bathroom.

Avalanches roared in the distance as we jümared up the ropes and hauled the bags. Black ran out a pitch so far that we had to unclip his rope from the anchors and tie on the haul line. I jümared over an overhang on a rope that we had left during our escape four years before. After 18 hours, we reached our previous high point and found our haul bag and equipment, mysteriously just as we had left it. The side of the bag that was against the wall was bright orange. The side exposed to the sun had been bleached white.

Leading quickly, Schunk disappeared over a small roof and broke into new territory. The first rays of sunlight nicked the summits of Augustin and Gurney. Every major peak within 160 kilometers was visible. The weather was perfect.

Too perfect. Loosened by the sun's warmth, blocks of ice broke off from near the summit and like a flock of doves, flew past our belay. In a matter of minutes, our crack turned from a drip to a small waterfall. Leading as fast as possible, Black angled left toward cracks that appeared safer. A piece of ice exploded in his face and left a small cut on his cheek. Meanwhile, Schunk and I put on all our Gore-tex and scrambled to avoid getting soaked.

We traded leads up awkward, overhanging cracks. Our energy began to fade—we had been climbing continuously for over 30 hours and we were badly in need of a ledge. Using tied-off knifeblade pitons, Schunk angled a few meters across a 65° slab to a jam-crack and free climbing. Black and I were dozing when Schunk yelled down that he had reached a ledge.

When we arrived at the ledge, I saw that although not big, it had potential. While I melted snow on the stove, Black stomped and kicked away at the snow to make a suitable spot for two and Schunk arranged the third sleeping spot—a Porta-ledge hanging to the side of us. Around midnight we finished dinner and passed out.

Photo by George Schunk

Graber at the top of the ninth pitch on KICHATNA SPIRE.

I woke three hours later from cold feet in wet socks. As the sun came up, the summits of nearby peaks turned bright orange and then immediately faded to a dull grey. High clouds were moving in from the south. The party was over. I tried to go back to sleep but ended up staring at the sky and worrying about the weather.

We munched granola and Black took the lead while Schunk and I packed the bags. The right-facing corner required our largest pitons lengthwise and all of our tube chocks. Schunk and I were singing Jackson Browne songs when we heard the telltale "pop" and the jingle of weightless hardware. We looked up and saw Black in the middle of a backwards swan dive. The rope came tight and he pendulumed into the wall, head first.

Unhurt but shaken, Black came down to gather his wits and Schunk went up to finish the pitch. Above Schunk's belay was another wide chimney, full of ice and ominously dripping. Doing anything to avoid this chimney, I aided up cracks to its left and then stemmed across the chimney to cracks on the right. I was in the chimney only a few moments, but this was sufficient time to be struck by a sizeable piece of ice.

The sky grew darker, the cloud ceiling got lower, but we were moving well. It was going to be tight but I felt we had a good chance in our race against the weather. Besides, the quickest and safest way down from where we were then might well have been from the summit and down the north ridge. There was no question of retreating.

Finishing the sixteenth pitch, Schunk mantled onto a ledge, only the second such refuge we had thus far found. A stiff wind brought spindrift down on us as Black rapidly aided up another leaning dihedral. At the top of the dihedral, a large icicle loomed perilously, forcing Black to the left to avoid it. Above his belay we found a steep gully which allowed easier climbing. Expecting more of the same, Schunk charged around a corner but there found one of the climb's more difficult pitches; a F10 offwidth. The next pitch was ice. Hanging from Jümars, I strapped on our only pair of crampons, pulled out our only ice-axe and led what we hoped was the last hard pitch. My only thought was to get the hell out of this icy chimney. The rock was crumbly but the ice was good and I climbed to a keyhole underneath a large chockstone. As I poked my head through the window, I could see the summit only a pitch away.

I found a sheltered ledge on the lee side of the ridge and belayed the others up to discuss our next move. We felt like zombies as we tried to talk, spent from 75 hours of climbing with very little rest. Embick, who had done the second ascent, had told us that the summit ridge would be tricky and we could see that he was right. Everything that we no longer needed was tossed back down toward the start of the route. We climbed simultaneously, I with the axe in one hand and a haul bag in the other and Black and Schunk with monstrous loads. Feeling the press of time even stronger, we had sacrificed safety for speed. More than on the steeper climbing below, there was no room for the slightest error as we threaded our way around rock towers on the narrow ridge to the top.

One by one, we arrived at the summit and collapsed. A mixture of feelings flowed through us from exuberance to a nervous concern over the descent. The summit had been reached, but our race with the weather was not over.

We gathered our gear and carefully traversed the corniced north ridge, Black and Schunk without crampons. The ridge widened and we moved together until an icy section and strong winds forced us onto the north face. The wind continued to trouble us for the entire ten rappels. Even so, we were so exhausted that while waiting our turns to rappel, each of us kept falling asleep. Obviously concerned with this potentially dangerous state, we passed around a bottle of amphetamines and faced the last few rappels.

We kicked steps down the Secret Passage and walked out onto the glacier. After 90 hours of climbing with only five of rest, we felt safe at last. Jabbering and laughing, we skied back to camp for a celebration of warm food and hot tea. After our energy finally fizzled and we fell into a long and badly needed sleep, our victory was made even more poignant by the storm which settled in and kept us tentbound for the next six days.

Summary of Statistics:

AREA: Cathedral Spires, Kichatna Mountains, Alaska Range.

ASCENTS: Kichatna Spire, 8985 feet, fourth ascent, new route on east face, June 23-27, 1982, (NCCS VI, F10, A5).

> "Kathryn Minaret," 6300 feet (½ m. north of P6847), first ascent via south ridge, June 4, 1982, (NCCS III, F9).

> "Whale's Back Peak," 6500 feet, third ascent, first descent of north ridge on skis, June 7, 1982 (Graber) (Listed fifth in Embick's list on p18, *A.A.J.*, 1982 as P c6500).

> "Sequel Spire," 6400 feet (½ m. south of P6847), first ascent via southeast face, June 7, 1982, (NCCS II, F9) (Black, Schunk).

PERSONNEL: David Black, M.D., Michael Graber, George Schunk.

Alone on Denali's
South Face

MARK HESSE

I WAS AT AN IMPASSE. Seated on my pack with my elbows on my knees and my chin buried in the palms of my hands, I stared intently at the face. I had ventured out across the glacier only two hundred yards before fearfully retreating back to Michael Covington's South Buttress party. Despite their preoccupation with crossing a large crevasse, they no doubt sensed my indecisiveness. I sat for a moment and then, on an impulse, stood, shouldered my pack, adjusted the twelve-foot aluminum pole that I had fashioned to protect me on my solo treks across the glaciers, and began again the final mile to the base of the face. I carried with me 55 pounds of food and equipment, one rope, my ice tools, and one thousand questions and fears. A solo ascent of any magnitude demands a certain mind-set. One must be mentally ripe for it. As I strode up the valley below the tremendous objective that I had so audaciously come to climb, I wondered if it was for me such a time.

I had arrived at Denali in late April. After a futile attempt at the West Buttress with my brother Jon, I reorganized my gear for an attempt at the mountain's South Face. My plan was an ambitious one. The 9000-foot face was first climbed in 1967 by an American team over the course of one month. They employed 7000 feet of fixed rope. In 1976, Dougal Haston and Doug Scott, fresh from Mount Everest, followed the first-ascent party's route to 16,800 feet, then ventured out across and up the upper icefield to the summit ridge. They completed the route in six-and-a-half days. Their ascent was the harbinger of a new standard on Denali and in the Alaska Range, the climbing of major faces and ridges alpine-style. The South Face was climbed twice after the 1976 ascent, by the Japanese in 1977, who made a new direct start to the American route, and by the Slovaks in 1980, between the American direct and the South Buttress. It was my intention to push the standards on the face one step farther by following in Haston's and Scott's footsteps, alone.

The initial problems that I had encountered were negotiating the long approach up the east fork on the Kahiltna and finding the face in proper condition. Michael Covington invited me to join his team for the approach which solved my first problem. And I was fortunate enough to find the face in excellent shape. The mountain appeared to be at rest, tranquil in mood. The fury that had enveloped the peak during the previous weeks and which had spelled defeat for my brother and me had subsided. It appeared that there had been but a dusting of new snow above 12,000 feet and that the arctic winds which had blown incessantly until that time had worked to sweep and tightly pack the face.

I was standing in the bergschrund at the base of my route when I heard the ominous sound of falling séracs. Great billows of snow and ice fell from the sky, swept out across the entire breadth of the valley, rose high into the air and slowly settled back onto the glacier. After leaving Michael's company, I had kept to the east side of the valley, moving as quickly as the weight of my pack would allow me. I reached the safety of the schrund only moments before Big Bertha, the tremendous icefall situated halfway up the South Face, let her true might be known. I had never been so close to an avalanche so large. Fortunately, I was well out of harm's way. Nonetheless, it left me extremely shaken and even more anxious about the coming days. As I shoveled out a platform for my tent, I tried often to locate Michael's party, but in vain.

The following morning I forced myself from my sleeping bag as soon as possible and was soon ready for my first day of climbing. A short step over the schrund brought me onto the expansive lower icefields. The snow that covered the ice was unconsolidated in places and, consequently, the climbing was tedious. Much of my apprehension, however, was lost as the overall enormity of the climb was reduced to a series of individual moves. I climbed throughout the day, reaching the first rock band late in the afternoon.

I had anticipated some difficulty in finding spots where I could bivouac, especially on the first half of the route. As I expected, there was not a ledge that wasn't encased in ice. Despite the fact that I had several hours of daylight left, I stopped early to begin my search for an accessible sleeping site. I soon located a small step and after an hour and a half of chopping, managed to fashion a small trench large enough to lie down in. As I peered out across the arctic wasteland from my tiny ledge, the protection afforded me by my sleeping bag and bivy sack seemed ever so meager.

Early the next day, I descended from my perch and back onto the icefield. As I climbed higher and the glacier slowly fell away below me, the exposure grew more taxing. Continuous front-pointing on the 55° to 60° ice with my heavy pack worked me into a state of acute physical and mental exhaustion. The afternoon of my second day found me scrambling around once again on steep rock and ice at 14,000 feet, looking for a ledge on which to situate myself for the night. After some difficult mixed climbing, I gained a small bench and began the task of shaping out a trough.

I arose the following morning still fatigued. My night's sleep had done little to assuage the strain of the previous day. As I rappelled down from my bivouac ledge, I became particularly anxious about the next section of the icefield. It was entirely free of snow and glistened in the morning sun. After 300 to 400 feet, I began to question my endurance and sought out a variation through the

PLATE 38
Photo by Bradford Washburn
Hesse's route on the South Face of
MOUNT McKINLEY.

rocks. It was a costly decision for I spent the next two-and-a-half hours belaying myself and hauling my pack up a series of short vertical cracks. I was finally able to traverse to a ledge at the edge of the icefield. My confidence was battered and I began to contemplate the extraordinary position in which I had succeeded in placing myself. I had expected to complete the climb in four or five days, in approximately the same time that Chris Reveley and I had taken on the Cassin Ridge three years before. Based on my progress, I estimated that it would take me two to three days longer than I had originally predicted. With only ten days of food, I would not be in the position to sit out a storm should one occur. I was also nearing the point of no return. A retreat from much higher on the face would be extremely difficult, given the conditions and my limited amount of equipment. The next section involved a traverse to a narrow couloir. It was impossible to see into it from my vantage point. An hour later I still sat, locked in indecision.

In the same fashion that I had ventured out across the glacier to the base of the face three days before, I finally struck out across the ice. Never had I felt so extended on a climb; however, despite the degree to which I was pushing myself, I could not in the end turn from the challenges above.

The further out I climbed, the more the couloir came into view. Despite its 70° to 75° angle, it appeared to be chocked with snow. A tension traverse through a rock-and-ice section brought me to a platform at the base of the couloir where I chopped out a bivy ledge. As during the two previous evenings, the air was still and the peaks to the south presented themselves in full grandeur in the setting sun. The day had been without question my nadir up to that point and I had come ever so close to retreating.

The following day was magnificent: clear and warm. The climbing up the couloir was varied in nature and its complexity kept me absorbed. After 500 to 600 feet the couloir steepened in a nearly vertical headwall that brought me to a rather large platform. It was here in this place at 15,000 feet that Haston and Scott spent their horrid night, ravaged by the wind. They described it as the most difficult night that either of them had experienced in the mountains. From my past experiences, I knew full well what misery the weather on Denali can inflict. I remembered the day and night that Chris and I spent at 17,500 feet on the Cassin in our bivy sacks huddled amongst the rocks in similar conditions. The wind and severe temperature, which combined have earned the peak the reputation as being one of the coldest major mountains in the world, are a constant threat. I had been extremely fortunate in most respects. The weather had remained clear and stable.

The spiral couloir branched out left from the platform. It presented the most difficult climbing that I had yet encountered. Encased in hard, brittle ice, it steepened to nearly 80° at the top. I attacked it full on, reaching a snowy knife-edged ridge, close to total exhaustion. I rested briefly then continued on in the fading daylight, as at peace as I have ever been in the mountains. I reached a large overhanging boulder and climbed under it for the night. It grew horribly cold. Later I learned from a party on the West Buttress, who were at roughly the same elevation as I, that the ambient air temperature on that evening at 10:30 P.M. was $-50°$ F. Who knows to what ungodly depths it fell later that night!

I slept into the next day, waiting until the sun was fully upon me before crawling from my sack. I elected to climb up to the First Buttress, the large triangular shaped rock at 16,800 feet, rather than traverse out across the top of Big Bertha. I hoped that the buttress would afford me room and protection enough to set my tent. The climbing proved difficult in sections but most interesting. As I meandered in and out of the rocks on the ice my ascent began to take on a new perspective. The difficult ground was for the most part behind me and for the first time success, though at best two days away, seemed less a pipe dream and more a reality. Once below the buttress, I was able, as I had hoped, to erect my tent and was soon settled in for the night.

The next day I traversed down and left across the snow to rejoin Scott and Haston's line of ascent. The snow was firm and in excellent condition. There was little avalanche danger and the crevasses were easy to negotiate. After a full day of climbing, I set my tent in a crevasse at about 17,500 feet. Just before sundown, as I was finishing my dinner, I heard the distant drone of a small engine. I soon spotted a plane several thousand feet below me. I guessed that it was Doug Geeting out checking on my progress. His visit exacerbated the great loneliness that I was beginning to feel. In that moment I felt as if I had left the entire world behind me.

I had hoped to reach the summit the following day. The climb, however, was taking its toll. The altitude was now robbing me of the opportunity fully to recuperate at night. What I thought was going to be an easy day turned into a most trying one as I labored up the frozen snow. I reached 19,200 feet before exhaustion overcame me. I made my bivy site on a small ledge and crawled into my sack with everything on save my crampons.

I awoke the following day to blowing snow. A storm had developed during the night and was growing in intensity with each passing moment. It was as if my challenge to gain the summit had awakened this sleeping giant from its repose. Fear grew inside me, usurping my fatigue and driving me to action. Never had I felt so utterly vulnerable. I had no choice but to make my bid for the top and within minutes I was off the ledge and out onto the snow. I could see absolutely nothing as I front-pointed up the couloir. Up and up I climbed into the thick of the storm. My fingers and toes grew numb and the fear of frostbite entered my mind. I struggled on in desperation. After three to four hours of toil the angle of the slope steepened and I realized that at last I was nearing the end of my ascent. Indeed, within a short distance, I found myself standing on what I presumed was the summit ridge. After a few moments I recognized the very place where Chris and I had stood so proudly years before. After a few moments, I located the route down the West Buttress and immediately began my descent.

Tears welled into my eyes as I scrambled from the top of North America, half frozen by the storm. In that moment, despite a most fleeting return visit to a summit that I couldn't even see, I knew that it would be a long time before I would truly descend from the height to which the mountain had once again pushed me.

Summary of Statistics:

AREA: Alaska Range.

SOLO ASCENT: Mount McKinley, 6193 meters, 20,320 feet, via the Scott-Haston route on the South Face, May 12 to May 19, 1982 (Mark Hesse).

Cassin Ridge in Winter

MICHAEL YOUNG, *Colorado Outward Bound School*

OUR INTENT had been to climb Mount Logan in winter. Seldom visited in summer, we knew of no winter attempts on North America's second highest peak. Only weeks before we were to leave for the Yukon, our fourth climber opted for warmer activities. The Canadian Park Service refused to let groups of less than four enter Kluane National Park. Even farther north, Mount McKinley was a logical alternative.

McKinley's first winter ascent was in 1967. In his book *Minus 148*, Art Davidson details the grim adventure of that ascent where one climber died falling unroped into a crevasse and the rest of the party nearly perished while trapped in a blizzard near the summit for several days. Horror stories like this did not seem to inhibit other winter attempts over subsequent years, but few made it further than the glacier below the mountain. Stories circulated of arctic conditions with sustained 100-mph winds and temperatures of $-70°$.

Why climb Mount McKinley in the winter with its arctic storms and minimal daylight? After most of the great mountain summits around the world had been climbed, the focus changed to climbing mountains by their most difficult routes. In the 1970s the emphasis changed to "classic" routes in parties of one to four without porters and with lightning speed. A winter ascent of a difficult route in a subarctic region would perhaps further extend the boundaries of mountaineering.

As climbers gain confidence and experience, they often wish to simplify their gear. Ironically, as they improve, they attempt more difficult climbs requiring more sophisticated equipment. During the planning stages for our arctic winter climb we knew that our gear could easily be a limiting factor. Much of it required extensive modifications. Wool and natural fibers were used minimally. We wore polypropolene underwear next to our skin and then a one piece Dumart suit. Covering that we had pile suits. Our outer layer was of double thickness Thinsulate covered with Gore-Tex. Our faces were hidden by goggles, silk and wool balaclavas. In the coldest conditions we used neoprene face masks and a large hood attached to the oversuit. Footwear was our greatest concern. Vapor-barrier boots are warm but too floppy for the difficult climbing we anticipated. We used plastic double boots with vapor-barrier liners and neoprene over-boots. For hand protection we brought thick wool mittens with fiber-filled outer shells.

After the typical last-minute crises of gear sorting, food purchasing and equipment modifications, in the middle of February Roger Mear, Jon Waterman and I made our way to Talkeetna. With only a minimal delay we were flown to the "airstrip" on the southeast fork of the Kahiltna Glacier. As we arrived, a party of four were vacating the airstrip after an unsuccessful attempt on the West Buttress of McKinley. They had struggled with the winds for two weeks only to make it six miles up the glacier. We stashed our things and ourselves in their old snow hole. Eager to test our gear, we attempted to assemble our new large-dome tent. In the severe cold the shock cords lost their elasticity and were unusable. A pole snapped. The tent was retired. Our alternative was Roger's two-man tent made for people five feet seven. Roger is five feet seven. Jon and I are six feet two.

In surprisingly mild weather (temperatures of $-12°$ to $-30°$ F) we moved up-glacier carrying loads to the base of the Cassin Ridge. We hauled plastic sleds and wore skis with skins. To avoid the cramped quarters of our mini-tent and the winter winds, we routinely dug snow holes. Each day we learned more of the tricks of keeping warm and dry. Our days were broken down into cycles of eight hours of sleep time, ten hours of maintenance tasks and six hours of walking or climbing. Daylight was less of a problem than we anticipated. We had nearly ten hours of traveling light and our small lantern illuminated our snow homes.

Leading up to the Cassin Ridge is the Japanese Couloir, a 2000-foot, 40°-to-50° gully of rock and smooth water ice. We determined to climb the mountain in alpine style. Shouldering enormous packs, we ascended the gully, ignoring the dozens of partly buried and chopped fixed ropes left behind by previous parties. The advent of front-pointing and drooped picks has eliminated the need for fixed lines on nearly all ice routes. The thought of 2000 feet of step-chopping on ten-point crampons seemed awesome to us. At twilight we reached the ridge crest, a knife-edged cornice, dropping away to the glacier 2000 feet below us. We traversed to a rock buttress providing a two-foot ledge over 30 feet in length. Fatigue tempered our concerns about our exposed bivouac site. Too soon it was time to melt chunks of snow and ice for breakfast cocoa.

The technical crux of the climb presented itself to us early the next morning. For years climbers have argued about the difficulty of the rock on the Cassin. It is frequently described as 5.7 or 5.8. As we grunted and scraped our way with crampons over the granite slabs wearing 70-pound packs, I was sure the climb was easily 5.10. In Yosemite wearing EBs on a summer day it might be graded as 5.1.

The long nights gave us time to discuss many things, including the difference between winter and summer climbing in subarctic regions. Despite the weakness of the sun, icefalls still released blocks the size of trucks with about the same frequency as in summer. The snow on the glaciers was predictably less packed in winter but above 11,000 feet there were no consistent differences. The ridge itself was mainly blown clear of new snow and the clutter and waste of previous parties was grossly apparent. During our month the most profound contrast with summer was that the temperatures never warmed to above $-12°$ F. There was seldom a time when we could sit outside comfortably for more than a few minutes. Our sleeping bags became crusty and meticulous attention to clothing was needed to stay dry. Discipline is needed to avoid frostbite to the extremities and it was only moments of inattention that brought me superficial frostbite later on the trip.

Above the rock ridge, the route narrowed to an arête of rock and snow. We moved steadily across the arête kicking steps under the brilliant sun until mid-afternoon when we uncovered a crevasse for our evening headquarters. In another two days we reached 16,000 feet and were able to make contact with a CB operator named Kansas Sunflower who lives just north of Anchorage. He relayed our progress and departure plans on to our pilot. Roger and I spent that night in the tent and Jon slept outside in his bivouac sack ecstatically describing the brilliant northern lights sweeping across the mountain. Satisfied with his description, I burrowed further into my sleeping bag.

Most of the climbing above 16,000 feet on the Cassin is on moderate snow-and-ice slopes. Up to that point we had moved together through the technical terrain placing occasional runners and infrequent belays, perhaps more out of habit than logic or need. Weaving in and out of the rocks in the ice gullies over short rock ramps reminded me of Scottish winter climbing. On the final 4000 feet to the summit we abandoned extra gear and, unroped, we walked up the final steep slope.

Gaining several thousand feet of altitude a day, we were far from fully acclimatized. Except when confronting freeze-dried dinners, my appetite was good and I was able to sleep at night. Sleeping fully clothed has its advantages. Morning departures, however, were slowed by our cramped tenting quarters and inertia. We had one tent for the three of us. One by one, we put on our boots while those waiting savored another few moments of warmth in their sleeping bags.

On our fifth evening on the ridge we chopped out a small platform among rocks covered with rime ice. Jon was not feeling well and woke up with a nightmare about suffocation. The next morning was clearly our coldest but the thermometer was lost or broken. Roger and I both complained of numb toes and started up the slope. In about 30 minutes we reached the summit ridge. Dropping our packs the two of us walked up the 400 feet to North America's highest point. Approaching the summit cornice I briefly reminisced about broken relationships, family and the green world below. I noted the bamboo and aluminum rods staking out the highest snow block. Instead of exultation I felt irritation at earlier climbers for marring a sculpture finer than any art work.

Back at our packs we saw Jon struggling up the last few hundred feet to the summit ridge. I walked down to him and relieved him of his pack. He was too fatigued and we were too cold for him to climb the final section to the summit. We started down the West Buttress route. Jon resembled a man living a nightmare with sunken eyes staring at the ground. He took prolonged rest stops while Roger and I danced up and down to stay warm. At 17,200 feet we camped in brilliant sunshine. During the night the weather deteriorated. In near white-out conditions we broke camp. Jon was still suffering from fatigue. I helped him dress and pack while Roger organized the group gear. Roger walked with Jon encouraging him on while I fumbled ahead looking for wands and the best footing down the windy descent route. Jon stated that he would descend no further than the crevasse at 15,000 feet. Since we had only one day of food and fuel, Roger and I independently concluded that we would have to leave him if he refused to move further down-glacier. We were spared that choice when we spotted a party moving up the glacier. Five British mountaineers shared an enormous snow cave with us that night, as well as the English cooking that horrifies the world. Jon recovered his strength during the night. He felt that he had been suffering from pulmonary edema, but it may have been other forms of acute mountain sickness with nausea, lassitude and fatigue. His respiratory rate and pulse were normal, he had normal airway sounds and was able to sleep at night with his head lower than his feet.

Our longest day was after leaving the British party and walking the 12 miles back to the airstrip. The final mile was sadly uphill. I wore snowshoes picked up from a previous camp to protect my toes which were beginning to blister with frostbite. Ahead of me Roger and Jon post-holed but moved steadily ahead with the patience of Job.

The airstrip in summer is often a tent-city with as many as several hundred temporary residents. Except for a forlorn wooden pole guarding the entrance of our snowcave, the glacier was deserted. We dug our way down to our subterranean home where bagels and a canned ham formed our victory dinner. Exhaustion dulled our sense of accomplishment. Decreased mutual dependency diminished our tolerance for each other's oddities. Irritably we tolerated each other's presence over the next few days waiting for the plane. Incredibly, our pilot flew in late one afternoon, dropping off three Spaniards who hoped to climb the north face of Hunter. Later we found that he had shouted down our snow hole but the snores of two sleeping climbers and the sounds of a walkeman radio drowned out his call. He flew away believing us still on the mountain.

After five days of waiting, Roger went with one of the Spaniards to rescue gear abandoned up-glacier. Less than a mile from Base Camp, he fell 30 feet into a crevasse, tearing knee ligaments. The Spanish climbers hauled him back to camp. Jon, like me, was nursing frostbitten toes. And so we three cripples sat in our snow cave with its blackened ceiling from the lantern smoke, eating macaroni and cheese. The following day another pilot, flying up glacier to rescue gear from an airplane that had crashed earlier that winter, spotted our huge S.O.S. and initiated our evacuation to civilization.

Summary of Statistics:

Area: Alaska Range.

First Winter Ascent: Mount McKinley, 6193 meters, 20,320 feet, via Cassin Ridge; on the glacier and mountain from February 17 to March 13, 1982, on the Cassin Ridge from February 27 to March 4, 1982.

Personnel: Roger Mear, Jonathan Waterman, Michael Young.

Plate 39

Photo by Jonathan Waterman

Young and Mear digging in on McKinley Winter Ascent.

Mount Blackburn's East Ridge

CRAIG GASKILL

On MAY 21, 1982, we stood on the summit of Mount Blackburn. The mountain rises to 16,390 feet (4996 meters) in the Wrangell-Saint Elias National Park and Preserve in southern Alaska. Michael and Glenn Ruckhaus, David Johns and I took in the views and experiences from this high point and began our descent.

Our expedition had started on May 2 when we were flown from the Galkona airport to 7000 feet on the Nebesna Glacier, below Mount Blackburn. In less than twelve hours after we had left Denver and our civilized lives, we had been transported to a vast expanse of snow and ice, where the word civilization was a thought buried by crashing avalanches. Our route would take us up the unclimbed east ridge of Blackburn via Rime Peak and the east summit of Blackburn.

Our first three camps were established without problems. A minor storm, hidden crevasses and deep snow hampered our progress a little, but after five days we had gained 4900 feet, climbing with 500 pounds of gear between the four of us. Camp IV was established by climbing the north face of Rime Peak and descending onto the east ridge of Mount Blackburn. We put in 1500 feet of fixed rope to ease the carrying of our gear to the camp.

Camp IV was situated on the low side of a long and difficult ridge which we had to cross. We nicknamed it "Phantom Ridge" because when we first saw it in a blizzard, the snow towers on the ridge loomed through the mist like snow phantoms. Signs of trepidation were noticeable throughout the group after seeing the ridge. For two-and-a-half days we were stuck in the tent as a storm raged. Yet, we lounged about in easy thought and relaxation as the storm masked the ridge and our fears. When the storm finally subsided, we were mentally ready for the challenge of Phantom Ridge. It was windy, exciting and feasible. Climbing the ridge was a slow process which took careful stepping and utmost concentration. We fixed 2000 feet of rope on the knife-edged, corniced ridge. When we finally established Camp V on the high side of the ridge, we believed the crux of the climb was behind us.

From a technical standpoint, the crux was passed, but the hardest was still to come. At Camp VI, on a spin-drift knoll at 15,700 feet, a howling storm stranded us for four-and-a-half days. We could not see the ridge, just ten yards away. We were unable to cook outside. Cold blasts of wind and snow pene-

Photo by Craig Gaskill

East Ridge of MOUNT BLACKBURN.

PLATE 41

Photo by Craig Gaskill

Mike Ruckhaus on the approach to Phantom Ridge on BLACKBURN. Camp IV is in upper right.

PLATE 42

Photo by Michael Ruckhaus

Above Camp V on BLACKBURN, looking toward Rime Peak.

trated whenever a tunnel tent door was opened. We exhausted our books and grew tired of card games and oblivious to the flapping of the tent, dreaming of chocolate bars and steak. I huddled for 105 hours in my sleeping bag. I was pleased to be there and glad to be warm. Climbers do not conquer mountains. Mountains conquer climbers.

The storm finally broke. The day we left Camp VI, we made the summit and looked down upon the world below. What a view, what a sense of triumph, of exultation, of accomplishment! We left the summit full of good feeling and camaraderie. Our descent down a different ridge, the north "Japanese" ridge, began with an easy walk but soon turned into a climbers' nightmare. A ground blizzard moved in with zero visibility on the slope. We could see distant peaks, but not a crevasse three feet in front of us. As the ridge got steeper, more ice séracs and crevasses appeared, forcing us to camp on the windy ridge far above our destination. The next morning was stormy, but at least we could just see a route down a face and off the side of the ridge. Despite the avalanche danger, the alternatives were worse. We descended as quickly as possible out of danger.

For the next five days we skied and hiked out the Nebesna Glacier to our pickup point, 50 miles distant. Though anticlimactic after the climb, it would have made an excellent trek with light packs. Mount Blackburn, Rime Peak, the Atna Peaks, Mount Sanford, Mount Jarvis and the smoking volcano, Mount Wrangell, loomed above us. The upper reaches of the Nebesna Glacier were smooth and snow-covered; the lower sections of rock and ice were jagged. Hundreds of Dall sheep danced on the cliff tops. The wild glacier streams gouged out canyons in the ice. There were the high alpine reaches where the tundra began and the forested expanses where the grizzly ran wild.

When we finally were flown out from Orange Hill, we were tired, restless and sad about leaving, but we shall never forget the twenty-six action-packed days.

Summary of Statistics:

AREA: Wrangell Mountains, Alaska.

NEW ROUTE: Mount Blackburn, 4996 meters or 16,390 feet, over Rime Peak and East Ridge, descent via North Ridge, Summit on May 21, 1982 (whole party).

PERSONNEL: Craig Gaskill, Michael Ruckhaus, Glenn Ruckhaus, David Johns.

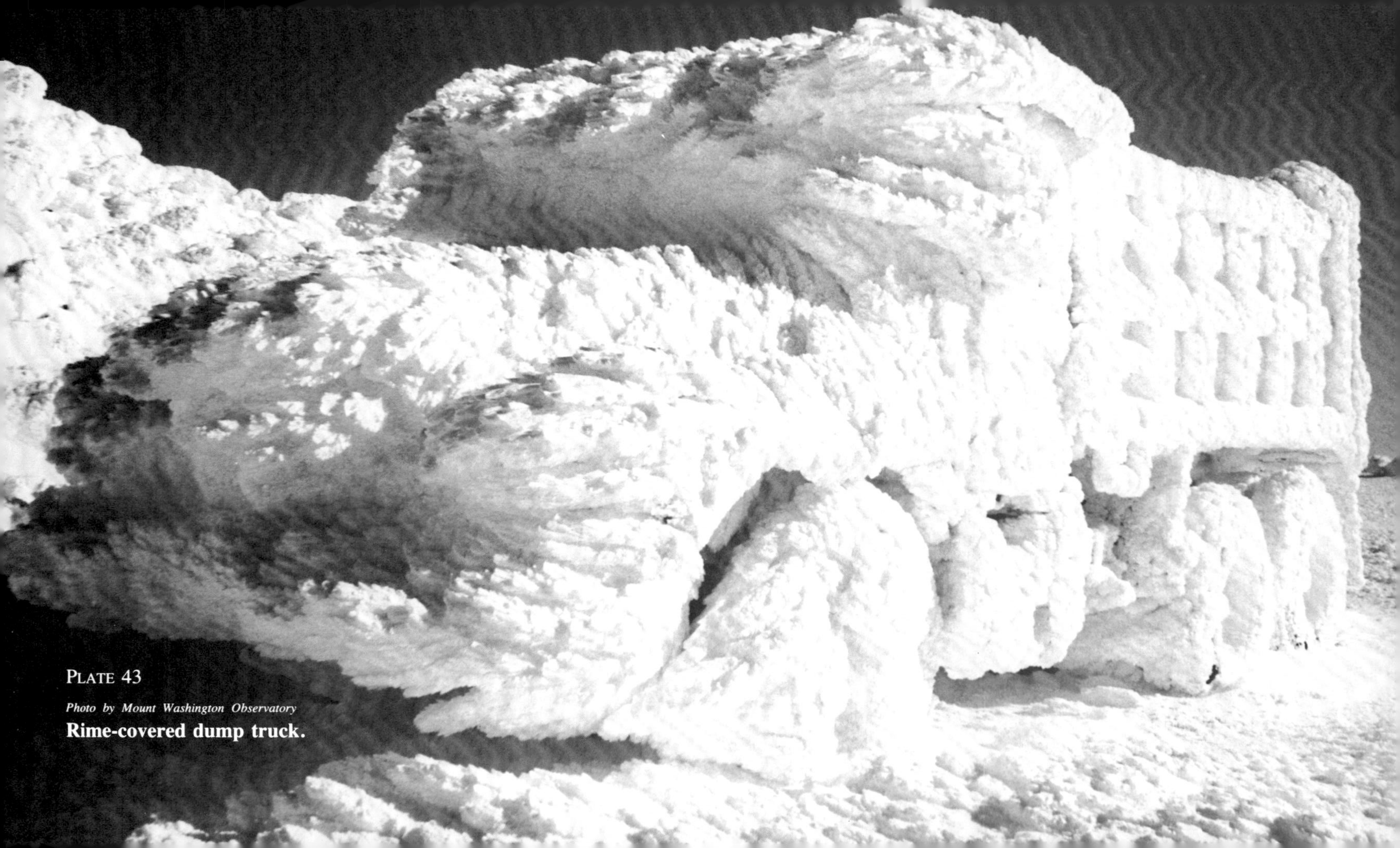

PLATE 43
Photo by *Mount Washington Observatory*
Rime-covered dump truck.

"The World's Worst Weather"

ALAN A. SMITH*

OUNT WASHINGTON, in New Hampshire, is said by many to have "the worst weather in the world." The point is arguable—Fitz Roy in Argentina and Mount McKinley come to mind—but it is true that clouds, high winds and icing prevail at Mount Washington during most seasons of the year, despite its relatively low elevation of only 6288 feet (1917 meters) above sea level.

One of the major rewards of climbing is surely the view from the summit, or along the route. Yet, the summit of Mount Washington is in the clouds about 55% of the time, year round. That obviously affects the tourists who visit the top by trails, the Auto Road or the Cog Railway, but it also frustrates technical climbers in the mountain's ravines and gullies, where many an alpinist has gotten his first training.

There are good meteorological reasons for such bad weather at the Mount Washington Observatory on the summit, and we summarize them below. But first, to show that the perverse climate is not merely a matter of localized Observatory pride, we quote three respected alpinists.

—Brad Washburn, as reported in the *New York Times* for January 13, 1981: "With the exception of some isolated peaks in the Arctic and Antarctic, Mount Washington has the most severe weather in the world."

—Chris Jones, in *Climbing in North America* (published for the American Alpine Club by the University of California Press, Berkeley, 1976): ". . . in the winter, Mount Washington has weather as bad as any in Alaska . . . Snow-and-ice climbing on Mount Washington can be a survival exercise . . ."

—Noel Odell of Mount Everest fame, private communication: "I made several winter ascents of Mount Washington and, during one of these, accompanied by Dr. Terris Moore, we experienced as fierce conditions of strong wind and low temperature as I can remember on any high mountain."

---

*The new (1980) Observatory tower, where wind speed measurements are made, reaches

PLATE 44
Photo by Bradford Washburn
MOUNT WASHINGTON from the
southeast.

The Facts

Weather conditions at Mount Washington (lat. 44° 16'N) approximate those encountered at much higher latitudes.[1] Prevailing winds are from the west and west-northwest, although the most severe storms are usually from the southeast. Temperature extremes are not excessive; the maximum ever recorded was 72°F (22°C) in August 1975 and the minimum was −47°F (−44°C) in January 1934. The yearly average, however, is only 27°F (−3°C) —the lowest annual normal temperature for the lower 48 contiguous states.

The wind regime at the summit is severe; wind speeds measured at the Observatory are higher than at the same elevation at some distance from the mountain. The world's wind speed record was established on Mount Washington on April 12, 1934, when a peak gust reached 231 mph (372 kph). So-called "century days," when peak gusts exceed 100 mph (161 kph), are most frequent in winter, but occur in every month of the year. The annual average wind speed for 1981 was 34.9 mph (56.2 kph).

Two other data points contribute to the overall picture: Over the last 43 years, the percentage of possible sunshine was only 33%, and the summit was in cloud or fog (visibility ¼ mile or c. 400 meters or less) for part of 313 days out of each of the last 49 years. And finally, freezing fog is an important part of the local climate; deposits of rime ice—"frost feathers", pointing into the wind—often grow up to several feet in length on exposed structures.

Comparisons are always of interest. To place Mount Washington data in perspective, Dr. Charles F. Brooks, first President of the Observatory, compared his information with that available from other stations some years ago.[2] Specific reports were available to him from Pike's Peak, Mount Rose (central Sierra Nevada), Sonnblick Observatory (Austria) and Mount Nordenskjøld (Spitsbergen). In no case could Brooks match Mount Washington's overall performance but, considering the limitations of his data base, he came up with the following modest conclusion: "It is probable that there are worse mountains than Mount Washington, but observations do not seem to have been made upon them."

The Causes

Wind-speed figures indicate the horizontal motion of air; vertical motions are referred to as ascending or descending currents, updrafts or downdrafts. According to Ludlum,[3] a recent survey of surface winds at the standard 33-foot height for anemometer exposure showed that 130 mph (209 kph) would be the maximum speed expected at United States locations—but, he continues, "It apparently requires an ascending or descending flow on a mountain slope for extreme speeds."

"Uplift" is one reason why wind speeds are so high on Mount Washington; the mountain presents an extended upslope to the prevailing winds from the west. And it is the same uplift—referred to by Schaefer and Day[4] as "oro

Photo by Mount Washington Observatory

Mount Washington Observatory covered with rime.

graphic lift"—which accounts for the prevalence of clouds at the summit; moisture-laden air will reach its condensation level as it travels up the slope toward lower temperatures, and cloud droplets will form at an elevation just below or immediately above the summit.

The second reason for high winds is the Bernoulli effect, according to which an air mass speeds up as it passes over an obstacle, just as water in a stream speeds up when it must pass through a constriction between two rocks. The air masses that traverse Mount Washington may have proceeded at a leisurely fashion when they could extend downward to the valleys at 2000 feet, but must accelerate to pass over the mountain at more than 6000 feet.*

Air mass movement on the national scale is probably the most important factor in determining Mount Washington's bad weather. In general, weather systems travel from west to east across the United States and Canada, but there is another broad-scale path up the Atlantic coast. Further, there are smaller-scale and quite specific storm tracks across the country; they vary from season to season (see Ludlum), but many of them converge upon, or traverse, the northeastern United States, bringing their mixed blessing of precipitation and wind to the highest peak in the Presidentials.

Accidents

One aspect of Mount Washington's bad weather is of particular interest and concern to climbers—it "produces" accidents. Granted, some of the victims are inexperienced and ill-equipped summer "goofers" who fail to heed the White Mountain National Forest weather-warning signs at timberline. But not all— even the veteran driver of the snow vehicle most often used for rescue on the mountain found himself bewildered in a whiteout of high wind and blowing snow in December 16, 1981; it took him over five hours to walk out, and he spent four days in the hospital, recovering.

Is the lure of "mountaineering" on the northeast's most accessible peak a contributing factor? Perhaps it is and, to close, we quote a paragraph from the Mount Washington Observatory News Bulletin for Summer, 1982, prepared by Charles B. Fobes, with information supplied by the Appalachian Mountain Club:

> There have been 27 fatal accidents in Tuckerman Ravine (a glacial cirque on the east side of Mount Washington) since 1849. The total number of lives lost on the Mount Washington Range is ninety-one. This number includes all types of accidents. If we consider mountaineering to include those persons who hiking, skiing, rock, snow-and-ice climbing, then 61 fatalities may be attributed to "mountaineering."

---

*The new (1980) Observatory tower, where wind speed measurements are made, reaches 6309 feet above sea level, about 30 feet higher than the old tower, and it is in a much more exposed location, some neighboring buildings having been removed. Peak wind gusts at the new location average 8-10% higher than at the old one.

PLATE 46
Photo by H. Adams Carter
Early October Rime on upper slopes
of Mount Washington.

Information for this article was drawn from Kenneth Rancourt, Staff Meteorologist for the Mount Washington Observatory, and from the following sources:

(1) *Local Climatological Data, Annual Summary with Comparative Data, 1981, Mount Washington Observatory, Gorham, New Hampshire,* pub. by National Oceanic and Atmospheric Administration/Environmental Data and Information Service/National Climatic Center, Asheville, N.C.
(2) "The Worst Weather in the World," by Charles F. Brooks, in *Appalachia,* December, 1940, pp. 194 ff.
(3) *The American Weather Book,* by David M. Ludlum, Houghton Mifflin Company, Boston, 1982.
(4) *A Field Guide to the Atmosphere,* by Vincent J. Schaefer and John A. Day, Houghton Mifflin Company, Boston, 1981.

Letter to the Editor— Climbing Ethics

Thomas Higgins

IN THE 1982 ISSUE of the *American Alpine Journal,* Bruce Morris wrote a historical and interpretive article on face climbing in Yosemite and Tuolumne Meadows. As a contributor to the face climbing tradition of these areas, particularly Tuolumne, I suggest Bruce Morris has done a very poor job of telling the story.

First, he has omitted much of the relevance in the history of routes and the ethical traditions of the areas. Second, in addition to these omissions, there are confusing discussions about the experience of face climbing and rationales for climbing styles, all suggesting the author either doesn't believe what he is saying or isn't clear what he is saying or both. Finally, and most disturbing in the pages of the *Journal,* the author sets out very unconvincing, if not preposterous, arguments in support of certain climbing styles clearly aimed at murdering the impossible.

Let's begin with the omissions in the article, some factual, some interpretive. If I had to name my favorite face climb in Tuolumne, it would be *Pièce de Résistance.* It is a long, direct line on the largest dome in the area, Fairview. It entails progressively harder face-climbing (some say 5.11, some 5.12) and crack-climbing, and follows a spectacular arch in the middle of the wide-open west face. Bob Kamps and I worked on the route several times in the early 1970s, always turning back at a blank headwall about midway up. We had no desire to aid the headwall. Our climbing styles (mine was learned from his) were founded on the belief one should leave the impossible for another time or for other climbers who might someday free-climb it. In 1974, Vern Clevenger and Bob Harrington did the headwall only and then retreated. They placed several bolts, at least one of which was used for aid. Later, Vern Clevenger and I returned, free-climbed the headwall and finished the route. I named the route as I did since I felt it was my finale in Tuolumne. I also wrote an article about it for the Sierra Club publication, *Ascent.* In part, the article was a tribute to Bob Kamps as my mentor, to our friendship and to our many attempts together on the route.

Bruce Morris tells us *Pièce de Résistance* is "one of Vern Clevenger's best routes." We are told, "Where Higgins and Kamps had met defeat, Clevenger and Harrington eventually prevailed." I don't routinely call routes "mine," nor do I think *Pièce de Résistance* is Clevenger's route. I suspect Vern Clevenger doesn't feel the route is "his" either. But the main point and serious omission relates to who did the first ascent. Vern Clevenger and Bob Harrington did not do the first ascent of *Pièce de Résistance*. Tom Higgins and Clevenger did.

Obviously, Bruce Morris has made another omission about *Pièce de Résistance,* this one interpretive. For years, when the route repelled attempts, it underscored the climbing style of the 1970s: if aid bolts were necessary, turn back. Leave it for later. For others. Or, for never. Morris has chosen to ignore the significance of Resistance, as well as the entire ethical tradition behind its development.

When the article moves from discussion of specific routes to a discussion of style, the omissions about traditional style are even more apparent. Again, writing about Tuolumne, "Here, at the present moment, and for many years past, aesthetic considerations have displaced most questions of style . . . the goal has remained . . . a line of technical difficulty at almost any price." Shouldn't readers be told about the many aesthetic routes done when and where it mattered how they were done? For at least a decade in Tuolumne, fabulous routes were created without aid, previewing, preprotection or what Morris calls "selective cheating." Readers should know not only a different and earlier style once existed, but what routes represent the style, who did them, and why the style once prevailed. Morris also might have mentioned some of the younger generation who even today create aesthetic routes without "selective cheating."

Aside from omissions, Bruce Morris has given us lots of confusing discussions. For example, this statement makes no sense to me: "If good drill stances are passed up simply to make a route more committing, the crux moves, no matter how frightening, are never as hard as they might be if better protected." Following this logic, the lesser and lesser protection we use, the easier and easier crux moves become. Does anyone really subscribe to this logic? I have done several of the Yosemite face climbs Morris refers to as having "economical protection," such as *Quicksilver*. They seemed challenging to me just because the protection is sparse. More protection would make them easier, not harder. In England, poor protection even gets reflected in higher, not lower, ratings. Who really experiences the inverted reactions Morris claims can be found on the routes he names?

Here is another confusion, again relying on a kind of inverted perspective of things. *Handjive* is a route on Lembert Dome in Tuolumne. It was done by placing bolts on rappel, preprotected, as they say. When it was first done, it was an oddity in Tuolumne and I chopped the bolts hoping to nip a trend in the bud. I even lectured the first-ascent party about violating a long-standing tradition against such climbing styles. Bruce Morris tells us the bolts were replaced after I chopped them, again on rappel. Why? Not as a slap back at a self-righteous Tom Higgins, but as a "fitting memorial" to Tim Harrison of the first-ascent team, who was so "popular" and "self-reliant." Have I been on Pluto for the last few years or is there a very sorry irony here? Even if you feel preprotection is an acceptable form of selective cheating, do you use it to create a *memorial* to a self-reliant climber? Would all the self-reliant climbers wishing a memorial climb protected on rappel please step forward?

The same confusion is compounded elsewhere in the article. Morris tells us Vern Clevenger battled his way up *Golden Bars* with "persistence" and "grim determination," but ". . . no one will ever know whether he drilled all the bolts strictly on the lead." Why will no one know? If standing on bolts or putting them in on rappel creates fitting memorials, why won't we ever know how *Golden Bars* was done? Perhaps Bruce has stumbled upon the essential issue without knowing it—climbers "selectively cheating" have a very hard time justifying their actions, and they know it. They are reluctant to reveal the style of their ascent, even while loudly defending their styles in articles and discussions.

Finally Morris has given no credence whatsoever to "selective cheating," even while setting out to do so. He quotes Claud Fiddler, a "notorious local," who apparently supports such actions as placing bolts on rappel, rehearsing moves, previewing possible routes, and drilling aid bolt ladders to allow free-climbing. Asks Claud, "How can a route be worthwhile unless 'questionable methods' were employed on its first ascent?" Morris then goes on, "After all, can temporal ethics ever be successfully reconciled with a mandate to extend contemporary standards beyond the merely human? Like *Pantanjali's Yogasutra*, the moves on a difficult face-climb should outline the mystical steps toward achieving a deathless super-consciousness." Who among the ascribers to new climbing styles understands—never mind believes—such rubbish? There are hundreds of *worthwhile* routes done without questionable methods! And who is *mandating* an extension of contemporary standards? Or, who has the gall to say they are reaching toward a *deathless superconsciousness* beyond the *merely human* in climbing when they stand on bolts to place others? Or when they rappel down to check out the difficulty of a possible new route? Or place bolts on rappel for later protection in free climbing? One can usefully discuss the appropriateness of these climbing styles based on how they affect other climbers ascribing to different styles. But it is laughable to defend the style on the basis of their abilities to transform us into gods. What is this stuff doing in the pages of the *Journal*?

Nowhere in the article has Bruce Morris explained or defended the climbing styles he discusses. Perhaps such a defense is possible, though I have yet to see it. I'm not alone in wondering how cheating selectively, as Morris says Clevenger has done, can be justified to form an "artistically satisfying whole." I'm unconvinced Cantwell has created a better climb in the *Hall of Mirrors* by placing an aid bolt ladder up the "line of strength" and then free-climbing it, rather than climbing a ramp to the right without a ladder. I still ask why Ray Jardine feels justified in "sculpting" holds on El Cap, if in fact he did so, to make an area of rock go free. Nothing in the article convinces the reader that these methods either make good routes, or are justifiable no matter what the resulting route. Who wants to climb aid ladders free? Or climb on sculptings? Or on gymnastic problems next to a more natural path of holds? And who so completely can disassociate ends from means as to ignore how holds were made or bolts placed, and climb like a dullard, unaware or uncaring of who first did a route, how and why?

In sum, omissions, confusions and unconvincing or preposterous assertions abound in "Methods & Madness." I hope readers are treated to better fare in the future.

Color Plate 3

**Classification of High Altitude
Retinal Hemorrhage.**

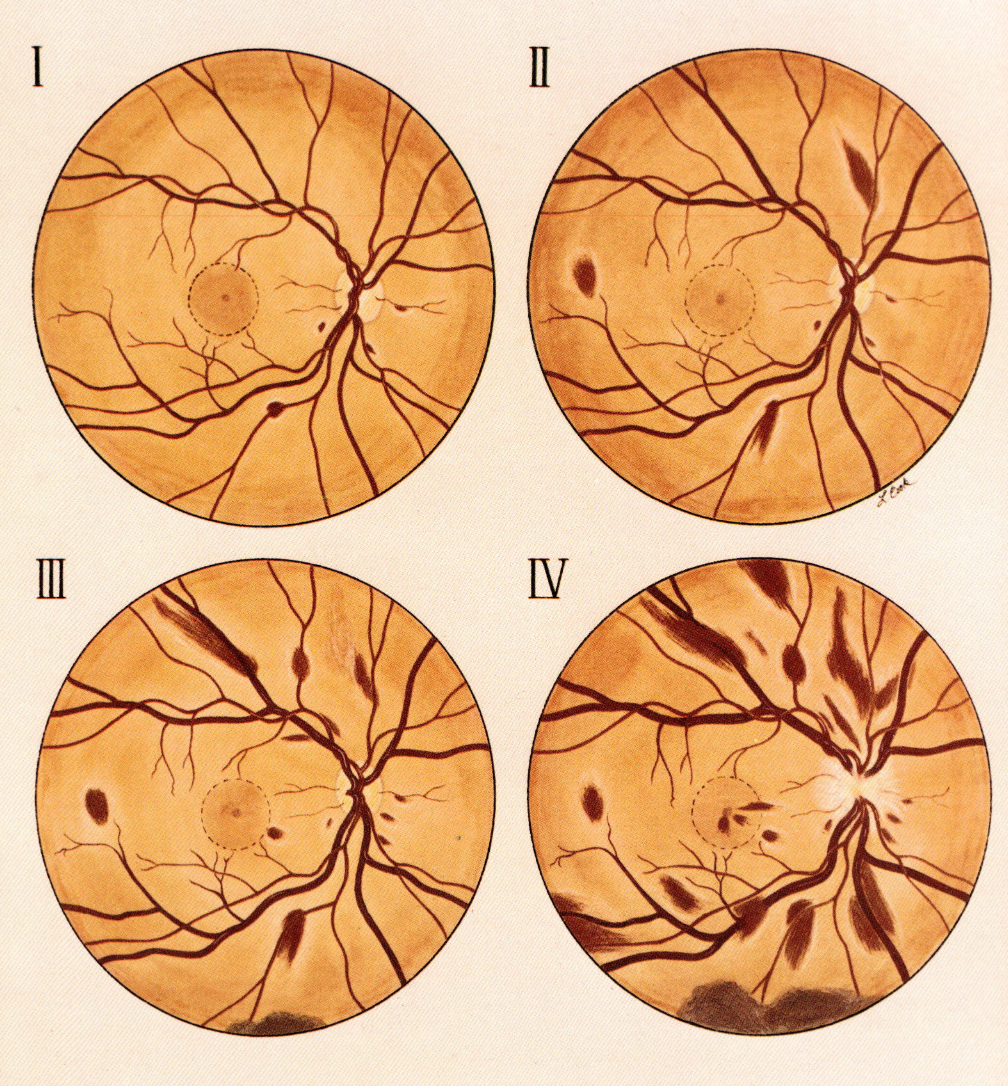

I
II
III
IV

Scientific Notes

Classification of High Altitude Retinal Hemorrhage (HARH)

Method of Reporting Findings and Request for Collection of Data on High Altitude Retinal Hemorrhage. Dr. Michael Wiedman, Harvard Medical School, 243 Charles Street, Boston, Massachusetts 02214, urges doctors who will be members of expeditions going to high altitudes to assist him in his study of High Altitude Retinal Hemorrhage. He stresses that retinal examination of the gross features is within the scope of any physician and may be learned by ancillary medical personnel. The reason for the study is to determine the relationships of retinal hemorrhage to altitude illness and cerebral edema. Additional detailed description, report forms and possibly lightweight ophthalmoscopes are available on application to him. Examiners are invited to submit information, which will be computerized and collated data will be shared with the sender.

A complete description of the facing page illustration will be sent on application to interested examiners.

MICHAEL WIEDMAN, M.D.

Charge of Hoax Against Robert E. Peary Examined

Terris Moore

VER SINCE the return of Dr. Frederick A. Cook and Commander Robert E. Peary from the Arctic, within a week of each other in September 1909, both claiming to have reached the North Pole, partisans of the two have been at each others' throats. Because both men were founding members of the American Alpine Club—as was also Peary's wife, Josephine Diebitsch (women were admitted into the Club from the beginning)—the subject in those years very much gripped the attention of Club members. Investigations were made, Dr. Cook was formally expelled from the Club in 1910. Peary, an Honorary Member from earlier years was continued on as such until his death in 1920, with no indication that the Club—except perhaps for one or two members—accepted any of the charges made against him. These have continued sporadically; but principally in what one might call the "yellow press," of sensationalist editors skating the edges of truth, grasping to increase their readership. But now that the Sierra Club has published *Great Exploration Hoaxes,* by our fellow member and well-known author, David Roberts (see book review), the charge against Peary must be examined with a freshly open mind.

On the jacket of this new (1982) book, we see Peary's polar party featured at their goal the North Pole, over the word HOAX in giant capitals. And inside we study Roberts' map showing the Peary party sledging to 87°47′N, the latitude of Bartlett's return; but from there northward only dotted lines labelled "probably spurious" indicate where Peary with Matthew Henson and four picked Eskimos reported that he had continued on to the Pole. This historic dog-sledging dash the author decries as "pretense of having made the actual achievement . . . a grimly serious effort to fool the whole world;" and he equates the whole thing with "Rosie Ruiz, the runner who tried to fake victory in the 1980 Boston Marathon [but] made a very bad show of it compared to men like Peary. Cross-examined . . . she took refuge in tears and a short memory." And equating Peary with Cook, the publisher promotes this book with: "Historians now believe that both men falsified their evidence."

114

This is all so completely at variance with the A.A.C.'s view of it all from the individuals themselves at the time that we must ask why this utterly different conclusion? Has some heinous behavior by Peary emerged, not known before?

This reviewer has made an exceptionally careful study of the author's sources and argument, but cannot find that at all. Instead, curiously, the one new and really important piece of information which has emerged in all these years is *supportive* of Peary—but the book's author and publisher seem unaware of it.

On just what basis, specifically, is the 1909 Peary expedition charged with fraud, fake, hoax, etc., and judged guilty by this new book? Also, do these charges differ at all from the original anti-Peary publications? Masses of detail of course in argument on this in the vast literature of the Cook-Peary controversy which has raged now for 74 years. But essentially the early charges against Peary and those in this new 1982 book can be summarized under the same three headings.

The First Charge: Peary Did Not Make Longitude Determinations, necessary to steering the sledges true north. Roberts in *Great Exploration Hoaxes* says: "In 1973 Dennis Rawlins published a book* that must be regarded as the definitive analysis of the Peary controversy . . . the crux of this fairly technical matter is [that] Peary's observations are most suspect in the matter of direction-finding." And Dave Roberts' chapter of 18 pages is essentially a readable, workmanlike summary of Rawlins' rambling repetitious book of 320 pages. The essence of their number one charge is that although Peary did make observations for longitude at many key locations on all his preceding expeditions, in 1909 he made no observations for longitude anywhere between leaving land at Cape Columbia and what he asserted at his farthest north was 89°57'. So how could Peary have made corrections en route for transverse motion resulting from inevitable aiming errors in his simplified direction-finding by compass and dead reckoning?

The answer is that Peary's method was actually the same as the simplified navigational method subsequently employed by Amundsen and his navigators in their attainment of the South Pole in 1911. And what was that?

The clearest description of this method which both used may be found in the article "Amundsen's Route to the South Pole" published in the January, 1979 issue (page 331) of the *Polar Record* (Cambridge University's Scott Polar Research Institute). Specifically: ". . . Amundsen's system of navigation. He took no longitude sights during the whole polar journey . . . he trusted to latitude observations alone, combined with dead reckoning based on compass courses and distances run. The compasses were checked by frequent azimuth observations, the logical method at high latitudes. Amundsen's navigation was specifically designed for simplicity and time-saving on the march, based upon the comparatively easy meridian observation. In contrast, Scott used con-

---

**Peary At The North Pole Fact or Fiction?* D. Rawlins, Washington, 1973.

Photo by Admiral Robert E. Peary
Courtesy of Edward P. Stafford
MATTHEW HENSON

ventional marine navigation as employed at lower latitudes. His navigator, Henry Bowers, made ex-meridian observations and longitude sights, spending considerable time and effort on calculations for a few kilometers, sometimes a few hundred meters, of meaningless accuracy."

Both Peary and Amundsen were criticized for failing to bring back scientific results. Scott was praised for his scientific materials obtained, including of course the "unnecessary" longitude determinations—but he perished at the end of a thousand mile round trip sledging journey, only 11 miles short of safe return!

The Second Charge: Peary's Dog-Sledging Speeds Were Impossible. Roberts says: "From Cape Columbia outward to 87°47', Bartlett's turnaround point, Peary averaged only 9.3 miles per day. His six best consecutive days yielded an average of 15.3. Suddenly, once there were no witnesses who could make observations [referring to Matt Henson and the four polar Eskimos] Peary made five days in a row to the Pole at an average, by his own reckoning, of 26 miles per day. . . But the most astounding feat of all was Peary's alleged return from the Pole to 87°47'—133 miles at the very minimum—in 2¼ days. Between April 2 and April 9 . . . Peary [Henson and the four polar Eskimos] are supposed to have averaged more than 53 miles per day. . . ."

For comparison Roberts offers us ". . . one of the greatest Arctic explorers, Knud Rasmussen, [who] averaged 36.6 miles per day in Greenland in 1912 which may be the legitimate all-time record . . . the impossible distances [are] proof enough that Peary failed to reach the Pole. Certainly no one since has been able to approach Peary's apparent sledging times."

Sorry, but this statement is dramatically unacceptable. As far back as the rushing of the diphtheria serum to Nome in 1925 there are records of desperate dog-sledge racing, greatly in excess of Knud Rasmussen's figure. The Nenana to Tolovana run of 52 miles, on the first day of the 674 miles to Nome was done by the first driver in *half* a day of 13 hours. The entire distance, by some fifteen drivers in sequence, was done in 127½ sledging hours: a rate of far over a hundred miles per 24 hours. Not comparable of course except to demonstrate the maximum possible speeds of work dog-teams and drivers. (The already in-place U.S. Mail run teams were used).

Much more recently, and far more comparable to the thousand mile distance from Cape Columbia to the Pole and return—especially the return as we shall see—is the annual Alaskan "Iditarod" race of 1047 miles from Anchorage to Nome. In the "Iditarod" many drivers, at least one of them a woman, have consistently done over 75 miles per day carrying sleeping gear, tent, and the necessary food provisions. In 1981, the winner, Rick Swenson, set the course record of 12 days, 8 hours, 45 minutes and 2 seconds. This would seem to be *84.8* miles per day, *day after day!* The times and distances have all been publicly verified. Just who has been getting hoaxed by whom in this matter of dog-sledging speeds?

Third Charge: Matt Henson and Eskimos Were Not Credible Witnesses, for Peary after Bartlett's turnaround from 87°47'. In *Great Exploration Hoaxes,*

Roberts introducing Matthew Henson, refers to him as "Peary's oldest accomplice, a former manservant . . . neither the Eskimos nor Henson knew how to take observations of latitude and longitude . . . was Matthew Henson privy to the fraud? Rawlins thinks not." The book condescends: "Like the Eskimos, Henson had no independent way of knowing whether he was at the North Pole or not." It then asserts: "He never directly confirmed the astounding sledging distances claimed by Peary."

Sorry to have to differ again, but Matt Henson *did* know how to determine latitude and longitude, and *did* confirm Peary's sledging distances. I knew Matt Henson well for a period of close to twenty years—which is the principal reason for my writing this piece. I knew him from the time Vilhaljmur Stefansson, during Stef's second presidency of the Explorers Club, in the mid-thirties succeeded in getting Matt into its membership (I had the opportunity of voting for this), until in 1954 at the Annual Dinner that year I had the pleasure of sitting with Matt on the dais, his last time.

Matt knew how to determine latitude and longtitude from solar sights at the noon and midnight meridian passages: Professor Ross Marvin of Cornell's College of Engineering taught him this during the long winter of 1908-9 aboard the *Roosevelt*. Matt would not have been able to reduce *ex-meridian time sights* for longitude because they are much more difficult, time consuming, uncertain, unnecessary and Peary's navigators were not going to bother with them. But he fully understood the use of GMT, GHA, and the Equation of Time to obtain longitude at simple meridian passages. He also knew that the Analemma, found on most globes in those years is simply a condensed scale for the sun's Declination and the Equation of Time. He never actually used any of this. But like the Eskimos, he knew that the sun *is* due south at its noon high point and due north at its midnight low point, and that no one can walk or steer a sledge closer than about 5° to a compass course anyhow. But if you check your compass for deviation at every noon or midnight opportunity, and have a reasonable number of such opportunities, for which Matt is witness that they did—then, contrary to what Rawlins in *Peary At The North Pole Fact or Fiction* would have us believe—the error in using this method of steering north is *not* cumulative. It is instead self-correcting. Even if you have no idea what longitude meridian you're on, you can still continue to steer north in this way, wandering 5° to 10° in your "pointing" back and forth, but pulled back constantly to averaging true north by your compass and by the periodic check of the sun to correct for any observed change in the magnetic deviation.

The accuracy essential to any *scientific data* collecting for magnetic deviation requires exact longitude, latitude and a precision magnetic device to record "dip" as well as azimuth. It is far out beyond what is adequate for merely steering north. In contrast the navigation for return *is* potentially difficult, and indeed just as demanding as Rawlins stipulates—unless, as Peary's polar party succeeded in doing, they merely follow their outward tracks back.

As persons, Matt Henson and the four polar Eskimos, Ootah, Ooqueah, Seegloo, and Egingwah certainly seem reasonable witnesses. In that day, as

Bartlett points out "the Eskimos never keep a secret." Peary, indeed, not being really fluent in their language (though Henson was) could not have organized them into some conspiracy of fraud even had he wanted to. The five of them were there; they can certainly tell us the essentials about Peary beyond Bartlett. For example, that during the five days April 2, 3, 4, 5, and 6 they travelled north, not some other direction. Henson himself, during close to thirteen thousand miles of sledge travel with Peary on all Peary's expeditions was every bit as familiar with the use of the compass—corrected from the sun at noon and at midnight for magnetic variation—as anyone.

Bartlett turns back at 87°47' on April 1st. Onto their five sledges the six of the polar party now take Bartlett's polar provisions of pemmican, fuel, etc. The same was done when the other support parties, Marvin, MacMillan, and Borup turned back—indeed this is what the support parties came out on the ice to do: keep the Peary polar party moving forward. Also Bartlett's return makes it possible to kill one of the dogs, splinter up the poorest sledge, and cook the dog meat with that to strenghen the four Eskimos. "It was a change for them from the pemmican diet. It was fresh meat, it was hot, and they seemed thoroughly to enjoy it." Peary says that though he had eaten raw dog meat in emergencies he did not participate this time.

The very low sun, constantly in the sky now rolling around the horizon, is *nine* solar diameters higher at noon in the south than when grazing the horizon at midnight to the north. South, where Bartlett and his Eskimos have disappeared on their return to land and safety: Ootah (Henson's closest friend), Ooqueah, Seegloo, and Egingwah (the youngest, on whose sledge Peary himself would ride) do notice. They know very well which direction is north, into increasing danger. Even at the 89th parallel the sun is still *four* solar diameters higher behind them at noon than at midnight before them. Beyond 89° the difference becomes so slight they cannot really tell, and Ootah becomes more interested in talking to Henson about the compass by which he and Peary are choosing course, sighting on distant pressure ridge features, from time to time.

On the last day, Henson with Ootah, instructed by Peary—who because of the increased speed has mostly been riding on Egingwah's sledge ever since Bartlett's return—goes the final estimated distance fast as he can, and stops. By the time Peary and Egingwah, slowed by Peary's weight in that sledge, pull up forty-five minutes later, Henson and Egingwah have a snow igloo almost finished (an hour is standard time for doing an igloo start to finish). "I think this is it," Henson says to Ootah, starting over to Peary, meaning that at least this is where Peary will be sure to make the last camp. If it's the Pole, Henson got there first; but there's no point about that. Peary says nothing but unpacks the sextant, and the artificial horizon box, turns it toward the sun, pours in the mercury, lies down in the snow. Satisfied for a first reading, he gets up and says to Henson: "Eighty Nine degrees, fifty-seven minutes." Back, the day before, he had got 89° 25'.

Then, according to Matt, Peary went into the now fininshed igloo and fell into exhausted sleep. All accounts agree they spent in total about 30 hours around this camp. Peary, after a few hours of rest only, found according to his account, he could not sleep long; got up and then taking two Eskimos and a light sledge probed ten miles in one direction, and then in another, making altitude observations of the sun. He reports that in total he took "thirteen single, or six-and-one-half double [upper limb-lower limb], altitudes of the sun at two different stations, in three different directions, at four different times." For probable error on any one of these he estimates "an arbitrary allowance of about ten miles for possible errors of the instruments and myself as an observer" and as to all of them taken together "an allowance of five miles is an equitable one." For the considerable sledging back and forth between the observation spots, he makes a much closer claim—and this one propelled him into great controversy— . . . "no one, except the most ignorant, will have any doubt but what, at some time, I had passed close to the precise point, and had, perhaps actually passed over it." Very doubtful; and "most ignorant" surely arouses the doubters.

Henson, among whose many jobs the keeping of the sledges in repair was a very important detail at this point, never seemed to feel that Peary should have had him check all these sextant readings—which Henson could quite capably have done. To Henson at the time, what value would there have been in that? Or even to Peary: he had Borup, Marvin, MacMillan, and Bartlett for confirmation of latitude to within 133 nautical miles and Henson for the direction and short distance after that. Neither Henson nor Peary at the time had the slightest conception of the bitterness and intensity with which Peary was going to be attacked; and Matt was very busy with urgent sledge maintenance.

He did happen to be in on the last sextant reading. "Matt lay in the snow beside Peary writing down his readings as Peary called them off. At last Peary snapped shut the vernier, rested his eyes a moment, picked up the pad with Matt's figures, and finished his calculations."

The Eskimos had been astonished and quite let down, pleased though Henson and Peary obviously were, to have reached the goal they had so long been pursuing, that nothing tangible or even different was to be seen. "We have found what we hunt," Matt said to Ootah. Bewildered, Ootah stared. Finally he shrugged: "There is nothing here. Just ice, just ice!"

Returning to Peary, Matt found him lying on his, Matt's, sledge "utter exhaustion engraved on the man's face. Now that his goal had been reached, the energy with which he had driven himself . . . had suddenly abandoned him. Touching Peary's shoulder lightly, Matt held out his hand. 'Let me be the first to congratulate you, sir.' . . . Peary shook Matt's hand weakly and then lay back on the sledge. . . . 'Let us go home, Matt, let us go home.' " This is what Henson remembers.

Now began the wild flight for their lives, a furious retreat, led in effect by Henson; sledges light, everything except food and fuel thrown away. Peary in his fifties, much the oldest and most worn-out of them all, and with feet damaged beyond the possibility of keeping up at the now much higher speed over the well packed trail leading south, must ride on Henson's sledge.

Now it was Matt who would bang on the ice in the morning after a minimum of rest hours—whatever the actual time—to wake up and start the five sledges on another double-day south. In fact the first time going south Matt led them the full distance of the last *three* of their northward "marches". No "day" really about that one, sun circling low, endlessly in the sky; Matt simply kept them on their feet, and the dogs going, until they got there: two empty igloos—and too much for one session on their feet without a ration of real rest. After that, double days only, resting in every other one of the empty igloos they had constructed on the way going north, sleeping in their fur clothes, racing desperately to get shore-ward of the "big lead" over the edge of the continental shelf below, where currents are most likely to open up large stretches of sea-water.

On and on, still they do not slacken the exhausting speed. Actually it was either do two stretches in one, or stop at one and a half and waste time building snow igloos.

As they approach the "big lead" area, fortunately a north wind is at their backs closing the lead, and they find it possible to cross by rafting over on ice-floes. Now their big worry is behind them, but still they keep up the relentless pace, their eyes beginning to strain to pick up the mountains behind Cape Columbia. At last they see mirages of these mountains which vanish. Suddenly the next day, there they are: white peaks unmistakably etched against the blue-gray sky! Still Henson continues the "impossible" pace, until they drag themselves into the empty igloos at Cape Columbia, "6 am, April 23:" sixteen days for something that can be called half a thousand statute miles.

In perspective, what do we see? That for the time, 1909, there could be no proof—short of a separate party such as Scott's confirming of Amundsen—for having reached any point in the Arctic Ocean out of sight of photographically identifiable land. From the primary evidence—and rejecting carefully examined but unreliable assertions from secondary sources—it appears that our Honorary Member R.E. Peary may indeed reasonably be regarded as the "discoverer" of the North Pole in the sense of having reached within five or ten nautical miles of 90° North. From the top of ocean pressure ridges which he did reach, had there been land at the North Pole, then unknown, it would have been visible. Despite assertions to the contrary, there was in fact adequate witnessing for his attainment of this location. The unnecessary parading of flags of narrow special interest groups at an historic moment, was a great waste of valuable limited time, and stirred much understandable resentment against Peary. No real evidence of HOAX or fraud can be found in the primary accounts of the expedition, and the primary accounts are adequate to reveal any of consequence had such been present. In our society where the presumption of innocence is accepted unless proof of guilt is shown, the featuring of a photograph of Peary's party over the word HOAX—in our opinion—verges on the irresponsible.

Literature References. The enormous volume of literature references on our subject is daunting. Rawlins' admirable list offers some 235! But published in

1973 it could not include the very important 1979 article in the *Polar Record* quoted at length earlier here.

Much the most important other literature reference, not mentioned at all in *Great Exploration Hoaxes'* list of seven, is *Dark Companion, The Story of Matthew Henson,* by Bradley Robinson, New York, 1967, Fawcett (publisher), first copyright 1947 by Robert M. McBride Co. This is primary material for me because of my nearly twenty year friendship with Matt Henson, who consistently to Capt. Bob Bartlett and others, in my presence, in the nineteen-thirties outspokenly repudiated the many "interviews" and articles over his name which had outrageously been published during the early Cook-Peary controversy for the purpose of attacking Peary. Finally at Vilhjalmur Stefansson's suggestion Henson sat down with his close friend Bradley Robinson and the result, introduced by Stef himself, is *Dark Companion.* Matt afterward always confirmed that everything in it definitely was his as if he himself had personally written it. Everything of interest I remember which Matt told me, I have put in quotes and is confirmed in *Dark Companion.*

The North Pole, by Robert E. Peary, New York, 1910 Stokes, publisher, is not accepted by Peary's critics, presumably because there was a "ghost" assistant. But I can find no slightest deviation between its presentation and what Bartlett, MacMillan, and Henson personally related to me. And regardless of whatever effect the "ghost" may or may not have had upon the text, the many excellent and very informative photographs of the Peary sledges in operation during the course of the expedition cannot remotely have been touched up, and are well worth careful study.

The final essential reference, for any reader further pursuing this subject, is the 1934 personal letter from Peter Freuchen to Vilhjalmur Stefansson, describing at length Freuchen's frequent accounts in Eskimo from the four who accompanied Peary and Henson after Bartlett's return. Freuchen was a North Greenlander who lived in the Smith Sound area in his youth, and was fluent from his earliest youth in the Eskimo language. This letter appears to be the *only* available account direct from the four polar Eskimos. It fully confirms the Peary-Henson-Bartlett version of events: *To Stand At The Pole,* by Dr. Wm. R. Hunt (University of Alaska history professor), New York, 1981 Stein & Day, p. 259-266.

Answer to Terris Moore Article

David Roberts

Terris Moore was and is one of my climbing heroes, and I've also been proud to count him a friend since 1979, when he kindly gave me a lot of his time while I was researching an article on the Harvard climbers of the 1930s. It is, therefore, doubly daunting to find one's published work subjected to such a sharp critique by a great and good man who is also one of the pioneers of Arctic navigation. To many in the AAC, the debate over Peary may seem arcane and technical; but to those who care, the controversy stirs the blood almost as much as it did in 1909. I wonder, then, whether Moore's unstinting loyalty to Matthew Henson—who was *his* hero and friend—has not helped persuade Terris that Peary's critics have a thin case.

Three points, in brief:

(1). The debate about steering and observations of latitude and longitude is extremely knotty, and Moore knows far more about this business than I do. His comments here amount to the only substantive rebuttal in print to Dennis Rawlins' detailed attack in *Peary at the North Pole: Fact or Fiction?*—a book that convinced me. The interested student should read Rawlins, then Moore's rejoinder. However, the argument about navigational method seems far less important to me than Peary's admission before a Congressional subcommittee that he made *no* observations between his last camp with Bartlett (87°47' N.), and the Pole, combined with the fact that Henson did not independently verify Peary's reading that gave a supposed latitude of 89°57' N. on April 6.

(2). The distances for daily travel required beyond 87°47' still seem to me utterly improbable. Having averaged only 9.3 miles per day up to that point, Peary must have averaged 26 miles a day to get to the Pole, then an astounding 59 miles a day back to 87°47'. Moore cites the daily records of mushers in recent runnings of the Iditarod Race. These are not comparable, I think, because in the Iditarod the racers have pre-cached food, use each other's tracks, have modern sledges and extra dogs, and follow a well-known marked trail. Peary was *riding* his sledge and traveling over unknown pack ice, with worn-out dogs.

(3). Moore thinks that if Peary pulled off a hoax, then logically Henson must have been in on it, and finds condescending my suggestion (and Rawlins') that Henson could have been duped by Peary. I never meant to suggest that Henson or the Eskimos were in on Peary's hoax. It is interesting to learn from Moore that Bradley Robinson's *Dark Companion* represents, as it were, Henson's authorized version of the story. That book makes no claims as to daily sledging distances, except to note casually that the last 133 miles to the Pole were covered in five days. As for the Eskimos, Henson (through Robinson) relates that on April 5, "Only the Eskimos slept, and theirs was the blissful sleep of exhausted, innocent children. Geographically ignorant of the world's form, they never could comprehend what matter of madness brought their two civilized friends to this desolate, fearful place. And so they slept, completely unaware that the white man and Negro whom they called brother were soon to make a great discovery. . . ." And speaking of condescension, Peary claimed that Henson, while a great sledger when directed by his leader, "had not, as a racial inheritance, the daring and initiative of Bartlett, or . . . MacMillan, or Borup."

I believe, as Terris Moore does, that an explorer should be innocent until proven guilty. Both he and I have had the truth of our own ascents questioned by others who were not there. I'm still convinced, however, that there are too many holes in Peary's story to be compatible with his arrival at the Pole. I invite those who wish to form their own conclusions to look at Rawlins' and my books and then to reread Moore's rebuttal.

The Czechoslovakian Exchange

MARK WILFORD

EING A SELF-CONFESSED sandstone and adrenaline addict, I'm continually looking for my next fix. Having such traits, a visit to the spawning grounds of my obsession would be quite a treat. That is, as long as I didn't overdose there.

Recently I took the opportunity of such a trip, via an American Alpine Club exchange, and visited the somewhat unknown climbing regions of Czechoslovakia. For five-and-a-half weeks Matt Kerns, Rick Powell and I participated in, and were awe-stricken by, some of the oldest and most traditional climbing in the world.

Geographically, Czechoslovakia lies in the Eastern Bloc of Europe. For obvious and not so obvious reasons, few Western climbers have explored the many climbing areas Czechoslovakia has to offer. Really a shame for all parties concerned!

Basically, Czech climbing can be divided into two main regions. These centers are the granite walls of the High Tatras and the sandstone pinnacles of Bohemia. Besides these two main regions, many smaller areas of basalt, limestone and granite abound.

By far the most significant and impressive of the climbing is on the Bohemian sandstone. It is this region which offers amazing pinnacles combined with unbelievable ethics and rules resulting in some of the boldest and most well-defined climbing anywhere. The idea of rules and regulation in climbing will come as a surprise to most climbers. Nobody tells *us* how to climb. Czech sandstone climbing is different. Entrenched in a very old tradition are a set of rules governing and protecting this climbing and rock. With the printing of the 1958 guide book to the sandstone came the first occasion for the rules to be written down. These rules are the common sense and opinions of the majority of sandstone climbers. Following are the general rules accepted after discussions in 1968. This should help in understanding the confusing nature of the sandstone sport.

Rules:

1. One may climb using only natural hand- and footholds while incorporating one's own strength and technique.

Photo by Mark Wilford

Towers of ADRŠPACH in Northeast Bohemia.

2. It is strictly prohibited to:
   a. change the nature of the rock intentionally.
   b. use chocks, pitons, friends or other metal protection devices in cracks or pockets.
   c. climb on wet sandstone (Suché Skály excepted).
   d. use hard-soled shoes, i.e., Vibram.
   e. use alcohol, drugs, etc., which might affect the safety of the ascent.
   f. use magnesium. (This was included after 1968.)
3. The rope can only be used to belay from under the rock. No top-roping.
4. The placing of protection knots and slings has to be based only on the natural properties of the rock. It is also necessary to protect the rock from damage by using slings to eliminate friction over the rock. Slings can only be used for protection. Resting on a sling lowers the "sport value" of the ascent.
5. A shoulder-stand by one's own strength, so called "clean shoulder-stand", is allowed only at places where it was, with good reason, employed during the first ascent. A shoulder-stand using a ring (bolt), sling or knot for aid is prohibited. The areas in northeast Bohemia are officially excluded from this rule.
6. a. Rings (bolts) are to be used only for belaying and protection. Use as a handhold/foothold is prohibited.
   b. The criteria for proper placement must be followed. i.e.—proper depth of hole and packing of the ring upon placement. Whoever places the ring is responsible for its safety.
   c. During the first ascent the ring must be placed from a free position. During the drilling one is allowed to rest on the drill. The ring must be placed in the original hole started. A second hole denotes that it was used to rest on while drilling the main hole. Again, northeast Bohemia is exempt from this rule. Regarding this exemption, the distance between the two holes cannot exceed 30 cm.
   d. One is not allowed to change the place of or add more rings to an established climb. The exception to this is when the ring's position is such that the friction of the rope over edges damages the soft rock.

Enforcement of any violation which might damage the rock is possible by forest ranger/park warden types. Local climbers will also discourage infractions as I found out by using chalk on my first climbs. In certain areas, climbers will form ethics committees. If, for some reason, there is doubt about the style of a first ascent, the committee can request that the first ascentist reclimb the route in front of them. If it can't be repeated legitimately, the climb is deemed impure and the rings removed from it.

The subject of grades and grading is a fairly difficult one. It seems that the Czech grading system suffers too much from the old guard's ego as it is closed at 7c. 7c then contains quite a variety of grades and means little else than it's harder than 7b. Unfortunately, 7b starts to mean less and less as old 7cs are

PLATE 49
Photo by Mark Wilford
Rick Powell on "The Whip," Teplice
(5.10a).

down rated to 7b to make room for the new 7cs. Generally 7a is 5.7, 7b is 5.8 and easy 7c around 5.9.

Fortunately, the neighboring East Germans have remained open-minded and open-ended. After 7c, the scale continues with 8a-c and 9a-c. 9c is currently the limit in both East Germany and Czechoslovakia. An approximate correlation between East German and U.S. grades is: 8a = 5.10 − , 8b = 5.10, 8c = 5.10 + or 5.11 − , 9a = 5.11 − or 5.11, 9b = 5.11 or 5.11 + , 9c = 5.11 + or 5.12 − . These grades are further complicated when protection factors are taken into consideration. A certain climb may technically be 8c but because it has a 50-foot run-out off the ground it is given 9b.

Another factor regarding grades is the rings. It is stated that the rings cannot be used as hand- or footholds. They can, however, be used for rest points. This is a major difference from the U.S. view on free-climbing. Czech and East German grades can have little or no meaning when attempting something with a Western attitude. It's quite easy to transform an 8c climb into an arm-pumping 9b when trying to free-climb past these rings. It would be comparable to climbing Yosemite's "Butterballs" in three sections and grading it 5.10.

As interesting as the rules and strict ethics of the sandstone climbing is its seemingly ancient history. Czech sandstone climbing is separated into three main areas of Bohemia. The westernmost area, northern Bohemia, lies along the Elbe River on the East German border. Just to the east, in north-central Bohemia, is the Czech Paradise (Český Ráj) region. Further to the east, near the Polish border, is the northeastern Bohemian area. Although relatively close, each of these areas has different histories and developments.

Before most of us were even a gleam in our grandfathers' eyes, Czech sandstone climbing was maturing. Initial development started in northern Bohemia in the early 1880's. Responsible for this primitive insanity were Saxon Germans who lived nearby. These Germans monopolised the area for half a century with their first ascents. It wasn't until 1950 that the first significant Czech climb appeared. Because of this lengthy German occupation, a very strong Saxon influence can be seen in northern Bohemia's ethics.

The Czech Paradise region saw a slightly later development, again by Saxon Germans. Between 1920 and 1930 most of the main pinnacles had been climbed by the Germans. The Czechs were quicker in this area. Just before World War II they had produced their first climbs.

Northeastern Bohemia saw the latest exploitation of the sandstone regions. In 1925 the Germans, again, began development of this vast region. Activity was slow and by 1937 no more than 40 of the 1000 towers were climbed. The years just after World War II saw the boom of Czech climbing. Because of this late and slow development the Saxon ethics and traditions are weakest in this area.

Faced with such radically different ideas on free climbing, you can imagine the anxiety that beset our humble group as we began our sandstone journey. Introduction to the rock came on a typically hazy day at Suché Skály, in the Czech Paradise. After a warm-up on "Photographic Arête," 7b, I knew a good

Photo by Mark Wilford

Roman on the Traverse Pitch of "Crazy Project" (5.12) in Adršpach, Czechoslovakia.

time was going to be had. Declaring 7b to be too easy, I was given to a local expert for initiation into the terror zone of 7c.

With my first 7c, "Vega," I also received my first lesson in knot technology. I've never trusted nuts in opposition, but knots? Surely someone jests. I think the whole knot business is to inhibit falling. I will admit I cheated on "Vega," however. Being the kind souls they are, our "guides" forgot to take our chalk away from us. Unfortunately, the brightly-colored bags of courage were soon noticed by self-appointed "ethic enforcers." The show-down came swiftly as I was climbing "The Overhanging Arête," 5.11. While indulging in my habitual dipping, the air was suddenly shattered with "Nicht, nicht magnesium". Looking down I saw a scrawny yet serious figure gibbering at Matt and me. My life was crushed. I mean I can't even get out of bed without my chalk bag.

The next few days saw us sampling many of the pinnacles in a variety of the Czech Paradise's sub-areas. As a rule, most of these climbs were on soft, vertical and highly pocketed rock. By now knots had become an accepted and somewhat trusted necessary evil. Giving up chalk wasn't quite as easy. Giving up a two-pack-a-day-cig habit would have been easier. Eventually the inevitable was realized; we did as the Romans.

After having collected a good number of routes, it was time to move on. Next stop was northeastern Bohemia featuring its two subareas Adršpach and Teplice. This region of pinnacles, although similar in appearance, varies greatly from the pocketed, soft towers of the Paradise area. Typical of most climbs are rough, wide cracks coupled with smooth, bulging friction walls. Even Yosemite would be hard pressed to offer more fist, off-width and chimney cracks. So much for my love of face climbing.

First day in Adršpach saw me teamed up with local hardman Roman. By now I was getting used to thrifty conversations. "Sieben c, gut, nicht so gut, classic sieben c, kein magnesium, sieben c, gut material, kein magnesium, gut sieben c, kein magnesium etc." As Roman and I were both monolingual, little was to be gained from the intellectual stimulation of conversing. Fortunately, you don't really have to talk to climb. If you pull hard enough on the rope, something is bound to happen. In keeping with the brotherhood of climbing and international good will, I was honored with a "classic 7c" as an introduction to Adršpach. It wasn't until I was halfway up the off-width, clad in shorts, that I wondered if classic and brotherhood held the same connotation world wide. They were smiling at me anyway. Classic or not, I had little difficulty, unlike the climb, in expressing my displeasure for any further swimming expeditions up wide cracks.

After testing a few reasonable hand cracks, Roman shepherded me to an isolated tower sporting the unrepeated "Crazy Project". Sickening can best describe my feelings as I peered up the 80-meter, overhanging wall. Because of our language barrier, my usual response was pointless. I had no way of describing the flare-up of an old injury, the late hour of the day or the possibility of a sudden thunderstorm. I was doomed to climb.

Photo by Mark Wilford

Petr Cermak on the First Ascent of "Coloradical" (5.11) at Suché Skály.

The honor was again mine as Roman "gave" me the first pitch. The climbing started out easy but, sooner than hoped, fear replaced pleasure. Above me the wall turned roof and I was forced onto an overhanging traverse. It was all there, except for the protection. Each time I ventured out the traverse the thought of a 10-meter pendulum pulled me back. Finally, concentration conquered fear and I managed the moves to find the salvation of the belay ring. The smiles were now mine as Roman arrived to ponder the next pitch. The climb was just beginning to show its teeth. Rising above us, on the 95° wall, was a short hand crack. Now I think hand cracks are always nice, except, on the rare occasion, when they end in a blank face. This was such an occasion. Roman was unfazed. Halfway up the crack he fired in the only protection, an 8mm knot. As it turned out, the face above wasn't completely blank. There were holds. The problem being, a matter of meters separated the holds. Knots do hold. This I can testify to as Roman began a series of nerve-shattering plummets while measuring the distance between the handholds. After more than enough of these wingers, my true ambition to be a secured second was replaced by the sharp end of the rope.

Why the protection knot was good I don't know. Better judgement denied my visual inspection. As I arrived at the top of the crack Roman's flight time was explained by the substantial void from hand-jam to fingerhold. Not one to duplicate the unpleasant, I broke sacred laws of statics and lunged for the goading hold. The gamble paid and I cashed in on the richly pocketed climbing above.

The next pitch refused to relent and so did we. After a short traverse, a flaring crack split the wall above. Placing protection at the bottom of said crack, Roman went for it. There is no fear of flying here. Five meters of overhanging laybacking insured no time for protecting and lots of time for sweating. Roman was not protecting and I was sweating. My comrade prevailed. Soon I found myself cranking up the crack.

Although the angle had now laid back some, the climb still wasn't over. To be dealt with next were two devilishly deceiving pitches of vertical and horizontal breaks. All the remaining holds involved friction. No jams or edges, just friction. No matter how close the protection is, and it wasn't, nothing is worse than slipping up a climb. This was a typical feature of most last pitches in northeast Bohemia. Frictioning for the top was usually as hard as any of the crux sections below. After many less-than-graceful maneuvers (i.e. groveling), we were allowed the summit. "Crazy Project" was ours for the mere fee of a couple of extra heart beats and a few white hairs.

Besides surviving the constant climbing, I was also becoming quite proficient at the number one sport in Czechoslovakia, that sport being beer drinking with the ability to stand after six pints of Pilsner. At 25 cents a pint, beer was becoming a major staple in my diet. Just as bouldering, nuts and good ropes are an integral part of our climbing, beer drinking contributes many necessary requirements to sandstone climbing, the obvious being courage and as a pain killer. After a week of primo climbing intermixed with great drinking

Photos by Vladimir Weigner

Mark Wilford and Matt Kerns on the Hlaska Pinnacle, Teplice, Northeast Bohemia.

sessions, it was time to move on. The mountains were calling and we had to answer.

Located in the northeastern section of Czechoslovakia, along the Polish border, is the smallest alpine range in the world, the High Tatras. This range is actually shared by both Poland and Czechoslovakia with Polish Tatra climbing being more publicized. Unlike the highly regulated and well defined sandstone climbing, the Tatras have the all-important summit syndrome. Anything goes in the no-holds-barred climbing. Tactics and styles are reminiscent of most West European areas. Bolt ladders, pitons and nuts. Everything short of air compressed drills and scaffolding goes, even chalk! You can imagine that this came as quite a relief to our sandstone tried-and-fried brains.

The beauty of the Tatras is vast and sudden. Unfortunately, my initial opinion was adversely affected by the combination of my intense laziness and the lengthy trudge to our Base Camp. My heavy load only seemed to dim the warm sunlight. All things come to an end, as did our death march, and the true majesty of the Tatras appeared to me just as I stumbled into camp.

Since we were in an alpine range, an alpine start for the next day seemed in order. Again, the splendor of the Tatras was being tested. Four A.M. starts and I mix like oil and water. In self-defense I slept on the approach hike to our climb.

The walls of the Tatras are not spectacular in a Yosemite sense. Often, the climbs appear to be shattered and loose. It's not until you're 200 meters up and find it *is* straight down that you realize respect is in order. In general, the rock is good granite offering fine face climbing with adequate protection from crack systems stuffed with fixed pins.

Besides occasional rockfall, a major hazard of the Tatras is its unpredictable weather. Storms can blow in quickly, leaving climbers in serious situations. A fear of some Czech climbers is being caught, two-thirds up a climb, in a storm and being drowned. Apparently, this has happened. It seems the large dihedrals near the tops of climbs funnel rainwater, very quickly, down crack systems and onto hanging belays. Hopefully our early start would be early enough since I'd left my life-preserver back at camp.

Accompanying me on my first Tatra climb was rat-urologist Yeti Hausman. Our objective was the 300-meter "Studničkova cesta" on the Galerie Ganku. Yeti was a horse of a man and quite a good climber. His brain just had a great desire to keep the rest of him alive. For this and other reasons, I was to do all the leading and Yeti was to carry the pack. O.K. by me.

The first pitches of our climb were about 80° and in the 5.7 to 5.8 range. We quickly gained altitude as I ran out the rope on the moderate climbing. After 150 meters, the wall started bulging and dripping. The next pitch completely changed the nature of the climb. In a dry state, it would have gone at a reasonable 5.9. Unfortunately, a small waterfall was seeping out above us, sliming up the whole pitch. Out came the rain gear. I started the lead up a slab to the overhangs above. Every hold was wet and glassy. My chalk was becoming a worthless paste. Upon arrival at the overhangs, I was forced onto a traverse across the walls of a large, vertical dihedral. This was also soaked. Luckily, protection was in situ and abundant. The handholds were jugs but just as their namesakes, they also held water. Each time I used a jam or clipped protection, water would run down my arm. Just as agonizing was the serious rope-drag I had acquired from all my zigzag climbing. I hollered down for a belay on the 7mm haul line and went onto a double-rope belay. Big holds or not, I was gripped. After 30 meters of slip-slide traversing, I found a hole protected from the waterfalls. It was now Yeti's turn for an exciting bath as he began the traverse. Long swings stared at him each time he unclipped a piece of protection. Fortunately, steel handholds are legit in Yeti's book. More than one screamer was saved by the fixed protection.

Like the rats Yeti tested, we clawed our way out of the hole and up to the base of yet another large dihedral. Our situation was a spectacular one. Two hundred meters of air below and the looming walls of the dihedral above. The climbing was perfect now. All the wet sections were below us. Piercing the left wall of the dihedral were thin finger-cracks accompanied by pleasantly spaced, square-cut edges. After salvaging some dry chalk, I attacked the cracks and face-climbing. All the protection was in and I was playing clip-and-go. Much to Yeti's dismay, I didn't clip into all the pitons, making long run-outs instead. It was quite an ordeal for Yeti when he was left with one nice hold only to find the next one unclipped and therefore much too small. These "blank sections" of unclipped pegs often produced a tremendous scream of "Big tension" from a usually quite calm Yeti. After two long pitches in the dihedral the talus slope of the summit met us. Just in time as well. Like a synchronized movement, the clouds rolled in and we moved out.

Adventures of this type were to become typical of the rest of our Tatra climbs. Something was always being thrown in to make a normally humdrum, 300-meter climb exciting. Racing clouds and thunderstorms, wet and loose rock, the freeing of aid sections, 10-meter roofs and the labyrinth of a descent were all ingredients of one climb or another.

With our departure from the Tatras I again felt the loss of a brutal yet passionate relationship. Still, I was satisfied. Our imaginations, abilities and styles had opened up new doors to extreme climbing on the massive granite walls.

As a last reminder of who was really in charge and who was just along for the ride, Matt and I lost the trail on our way out. The extra miles of stumbling about in the dark seemed fair retribution for our brash exploits on the lofty peaks.

After the Tatras, we still had another week in which to dismember ourselves. The Elbe valley of East Germany and Czechoslovakia was next on the agenda. We all had great expectations of what was to come. Rick Powell was expecting to live through our stay, I was expecting another beer with dinner and Matt Kerns was expecting a child *soon*, like yesterday. I was the only one who was immediately satisfied. Matt and Rick would have to wait a couple more days for their results.

PLATE 53

Photo by Petr Brzak

Mark Wilford on the Second Ascent
of "Contact" (5.11) in the Czech
Paradise region.

The climbing of the Elbe valley is on nearly perfect sandstone pinnacles set in a beautiful countryside. On the German side are the humbling test pieces of the god-like and barefoot Bernd Arnold. Impossible lies in another dimension when it comes to 9c and Bernd. Through personal experience, I found barefoot 9a to be both mentally and physically ridiculous. Only by digressing to an instinct-driven and prehensilely-toed Neanderthal creature, was I able to enjoy the fruits (usually a banana) of success.

Northern Bohemia offers the same spectacular and difficult climbing. It seems to go on forever. In regards to the climbing, my only regret was the inability to climb all of the pinnacles. But then I'd have no reason to return. You see, besides the excellent beer, friendly and hospitable people, tremendous scenery and beautiful girls, collecting pinnacles makes Czechoslovakia a true climbers' paradise no one should miss.

PLATE 54

Photo by Mark Wilford

Roman on "The Whip Direct" at Teplice (5.10).

Climbs and Expeditions, 1982

The Editorial Board is extremely grateful to the many people who have done so much to make this section possible. Among those who have been very helpful, we should like to thank in particular Michael J. Cheney, Kamal K. Guha, Harish Kapadia, Mohan C. Motwani, H.C. Sarin, Józef Nyka, Tsunemichi Ikeda, Toni Hiebeler, Naseer Ullah Awan, Taleh Mohammad, Trevor Braham, Renato Moro, Paolo Panzeri, César Morales Arnao, Vojslav Arko, Aleš Kunaver, Franci Savenc, Tim Lewis, Doug Scott, José Manuel Anglada, Josep Paytubi, Elmar Landes, Alois Furtner, Claude Deck and Anders Bolinder.

METERS TO FEET

Unfortunately the American public seems to be resisting the change from feet to meters. To assist readers from the more enlightened countries, where meters are universally used, we give the following conversion chart:

meters	feet	meters	feet	meters	feet	meters	feet
3300	10,827	4700	15,420	6100	20,013	7500	24,607
3400	11,155	4800	15,748	6200	20,342	7600	24,935
3500	11,483	4900	16,076	6300	20,670	7700	25,263
3600	11,811	5000	16,404	6400	20,998	7800	25,591
3700	12,139	5100	16,733	6500	21,326	7900	25,919
3800	12,467	5200	17,061	6600	21,654	8000	26,247
3900	12,795	5300	17,389	6700	21,982	8100	26,575
4000	13,124	5400	17,717	6800	22,310	8200	26,903
4100	13,452	5500	18,045	6900	22,638	8300	27,231
4200	13,780	5600	18,373	7000	22,966	8400	27,560
4300	14,108	5700	18,701	7100	23,294	8500	27,888
4400	14,436	5800	19,029	7200	23,622	8600	28,216
4500	14,764	5900	19,357	7300	23,951	8700	28,544
4600	15,092	6000	19,685	7400	24,279	8800	28,872

NOTE: All dates in this section refer to 1982 unless otherwise stated.

Correction about the Photographer of the Cover Photo of the A.A.J., 1982. Unfortunately the wrong person was credited with the cover photo of the *A.A.J.*, 1982. Although it was submitted to the *Editor,* by John Evans, it was not taken by him. Evans has kindly given us the following pertinent information about the photograph. It was taken at about 5:30 P.M. on October 24, 1981 by Christopher Pizzo, M.D., a member of the American Medical Research Expedition to Everest. Dr. Pizzo had reached the summit of Mount Everest at about noon with Sherpa Yong Tenzing and collected physical and physiological data there. On the descent they were met at 28,500 feet by Peter Hackett, M.D., who was climbing alone. After a brief conference, Hackett decided to make a solo ascent and Pizzo agreed to wait for him a bit lower on the ridge. Tenzing descended to camp at 26,500 feet to melt snow for hot drinks. At dusk, realizing that neither he nor Hackett would be likely to survive without the other, Pizzo completed a set of scientific observations and left instructions for the disposition of his records. At this time he also took the photograph of the last rays of the sun on the neighboring peaks. Just then, at 5:45, Hackett came into view above him. Together they descended in the dark to the safety of the camp. Makalu (27,825 feet) is the world's fifth highest mountain; in the distance is Kanchenjunga (28,208 feet), the third highest. The prominent ridge forms the border between Nepal on the right and Tibet on the left. Kanchenjunga is 80 miles east of Everest on the border between Nepal and Sikkim.

UNITED STATES

Alaska

Denali National Park and Preserve, 1982 Mountaineering Summary. During the 1982 climbing season, more climbers were on Mount McKinley than ever before, but surprisingly, the summit saw fewer climbers than in several previous years. Of the record 696 climbers who attempted the mountain in 1982, only 310 (44%) successfully reached the summit. In 1981, 321 climbers (52%) made it to the top; in 1979, 351 (66%) were successful; and in 1976, 339 (67%). Why were so few climbers successful this year? There were no long periods of consistently bad weather. Were the climbers of 1982 attempting more difficult routes, or were they more inexperienced? Or were they simply less summit oriented and more concerned with enjoying their climb? Another possible reason may be that every year more climbers choose to begin their climbs in April, an extremely cold and bitterly windy time for a climb. Presumably most of the climbers choose April in order to avoid the "hordes" of climbers that are on the mountain in May, June, and July. But as April

Photo by Jack Tackle

The Southeast Face of MOUNT McKINLEY, the Isis Face.

becomes more popular, these climbers may find that, instead of avoiding the hordes, they may in fact be part of the hordes of April. Despite the lower success rate, some impressive climbs were made in 1982. A party of three completed the first winter ascent of the Cassin Ridge route (and only the second winter ascent of the mountain) in February and March. This climb was extremely difficult and dangerous, and the three climbers were lucky that the weather was basically stable the entire time they were on the mountain. Other significant ascents were marred to some degree. An American climber made a very impressive solo ascent of the Scott-Haston route on the South Face of Mount McKinley, but suffered badly frostbitten hands and ended his climb being evacuated back to the Kahiltna Base Camp by dog team. Two other climbers completed a new route on the Southeast Face of the South Buttress—a route that they named the Isis Face. Though they completed their intended route, they stopped their climb on the South Buttress and did not continue to the summit of the mountain. And finally, a party of six completed the second ascent of the Northwest Buttress (first ascent in 1954) by making the questionable decision of sending two members to the summit while another member was suffering from cerebral edema. Whatever the reasons for the lower success rate on the mountain, they were *not* responsible for a corresponding increase in the number of accidents on the mountain. For only the fourth time in the last fourteen years, there were no deaths on Mount McKinley. Helicopters flew to Mount McKinley for rescues only four times, compared to fifteen times in 1976.

However, there were *some* serious incidents. Two Japanese climbers nearly perished when they fell an unknown distance down the West Rib route. The two owe their lives to the High Latitude Research Project, a team of doctors doing medical research on the mountain, who spotted the two climbers, evacuated them to their camp and cared for them for several days until the weather improved and helicopters could reach the camp. A large German expedition faced a near tragedy when they climbed from 17,000 feet to the summit in very poor weather. Other climbers at the same camp refused to go to the summit in such weather. The bad weather got worse and the party was forced to bivouac on their descent. The next day they struggled back into the camp, several with frostbite and one with a back injury. Had there not been other climbers at the 17,000-foot camp to care for the German climbers, it is probable that some would have perished. The same severe storm compounded another climber's problems. A young English climber, out for a day's solo ice climb on the West Buttress, fell when a cornice collapsed beneath him. He lost most of his equipment and was forced to spend a night out in a shallow snow cave. During the bivouac, both hands were very badly frostbitten and he eventually lost most of his fingers. Many other climbers suffered frostbite in 1982. From our after-climb reports, it appears that at least 15% of all the climbers on the mountain received some degree of frostbite. Many of these were those who chose to climb in April or early May, although frostbite injury is possible at any time. Even though many of these frostbite cases were minor, the figure is

DENALI NATIONAL PARK AND PRESERVE
1982 MOUNTAINEERING SUMMARY

Mount McKinley	*Expeditions*	*Climbers*	*Successful* *Climbers*
West Buttress	97	352	129
West Buttress (Guided)	17	146	82
Muldrow Glacier	4	19	13
Muldrow Glacier (Guided)	1	20	18
West Rib	20	64	23
Cassin	17	43	23
South Buttress (Guided)	1	11	10
NW Buttress (Guided)	1	6	2 (N. Peak)
Wickersham Wall	3	14	0
East Buttress	2	5	3
Messner Couloir	2	4	4
SE Face (Isis Face)	1	2	0
South Face	2	6	1
Reality Ridge	1	2	2
SW Face	1	2	0
	170	696	310
Mount Foraker	5	14	4
Mount Foraker (Guided)	1	2	0
Mount Hunter	6	16	0
Mount Huntington	6	15	0
Mooses Tooth	4	8	6 (W. Peak)
Kitchatna Spires	3	8	5
Mount Russell	1	3	0
Little Switzerland	1	2	2
	27	68	17
TOTAL	197	764	327

Robert A. Gerhard, *Denali National Park and Preserve*

far too high. Even a relatively minor case of frostbite can result in impaired circulation and a greater risk of subsequent injury. Virtually all frostbite injuries should be preventable. Wearing the proper clothing is, in itself, not enough to prevent frostbite. Proper nutrition, proper hydration, and proper mental attitude are all equally important. In addition to the two Japanese climbers on the West Rib route, the High Latitude Research Project may have saved other lives, or at least prevented some accidents. Teams of doctors spent most of May and June at two camps on the West Buttress route—one at the 7000-foot Kahiltna Base Camp and one at 14,300 feet. Though their primary

From Camp IV on the Isis Face on
McKINLEY, looking at Huntington.

mission was to conduct medical research, the doctors also assisted numerous climbers with minor to major medical problems. Some climbers with minor altitude problems were cautioned to remain at the 14,300-foot camp for a day or so before continuing their climb, perhaps preventing more serious altitude illness higher on the mountain. The High Latitude Research Project plans at this time to return to Mount McKinley for the 1983 climbing season. A few other statistics about the 1982 climbing season on Mount McKinley may be of interest: 42% of the climbers came to the mountain from outside the United States. In addition to the United States, 23 separate countries were represented. It is truly an international mountain. 498 of the 696 climbers who attempted Mount McKinley did so via the popular West Buttress route. Thus nearly three out of every four climbers on the mountain can be found on one route. 183 (26%) of the 696 climbers were guided on their climbs by professional mountain guides. Most of these climbs were on the West Buttress route, but guided climbs were also made on the Muldrow Glacier, South Buttress, and Northwest Buttress routes. For more information, please contact: Mountaineering Ranger, Denali National Park and Preserve, P.O. Box 9, Denali National Park, Alaska 99755.

Thunder Ridge, West Buttress, Mount McKinley. Bill Holton, Stan Olsen and I left Kahiltna Base with plans to climb a new direct variation between 12,000 and 16,000 feet on the West Buttress proper, a steep section of ice and rock. We set up camp at 12,300 feet and prepared equipment and supplies for ten days. Directly above us was a broken ridge of rock and ice leading to the final knife-edged ridge nearly 4000 feet higher. Early on the afternoon of June 24 and in beautiful weather, we hiked across the base of the basin to where it drops off onto the Peters Glacier. We roped at 12,700 feet to climb in a prominent narrow ice gully on the right side of the ridge. We climbed six pitches of excellent ice and occasional snow and rock to where the gully merged with a large ice-and-snow ramp. These first pitches were among the steepest on the climb and averaged from 50° to 60°. At the end of the sixth pitch we found enough snow to level a tent platform for Camp I at 13,300 feet. In flawless weather on the 25th, we continued for four pitches on the ramp to a narrow col separating us from a large couloir on the right, "Windy Col." From there we climbed mostly on snow with some rock for 300 feet to the base of a snowfield visible from the base of the climb. We climbed for 200 feet up this and then 300 feet along the ridge to a perfect niche between two rocks just big enough for our three-man dome tent. We placed Camp II at 14,400 feet and remained there the following day as the weather appeared to be deteriorating. On the 27th we were above the clouds and so we resumed climbing. Just above camp the ridge merged with the couloir we had seen from Windy Col and soon we found ourselves traversing to the right across the top of it to gain the base of a large rock band leading to the summit ridge. The winds picked up and blowing snow driven by violent winds made progress slow. At six P.M., as things were starting to look grim, we found a small shelf somewhat sheltered

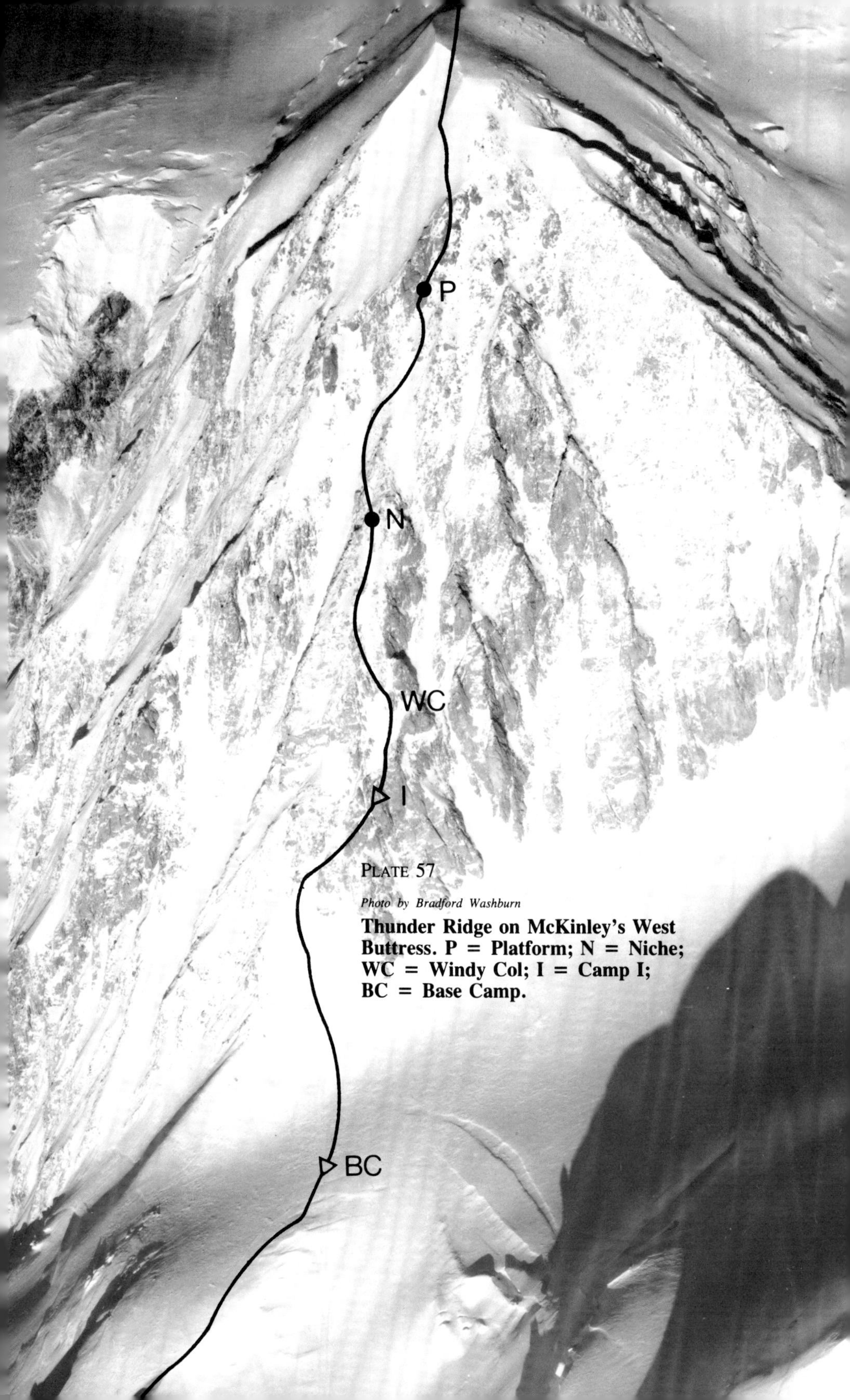

PLATE 57

Photo by Bradford Washburn

Thunder Ridge on McKinley's West Buttress. P = Platform; N = Niche; WC = Windy Col; I = Camp I; BC = Base Camp.

from the wind. After three hours of nerve-racking work carrying snow blocks across a 40° slope, still roped up, we finished the platform. We could barely erect the tent, which we lashed to the cliff before climbing inside. We were astonished to be able to have our brews and to awaken in the morning with the tent still intact. The winds began to subside later in the morning, but we stayed put for the day. July 29 brought a brief window in the storm, and we hurriedly packed up. The tent poles resembled cork screws; what had saved us was tying up the tent with our ropes which prevented the poles from bending to the breaking point. We continued along the base of the rock band on 50° ice for four pitches to round a corner and enter a large couloir which we followed for 400 feet to gain the ridge where it turned to snow and became knife-edged. We continued on for another four pitches to where the climb suddenly ended on top of the buttress at just over 16,000 feet. We hoped to camp at 16,300 feet above the headwall on the regular West-Buttress route. We marveled at how the wind had completely removed the snow from the ridge, leaving sparkling blue ice. Just short of the top of the headwall, Holton was unable to go further and so we camped in a small hollow on the ridge. In increasing wind Olsen and I built a wall around the tent. This effort took us until 1:30 A.M. when we could relax, brew up and eat. The second storm kept on until July 2 when we descended the headwall because Holton could not carry on. *Statistics:* 4 short climbing days, 3 camps and 34 pitches of interesting but never difficult climbing, mostly on snow and ice. Recommended hardware: 4 ice tubes, 5 pitons up to 1″ and 5 chocks up to a N° 8 Hex. Two snow stakes were helpful for anchoring the tent and were used on the final four pitches. I recommend this as a technical route without the objective danger involved in reaching the West Rib, the Cassin Ridge or the South Buttress.

Michael Covington

Mount McKinley. Bill Krause, Ted Waltman and Mike Danaher in alpine style made the fourth ascent of the East Buttress, reaching the summit on June 8 before descending the West Buttress. They had very severe weather conditions on this difficult route. They were nine days on the East Buttress and then were pinned down by storms for days on the upper slopes of the peak. In May Gary Bocarde and others made the second ascent of the Northwest Buttress.

Foraker and Crosson, Ski Descents, 1981. On May 22, 1981 we landed on the Kahiltna Glacier. The team was Pierre Beghin, James Merel, Jean-Luc Ruby and I. We left for Base Camp four hours later. After three days of looking for a suitable route on the east ridge, we finally decided to climb the southeast ridge. Before leaving Anchorage, we had asked several American climbers if they thought it was possible to make a ski descent of the southeast ridge; they just looked at us and laughed. We left for the climb with ten days' food and *one* pair of skis. To reach Camp I was not without danger. It was steep and we had to cross an avalanche area. I was nearly caught in a big ice avalanche. The good weather was so warm that we were obliged to climb after sunset. The second day was foggy but the face was not quite so steep. That second evening we found a snow cave. In the morning we had to dig our way out as the cold winds had drifted the entrance in. The weather on the third day was extremely clear and we could see our Base Camp 6000 feet lower on the glacier. This was our longest day. Though we thought it would take us five hours, we finally reached the summit after twelve hours. With only one pair of skis, Beghin skied from the summit to Camp II, which was the easiest and best of the descent. It was difficult for the three on foot in the thigh-deep snow. We reached camp at eight P.M., exhausted. As we headed for Camp I the next day, the skiing became dangerous, some of it on 60° slopes. We had to ski roped to cross several steep sections, crevasses and avalanche areas. It snowed on the third day of the descent, from Camp I to Base Camp, which we reached late in the afternoon. Later we skied from the summit of Mount Crosson before crossing the pass to arrive after 28 days at Wonder Lake.

RÉMY POCCARD, *Club Alpin Français*

Mount Foraker. Mount Foraker was climbed by its southeast ridge, first by John Tuckey and Rob Kimbrough and then by Glenn Randall and Peter Metcalf.

Mount Hunter, Northwest Spur Variant. On April 12 Gary Bocarde, Nick Parker and I started on a new variant on the west ridge of Mount Hunter. After skiing around from the southeast fork of the Kahiltna into the basin north of the west ridge, we set up Base Camp below the prominent icefall and bowl that indents the lower northern part of the west ridge. We worked through the heavily crevassed lower section of the bowl and onto the western face of the northwest spur, where we climbed 45° to 50° stable snow slopes to camp on a narrow platform below the lower rocks of the spur at 8200 feet. The next day we proceeded along below the crest on steepening slopes to 9400 feet, where we cut a narrow platform and slept roped in cold April weather. The next morning we were treated to a spectacular display when a large section of the icefall, just a few hundred feet over on the ridge and level with us, broke and avalanched. Bocarde continued the lead, the last three pitches being 60° to 70° rotten ice, and reached the ridge at the point marked 10,610 feet, where we spent the night on a broad flat area just off the west ridge. Bocarde next led over the cornice problems to the ice slope at 11,000 feet, where a storm stopped us for a day. We left for the summit on the sixth day in unsettled weather. While Bocarde blissfully led the second pitch on ice at 11,200 feet, Parker and I watched ominous lenticular clouds descend on Denali, Foraker and our summit. We retreated to camp in worsening weather and strong winds, decided to descend and stopped for the night at our Camp III. We descended in rappels from the ridge. The lower slope was moderately loaded by the storm, reminding us how unsavory the lower route would be in heavy snow.

LANCE S. OWENS

P 11,300, West Face Couloir, West Fork of Ruth Glacier. Bob Crawford and I flew to the Ruth Glacier on April 17. After several days of storm and reconnaissance, we climbed a hidden couloir on the west face of P 11,300. The couloir was 2500 feet long, with 1500 feet of continuous, undulating ice, averaging between 55° and 80° in steepness. From the top of the couloir we followed the southwest ridge for several pitches to descend the southeast ridge. The climb occurred between April 30 and May 3. During the same period Donnie Black and Scotty Wade climbed an obvious couloir to the left of our couloir, directly to the summit.

DANIEL CAUTHORN*

Broken Tooth. "Broken Tooth" is the unofficial name that Alaskan mountaineers have applied to P 9050 on the divide between the Buckskin and Coffee Glaciers, 20 miles southeast of Denali. On May 7 Bob Plumb and I made the first ascent of Broken Tooth, climbing the southeast ridge. Our route from the Coffee Glacier ascended a 45° snow slope for 2000 feet before coming to grips with the main technical difficulties. The upper southeast ridge rises for another 2000 feet at an average of 55° and comprises difficult mixed climbing. We made 24 belays, placed five bolts to anchor belays and rappels and bivouacked three times on the upper ridge. The technical part of the climb required four days. (VI, 5.8, A3.)

CURT HAIRE

Tordrillo Mountains Ski Traverse. In late March and early April Mark Jonas** and I flew to Beluga Lake to begin the first 3-pin ski traverse of the Tordrillo Mountains. These stretch for over 100 miles from near Mount Spur to the Cathedral Mountains. Our route lay up the Triumvirate Glacier, across a major pass to the Hayes Glacier, over the Black and Tan Glacier and down the Skwentna River to Rainy Pass Lodge. We were to have ascended Moose Creek to the Cathedral Mountains. Unfortunately Jonas developed frostbite on his toes while crossing the Triumvirate-Hayes pass, which forced us to fly out from Rainy Pass Lodge, only 15 miles from our goal.

SCOTT WOOLUMS

"Mount Titanic," Revelation Mountains. In late May and early June 1981 we visited a group of unnamed and previously unvisited peaks in the northern portion of the remote Revelation Mountains. Doug McCarty, Craig Tillery, Dan Hogan and I landed on a gravel bar alongside an upper fork of the Big River. After a trip to Mount Hesperus, where we found snow and rock stability conditions intolerable, we set as our goal the bulky rock and ice peak at the head of a glacier several miles to the east (9300 + feet). Interesting canyon and

---

*Recipient of an AAC Mountaineering Fellowship Grant.
**Recipient of an American Alpine Club Climbing Fellowship grant.

alp slope traverses led to the glacier, where we placed a camp near the edge. Facing us was a major granitic rock wall, a climbing opportunity we did not have time to undertake. The best route to reach the summit was to continue along the glacier, outflanking the peak on the south, then to climb an ice rampart beneath cliffs of the east face. There were a few steep sections and crevasse problems, but otherwise the route led to the broad summit dome without difficulty. Clouds and a few snow flurries blocked distant views, but the cool temperatures made for good climbing conditions. Poor weather prevented serious attempts on attractive neighboring peaks. We left the area by aircraft pickup on the gravel bar.

FRED BECKEY

Mount Deborah, West Face, A Third New Route. Though virgin summits are fast disappearing, new routes are everywhere and the aura of Alaska retains its remoteness. Remoteness and grandeur increase challenge and reward. A high-mountain bivouac which looks 70 miles to the nearest habitation is true in its wildness, where humanity is on an island and not in a polluted sea. And so we skied the 60 miles to Mount Deborah to savor our Alaska Range in its entirety. Peg Whillet skied with Steve Will and me, while Pete Bowers mushed food, fuel and gear to the Yanert Glacier moraine. Nightly campfires of cottonwood, spruce and birch made a merry scene, complete with eight husky dogs for porters, protection and entertainment. This pleasure skiing ended in the moraine. Big glacial moraines are best avoided, but rarely can be on treks into or out of the mountains. Our pile of gear dumped beneath a granite boulder was as depressing as our short good-byes. Steve and I were to carry our 75-pount packs the remaining 25 miles, alone, in heavy, deep, fresh snow. A single rest-day in honor of the vernal equinox bolstered our spirits. Then the weather cleared and the temperature dropped, sending our commitment high. Dawn of the ninth day was frigid. We walked a mile up the glacier in gale-force blasts, which occasionally knocked us to our knees. In the gully to the left of the first icefall, we kicked steps easily and, sheltered from the wind, made good time. Wandering through the second icefall in the heat of the afternoon, we got our first view of the entire west face. Beneath the bergschrund we dug our cave. The next day we arose late and started for the bergschrund's bridge. Bad ice and bulges beneath dollops of frothy snow slowed us considerably. Steve's lead over the schrund was the most difficult of the climb. Once on the face, we moved together on white ice and snow. The ice became gray, then blue and then, in the rocks, became green. Torquing in a screw, I left my ice axe unattended, stuck in the green rock ice. Inadvertently, I knocked it off and watched with an uncanny blend of relief and disbelief as it bounced down. I yelled, "Catch it!" and somehow, 150 feet below, Steve did. Steve swung by and we moved together, first on grey ice and then again on crunchy snow. We had moved only ten rope-lengths when the sun went down. Pretty soon our belay stances were chopped to bivouac platforms as we scratched down to the ice. In the morning the sun chased the shadow up the glacier, and the west face, to us. Leaving the deep snow of the face, we entered the rime-ice crackerjack realm of double cornices of the south ridge. After dumping our packs on the ridge at 12,000 feet, we stepped out onto climbing that was as exhilarating as it was breath-taking. We went over, under, around and through the summit mushrooms for three pitches over rime-covered green ice so hard that a screw would penetrate only halfway. Steve took the third gully to the summit. I swung up and we walked together to the top (3761 meters, 12,339 feet). It was March 27. Our route was the third one on the face. It rose to the right of the Gee-Wisdom route and emerged on the south ridge about 300 feet below the summit. A final aurora-illuminated traverse put us back to our packs and into a cornice crack for the night. We abseiled straight out of our drafty cornice cave with the last of our hearty nourishment in our bellies. The Beckey ridge is spectacular with fine views of both the gargoyle-clad gullies of the east face and the scalloped sweep of the west. We dropped off the basal cornices and climbed down to the third icefall. The ski out was brutally beautiful and cold. We reached the road 19 days after we had left it.

ROMAN DIAL, *Alaska Alpine Club*

Mount Fairweather, 1981. Kim Grandfield, Dave Lunn and I climbed the classic south (Carpé) ridge in a light-weight expedition which began with a beach landing on May 17, 1981. Due to bad flying weather and confused geography, we landed at the next major creek north of our intended landing at Sea Otter Creek, not discovering our mistake until four days later, when we arrived at the Sea Otter rather than the Fairweather Glacier. We carried loads through the wildest and most difficult terrain any of us had experienced. We turned south and explored the bizarre glacier that parallels the coast along the Fairweather Fault, in Desolation Valley. After a very difficult traverse of the Fairweather Glacier, we finally joined the normal approach path. Leaving our sixth approach camp at 3100 feet, we began the climb around noon. Upon gaining the ridge, we traversed right to a good camp site at the right edge and just below the major rock band at 7250 feet. The next camp was at 11,800 feet on the knife-edged ridge below the main shoulder. After a rest day, we climbed on May 27, 1981 to the summit in conditions that deteriorated all day. We made a bivouac perched on a platform we chopped into the wall of a covered crevasse directly below the summit. After one more night on the ridge we reached the glacier. Our return path led directly off the end of the Fairweather Glacier close to its north margin. Although shorter than our approach, the terrain was even more difficult, the final 2½ miles requiring a full day's effort.

GARY CLARK

Fairweather, Carpé Ridge, and "Sabine." On June 5 Ton Hoeneveld, Roel Mulder and I were flown to the beach just southeast of Cape Fairweather. It took us eight days to transport our loads through the woods and over the Fairweather Galcier to Base Camp at 4700 feet above the upper icefall on the south of the glacier just opposite Fairweather. Till then, the weather had been unsettled and more rain and snow followed. Fortunately on June 21 the skies cleared. We left Base Camp at four A.M. on June 22, crossed the glacier and followed the Carpé Ridge to camp at six P.M. below a 50-foot rock spur. After a 4:30 start the next morning, windpacked snow gave ideal conditions. The weather still was magnificent, with so little wind that we nearly got sunstruck. Mulder didn't feel well and decided to stay behind. At 6:30 P.M. Hoeneveld and I arrived at the summit. We were back in our high camp at midnight. The weather stayed beautiful to our surprise for the next five days. We stayed in our high camp for another day to enjoy the views. On the way down we took a line east of the Carpé Ridge, mostly through snowfields that brought us to a rock buttress, where we needed one abseil to get down. On June 28 Mulder and I left Base Camp for the northwest ridge of "Sabine" (3172 meters, 10,405 feet). We hit the ridge a few hundred feet above Base Camp. It was a very pretty, classic snow ridge with a few rock steps and a few steep ice sections at the end. On June 30 we headed out to the ocean. Just below the icefall Mulder broke his shinbone, and so it took us four days to get back to the beach.

HAN TIMMERS, *Koninklijke Nederlandse Alpen Vereniging*

Mount Huxley Correction. On page 161 of *A.A.J.*, 1982 the *Editor* surmised that the peak climbed west of Windy Peak might have been Mount Huxley. After poring over photos and maps, I have come to the conclusion that the mountain the Feichtners climbed could not have been Mount Huxley. It was probably either the Hump or a western summit of Windy Peak.

WALTER A. WOOD

Haydon Peak on Skis. Our group, consisting of Pierre Beghin, Christian Bougnaud, Jackiepolo Duliand, Alain Gaimard, Michel Poencet, Maurice Poulain and me, landed on May 6 at Yakatat in very bad weather. On May 8 we made a reconnaissance flight of the south face of St. Elias, our original objective, but were prevented from landing at Base Camp by a sea of clouds covering everything below 3500 feet. On the evening of May 14 we could finally fly by plane to the Chaix Hills and helicopter to Base Camp on the Tyndall Glacier at 25000 feet. Our route was the long ridge that rises in a huge curve and finally reaches the summit of Haydon Peak from the west. In heavy snow but with good weather, we climbed to Camp I at 4600 feet on the 15th. The next day Beghin and I climbed a steep rock rib, then avalanche-prone slopes to the ridge and along it to Camp II, but not having enough food, returned to Camp I on the 17th and, after 18 inches of new snow, to Base Camp on the 18th. It stormed until May 22 when we plowed through a meter of new snow to Camp II. It stormed for the next two days, but on May 25 we climbed to make Camp III at 10,000 feet. A huge avalanche broke away from the ridge under our feet. On May 26 we climbed to just beyond Haydon Col, but the weather became bad at noon and the snow was waist-deep; we returned to camp on the col. On May 27 we gave up the idea of climbing St. Elias and climbed Haydon Peak (3633 meters, 11,920 feet) in bad weather. The weather was good on May 28 and we climbed Haydon Peak again for a movie. On May 29 the skiing to Base Camp was fantastic, some of the slopes being 55°.

JAMES MEREL, *Club Alpin Français*

Mount Emmerich. On July 29 and 30, with two companions I climbed Mount Emmerich (6405 feet), which is just northwest of Haines. We completed the ascent of the northeast ridge, which had been unsuccessfully attempted by Fred Beckey and party in 1976. (They then made the first ascent of the mountain via the southwest ridge. See *A.A.J.*, 1977, page 169.) This involved 17 roped pitches averaging 5.7. We traversed the summits, descending Beckey's route.

DAVID L. BURGER, *Colorado Outward Bound School*

Devils Thumb, Northwest Face Attempt, Coast Range. Michael Bearzi and I attempted the northwest face of the Devils Thumb. The climbing halfway up the northwest face was hair-raising, whereas the rest would have been impassible. Avalanche danger was terrible and the weather was even worse.

DIETER HANS KLOSE

Washington—Cascade Mountains

Mount Logan, Winter Ascent. Mike Hill, Troy Ness, and I did the first winter ascent of Mount Logan on December 29, 1981. From Junction Camp, we ascended and ran the ridge on Soldier Boy to the base of a steep couloir, where we made our high camp on the third day. The next morning we ascended the couloir which gave us access to the Fremont Glacier. The 200 feet from the glacier to the ridge notch, and then the ridge to the summit, was steep thinly-ice-covered rock, and provided some very interesting climbing.

JERRY CROFOOT, *Everett Mountaineers*

The Blockhouse, West Face. In early August Pat McNerthney and I climbed a route on this face in the Cashmere Crags. The route began on the left, climbed to a ledge with a tree, moved up and right, finishing up and left. (NCCS III, 5.10.) In late August Doug Klewin and Todd Bibler did a more direct line on the same face, following obvious straight cracks. (NCCS III, 5.10 + , AO.)

DAN CAUTHORN

Mantis Peak, North Couloir. On May 15, I climbed the north couloir on Mantis Peak, after making a ski descent from the Colonial-Névé Glacier Col. Access to the couloir was gained by ascending a narrow snow chute, just right of a restricting rock band. Once in the couloir the climbing was straight-forward on 40°-55° névé, and then through the cornice to the top. (Grade II.)

GORDY SKOOG

Nooksack Tower, Northeast Couloir and East Ridge. On May 30 Chuck Gerson and I made this climb in one long day (18 hours) from our camp on the ridge above Price Lake (5800 feet). Our route continued up the ice ribbon where the main couloir narrows down, and the original route traverses right. We had one good pitch of ice before the angle eased off and then it was snow the rest of the way to the notch. From the notch there were probably eight pitches on rock. The rock was quite reasonable except for one pitch on the south face. The descent found us rappeling down fantastic ice gullies on the 1946 route. Here was the ice we had hoped to find on our route. About 10 rappels put us back in the main couloir, which we climbed down by head-lamp. (IV 5.7.)

JIM NELSON

California—Sierra Nevada

The Parapet, South Face. Our unofficial naming of the imposing central crag of the Mount Bago jumble above Junction Meadow along Bubbs Creek came after a most enjoyable frolic on the solid rock of this formation. In May, Rick Nolting and I climbed a central line. A long chimney-gully system led to a headwall where Rick led the hardest pitch—a vertical and sometimes over-hanging system of flakes. The moves would be classic anywhere, and the stopper protection was good if strenuous to place while "hanging on." The climbing drifted onto a long, easy ramp to the main corner, then became serious again: we took a zigzagging line up a headwall, then a leftward traverse across small bathtub holds to a shallow crack system. After the highest point was eventually reached, the descent was made by a long snow gully to the west. A few exposed rappels allowed us to escape from the walls. The climb, as well as adjacent new-route possibilities, is to be recommended. (Grade III, 5.8.)

FRED BECKEY

Penstemon Dome. Jerry Coe and I apparently made the first climb of this prominent rock formation, the second dome east of Courtwright Dam, in the spring. The climb features a system of continuous cracks on firm granite (with a few wild flowers) and an apron-type slab (one protection bolt) which led to easier terrain. (Grade II, 5.8.)

FRED BECKEY

North Guard, East Face, 1981. North Guard, near better-known Mount Brewer, has a provoking, craggy shape. There is a short but quite steep east face that looms above many acres of glacier-polished rock slab. In June 1981 Rick Nolting and I made the first climb of the challenging face. Steep, unroped climbing led to the crux about midway. Here we climbed an exposed edge, made a difficult rightward exit, then took to an outside corner that had a scarcity of holds and protection. The remainder of the climb was steep but well broken by good jointing in the granite. (Grade III 5.8.)

FRED BECKEY

Finger Dome, South Face, 1981. When making the hike from near Wishon Dam to Crown Valley, the usual route to Tehepite Dome and the Obelisk, the seemingly misplaced rock formation of Finger Dome is a magnet to the eye. Not knowing of any visitation by rock climbers, the dome's steep south face came to mind as the perfect idea for a late fall (1981) weekend. Fresh snow had already fallen well below timberline. A short hike from the road brought Rick Nolting and me to a campsite in pines where we studied the 700-foot face with some concern. It appeared all reasonable routes would end on a mid-face pillar several hundred feet short of the summit. Yet a climber must investigate possible weaknesses in the blank slabs not detectable to the distant eye. In the morning we stood at the base wondering where to begin. The possibilities seemed impossible or unappealing until we investigated a great chimney which split the center of the pillar. Two pitches of serious climbing—some of it wonderful stemming exercise—brought us to a place where we were almost certain the climb would end. But no, an easy ledge angled rightward above the big drop. The ledge ended in a blank wall, but from an isolated ledge tiny holds and cracks offered hope. After an unprotected aid move from a tied-off knife-blade, I was able to move upward on small holds, fairly desperate for a few minutes. On the next lead Rick solved a continuing crack problem and the leftward traverse of a steep, holdless slab. Moderate climbing on a distinct rib continued, then slabs took us to the summit. (Grade III, 5.8 or 5.9.)

FRED BECKEY

Mount Hoffman, Crimson Corner and Hoffman's Turret. To the right of the Merle-Alley route on the north face of Mount Hoffman is a large, left-facing, reddish-stained corner starting about 200 feet off the ground. Two pitches led to the base of the corner, which was followed for three more pitches to the top. Often, cracks on the right wall of the corner were quite useful, and the crux was an offwidth section of the fourth pitch. Terri Counts and I climbed this route in August, (Grade III, 5.9.) Also in August, Terri Counts and I made what we believe to be the first free ascent of Hoffman's Turret, an enjoyable two-pitch route. (Grade I, 5.9.)

ALAN BARTLETT, *Buff Alpine Club*

Homer's Nose, Where Eagles Dare. In July 1981 Patrick Paul and I completed another four-pitch route on the southwest face. This route lies a couple of hundred yards west (left) of the original south-face route (The Dance of Topo-Usha 1980). It follows an obvious crack-and-flake system just left of a long, awesome right-facing dihedral. The crack on the first pitch is formed by a 200-foot extremely expanding flake (hence the name). 3 bolts. (Grade III, 5.9, A1.)

DICK LEVERSEE, *Unaffiliated*

Middle Fork, Tule River Area. In the winter of 1980-81, Patrick Paul, Gary Kunkel, Randy Powers and I made the first ascent of the "Powerhouse Wall", just south of the powerhouse on the Wishon Fork of the Middle Fork of the Tule River, east of Springville. We followed the obvious central line for four pitches under many ceilings and eventually through the summit overhangs. 3 bolts. (Grade III-IV, 5.10, A4.) In November 1980, Patrick Paul and I completed the first ascent of the "Sky Garden Wall", a 700-foot cliff on the north side of the Middle Fork of the Tule River, just east of Springville. We climbed a continuous crack system for six pitches just right of the center of the wall.

DICK LEVERSEE, *Unaffiliated*

Jordan Peak Area. In late spring 1981, Eddie Joe and I discovered and climbed the first routes on a triple rock formation on the south side of Jordan Peak, just north of Camp Nelson. In the following month, Eddie, Randy Jewitt, Patrick Paul, Gary Kunkel, Debbie Winney and I put up 12 new one- to two-pitch routes from 5.8 to 5.10 + . We called this rock formation "Trilogy" and the major buttress/tower on the southeast side "Aerie Pinnacle."

DICK LEVERSEE, *Unaffiliated*

Bear Creek Spire, Complete East Ridge. From the air, this long knife-edged arête is one of the most spectacular features in the entire range. In August John Martinek and I spent a very long day on this 22-pitch route with an overall rating of Grade IV, 5.8. The climb is not mentioned in early editions of *The Climber's Guide to the High Sierra,* but is listed as "cnjoyable and lengthy . . . moderate class 5 . . . first ascent unknown" in the 1976 edition. A little investigation showed that the source of this listing was someone who thought that someone else knew someone who had climbed it. I talked to one of these "someones" who had it on his own list of new routes to do! In retrospect, the guidebook entry was entirely accurate: the route was lengthy, enjoyable, fifth class, and the first ascent was indeed unknown.

GALEN ROWELL

PLATE 58

Photo by Galen Rowell

Bear Creek Spire's East Ridge, Sierra Nevada.

Peak 12,563, Northeast Ridge. On Fourth of July weekend I soloed this prominent prow in Granite Park near Pine Creek Pass, finding no evidence of a prior ascent. (Grade II, 5.6.)

GALEN ROWELL

Peak 13,198, Ruby Wall. The east face of this peak is a vertical, 900-foot wall that is reflected in the waters of Ruby Lake, near the Mono Pass trail. On July 10, Mike White and I approached the face entirely on snow for the last 1500 feet, due to the extreme winter. The climb begins near the middle of the wall in a chimney system that is not obvious as seen from the lake. Continuously challenging pitches of 5.8 to 5.10 led us to the point where a scary ramp slanting leftward allowed us to traverse into the easy summit dihedral two pitches below the top. (Grade IV, 5.10.)

GALEN ROWELL

Mount Whitney, Northeast Ridge. After more than a dozen ascents of this mountain by what I assumed to be all different sides, I was most surprised when Claude Fiddler pointed out an unclimbed ridge on the highest peak in the 48 contiguous states. On the morning of July 26, I awoke to lightning and storm clouds at a 12,000-foot camp under the east face of Whitney with Claude and Vern Clevenger. We were about to give up and descend when a spot of blue opened in the western sky. By the time we reached the base of the route just south of the Whitney-Russell col, the upper air was clear and mist was rising from every peak and valley. Difficult pitches of 5.9 and 5.10 alternated with scrambling along one of the most spectacular arêtes to be found anywhere. A rappel was necessary in one place to drop fifty feet over an overhang into a notch. The three-and-a-half hours of roped climbing ended at the top of the Mountaineer's Route, ten minutes from the main summit. What had looked like a bust turned into one of the finest Sierra days any of us had experienced. We glissaded 2500 feet down the east side back to camp, ran through flowers and late spring melt back to the valley, soaked sore muscles in a hot spring, and watched our window in the week's bad weather close again as a double rainbow glistened in the first evening raindrops. (Grade III, 5.10.)

GALEN ROWELL

P 9011, "Leopold Dome", Burt Miller Route, 1981. After hiking six miles around Courtwright Reservoir, climbing a few pitches and sitting out a rainstorm, Alan Swanson and I were nearing the summit of the "unclimbed" P 9011. Upon seeing a hook hole and an aid bolt above, we realized the route matched the description of the Burt-Miller route on the south face of P 9547, Maxson Dome (*A.A.J.*, 1978, p. 525). The only difference is that the route is actually on the southeast face of P 9011. This was perhaps the first free ascent. We refer to the formation as Leopold Dome in honor of conservationist Aldo Leopold. (NCCS III, F10.)

STEPHEN MCCABE, *Manx Mountaineers*

Humdinger Dome. No Zukes follows a small, easily visible dihedral on a dome just southwest of P 9053. When the left-facing dihedral merged into a shallow groove, we climbed right past a bolt, left past a bolt up to the crack. From here Alan and I climbed one more pitch and unroped. (NCCS II, F9.) A few days later, still in August, I returned with Gerri Dayharsh and climbed *Crooked Neck*. Traverse right past a pine growing horizontally out of a narrow ledge. Climb a flake, then face-climb, and follow a crooked crack up and left. The route continues for a few more pitches to the summit. (NCCS II, F8.) In 1981, the day after climbing the Burt Miller route, Alan and I had a few hours to look at the southwest of Power Dome. The armed guards at the Helm's Creek Power Project construction site let us know which approaches to this dome just below the dam would be acceptable and would be out of the blasting zones. From the top of the first pitch, the intimidating steepness of the second and third pitches made us glad there would not be enough time until the next year to make a full-fledged attempt. *Helm's Deep* follows a line in the area of the right margin of a prominent black water streak which drops from near the summit straight down to a huge ledge at the base of the dome. In August 1982 we returned and reclimbed the first pitch, passing our bolt and fixed pin just above the huge ledge. From the belay on a steeply sloping ledge, we traversed right to a thin flake and then up (bolt) over a small roof. We continued up and slightly left (bolt) to a double-bolt belay. On the third pitch we traversed right and then climbed straight up for about 50 feet to a small flake. The next 80 feet of climbing up and right to the end of a large sloping ledge were steep and unprotected, though not as difficult as we had anticipated. After traversing left on the ledge to a ten-foot-high flake, we face-climbed the fourth and fifth pitches up the water streak to the summit. Careful route-finding allowed some protection and probably only one F9 move on these last two pitches. (NCCS III, F 10.) On the right side of the southwest face, a faint light-colored water streak can be found on a line directly below where the summit meets the sloping south side of Power Dome. On a hot, sunny day, Gerri and I started *Solar Energy* from solution pockets in two large white dikes and climbed three pitches up the water streak, placing three protection and four anchor bolts. The third belay was in a right-facing, sloping ramp. We continued up and left for four more pitches to the summit. (NCCS III, F9.)

STEPHEN MCCABE, *Manx Mountaineers*

Sierra Buttes, Sea Lion Buttress, 1981. The Sierra Buttes may deserve more attention from climbers. In May 1981 Joe Kiskis, Tim Butler and I climbed the northwest buttress of the highest tower in the southern group that is prominent from Highway 49. This was an enjoyable 10-pitch climb on dense metavolcanic rock that turned out to be quite solid. (5.6 to 5.7 with some 4th Class.)

BOB GROW, *Unaffiliated*

Nance Peak, Supercleavage. This peak, actually a dome, rises out of some of the most rcmote territory in Yosemite National Park. The 1500-foot south face is split by an enormous couloir leading straight to the summit. Tim Butler, Joe Kiskis and I climbed the couloir in early September. (5.8 to 5.9.)

BOB GROW, *Unaffiliated*

Bear Dome. Ian Raistrick and I climbed a prow on the west face of Bear Dome in August. The buttress is quite steep and imposing, and only the unglaciated nature of the rock lends plausibility to the climb. In fact, the route is quite easy, with the crux—a 5.8 crack—coming on the second pitch.

GREG DONALDSON

Chiquito Dome. The route named "Archline," as reported by Conrad van Bruggen and Fremont Bainbridge in *A.A.J.*, 1981, page 174, had been previously climbed in 1974 by Ian Raistrick, Darien Hopkins and Hugh Woodland. They had placed no bolts and there was no evidence of their climb on the rock.

GREG DONALDSON

Crystal Crag, East Face, 1978. Chuck Calef and I climbed a route on the east face of Crystal Crag in April 1978. We began in a dihedral above a large pine tree just uphill from the Rowell-Clevenger route. The first pitches are steep. Then the angle eases and the ridge is followed past a remarkable crystalline area to the summit. (I, 5.8.)

GREG DONALDSON

Temple Crag, Sunribbon Arête, Winter Ascent. Rising almost out of the shores of beautiful Third Lake, the north face of Temple Crag dominates the immediate area, its dark granite walls accented by snow-covered ledges and couloirs in deep winter. George Lowe and I had come to climb Sunribbon Arête, a thinly defined buttress cutting the main bulk of the cliff. (First attempted in winter in January 1978 by Jim Sedinger and me.) George and I held a brief discussion about the feasibility of climbing in − 10°F, but still packed our bags and made a short ski approach. We climbed bundled in all the clothes we had, moved quickly over the first steep pitch and the snow-covered fourth-class beyond. Then up the headwall, four pitches of clean granite with a wonderful diversity of cracks and face holds. As dusk approached, we reached the Tyrolean traverse. Finally we were able to flip a rope across the 15-foot gap over the horn and make the crossing as darkness descended. On the narrow arête, we "pitched" our small tent on the only level spot, a 2½-by-4-foot area with a clean drop on both sides. In the morning, the only sun we had on the north face moved off after one pitch, and a biting wind drove the cold through our clothing. The pitches broke down into short bursts of climbing activity, followed by finger-warming sessions. We raced the February

PLATE 59

Photo by Brock Wagstaff

Temple Crag, Sierra Nevada.

Photo by Ed Webster

**Monster Tower on left and
Washerwoman Arch on right,
Canyonlands, Utah.**

Lowe on headwall of Temple Crag.

PLATE 60

Photos by Brock Wagstaff

George Lowe after Tirolean Traverse (Pitch 9) on second day on Temple Crag.

daylight hours to the top, arriving with 15 minutes to spare. We descended in the dark over iced slopes on crampons. Steep couloirs led to drop-offs and delicate traverses. Unroped and careful, we finally reached a rappel which dropped us onto the snowfield at Contact Pass. By the time we got to our skis, my feet were numb, but I didn't realize until later that they were frostbitten as well. Two months of inactivity followed, a painful reminder of winter climbing in the "Range of Light."

BROCK WAGSTAFF

California—Pinnacles National Monument

Climbs in Pinnacles National Monument. At least three routes were added to the monument this year. *Cleaver Buttress* (F6) lies on a formation above and behind the Machete Ridge. It ascends a water chute to the base of a chimney. The second pitch ascends the chimney to gain an arête, which is followed to the summit. On the Discovery Wall, *Plague* (5.9) climbs the crack and black face to the left of *Trauma.* Most interesting of the new routes is *Lava Falls* (5.8) that ascends the Balconies Cliff to the left of *Shake And Bake* (A.A.J., 1977.) There are 14 protection bolts, some which were used as rest points immediately after placement. Unfortunately, *Lava Falls* has already lived up to its name and inflicted a serious rockfall injury. Let the belayer beware. A number of "NADS" participated in these climbs including W.V. Graham Matthews III, Peter Ruben, Keith Vandevere and myself.

JACK HOLMGREN, *NADS Alpine Club*

California—Yosemite

Charlotte Dome. John Liebeskind and I climbed *Shake it like a Bowl of Soup,* a beautiful 11-pitch route on the dome's 1000-foot south face. Our route left the classic Rowell-Jones-Beckey line after the first fifth-class pitch and angled far right for two pitches of face and jam-cracks. We then went straight up over slabs, solution pockets and chicken heads into the large depression at the top of the southeast face. There, we veered right, joining the 1970 south-face line on the summit ridge. (NCCS III, F8.)

ROBERT KAYEN, *Tufts Mountain Club*

El Capitan, Solo Ascent of the West Buttress. From April 21 to May 1, I made a solo ascent of El Capitan's west buttress via the classic Kor-Roper route. The first five days were straightforward climbing through the lower face's wet jam-cracks and chimneys, leading up to the White Dihedral. From there aid led up to the committing Grand Traverse, which connects the White and Black Dihedrals and cuts off any fast retreat from the wall. Up to that point,

I had been using the Barnett solo system until it failed on the roof of the Grand Traverse. This sent me on a 100-foot fall, which I checked by grabbing the rope with my hands. I covered the rope-burns with bandanas and strips torn from my pants, jümared back up to the roof and completed the lead with the clove-hitch solo system. Luckily the fall occurred near the route's first ledge and I was able to take a recuperating day's break away from my hammock. The climb continued through the Black Dihedral, slowly due to the difficulty I had in using my hands. I reached Thanksgiving Ledge and the summit on the eleventh day. I believe the climb was the last of the four classic siege routes to be soloed. It was made alpine style with no bolt kit.

ROBERT KAYEN, Tufts Mountain Club

Yosemite Valley, 1982. Rock climbing continues to flourish in Yosemite National Park, and each year there seem to be more climbers in the valley than the previous year. Certain areas are extremely crowded on the weekends in the spring and fall, notably Manure Pile Buttress, Five Open Books, Sunnyside Bench, Church Bowl and Glacier Point Apron. Even the Cookie Cliff, long known as having the most consistently difficult climbs of any crag in the valley, teems with climbers during these periods, despite the fact that a landslide destroyed the approach road in April. An excellent new guidebook written by George Meyers appeared at the end of the year, and it is hoped that this will serve to spread out the climbers, both neophyte and expert alike, in the years to come. One of the main differences between now and the scene of ten years ago is the ever-increasing number of foreign climbers. Americans are a distinct minority in Camp 4 (officially known as Sunnyside Campground, but still called Camp 4 by most climbers) during spring and fall seasons. New routes continue to be done, both big walls and short free routes. Some of the best are listed here: *El Capitan, Lunar Eclipse* (VI, A4). A 14-pitch route to the right of the Zodiac, climbed by Steve Schneider and John Barbella. *El Capitan, Mediterranean Route* (VI, rating unknown). This route starts to the left of the Salathé, crosses that route at the Half Dollar formation, then stays between the Muir and Nose routes to the top. It was climbed by four brothers from Spain, Miguel, José, Carlos and Javier Gallego. This is apparently the first all-foreign first ascent on El Capitan. *Liberty Cap, Direct Southwest Face* (V, 5.10, A5). A steep difficult route to the right of the original Harding-Rowell-Faint route, climbed by Rick Cashner and Werner Braun. *Mount Broderick, The Unemployment Line* (IV, 5.9, A3). An eight-pitch predominantly free climb which ascends the smooth southwest face of this dome, climbed by Alan Bartlett, Steve Gerberding and Jim May. *Higher Cathedral Spire, Higher Aspirations* (VI, 5.8, A4). Twelve steep pitches to the right of the Frost-Robbins route on the northwest face of the spire, climbed by Steve Bosque, Rick Derrick and Kelly Repp. *Tunnel Vision,* (I, 5.11 +). On the wall above the Cookie; John Bacher climbed this difficult direct line above Gait of Power. *Moongerms,* (I, 5.11 +). Another Bacher problem; this is the finger crack immediately right of Hairline on Elephant Rock. *Happy Days,* (I, 5.12 –). Climbed by Werner Braun, Chris Belizzi and Rick Cashner; this is a finger and hand crack on a wall to the east of Arch Rock. *Chow Chow Chow* (I, 5.10 +). This is a long thin corner on the east side of Loggerhead Buttress, climbed by Bruce Morris and Dave Yerian. *Skid Row* (II, 5.8). A three-pitch face climb on North Dome to the left of the west-face route, climbed by Dimitri Barton and Alan Bartlett. *Pure Essence* (II, 5.11). High up Eagle Creek on its left side is an unnamed wall containing this two-pitch overhanging hand and fist crack, climbed by Don Reid and Werner Braun. *New Testament* (I, 5.10 +). This climb starts with a hand traverse into an overhanging crack. It eventually joins Resurrection on the Chapel Wall, and was climbed by Don Reid and Rick Cashner. *Static Cling,* (I, 5.10 –). Located near the walk-on approach to the middle of the Rostrum; Don Reid and Rick Cashner climbed the left side of a giant flake. *The Laybacher* (I, 5.11 –). Adjacent to the first rappel leading to the base of the north face of the Rostrum is this perfect 90 × 90 degrees corner, climbed by John Bacher, Mari Gingery and Mike Lechlinski.

ALAN BARTLETT, *Yosemite Mountaineering School*

Tuolumne Meadows. In Tuolumne Meadows, face-climbing standards are being pushed higher and higher. John Bacher has almost singlehandedly rewritten the rules in an area where the bolt is the most standard protection device; many of his climbs involve 5.10 moves with little or no protection, and most have not seen second ascents. A number of underground guides have appeared to this area which has no official guidebook, and information is usually available at the Yosemite Mountaineering School to help visiting climbers find certain routes. Here are some of the best new routes done in 1982; *Harlot* (II, 5.10 –). Four pitches to the left of Hoodwink, climbed by Alan Bartlett and Alan Roberts. *Goldfinger* (I, 5.12). John Bacher finally solved this previously attempted problem, an overhanging finger crack immediately left of the Cooler. *Hurricane Betsy.* (I, 5.11 +). Climbed by John Bacher, this is a thin crack out a roof on the extreme left side of Low Profile Dome. *Steep Thrills.* (I, 5.10 +). A bolted, two-pitch face climb to the left of the Golfer's route on Low Profile Dome, climbed by Bacher. *King Midas* (II 5.9 +). Between Peter, Peter and Magical Mystery Tour on Fairview Dome; two pitches lead to the belay bolts at the end of the third pitch of Peter, Peter, climbed by Alan Bartlett and Gail Wilts. *Lamb Chops* (III, 5.10). On Lamb Dome, three pitches lead up the smooth face to the right of Hip Boots before joining On the Lamb; climbed by Bill Critchlow and Alan Bartlett. *Black Magic* (III, 5.11 +). This is the black streak to the right of the Yawn on Medlicott Dome. Bacher again. *Bacher-Yerian Route* (III, 5.11). This is one of the steepest routes in the meadows, and ascends the black streak to the right of Shambles, put up by John Bacher and Dave Yerian. *You Asked for It* (III, 5.10). Another black streak to the right of the Bacher-Yerian route, climbed by Bacher and Ron Peers. *Blacklight* (II, 5.10). Two pitches up a black streak in the center of the West Farthing Wall, climbed by Alan Bartlett and Terri Counts.

ALAN BARTLETT, *Yosemite Mountaineering School*

Montana

St. Paul Peak, East Face Direct, Cabinet Range, 1981. Brad Weller and I climbed a chimney and dihedral system directly up the center of the steep east face of St. Paul Peak in early July, 1981. The route consisted of 10 pitches of rock climbing, though we had occasionally to leave the dihedral for superb face-climbing to the right side. It is easily approached from St. Paul Lake and possibly is the best climbing in the Cabinets.

JOHN ROSKELLEY

Idaho

Mount Breitenbach, North Face, Lost River Range. From July 13 to 16, Bob Boyles, Mike Weber and I made the first ascent of the north face of Mount Breitenbach. Bill March has told me that some years ago his party was turned back by very severe rock climbing at the top of a large couloir. We easily identified the couloir and rock band. We also discovered a possible route to the west of that couloir but still east of the summit. We pieced our climb together. It consisted of small, steep snowfields intermixed with steep limestone. The crux was a short aid pitch next to a waterfall which led us into a 900-foot-long, 10- to 15-foot-wide hairline couloir that we followed to a bivouac on the skyline just east of the summit. In the dawn we descended the east-northeast ridge in two hours of fourth-class climbing. (Grade III, 5.8, A2.)

CURTIS OLSON, *Mountain Guides Inc., Boise, Idaho*

Utah

Climbs in Canyonlands National Park. Jeff Achey and I free-climbed the last aid route on Moses, a 500-foot sandstone tower in Taylory Canyon. Ironically, the route, though 5.11, was the easiest of the three routes on the tower. In the spring Charlie Fowler and Chip Chace had freed the Beckey route on the north face. The route had a pitch of 5.12 and three pitches of 5.10 and 5.11. A week later Kent Lugbill and I made the first free ascent of the 450-foot Candlestick Tower. Our route on the east face required seven pitches, many of them short. The hardest was a 5.10 wide-hands crack. Over Thanksgiving Charlie Fowler and I made the first free ascent of the Washerwoman in Lathrop Canyon, via a new route called *In Search of Suds* (5.10) on the right side of the south face. The tower had received only one previous ascent, in 1967, according to the summit register. We also climbed *Crack Wars,* a four-pitch 5.11 crack climb on the Nuns, near Castleton Tower.

GLENN RANDALL

Castleton Tower and Monster Tower, Wingate Spires. In October and early November Chester Dreiman and I climbed new routes on two Wingate Spires. On Castleton Tower, between the Kor-Ingalls and the North Chimney routes, we did *Star Dust Cowboy* (III, 5.11, A1), featuring a 5.11 crack and a long bolt ladder. The *Arrowhead* (5.10) is a two-pitch variation of this route. A week later we made the second ascent of 650-foot-high Monster Tower via a new eight-pitch 5.10 route up the south face, *Monster of Rock.* Layton Kor & party made the first ascent in 1963. We were benighted on the summit, and rappelled Kor's route in the dark. Luckily the rappel ropes only jammed once!

EDWARD WEBSTER

Wyoming

Devil's Tower. An excellent article on all climbs done to date on the Devil's Tower appeared in the July-August 1982 *Climbing,* starting on page 20. Several new climbs which were done too late to include in the article appear on page 6 of the same magazine.

Colorado

New Colorado Climbs, 1982. Despite the intense new-route activity of the last few years, climbers in the Boulder area continue to find first ascents on both new and established crags. In early spring, Alec Sharp and Matt Lavender climbed *Victim of Circumstance,* a 5.11+ crack just right of the *Campaigner* on Castle Rock in Boulder Canyon. The same team also squeezed *Dangerous Acquaintances* (5.10+) onto the face between *Temporary Like Achilles* and *Scary Canary* on Eldorado Canyon's Redgarden Wall. Sharp and Dave Weber inserted *Unnatural Desires* (5.10+) between *Temporary Like Achilles* and *Evangeline.* John Sherman, with Sharp following, put in *Tube Sock Tanline* (5.11) between *Scary Canary* and the *Wisdom.* Jeff Achey and Randy Leavitt freed the first pitch of *Apple Strudel* (5.11+) after replacing an old aid bolt. The second pitch had previously gone free to Joe Kaelin and me (5.11). Also in Eldorado, Bob Horan led *Johnny Belinda* (5.12), which climbs out of the cave on the Whale's Tail. Skunk Canyon, in the Flatirons area on Green and Bear Mountains near Boulder, saw much activity. Horan found *Anthem to the Sun* (5.12) and *Under the Influence* (5.11), both overhanging cracks. On the north side of Seal Rock, Jeff Achey, partnered by Roger Briggs, led *Archae-opteryx.* Achey spent 3½ hours on the poorly protected 5.11 face-climbing of the third lead. The south face of the Matron yielded *Warlocks,* a 5.12 hands/finger/fist problem with a four-foot roof to cap things off. Guerin and Ruckgaber made the first ascent. On the Veil slab on Bear Peak, Sharp added *Way Honed* and *Gnarly.* In July, Dan Hare and John Warren climbed *You'll Go Blind,* an overhanging, diagonal jam-crack on a rock near the Matron. The crack permits no rest for 80 feet and fades temporarily in the middle, forming

PLATE 62

Photo by Ed Webster

Brian Becker on McCarthy West Face Variation on DEVILS TOWER.

the 5.11 crux. In March, Jeff Achey and Chip Chace climbed a two-pitch direct variation on *Eavesdropper*, in the Flatirons near the Maiden. The route follows the Eavesdropper arête all the way. In June, Guerin freed the *Boot Lead* on Castle Rock (5.12) in Boulder Canyon, then continued straight up the wall above to the right of the second pitch of *Corinthian Vine*. The third pitch forced Guerin and partner Ruckgaber to use one bolt for aid. Also in Boulder Canyon, Dan Hare and Alfredo Len climbed *Acrophobia*, a one-pitch 5.10 face-climb on Chrome Dome, near Boulder Falls. Mark Rolofson and Eric Eliason completed a 5.11+ face-climb leading straight up to the Wounded Knee roof on Blob Rock. Hare and Joel Schiavone climbed *Specter*, a hand-crack on the Black Widow Slab. The crack led through a six-foot roof with an overhanging dihedral above (5.10+). Guerin and Ruckgaber climbed *Frogman* (5.12), a short face and finger-crack problem near the Elephant Buttresses.

New route activity has continued elsewhere in Colorado as well. Roger Briggs and Leonard Coyne climbed *Inner Limits*, a new 5.12 on an unnamed crag near the Barking Dog in South St. Vrain Canyon, north of Boulder. In the Garden of the Gods, soft sandstone pinnacles near Colorado Springs, Bob D'Antonio and Peter Gallagher climbed *Mission Improbable*, a 5.11, thinly protected face-climb which partially follows an old bolt ladder. D'Antonio and Ed Webster free-climbed the upper north ridge of Keyhole Rock at 5.11. The same pair also climbed *Patty the Pig*, a 5.10+ to the right of the Waterchute Route on Keyhole. Just off Rampart Road in the foothills northwest of Colorado Springs are a host of newly developing granite crags. D'Antonio pioneered three new 5.11s, *Scorpio*, *Lust for Kicks* and *Lost Cord*, all one-pitch crack climbs. On Sheep's Nose Rock, a granite dome near Turkey Rock in the South Platte region southwest of Denver, D'Antonio and Bob Robertston climbed *Sheer Sheep Attack*, with 5.11c face-climbing. The same pair climbed *For Wimps Only* (5.11a), *Space Cadet* (5.10+) and *Complications* (5.11−), all one-pitch face and crack climbs on Sheep's Nose. Malcolm Daly led Lumpy Ridge's first 5.12, *Red Man*, on Sundance. In Glenwood Canyon in west-central Colorado, Mike Kennedy and Jeff Lowe freed *International* (5.9+), a 10-pitch route that follows two granite buttresses and one limestone buttress to the top of the canyon. To Kennedy's knowledge *International* is the only route that climbs all the way to the Canyon rim. Kennedy and Gordon Banks also climbed *Night and Fog*, 5.11 A1, a route on the Night Buttress in Glenwood Canyon, near Glenwood Springs. The four-pitch route has two pitches of 5.9, a pitch of 5.10 and a pitch of 5.11, A1. In the Telluride area, in the southwest corner of the state, Bill Kees and Barry Rugo climbed a new three-pitch 5.10 called *Emotional Rescue* on the Wimpering Wall, a section of the Ophir Wall. On the same rock, Dave Bell completed *Nerf World*, an A4 that follows a network of incipient cracks. In the Independence Pass area, Mike Kennedy and Chip Lee climbed *The Hose Monster* on Pass Walls. The one-pitch route climbs a 5.11 finger-crack that took several attempts. In August Dan Hare and Joel Schiavone climbed the *Odessa File*, a three-pitch 5.10 near Odessa Lake in Rocky Mountain National Park. The crux was an undercling under a roof. Dan

PLATE 63

Photo by Mark Sommerfeld

Ed Webster on the Daub-Griffith
route in El Dorado Canyon,
Colorado.

Hare also climbed *Secret Agent,* two pitches, 5.10, A1, on Secret Crag south of Eldorado Canyon. This fall the notoriously desperate Genesis (5.12c) in Eldorado Canyon finally received a second ascent three years after it was first done. Britisher Jerry Moffatt made the second ascent, soon followed by Chris Gore and Skip Guerin. Though Jim Collins had devoted months to a rigorous training routine, then days of effort before making the first ascent, the repeats have been done in a matter of a day or two. Collins' 5.12 route on the Psycho Roof was also repeated by Moffat and Guerin.

GLEN RANDALL

Colorado Climbs, 1982. **Eldorado Canyon.** New route activity continues in Eldorado Canyon, although not at the feverish pace of the 1981 season. The canyon still refuses to be "climbed out", the same core group of locals, along with a variety of partners, being responsible for most of the new lines, namely: Carl Harrison, Sandy East, Jim Stuberg, Bob Horan, Skip Guerin and Chip Ruckgaber. On Quartzite Crag, Harrison and Stuberg found an interesting two-pitch line, *Little Egypt* (5.10). In the Pleasure Palace area, Harrison soloed two new routes, *The Snoz,* (5.8) and *Willie The Pimp* (5.6). Harrison and Nowell Harrison put up two good routes. *Desperados* (5.9, 1 pitch) and *Esquinita* (5.9, 2 pitches), both face climbs with little protection. On the West Ridge, Harrison and East found two new routes in the Inverted Vee area: *Office Hours* (5.9, 3 pitches) and *S.N.F.S.* (5.9, 2 pitches). Harrison and Stuberg climbed the arête immediately right of *Positively 4th St.,* and called it *Coniferous Types,* (5.10). On the recently discovered Midway Rock, located between the north end of Hawk Eagle Ridge and the Wall of a Thousand Eyes, Harrison and Stuberg have put up a dozen or more routes. The rock, although only 50 feet high, has some worthwhile climbs. All ascents were done solo. Of the more notable are *Batjam* (5.10, undercling to offwidth), *Geronimo* (5.9, face-climbing on solution pockets) and *Kornturner,* (5.8, handcrack). **Flatirons.** On the north face of the Matron. Harrison with Mike Brooks found *No Stranger To Danger* (5.9), a one-pitch route 250 feet west of the east-face route; it follows a poorly protected water groove. Harrison, with Al Torrisi, did *Pasta Man,* (5.9), a line beginning just left of the north-face route. On the west face of Satan's Slab, Ruckgaber made the 1st free ascent of the *Doric Dihedral* (5.12). Ruckgaber claimed the coveted "second-could-not-follow" award for this one, since he refused to belay off a No. 3 R.P. The climb has since repulsed several strong parties, including Ruckgaber himself, and remains unrepeated. Ruckgaber and Guerin also found *Slaughterhouse* (5.12), a crack and stemming problem, left of *Inferno.* Horan and John Baldwin made the 1st ascent of *Fire on the Mountain* (5.12) and *Lightning in the Sky,* both on the next ridge west of Satan's Slab. **Boulder Canyon.** On Broken Rock, Harrison and Torrisi added *Turkish Revenge* (5.10), a deceptive layback right of *Momentum Operator.* On Bell Buttress, Harrison and Torrisi put in two new lines. *Eat The Rich* (5.10), a one-pitch overhanging dihedral, right of *Tears* and *Christmas in L.A.* (5.7, 1 pitch), right of *Wrinkles. Dry Sobs* (5.10), a strenuous layback right of *Tears*, was added by Torrisi and Alan Bowman. **Estes Park.** Bad weather in the mountains restrained most of the new-route activity to the sub-alpine regions this season, with many new lines being added on Lumpy Ridge and the Crags. On Thunder Buttress, Scott Kimball and Carl Harrison found *Straight Arms* (5.10), a two-pitch slab route, the crux being a mantle over a roof. Another two-pitch slab climb, *Three's Company,* (5.7), was added by Kimball and Annegret Wroblewski; the second was seven-months-pregnant at the time. On the Book, Malcolm Daly and partner added *Deadboy Direct* (5.11), a thin-crack start to *Dead Boy.* Doug Snively and Bill Nickleson added a handcrack variation to the 1st pitch of *Possum Hang* on Alligator Rock. On the Bookend, Mark Wilford and Joseph put up *Static Cling* (5.11); it climbs a steep slab and roof right of *Winds of Fortune,* and is poorly protected. *Honkidori,* (5.9), a crystal handcrack, was added to Lens Rock by John Harlin. Two new routes were climbed on Checkboard Rock: *Non-Aligned* (5.10 +), a layback flake right of *Crystal Catch* by Kimball and Joe Hladick, and *Tim's Troubles* (5.10), a right-curving crack left of *Broken Wing* by Tim Hansen and Hladick. At the Crags, *Junk Pile* (5.9), a vertical crack right of *Treasure Island* was put up by Kent Lugbill and Kimball. *Rubble Rouser* (5.9), two pitch cracks and dihedrals left of *Midrib Route* was added by Snively, Kimball and Mike Kennedy. *Flesh Flagellation* (5.9), a classic corner crack left of *Consumption of the Ages,* was done by Kimball and Lugbill.

Carl Harrison, International Alpine School

Longs Peak, Solo Winter Ascent of the East Face. From January 13 to 17, 1983 I made the first solo winter ascent of the Lower East Face-Diamond combination on Longs Peak. On the Lower East Face I climbed the *Gray Pillar* (IV, 5.9, A4) up to Broadway. I then continued up the Diamond on *D7* (V, 5.9, A2). The climb took four days up and one on the descent. The weather was nearly perfect with clear skies but cold nights.

Mark Wilford

Black Canyon of the Gunnison, Three New Routes. In October, Chester Dreiman and I climbed three new routes here on consecutive days. The first climb, *Escape Artist* (IV, 5.11) scales a large buttress on the left side of SOB Gully. The next day we climbed the *Checkerboard Wall* (IV, 5.10 +), a route I had always hoped to do someday. This unlikely route ascends the center of the smooth wall to the right of Maiden Voyage. Criss-crossing bands of white pegmatite make the route obvious. Loose rock, poor protection, and getting benighted gave us a few exciting moments! The third climb, fortunately, was considerably easier. *Leisure Climb*, at 5.9 − is a good introductory route to the Black Canyon. Only six pitches long, well protected, and on very good rock, it ascends the wall on the right at the base of the Cruise Gully.

Edward Webster

PLATE 64

Photo by Ed Webster

Chester Dreiman on the crux (5.11) of "Escape Artist," Black Canyon of the Gunnison, Colorado.

CANADA

Yukon Territory

Climbing Season in Kluane National Park, Icefield Ranges, St. Elias Mountains. Mountaineering in the St. Elias Mountains was greatly reduced this summer as there were only ten groups in all. The following were successful. Americans Jim Himmes, David Rogers, Stanleigh Cole and James Thompson climbed Mount Logan by its east ridge. Canadians Willi Pfisterer, Ron Chambers, Rick Staley, Doug Burles, Darro Stinson, Claire Israelson, Bruce Sundo, Hal Morrison, Kevin McLaughlin and Lloyd Freese successfully climbed McArthur Peak. Americans Greg Grange, Peter Dea, Steve Monfredo and Andrew Lapkass traversed Logan, climbing the east ridge and descending the King Trench route. Canadians Will Black, David Charlebois, David Hammer and Calvin McDonald climbed Mount Steele by what is probably a new route between Mounts Steele and Walsh. Americans Franz Mohling, Turan Barut and Stephen Jensen were killed when their party was struck by an avalanche while in their camp at 15,000 feet on a north ridge of Mount Logan. The survivors, Paul O'Sullivan, Jim Ebersole, Doug Johnson and Kenneth Nolan were evacuated from the mountain at a later date. In all 56 people spent 906 man-days in the icefields of the park.

LLOYD FREESE, *Kluane National Park*

Tombstone Mountains Correction. On the last line of page 161 of *A.A.J.*, 1982 Mount Monolith is incorrectly given as Mount Mordith.

Coast Range

Noel Peak, Stikine Icecap. Between June 27 and July 18, Stacia Cronin, Jay McCubbrey, Peter VanderNailen, Tony Watkin, Beverly Wilson, David Wilson, Les Wilson, and I visited the northern Stikine Icecap of British Columbia. Our primary objective was Noel Peak (10,040 feet), which we believed unclimbed. We flew by float plane from Edontenajon Lake on the Stewart-Cassiar Highway to a Base Camp on Chutine Lake (1000 feet). I'd used this camp on previous trips in 1978 and 1980. We made an airdrop of food and fuel on the icecap at 6500 feet about ten miles south of the lake. Within three days we had gained the icecap and collected our supplies. Using home-made drags, constructed from heavy plastic sheeting by Les, we skiied south across the undulating icecap another twenty miles to the base of Noel Peak. A high camp was established at 7700 feet, just below an impressive rock buttress, on the northwest ridge. On July 6 all but Stacia and Peter crossed the glacier at the base of the west face to tackle the southwest ridge. Actually, this proved to be a series of parallel arêtes rather than a single ridge. We climbed a rotten gully between two of them to 9500 feet. Beyond, the ridge line consisted of a complex series of staggered gendarmes. The weather deteriorated suddenly. As it was nearly seven P.M., we bivouacked there. The next morning the weather showed no signs of clearing and we descended. When the weather was still poor two days later, we started back to Base Camp. On the return trip we made ascents of Boundary Peak 74 (7358 feet), Peak 8170, two miles to the northeast, and the east peak of the Sheppard Peak massif (8200 feet). Much to our surprise, Peak 8170 had seen a previous ascent by persons unidentified. Soon after our return to the U.S. the 1982 *Canadian Alpine Journal* came out and we learned that Noel Peak had been climbed the previous summer by the southeast face. Ours had been the fourth unsuccessful attempt of the southwest ridge.

PAUL TAMM

Ottarosko, Nuit Range, Coast Mountains. Ottarosko, a 10,000-foot massif near the northern end of the Nuit Range, east of Waddington, is featured by a large, cascading northern glacier and a long, serrated southern ridge. Its most striking aspect is the steep western ice face—a narrow, fluted slope that broadens and flattens into a small valley glacier draining into Nude Creek. In September Jim Nelson, Greg Collum, Bill Pilling and I flew to the outwash flat below the glacier by helicopter, then made an interim bivouac on the glacier edge near the second icefall. Our plan, to climb the main slope of the ice face, was enhanced by a recent snowfall that provided solid surface conditions atop the blue glare ice. Once across the bergschrund, the route went directly upward, in its higher portions requiring ice-screw placement for safety. The final portion of the climb followed the rocky south ridge, where two fifth-class pitches provided a few exposed problems. Descent was made by the west ridge and departure from the area by way of the pass leading to Ottarosko Creek, then following its valley to Tatlayoko Lake.

FRED BECKEY

Canadian Rockies

Mount Robson, Emperor Face; North Twin, North Face; Assiniboine, East Face. Tony Dick and I climbed a new line in the Emperor Face in August 1981. We went left of the Stumps-Logan line. There was much hard ice climbing, much rockfall and rock climbing up to 5.9, A3. In July 1982 Urs Kallen, Tim Friesen and I attempted to repeat the Lowe-Jones route on North Twin's north face. We were four days on the face but were unable to do the final wall as it was streaming with water caused by unusually warm conditions. Instead we traversed left to the ridge and followed this to the summit. We then crossed the icefield to the highway. We believe this is the most difficult face yet climbed in the Canadian Rockies. It still awaits a second ascent eight years after the first. Tony Dick and I made the first ascent of the impressive wall, the east face of Assiniboine, in September. The route took three days in perfect weather and is rated 5.9, A2. Snow and ice conditions were good at that time of the year but should be better in the spring or summer. The previous route in this vicinity takes a line much farther left and should more correctly be referred to as the East Buttress. (*A.A.J.*, 1970, page 148.)

DAVID CHEESMOND, *Alpine Club of Canada*

Mount Robson, Emperor Ridge Variation. On Mount Robson on September 17 Bryan Becker and I made an interesting and probably new variation to the regular north-face route. Instead of taking the normal start up the Berg Glacier, we climbed a narrow 45° ice gully up the left side of the Mint Glacier, crossed the bergschrund below the left rock buttresses of the Emperor Face, and circled left out onto the north face. We didn't rope up until we reached the Emperor Ridge, five pitches from the summit, which we reached after ten hours of climbing.

EDWARD WEBSTER

Canadian Arctic

British Empire Range, Ellesmere Island. From May 27 to June 10 Brad Albro, Bill Robinson, Rick Piercy, Jim Shedd, Paul Williams and John Petrie along with co-leaders Steve Trafton and me climbed and toured in northern Ellesmere Island. We flew from Resolute Bay on Cornwallis Island to a camp at 82° 1' N, 74° 31' W, north of Mount Whistler in the remote British Empire Range. We made the third ascent of Mount Whistler, 13 first ascents and the second ascent of Mount Barbeau (2732 meters, 8965 feet), the highest peak of Canada's Arctic islands. We enjoyed virtually flawless weather with crystal clear skies, continuous sunshine, calm winds and shade temperatures from 4° to 22° F and much warmer temperatures in the sun. Using nordic skis, we pulled individual freight sleds on a few inches of dry, powdery snow. We wish to name the group of peaks on this outing the "Maritime Group" in honor of the grand ships sailed by gallant seamen during the golden days of Arctic exploration. The peaks climbed follow: "Enterprise" (2347 meters, 7700 feet)[1] via southwest ridge by Errington, Robinson, Trafton and later by Albro, Piercy (The *Enterprise* saw Arctic service twice during the search for the lost Sir John Franklin expedition. The first was as Sir James Ross' flagship in 1848-49 in Barrow Strait and then as Captain Richard Collinson's ship in 1850-55 to Bering Strait and Victoria Island); Whistler (2685 meters, 8810 feet) third ascent via northeast face by Errington, Robinson, Trafter and later by Albro, Piercy; "Felix" (2493 meters, 8180 feet)[1] via east ridge by Albro, Piercy and via north ridge by Errington, Robinson, Shedd, Trafton (The *Felix* was Sir John Ross' ship in 1850-51 during his search for Franklin in Barrow Strait);

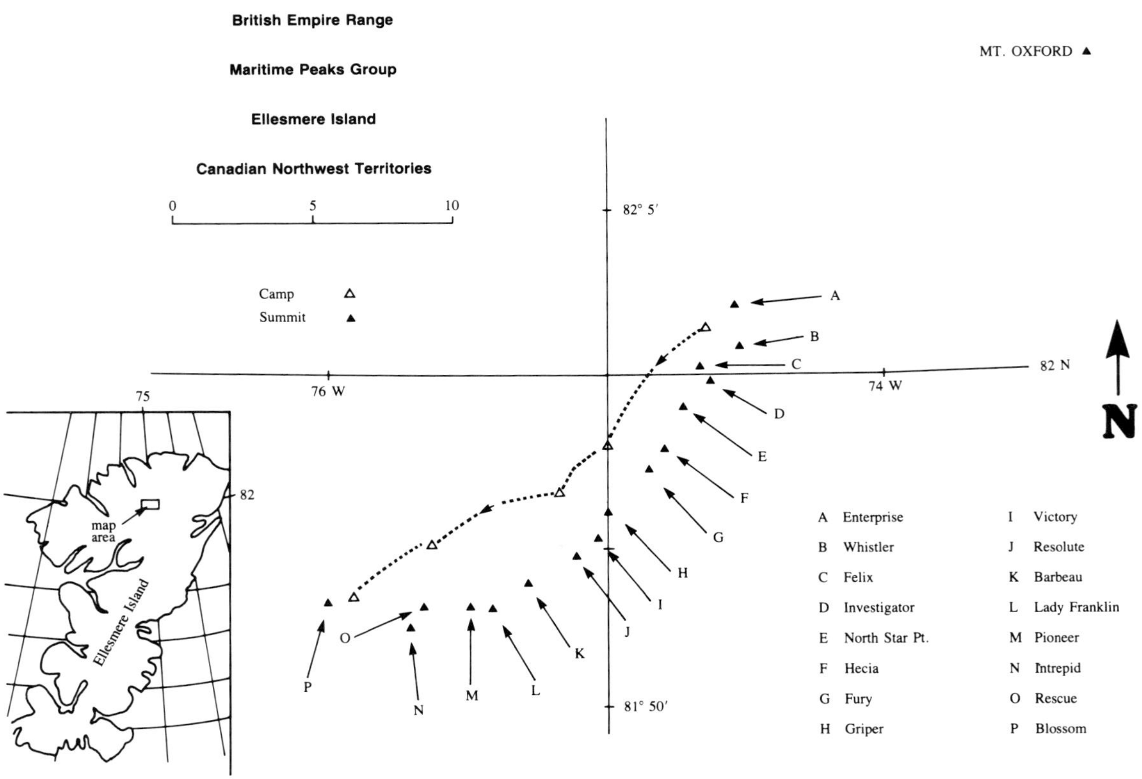

British Empire Range
Maritime Peaks Group
Ellesmere Island
Canadian Northwest Territories
MT. OXFORD ▲
0 5 10
Camp △
Summit ▲
82° 5'
82 N
76 W
74 W
81° 50'
N
map area
Ellesmere Island
75
82
A Enterprise
B Whistler
C Felix
D Investigator
E North Star Pt.
F Hecia
G Fury
H Griper
I Victory
J Resolute
K Barbeau
L Lady Franklin
M Pioneer
N Intrepid
O Rescue
P Blossom
A
B
C
D
E
F
G
H
I
J
K
L
M
N
O
P

"North Star" (2454 meters, 8050 feet)[1] traversed by Albro, Piercy during the ascent of Felix (The *North Star* saw duty twice as a Franklin search vessel, once in 1849-50 under Captain James Saunders to West Greenland and Lancaster Sound and later as Captain William Pullen's ship in 1852-54 to Beechey Island); "Investigator" (2423 meters, 7950 feet)[1] by Williams via north ridge and by Trafton via east ridge (The *Investigator* was the sister ship of the *Enterprise* on Sir James Ross' expedition and was Captain Robert McClure's ship during his voyage of 1850-54. She was lost in the ice on the north coast of Banks Island in 1854); "Hecla" (2545 meters, 8350 feet)[1] via north ridge by Albro, Errington, Piercy, Robinson, Shedd, Trafton, Williams (The *Hecla,* along with the *Griper,* was one of Captain William Parry's ships on his first Arctic voyage in 1819-20 and was also used, along with the *Fury,* during Parry's 1824-25 expedition); "Fury" (2585 meters, 8480 feet)[1] via west ridge by Albro, Errington, Piercy, Robinson, Shedd, Trafton (The *Fury* was Captain William Parry's vessel on his second voyage to the Arctic. She was abandoned at Fury Beach on North Somerset Island); "Griper" (2417 meters, 7930 feet)[1] via west ridge by Errington, Trafton, descent via north ridge (The *Griper* sailed under Captain William Parry on his first Arctic expedition in 1819-20 to Melville Island and again under Captain Lyon to Repulse Bay in 1824); "Victory" (2646 meters, 8680 feet)[1] via north ridge by Robinson, Shedd (The *Victory* was Sir John Ross' ship during his 1829-33 voyage to Prince Regent Inlet and was the first steamer in the Arctic. She was abandoned at Lord Mayor Bay on the east side of Boothia Peninsula); "Resolute" (2682 meters, 8800 feet)[1] via east ridge by Albro, Errington, Piercy, Robinson, Shedd, Trafton, and via north ridge by Petrie, Williams (The *Resolute* was Captain Henry Austin's flagship during his command of the Franklin search parties in 1850-51 to Barrow Strait); Barbeau (2732 meters, 8965 feet) second ascent via north face by Albro, Errington, Piercy, Robinson, Shadd, Trafton and via west ridge by Petrie, Williams; "Lady Franklin (2353 meters, 7720 feet)[1] via east ridge by Albro, Errington, Piercy, Robinson, Shedd, Trafton (The *Lady Franklin* was Captain William Penny's ship during his 1850-51 Franklin search to Wellingham Channel); "Pioneer" (2341 meters, 7680 feet)[1] via north ridge by Albro, Errington, Piercy, Robinson, Shedd, Trafton (The *Pioneer* was Sherard Osborn's ship. She was the steam tender to Austin's *Resolute* during 1850-51 and was ordered abandoned by Belcher in 1854); "Intrepid" (2439 meters, 8000 feet)[1] via west face by Albro, Errington, Piercy, Robinson, Shedd, Trafton (The *Intrepid* was Lieutenant J.B. Cator's ship. She was the steam tender to the *Assistance* and the *Resolute,* serving on Austin's 1850-51 expedition. The *Intrepid* was also ordered abandoned by Belcher in 1854); "Rescue" (2591 meters, 8500 feet)[1] via north ridge by Albro, Errington, Piercy, Robinson, Trafton (The *Rescue* was an American ship sent out by Henry Grinnell in 1850-51 under the command of Captain Edward DeHaven); "Blossom" (2259 meters, 7410 feet)[1] via east ridge by Albro, Errington, Petrie, Piercy, Rob-

---

[1] First ascent.

inson, Shedd, Trafton, Williams (The *Blossom* was Beechey's ship in 1826 when he sailed to Bering Strait in an unsuccessful attempt to meet up with Franklin's out-bound party from Great Slave Lake).

ALLAN ERRINGTON

British Empire Range, Ellesmere Island. Sponsored by the Explorer's Club, this expedition was aimed at exploratory ski-mountaineering on the northern coast of Ellesmere Island, above latitude 82°N. Our four-man advance party including Van Cochran, and Phil Trimble, John Stix and Sherman Bull, landed by Twin Otter on the sea ice of Yelverton Inlet on April 30. We spent the first week in reconnaissance of this little known area in cooperation with the Polar Continental Shelf Project, and in pursuing studies on the mechanics of sea ice. Temperatures were steady in the range of $-14°$ to $-20°F$. Operations on sea ice were hampered by unconsolidated snow which precluded travel to a climbing objective to the west. After climbing a coastal peak of 2500 feet, we began route-finding up a glacier at 82° 15′ N, 81° 50′ W on May 8. Problems with deep snow continued inland and were compounded by a maze of deep ravines cut by summer melt streams; nevertheless, a peak of over 3500 feet was climbed about five miles inland. Then, on May 15, another Twin Otter brought Dan Emmett, Eric Rosenfeld and John Bruno to our sea-level camp. During the ensuing 12 days, we completed a ski exploration of the glacier system from the sea to its head over 16 miles inland, near a divide leading to the Milne Glacier, reconnoitered a dominant group of peaks exceeding 6000 feet to the north (P 6258) and climbed a snow peak of over 4500 feet on skis. On May 25, our efforts culminated in a climb of P 5915 at the glacier head (as indicated on NTS 1:500,000 Map: Challenger Mts. No. 560N½ & 340N½). For details see *Canadian Alpine Journal* 1983. This expedition was the first to climb in north Ellesmere at this early season and, starting from sea level, penetrated a totally untrodden, high-relief area of the British Empire Range. Our furthest point inland approached an area explored by a Royal Navy Expedition which descended the Milne Glacier in the summer of 1972; they climbed several peaks southeast of our High Camp. We carried Explorers Club Flag #200.

G.V.B. COCHRAN

Northernmost Auyuittuq National Park, Baffin Island. I left Broughton Island in the company of three Eskimos on July 8. Travel by sled on the ice of Davis Strait was slow because of poor ice conditions. After four days, I was left alone near the entrance of a small fiord just south of Kekertaluk Island. I spent the rest of the summer alone, traveling by foot and inflatable kayak. August weather was fouler than usual, putting an end to ideas of serious climbing. I was picked up by an Eskimo in an open boat at the entrance to Okoa Bay on August 24 and returned to Broughton. I visited five summits, all first ascents I believe. They were P 2400 (68°07′N, 66°45′W) on July 17 via southwest slope; P 4000 (68°03'N, 67°00'W) on July 21 via west slope to a long crest; P 4000 (68°12'N, 66°55'W) on August 3 via south slopes from fiord head; P 2000 (68°12'N, 66°40'W) via south slopes; and P 3800 (68°03'N, 66°45'W) on August 9 via north slopes from fiord and then up glacier.

DAVID P. MACADAM, *Alpine Club of Canada*

Mount Thor, West Face, Rappels and Prusiking. During July eighteen American and Canadian men and women tackled the wilds of Auyuittuq National Park with its variable weather, rugged glacially carved terrain and continuous daylight. We successfully rigged, rappeled down and prusiked up the awe-inspiring west face of Mount Thor. In early May local outfitters drove six skidoos loaded with ropes, rigging gear and stove fuel up the frozen Weasel River to establish a cache. After our arrival, the summit team packed an enormous amount of material up the back side of Thor. We carefully selected the area where to lower our hoist line down the overhanging wall, slightly south of the dead center of the face. We then hauled up and rigged the rope. Utilizing single-rope techniques, we attained an uninterrupted pitch of 3250-feet. Pigeon Mountain Industries constructed a continuous 7/16-inch (11mm) nylon kern-mantle static rope, 5280-foot-long. Modified specifications included a super-tight sheath braid, one extra core strand and no splice closer than 30 feet to the next. Prusiks were accomplished both individually and in tandem, taking from 1½ to 6 hours. Rappels ranged from just over five minutes to 1½ hours.

STEVE HOLMES, *Atlanta, Georgia*

Loki, Asgard, Baffin Island. Our Australian Warren Lee, and I arrived at Summit Lake, in Auyuittuq National Park, on the last day of a two-week fine spell. From then on the weather continued to be generally poor with barely five fully fine days during the twenty-eight days of July that we spent in the area. However in this time we managed three ascents. The only ascent of Mount Loki since Pat Baird's 1966 first ascent was made via the south face. This new route, rated V, 5.10, followed a single crack and corner system for 2000 feet of flawless orange granite, taking some twenty hours of climbing time. Descent was made under stormy conditions in seven rappels down the north face. We also climbed the original Swiss route on Mount Asgard; superb granite climbing under a cloudless sky in an incomparable, remote alpine setting. The last ascent was of a previously unclimbed peak (MR 065820, 1:250000 Pang-nirtung) at the head of the Tuperaut Glacier, east of Summit Lake. We followed a classic alpine arête, (1V 5.9), directly to the summit, once again finishing in foul weather.

ROBERT STAVELEY PARKER, *New Zealand Alpine Club*

GREENLAND

Mount Forel and Other Peaks, East Greenland. On April 26 Bruno Klausbruckner, leader, E. Frosch, E. Gritzner, W. Hölzl, H. Hörhan, L. Krenn, O. Pletschko, F. Pucher, H. Wimmer and I were flown by helicopter from Angmagssalik to the Franche Compté Glacier and landed northwest of Lauper Bjerg. We traveled by skis with sledges over the Paris Glacier to the Bjørne Glacier. On May 3 Krenn, Klausbruckner, Hölzl, Pletschko, Gritzner and I climbed Mount Forel (3360 meters, 11,024 feet) via a new route, the southwest ridge. On May 6 Klausbruckner, Pucher, Hölzl and I climbed Perfektnunatak (3000 meters, 9843 feet), northeast of Forel. We then returned to Base Camp on the Franche Compté Glacier. On May 14 Hölzl and I made what is probably the second ascent of Lauper Bjerg (2580 meters, 8465 feet). We returned to Angmagssalik by helicopter on May 17.

PETER SCHIER, *Österreichische Himalaya Gesellschaft*

Glacier de France Region, Schweizerland, East Greenland. Our expedition was flown by helicopter from Angmagssalik to Base Camp at the junction of the Pourquoi Pas Glacier and the Glacier de France at 66°38′N, 36°30′W. We divided into three groups. Ferruccio Svaluto Moreolo, Marino Di Lenardo, Stefano Sinuello and I crossed the Femstjernen and the Kristian Glacier, where we climbed two virgin peaks northeast of Quervain Bjerg. Svaluto Moreolo and I on July 2 and 3 made a 33-hour ascent of P 3270 (10,728 feet), which we have proposed should be named "Alpe Adria." We climbed the northwest face, which had pitches up to 65°. The next highest peak of the group, P 3000 (9843 feet) was climbed by Di Lenardo and Sinuello in seven hours by the south face. The second group, composed of "free climbers," crossed the Pourquoi Pas Glacier to climb two peaks that divide that glacier from the Glacier de France. P 2350 (7710 feet) resembled the Badile. On July 1 Maurizio Dall'Omo, Gianni Pais De Gabriel and Daniele Zandegiacomo took 23 hours to climb the very difficult 3500-foot west face. That same day Gigi Dal Pozzo and Oliviero Olivier climbed the difficult south spur of the same peak. On July 4 Olivier and Pais De Gabriel climbed the tower, P 1900 (5234 feet), west of P 2350 by its northwest buttress. The third group climbed in the mountains between the Champs Elysées and Pourquoi Pas Glaciers, where between July 2 and 5 they climbed five previously unclimbed peaks: P 2080 (6824 feet), P 2050 (6726 feet), P 2010 (6595 feet), P 2000 (6562 feet) and P 1750 (5840 feet); and P 2010 (6595 feet), which lies northeast of Lauper Bjerg.

GIANNI PAIS BECHER, *Club Alpino Italiano*

Norsketinde and Other Peaks, Staunings Alper, East Greenland. Our expedition was organized both for science and for mountaineering as required by the government. The scientific program was carried out by Professors Luciano Luria, Giuseppe Alasonatti and Gian Luigi Vaccari. The other members were

Eugenio Ferrero, Sergio Martini, Franco Ribetti, Mario Salero and I as leader. We were flown by helicopter to our Base Camp at 4000 feet, east of Alpefjord, at the junction of the glaciers, Vikingebrae and Frihedsbrae. I was unable to take much part because of a back strain on the first day. On July 30 Martini and Ribetti ascended the Vikingebrae toward Helvedes Pass and turned up the second tributary glacier on the left to a couloir that led up to the rocky southeast ridge of P 2410 (7907 feet), which led to the top. The peak is southwest of Frihedstinde. P 1950 (6898 feet) is east of Base Camp between the first and second tributary glaciers on the left on the way to Helvedes Pass. On July 31 Alasonatti and Solero climbed moraine up the first tributary glacier to bypass an icefall and then climbed the west snow slope and the west rock ridge to the summit. "Norsketinde Dome" and "Norsketinde Teeth," north of Norsketinde, were climbed on August 1 by Martini and Ribetti in a 16-hour day. From Base Camp they crossed the Vikingebrae to the beginning of the northeast ridge that descends from Norsketinde. They climbed a steep couloir to a snow saddle and climbed a snow dome (2010 meters, 6595 feet). They continued south along the sharp rock ridge and climbed the two spires (2250 meters, 7382 feet) from the col that separates them. "Italytinde" was climbed on August 3 by Martini and Ribetti in 16½ hours. It lies north of Dansketinde. They ascended the second glacier on the right on the way to Helvedes Pass. They climbed the west face via an ice couloir. Where it forked they took the right fork to a notch and followed the ridge to the summit (2710 meters, 8891 feet). P 2200 (7218 feet) lies at the head of the first tributary glacier on the left of the Frihedsbrae, northeast of Mythotinde. It was climbed on August 6 by Alasonatti, Ferrero, Martini, Ribetti and Solero by its northeast side and southwest ridge. Martini and Ribetti on August 9 and 10 ascended the first tributary glacier on the right on the way to Helvedes Pass and from the west ascended an ice couloir that led to a col between the "Norsketinde Teeth" on the north and the "Norsketinde Spire" on the south. The 2500-foot couloir was difficult, especially the exit from it. They then traversed the east face and climbed the south ridge from the col to the summit of "Norsketinde Spire" (2400 meters, 7874 feet). They descended to the col between this peak and Norsketinde. They continued past rock gendarmes and up the north ridge of Norsketinde (2680 meters, 9383 feet), a new route. From there they descended the east ridge over various ice and rock towers to a wide col. They then climbed an ice slope to the top of P 2450 (8038 feet), east of Norsketinde. They descended the east ridge to a col at the head of the tributary glacier east of "Italytinde," which they reached via a rather dangerous couloir overhung by séracs and back to Base Camp. The difficulty was comparable to the Peuterey Ridge on Mont Blanc. The entire climb took 35 hours. All the climbs were first ascents except that of Norsketinde. In our final five days we were hampered by bad weather.

Giuseppe Dionisi, *Club Alpino Accademico Italiano*

PLATE 65
Photo by Geoffrey Monaghan
Turtle's Beak, Greenland.

Angmagssalik Region, East Greenland. Cormac Higgs, Colin Wootton and I arrived in Angmagssalik on July 20 where we met our sea freight. Our plan was to travel in our inflatable boat to the head of Kangertitivatsiaq Fjord, about 140 miles to the north and from there to sledge north for 70 miles to reach the range containing P 3060. This is an area of fine, big peaks almost totally unvisited due to its inaccessibility. Our coastal journey was hampered by the heaviest sea ice for many years. Kangertitivatsiaq was, in mid-July, still under winter ice! Our early attempts to complete the boat journey failed east of Sermiligaq and we altered our plan. We established a Base Camp at the head of Sermiligaq Fjord and set off to attempt to reach P 3060 with 40 days' supplies. We were stopped on the Haabets Glacier after 15 days of hard work. We then lost two days to a severe blizzard during which our tent was badly damaged. We made a protracted retreat to Base Camp and on by boat to Angmagssalik, during which we took opportunities to climb. Apart from several minor peaks, mainly around the head of the Knud Rasmussen Glacier (notable for their loose rock and stunning scenery) and north of Angmagssalik, we climbed the apparently virgin "Turtle's Beak" on August 18. This peak, west of the Knut Rasmussen Glacier (66°11′N) is approximately 2000 feet high and the summit is a frightful prow of rock, overhanging a vertical drop of 1000 feet. We climbed the northwest ridge and the west face of the summit tower. On September 1 and 2, in a 32-hour epic, we made the apparent first ascent of Nanerersarpik, a fine mountain rising from sea level to 1080 meters (3543 feet), northwest of Kingmiut. With a dawn start, we climbed the southeast buttress and then a superb sharp ridge to gain the summit (loose and serious; Grade 4). We had to sit out eight hours of darkness on the summit. It is worth noting that our flight to Søndre Strømfjord was delayed for five days due to bad weather. The record delay is 25 days!

Geoffrey Monaghan, *England*

Alfred Wegener Peninsula. Our expedition was made up of Emil Galehr, Heinz Grasbon, Berhard Grimm, Gerhard and Waltraut Huber, Helmut Koch and me as leader. We were carried by fishing boat from Umanak to Base Camp at Tuperssuatsiait on the western part of the south coast of Alfred Wegener Peninsula on July 14. P 1922 (6308 feet), P 1900 (6234 feet) and P 1850 (6070 feet), north of Base Camp, were climbed on July 16 by Galehr, Grasbon, Koch and me and on July 19 by Grimm and both Hubers. The latter two peaks lie west of P 1922. On July 19 P 1900 (6234 feet), which lies east of P 1922, was climbed via its south and west ridges by Galehr and Koch and via its southeast ridge (UIAA III or IV) by Grasbon and me. On July 21 and 22 Galehr, Grasbon and I traveled east and then traversed the ridge (UIAA IV) that tends northeast over P 1420 (4823 feet), P 1580 (5184 feet) and P 1833 (6014 feet). On July 24 Grimm, Koch and I climbed P 1100 (3609 feet; UIAA V), just north of Base Camp. On July 27 the Hubers and Koch climbed P 1600 (5250 feet; UIAA V), which lies near the northern coast on the western tip of the peninsula, while Galehr, Grasbon and I climbed the 1450-meter (4758-foot) tower just west of it (UIAA V). On July 9 Grasbon and I climbed P 1400 (4593 feet) northwest of Base Camp. We believe that ten of these were first ascents.

KARL MALIN, *Österreichischer Alpenverein*

SOUTH AMERICA

Venezuela

Pico Vértigo, East Face and Other Climbs. Venezuelan mountaineering has now entered a new phase, in which new routes on rock walls are sought. Local walls, granitic, are steep and at times vertical, albeit short, averaging 300 to 700 feet high. Artificial aid is often used. On June 22, 1981, together with four other climbers I made the ascent of the east wall of Pico Antón Goering (4550 meters, 14,928 feet), located between El León and El Toro. This name was given after a German artist who visited the Venezuelan Andes in 1868. On March 6, 1982, G. Gómez and I opened the east-face route on Pico Vértigo (c. 4900 meters, 16,076 feet), the "Dru" of Venezuela; in the upper part we changed around to the south face. Both peaks belong to the Sierra Nevada de Mérida. In the Sierra del Norte, situated north of the Andean city of Mérida, there are many unclimbed rock walls of interest. Quality of the rock varies. On March 14, G. Gomez and I climbed the east face of La Vieja III (c. 4300 meters, 14,108 feet). On November 14, the east face of La Vieja I (also c. 4300 meters) was also climbed, two girls, Rosa Pabón and Xiomara Rojas participating, plus A. Rángel and I. Finally, late in October, G. Reinosa and I climbed the east face of Pico La Torre (4311 meters, 14,144 feet). All these routes listed are new.

JOSÉ BETANCOURT, *Mérida, Venezuela*

Ecuador

Obispo and Fraile Grande, Altar Group, 1981. The Altar group consists of many peaks and pinnacles, which create the rim of a volcanic crater. Dave Jones and I climbed Obispo by its standard route, the south face. We bivouacked on the summit and then descended the long and difficult east ridge to the Obispo-Monja Grande col. From there we could descend to the glacier on the south side. This traverse took four days in late November 1981. In late December 1981 I returned with a Scot, Mike Orr and climbed the east ridge of the Fraile Grande, not a new route, and traversed the peak, descending the west ridge to a col from which we descended the glacier to the north.

CARLOS BUHLER

Peru—Cordillera Blanca

Puntancuerno. Our expedition was composed of Bernardo Davila, leader, Augusto Ortega, Jorge Pinatte, Ricardo Colonia, Alfonso Estremadoyro, Juan Miguel Alba and me. We placed Base Camp at 13,775 feet on the shores of Yuraccocha on August 14. We made a high camp at 18,375 feet on August 18. To reach this camp we had to climb the very crevassed, dangerous glacier. There were six vertical walls from 35 to 65 feet high. On August 19 we made a summit attempt that failed some 500 feet from the summit in bad weather, which we experienced 80% of the time we were there. On August 20 Ortega and I made rapid progress halfway up the summit ridge, thanks to the ropes we had fixed the day before. From there on, the ridge was even more difficult. The cornices were highly unstable. One particularly difficult rope-length was a vertical traverse where we climbed between the rock and ice. At four P.M. we surmounted the last great cornice, which was the summit.

AMÉRICO TORDOYA, *Club Andino Peruano*

Uruashraju, Northwest Face, Kashan Este, Northeast Face, and Other Peaks. Our expedition was composed of Pete du Preez, Tim and Janet Hughes, Jonathan Levy, Michael Scott, Dr. Robin Sandell, Antonio da Cruz, Des Watkins, Mrs. Felicity Eggelston, my 15-year-old son Alistair Schoon and me. We drove to the Pitec roadhead at the entrance to the Quebrada Qelkaywanka, joined by our Peruvian porter, Emilio Angeles. An easy two-day walk up the valley with equipment and food on 18 donkeys brought us to our first Base Camp at 14,100 feet below Laguna Tullparaju. For acclimatization we made the following climbs: Jatunmontepuncu (5415 meters, 17,766 feet) from a subcamp at 15,575 feet via southwest ridge on June 16 by du Preez, Sandell, A.F. and W.A. Schoon, Scott; Chopiraju (5475 meters, 17,962 feet) from a 16,400-foot subcamp via west shoulder on June 18 by T. Hughes, Levy; and Wamanripa (5243 meters, 17,530 feet) from a 15,425-foot subcamp via east slope and ridge on June 21 by Eggleston, J. Hughes, Sandell, Watkins. Then bad weather severely affected climbing done from the first Base Camp. Our attempt on Chinchey was stopped by high winds and snow. Unsettled weather persisted until we completed the traverse from Laguna Tullparaju to our second Base Camp in the Quebrada Rajuqolta. The traverse involved climbing over the high pass between San Juan and Kimarumi onto the Quebrada Shallap icefall, crossing the Wamashraju ridge west of P 5406 and into the Quebrada Rajuqolta. From a subcamp on the San Juan-Kimarumi col at 17,225 feet on June 28 Levy and T. Hughes climbed San Juan (5843 meters, 19,170 feet) via the northwest ridge while du Preez and Sandell climbed the east ridge of Kimarumi (5459 meters, 17,910 feet). On June 30 du Preez, Sandell, Scott and I climbed P 5406 (17,737 feet) from the 16,000-foot col via the north glacier and northeast ridge. On July 2 Levy soloed from the 14,100-foot Rajuqolta Base Camp the east ridge of P 5377 (17,641 feet) on the Kashan Ridge. On July 3

PLATE 66
Photo by H. Adams Carter
PUNTANCUERNO is higher sharp peak in center. Chinchey at right.

du Preez and Scott climbed via the east ridge P 5200 (17,061 feet) on the Wamashraju ridge from a 16,075-foot subcamp while J. Hughes, Sandell, my son and I climbed Yawarraju (5675 meters, 18,619 feet) from a subcamp at 17,400 feet via the northwest ridge and then traversed to Rurec (5700 meters, 18,701 feet). T. Hughes and Levy climbed Huantsán (6395 meters, 20,981 feet) via the 1952 route with four bivouacs, reaching the summit on July 7. Scott, my son and I made a new route on Uruashraju (5735 meters, 18,815 feet) from a 16,750-foot subcamp north of Uruashraju Norte. We climbed over Uruashraju Norte's northwest spur and by the northwest face to the summit. On July 10 Levy made a new route on Kashan Este (5723 meters, 18,777 feet) from the Rajuqolta Base Camp via the northeast face.

ANDRÉ SCHOON, *South Africa*

Ocshapalca, South Face. Bernard Francou, Jean Michael Cambon and I reconnoitered a safe route on the east face of Cayesh but we could reach only 17,000 feet because of very bad weather. We moved across the range to Huaraz and then made a new route on the south face of Ocshapalca. It took us ten hours on June 20 to ascend. We rappelled down the same route in five. The 2000-foot-high wall varied from 55° to perpendicular. This extremely difficult ice route is comparable to the south face of Chacraraju in difficulty. We attacked the face a little to the right of the summit just on the right of a rocky spur that rises diagonally to the left. Above the spur we climbed six ice pitches on an ice slope to a series of gullies. We then ascended one nearly vertical pitch and another of 75° to reach ice flutes. We climbed seven more rope-lengths of 60° to 65° to gain the nearly vertical exit to the summit. I also soloed the less difficult east face of Vallunaraju, a beautiful granite wall.

GIAN CARLO GRASSI, *Club Alpino Italiano*

Ocshapalca, South Face, Carás I, South Face and Other Peaks. Our group of Swiss were Vincent Banderet, Rafaël Rabout, André Duffey, Paula Scherer and I. In Huaraz we were joined by three Canadians, Jocelyn Ouellet and Isabelle and Thierry Legouis. Aside from classic climbs like Pisco, Huascarán, Huantsán Norte and Artesonraju, Banderet, Ouellet and I put up a new route on the south face of Ocshapalca on June 12. Our route was of technical ice with two vertical sections on the far left of the face. We tried Chacraraju Este but were turned back 350 feet from the summit by a storm. On July 28 Banderet and I made a route on the south face of Carás I, a 20-hour mixed climb which ended on the right summit. We had to descend the east ridge by moonlight and got back to camp at midnight. Thierry Legouis fell 125 feet down a sérac on Huascarán and was evacuated in a rescue that lasted three days. He has fully recovered.

BERNARD BALMAT, *Club Alpin Suisse*

OCSHAPALCA's South Face from Quebrada Llaca. French route on left, Italian on right.

Huascarán Norte, North Face Solo, 1981. The Belgian climber Johan de Schepper solved the French 1966 route on the north face of Huascarán Norte in July, 1981. He took two days to make this difficult climb.

Chopicalqui, Northwest Face, Solo in one day. From camp at 13,125 feet above Yurac Corral in the Quebrada Llanganuco, I decided to attempt a new route on the northwest face of Chopicalqui to the left of the route climbed in 1981 by Sigayret, the Rollands and Roberts (*A.A.J.*,1982, pages 176-7). I searched the route among the séracs with binoculars. Late in the afternoon, a huge avalanche swept the whole face and glacier. At three A.M. on July 24, I set out in the frigid cold with my headlamp. At dawn I climbed verglas-covered rock to set foot on the glacier. The avalanche had swept the whole glacier, filling crevasses. I rapidly ascended the resultant toboggan chute, letting me reach easily the icefall of the northwest face. Several nearly vertical gullies of blue ice led me to 18,700 feet. At eight A.M., I was at the foot of a chiseled wall of ice flutes, which averaged 60° to 70°. The ice was glassy and even black in the steeper pitches. After eating a bit, I chose the widest furrow and climbed without stopping to the very sharp north foresummit. Life took on a new savour, ice-axe, ice hammer and crampons were remarkably secure tools to give me confidence and a feeling of freedom. On the foresummit my altimeter read 6050 meters (19,850 feet). The main peak was cloud-covered. The last 1000 feet were torture. In heavy clouds I plowed up knee-deep snow. Finally at 10:30 A.M. I forced myself up the last meters to the summit (6345 meters, 20,817 feet). No visibility, but I delighted in the solitude and calm. I immediately began the descent. Through a hole in the clouds, Huascarán smiled at me. I left the north peak and descended to the glacier and made the long traverse off the glacier, thinking of yesterday's avalanche. Then rock, moraine, grass came. At three P.M. I found our porter, Pompeo, waiting for me by the stream.

ERIC DOSSIN, *Club Alpin Français*

Chopicalqui, East Ridge. Our expedition was composed of René Desmaison, Dr. Alain Vagne, Guy Giraud, David Autheman, Michel Arizzi and me. We had our Base Camp in the Quebrada Honda and established two more camps to acclimatize and to move up supplies. We prepared the route on the beginning of the unclimbed east ridge for three days, finding fixed ropes of a previous attempt in the first 650 feet. On August 17 Desmaison, Vagne, Arizzi and I set out. In the first part we had snow and ice with problems of huge cornices and varying snow-and-ice conditions. A section had rotten rock. The cornices were so high and thin that we had windows through to the other side, veritable labyrinths of ice. The climb was complicated by unstable weather and heavy loads. We each carried a rucksack and we had two haul sacks since we were making a movie. We made seven bivouacs and reached the summit on August 25.

XAVIER CHAPPAZ, *Compagnie de Guides, Chamonix, France*

CHOPICALQUI's Northwest Face.
- - - - = 1981 route of the Rollands, Sigayret and Roberts. • • • • • = 1982 Dossin solo.

Photo by Leigh N. Ortenburger

CHOPICALQUI from Northwest. Both routes reached sharp peak on the left and followed skyline to the summit.

Pisco Oeste, Chopicalqui, and Chacraraju. The Alpine Club Impol of Slovenska Bistrica expedition was composed of Ivan Šturm, Marjan Frešer, Franček Knez, Janko Korent, Matjaž Pečkovnik, Milan Romih, Dani Tič and Dr. Tone Žuntar. On June 4 Knez and Frešer made a new route on the south face of Pisco Oeste. This was later repeated by Italians. On June 8 Knez and Frešer made a new route on the south face of Chacraraju Oeste to the eastern foresummit. On June 11 and 12 this same pair made a new direct route on Chopicalqui's 3500-foot-high west face. On June 21 Knez, Frešer and Tič climbed the 1972 Japanese Chacraraju Oeste's south face, straight up the ice bulge to the left of the summit. That same day Pečkovnik and Romih repeated the 1976 Japanese route on the south face, which reached the summit ridge to the right of the summit. On each of the Chacraraju climbs, bivouacs were made low on the face.

FRANCI SAVENC, *Planinska Zveza Slovenije, Yugoslavia*

Routes on the South Face of Chacraraju. A number of routes have now been climbed on the south face of Chacraraju. These are marked on the photograph. *Chacraraju Oeste:* A. John Bouchard, Marie-Odile Meunier, Americans, 1977 (*A.A.J.*, 1978, pages 486-7); B. Yves Astier, French, 1979 (*A.A.J.*, 1982, page 178); C. Knez, Frešer, Yugoslavs, 1982 (This ascent stopped on the eastern foresummit.) (*A.A.J.*, 1983, above); *Chacraraju Este:* D. Kochi, Tanaka, Japanese 1972 (They fell when the cornice broke as they tried to emerge on the summit ridge. They obviously did not reach the summit.) (*A.A.J.*, 1973, page 457); E. Richey, Brewer, Americans, 1978 (*A.A.J.*, 1979, pages 230-2); F. Jaeger, French, 1978 (*A.A.J.*, 1979, page 234); G. Kondo, Yoshino, Japanese, 1976 (*A.A.J.*, 1977, pages 210-2.)

Chacraraju Este. French climbers Nicole Mazuir and Philippe Modéré climbed Chacraraju Este in August. They followed the route first climbed by Brewer and Richey in 1978 and probably made the second complete ascent of the route. (Japanese in 1979 reached the summit ridge but did not continue). The French also made several other climbs, including a full-moon ascent of Pisco.

Alpamayo, Chacraraju Oeste and Other Peaks. Viktor Jaralím, Miroslav Svoboda, Václav Zajíc and I on June 1 in five hours climbed the southwest face of Alpamayo by the Italian route. We also ascended Chacraraju Oeste from June 10 to 12 by the Bouchard-Meunier route on the south side directly to the western summit. Petr Hapala and Břetislav Husička climbed Huandoy Norte by the 1976 Polish route. Most of the party also climbed Pisco Oeste.

MIROSLAV ŠTĚPÁNEK, *Czechoslovakia*

PLATE 70

Photo by H. Adams Carter

Routes on CHACRARAJU's South Face. A = Bouchard-Meunier; B = Astier; C = Yugoslav; D = Japanese 1972; E = Richey-Brewer; F = Jaeger; G = Japanese 1976.

Quitaraju, Alpamayo, Artesonraju, Chacraraju Este and Other Peaks. While we were in the Cordillera Blanca, the weather was rather unstable. There was little snow, which exposed rock and black ice and left bergschrunds open. We placed Base Camp in the Quebrada Arhueicocha at 14,100 feet on July 7. We placed Camp I at 15,750 feet and Camp II at 17,725 in the Alpamayo-Quitaraju col. The last 125 feet to the col were very steep. On July 11 Gilles Léon and I climbed the north face of Quitaraju unroped in three hours. On July 16 we two climbed the southeast face of Loyaqjirca while Jean Louis Delourme soloed Quitaraju's north face. On July 17 Léon and I climbed the Italian route on the southwest face of Alpamayo, passing close to the body of my friend Serge Bériol, killed in 1980. By July 20 we had placed a light camp on the Artesonraju-Parón col. On July 21 Léon and I climbed the south face of Artesonraju, much of it 50° and 60° among séracs. We descended the delicate east ridge. An attempt on the west face of Pukajirka Sur failed in deep powder snow. We moved to the Quebrada Llanganuco. On August 2 an attempt on Bouchard's route on the south face of Chacraraju Oeste failed because of much exposed rock this year. On August 5 Delourme and I climbed Chopicalqui by the normal southwest ridge. On August 8 Léon and I climbed the south face of Chacraraju Este to the summit ridge but not to the summit. The climb was sustained and difficult with pitches of 80° ice. We followed the 1978 Brewer-Richey route, which did continue along the ridge to the top. We climbed up the lower face to the flutes, traversed left and then ascended straight up to emerge on the summit ridge west of the top. The ridge appeared impossible and we stopped there.

FRANCIS MOUSEL, *Club Alpin Français*

Taulliraju, Southwest Face, 1980. A strong Italian expedition in August 1980 climbed a new route on the left buttress of the southwest face of Taulliraju (5830 meters, 19,128 feet). The climbing was of great difficulty. They fixed rope on the first part up to an ice cave high on the spur. The summit was reached by Gianni Calcagno, Piero Perona, Ugo Vialardi, Costantino Piazzo, Tullio Vidoni and Stefano De Benedetti. They then climbed Artesonraju alpine style by its southeast ridge.

Rinrijirca, South Face. From a high camp at 16,900 feet, the Italian A. Paleari on June 3 climbed the south face of Rinrijirca solo in four hours with mixed climbing and ice up to 80°. From the top of the face, it took him another three hours to the summit (5810 meters, 19,062 feet).

Huandoy Este, East Ridge. Italians Massimo Marchini and Paola Gigliotti climbed the south ridge of Huandoy Este on June 3.

Nevado Parón, Huandoy Oeste and Other Peaks. Our expedition was made up of Boštjan Kekec, Franc Langerholc, Željko Perko, Stane Stanovnik, Damjan Vidmar and me as leader. On May 30 Langerholc, Stanovnik and I climbed the middle of the 1300-foot-high west face of Nevado Parón (5600 meters, 18,373 feet). At times it was dangerous since we were below huge séracs. We reached the face from the eastern end of Laguna Parón. After Kekec and Vidmar climbed Huandoy Norte (6395 meters, 20,981 feet) by the normal route on June 5, they made a new descent. From the col between Huandoy Norte and Huandoy Oeste they started in the séracs on the top of the southwest face and continued down the face to a very crevassed glacier, the first 350 feet of which were easy but which became progressively steeper. The middle section was really a hanging glacier before they reached the lower glacier and moraine. We also climbed the normal routes on Artesonraju, Pisco, Yanapatsa and Chopicalqui.

FRANC VICIC, *Škofja Loka, Yugoslavia*

Pukajirka Central, Northeast Face. Our expedition was probably the third to climb Pukajirka Central. We made a new route, the northeast face. We were Antonio Camozzi, Marino Giacometti, Antonio Magnanoni, Gian Battista Scanabessi, Dr. Annibale Bonicelli, Adalberto Frigerio and I as leader. We approached from Pomabamba via the Quebrada Jankapampa. We had the following camps: Base Camp, I and II at 12,150, 14,450 and 17,725 feet. Camp I was still below the very broken glacier. We fixed 1300 feet of rope to let the three porters carry loads. On July 7 Giacometti and Scanabessi reached the summit (6014 meters, 19,734 feet). They climbed the last 1300 feet in six hours and descended the same in ten rappels, which took four hours. The climbing was very difficult; the final pitch onto the summit ridge was of 70° ice.

PIERO NAVA, *Club Alpino Italiano*

Andean Museum, Huaraz. In July the first part of the *Museo Andino,* which I have founded, was opened on the corner of Los Sauces and Avenida Patay near the Hotel de Turistas in Huaraz. The museum will help fill in details of the Peruvian Mountain Ranges. For instance, all maps of the Cordillera Blanca are on exhibit from Antonio Raimondi's to the latest ones. There are climbing journals from 22 countries. Already completed are exhibits on Alpamayo and Huascarán with photographs from different sides. There is a small entry fee.

CÉSAR MORALES ARNAO, *Club Andino Peruano*

Mountain and Caving Film Festival, Huaraz. Acceding to a request of the *Revista Peruana de Andinismo,* the French Ministry of Youth and Sport sent 17 mountaineering and caving films to Huaraz. The famous French climber, René Desmaison, presented his film, *Huandoy Sur,* taken in 1976 and 1978 during the French climb of the south face. This received the Silver Trophy of the Club Ancash. The films were shown in the Regional Cultural Institute and attended by several thousand people, many of them foreign climbers. Other notable films were those of the late Dr. Nicolas Jaeger's 60-day solitary vigil on the summit of Huascaran, Jean Afanassieff's new route on Fitz Roy in Patagonia, Yannick Seigneur's attempt on Broad Peak, Lionel Terray's climbs and Maurice Herzog's films. A photographic exhibit by Jaeger and Richard List was also presented. The same festival was also put on in a number of other Peruvian cities.

CÉSAR MORALES ARNAO, *Club Andino Peruano*

Tsurup, Direct Southwest Face. The route climbed by Juan Antonio Lorenzo and me started up the southwest face the same as that climbed by Fear, Lahr, Malataux and Ridgeway in 1972, (*A.A.J.*, 1973, pages 325-7) but where they traversed upwards to the left two-thirds of the way up the face to meet the west ridge some 200 meters below the summit, we kept straight on up in a direct line to the summit. On July 24 we started up the couloir a little to the right of the center of the face, but rockfall drove us back. We started a second time on August 2 and followed up the face, not deviating at all from the direct line. The climbing was mixed with some ice slopes up to 75° and even 90° interrupted by rock of UIAA IV to V + . The climb took us eleven hours. We had to bivouac on the summit and suffered some frostbite on hands and feet. We descended the same route, making seven 200-foot rappels.

FRANCISCO JOSÉ PALACIOS, *Escuela Castellana de Alta Montaña, Spain*

Peru—Cordillera Huayhuash

Puscanturpa Group, 1981. (A brief report in *A.A.J.*, 1982 on page 182 was unfortunately not totally correct. The following was received too late for publication last year. See photos of Puscanturpa Norte and Sur in *A.A.J.*, 1975, Plates 59 and 60.) Our group of 14 from Varese had its Base Camp at the head of the Quebrada Huanacpatay at 15,425 feet, reached in four days from Chiquián since the shorter way through Cajatambo was interrupted by spring floods. Our principal objective was a new route on the north face of Puscanturpa Norte (5652 meters, 18,591 feet). We worked on the lower part of the route on August 8 and 9 and after a storm, Luigi Ossola, leader, Franco Facchinetti, Attilio Farè, Enrico Palermo and Carlo Vedani completed the climb on August 14 and 15, 1981. The face is 2500 feet high. They climbed the left side of the face to the left of the great cleft. The lower part was relatively easy (UIAA III and IV), the middle was of great difficulty (11 rope-lengths of UIAA V and VI and one of A1 and A2), and the last 350 feet were of scree and easy snow. We made two other one-day climbs from Base Camp. On August 14. 1981 Dr. Paolo Facchinetti, Ambrogio Cremonesi,

Mario Bramanti, Fabio Della Bordella, Giuseppe Picone and I made a new route on the south face of Puscanturpa Sur (5550 meters, 18,209 feet). From Cuyoc Pass we ascended the right side of the face and then followed the wide southeast ridge to the summit. On August 17, 1981 Ossola, Cremonesi, Marco Broggi, Picone, Luigi Tessari and I climbed Puscanturpa Central (5442 meters, 17,852 feet). We started under the northwest spur of Puscanturpa Norte, climbed the west face of Puscanturpa Central on snow to a col and ascended the snow-and-rock north ridge, which rose in three steps. All were new routes. Puscanturpa Norte and Sur were third ascents of the peaks and Puscanturpa Central was the second ascent.

LIVIO VISINTINI, *Club Alpino Italiano*

Ninashanca, Yerupajá and Jirishanca West Face. The Klub Wysokogórski Zakopane expedition was composed of Lech Korniszewski, leader, Maciej Pawlikowski, Zdzisław Kiszela and Bogusław Probulski. After acclimatizing in the Cordillera Blanca, they established Base Camp on Jahuacocha. From July 3 to 5 Korniszewski, Pawlikowski and Probulski climbed Ninashanca's west spur, previously climbed by Brian Hall and Alan Rouse in 1978. They had some 3500 feet of difficult rock and mixed climbing ending with seven rope-lengths of ice. On July 10 and 11, Kiszela, Pawlikowski and Probulski climbed the northwest ridge of Yerupajá (6634 meters, 21,765 feet), ascending on ice to the right of and parallel to the rock ridge. On July 16 Pawlikowski and Probulski made what is probably a new route on the west face of Jirishanca (6126 meters, 20,099 feet), to the left of the Cassin route, which they joined in the very upper part. After a mixed section, they climbed 3000 feet of 60° ice amid hanging séracs. After joining the west spur (Cassin) route, they found old ropes. After a 13-hour alpine-style ascent, they made fifteen rappels down the west face during the night.

JÓZEF NYKA, *Editor, Taternik, Poland*

Central Peru

Santa Rosa, West Face, Cordillera Raura. On June 28 Bernard Francou and I climbed for the first time the west face of Santa Rosa (5706 meters, 18,721 feet). The 1650-foot high face, which varied from 50° to 65°, took us five hours to climb. We crossed a crevassed area and attacked the very center of the wall. We climbed a long couloir to the left of the large, smooth rock rib to a wall of séracs, where we turned left to reach the summit triangle.

GIAN CARLO GRASSI, *Club Alpino Italiano*

PLATE 71
Photo by Gian Carlo Grassi
SANTA ROSA's West Face.

Tanraniyoc, Cordillera Central. Southwest of Huancayo, about 12 miles east of Yauyos, is a range of rock peaks and small glaciers that has received almost no mountaineering attention. In June Mike Stewart and I hiked in from Yauricocha on the north and camped at 15,500 feet between the two highest peaks in the range, both given on the map as 5431 meters (17,818 feet). We climbed the easternmost of the two, passing cliffs at the bottom via a couloir, climbing a glacier on the peak's southwest side and turning north on the very narrow summit ridge to a rocky summit. The Peruvian IGN map labeled the peak Tanraniyoc, but local people gave about four other names. We made only one first ascent, to afford as many other climbers as possible the same privilege we had.

Douglas Rice, *Unaffiliated*

Southern Peru

Jatunhuma I, West Face, Cordillera Vilcanota. Dave Wilkinson and I spent twelve days in the area, based at Ticlacocha. Apart from the rubbish piles, it was a delightful place and we were blessed with the promised good Andean weather. Campa I and Ccapana by the normal routes provided two easy training climbs before we tackled our main objective, Jatunhuma I (6094 meters, 19,994 feet). We made the first ascent of the west face, 2300 feet of ice steepening to 65° in the upper part. From a bivouac at the foot of the mountain, we climbed the face in 13 hours, bivouacking again under the summit cornices. The peak had no straightforward descent. We traversed the summit ridge southwards and then descended the east face and southeast ridge by a mixture of abseiling, down-climbing and traversing, bivouacking a third time near the bottom. Then a long, circuitous glacier plod took us back to Ticlacocha. We then went to Bolivia. (See that section.)

Stephen Venables, *Alpine Club*

Yayamari, Atun Paco and Pacco Loma, Southern Cordillera Vilcanota. In four days from Sicuani, we reached Base Camp at 16,250 feet on Laguna Amayani (a name unknown to the locals, who call the lake Cascara). Out of eleven days there, the weather was bad on five, preventing our climbing the original objectives. We made the following ascents: Yayamari (6007 meters, 19,709 feet) from the northwest on August 10 by G. Bosio, M. Meli, A. Panza, M. Salvi, M. Gavazzeni and me, on August 12 by A. Cattaneo, I. Galli, A. Chiappa and R. Chiappini, and on August 14 by Bosio, G. Ruggeri, G. Mainini, Meli, G. Sartori and B. Piazzoli; Pacco Loma (5454 meters, 17,894 feet) from the southeast on August 12 by Bosio, Rugerri and Mainini; Atun Paco (5672 meters, 18,610 feet) from the west on August 14 by Panza, Gavazzeni and me. This last peak is the summit south of Huilayoc and is called thus by local shepherds.

Santino Calegari, *Club Alpino Italiano*

PLATE 72

Photo by Stephen Venables

JATUNHUMA's West Face. The route ascended the face left of the sérac and curved upward through the couloir.

Helancoma, Huamarypayoc, 1981. Cordillera Urubamba. On March 13, 1981 Tom Hendrickson, leader, Nan Starbuck-Boardman, Wendy Weeks, and I entered the Cordillera Urubamba from the village of Tostayoc on the main Cuzco-Quillabamba road. We established Base Camp across from the beautiful pyramid peak of Cucullani. After a day of reconnaissance we were able to move up and establish a snow camp at 16,120 feet on the Helancoma Glacier. On March 15, 1981 we climbed a gentle "look-out" peak, very close to our camp, with an altitude of approximately 16,500 feet. We later found out that the local name for this peak is Chaipiurco. On March 16, 1981 we climbed to the summit of Helancoma (5212 meters, 17,100 feet) which we found marked by an aluminum wand. (The Scottish expedition of 1964 called this the northeast summit of Huacratanca—as described in *The Andes are Prickly* by Malcolm Slesser). From the summit of Helancoma we could see a slightly higher peak to the south. We attempted a ridge traverse to this peak but turned back due to lack of time. The 1964 Scottish expedition had also tried this traverse, had gotten farther than ourselves, but were also turned back, in their case, "by a great gap." We came down off the mountain to our Base Camp and on March 17, we hiked over two 15,000-foot passes to the other side of Helancoma where we established a second Base Camp at Chaipiurco Pampa. From Chaipiurco Pampa, in approximately five hours of climbing, we successfully reached the summit we had seen from Helancoma. It was in fact higher than Helancoma (5273 meters, 17,300 feet) and was unmarked by wand or cairn. The locals from the collection of houses in Helancoma Pampa (just below Chaipiurco Pampa) call this peak Huamarypayoc. As pointed out by Evelio Echevarría in his "Survey of Andean Ascents 1961—1970," the Huacratanca peaks offer a confusing situation. Apparently the Huacratanca northeast peak has also been called northwest in other sources by members of the same expedition. (Echevarría records the 1964 Scottish ascent as being the Huacratanca northwest summit). John Ricker (*A.A.J.*, 1971, p. 410) reports climbing a peak "east of Helancoma and considerably lower" which he calls Huacratanca, East Peak, also locally known as Sayhua Orco. Ricker guessed the mountain to be 5000 meters (16,404 feet). The Polish Mountaineering Club reports (*A.A.J.* 1975, p. 173) that three of their members climbed "Helancoma Norte (17,717 feet)" on September 13, 1973, and the next day four members "traversed the two Huarcratanka summits (17,470) from south to north." Echevarría also points out that it has not been determined exactly what peak was ascended in 1953 by the Ghiglione-Marx party. It is my conclusion that there are two separate peaks—Helancoma, which was positively identified by the people living below the mountain in Helancoma Pampa; and Huacratanca, slightly to the south of Helancoma, and known to the locals as Huamarypayoc. Although Echevarría records the 1964 Scottish climb as being the northwest summit of Huacratanca, in fact they would have climbed Helancoma (probable first ascent). The Poles would have a second ascent, and ourselves a third. The Poles definitely seemed to have traversed Huacrantanca or Huamarypayoc. We would be credited with a new route (possible second ascent) on this mountain. Ricker's information is confusing because Huacratanca or Huamarypayoc is definitely higher than Helancoma, and the mountain Ricker climbed was "considerably lower" than Helancoma. Perhaps Ricker climbed Chaipiurco.

JOHN E. SAUNDERS, *Alpine Club of Canada*

Huayanay V, 1981, Cordillera Vilcabamba. In 1976 the Scottish expedition to the Huayanay Range indicated that three peaks remained unclimbed, namely Huayanay III (Nevado Palchaioj), Huayanay V (Huayallabamba) and Nevado Esquina. It appeared that Huayanay III and V were located behind the main range. At Kilometer 88 on the Cuzco-Quillabamba railroad, there is a valley running north with snow peaks at the end of it. On April 30, 1981, Steve Amstutz, Robert Randall and I set out from Kilometer 88. Tom Hendrickson and Nan Starbuck-Boardman followed two days later. We managed to get on a trail passing through the village of Jacas. On May 1 we established Base Camp at the head of the valley. On May 2 we crossed a 14,500-foot ridge behind Base Camp. The next day, departing at 2:30 A.M., Amstutz, Randall and I climbed Huayanay V in five hours of straightforward snow climbing. Henrickson and Starbuck-Boardman that same day put up an entirely different all-rock route on the same peak. Our altimeter showed 17,000 feet (5182 meters). A local called the peak "Quimsa Kocha Punta."

JOHN E. SAUNDERS, *Alpine Club of Canada*

Chullunko, 1981. On July 29, 1981 Peter Getzels and I established Base Camp just below the Palcay Pass at approximately 15,000 feet. The following day we climbed Chullunko (17,127 feet) by the rock ridge which runs virtually from the summit back to the pass. The majority of the climb was on loose, very rotten rock that was impossible to protect. Getzels went on to solo Salcantay over the next two days.

JOHN E. SAUNDERS, *Alpine Club of Canada*

Bolivia

Cordillera Apolobamba, 1981. From July 10 to 12, 1981 Alberto Campanile, Giuseppe Pierantoni, Giambisi, Della Fina and I climbed the three main summits, P 5430 (17,815 feet), P 5380 (17,651 feet) and P 5340 (17,848 feet), in the long snow ridge between Paso Sánchez and Paso Riti. They were difficult snow-and-ice climbs. The local Indians call the region Macaro. We then moved to the 15,425-foot Peluchuco Pass and climbed the following peaks alpine style: Peluchuco Huaracha (5650 meters, 18,537 feet) via west ridge in ten hours by Giambisi, Pierantoni and me on July 18, 1981; Catantica (5530 meters, 18,143 feet) via west face in nine hours by Giambisi, Pierantoni, Della Fina and Campanile on July 20; and Macchu-Sutchi-Cuchi (5679 meters; 18,632 feet) by west face in eleven hours by all five of us on July 22.

Ostilio Campese, *Club Alpino Italiano*

Llihirini I, Ancohuma, Illimani and Other Peaks, Cordillera Real. We three reached Base Camp in the northern Cordillera Real from La Paz after two days' drive and two days' walk. Stephen Venables and I climbed Viluyo I (5638 meters, 18,500 feet) on August 11 via the southwest ridge. Joined by David Wilkinson, on August 14 we ascended Hancopiti I (5867 meters, 19,249 feet) via the north glacier and west ridge and descended the northwest face. All three of us climbed Llihirini (5970 meters, 19,587 feet) up the steep névé of the south face and then we traversed with mixed climbing along the interesting east ridge on August 13. This traverse may be new. Venables and Wilkinson made a west-to-east traverse of Espalda (c. 5700 meters, 18,701 feet) on August 21. An attempt on the east buttress of Ancohuma was thwarted by rockfall during a bivouac which temporarily incapacitated Wilkinson and me. In the interim Venables soloed the southeast couloir and south ridge of Ancohuma on August 23, descending the north side. In late August I soloed Illimani, starting up the west ridge and then continuing more directly to the summit on the west face.

Lindsay N. Griffin, *Alpine Climbing Group*

Pico del Norte, South Buttress and Gorra de Hielo, Cordillera Real. In the late spring we climbed in the Cordillera Real and made several new routes from Base Camp on the east side of Illampu. Alain Mesili, Bernard Chaux and I took three days to climb the extremely difficult south buttress of the Pico del Norte (6085 meters, 19,955 feet) in 27 pitches. The first three were of vertical Yosemite-type granite, followed by a roof. We fixed this part in six hours on the first day and left equipment above the overhang. On the second day we jümared up the prepared section, climbed broken slabs and then mixed terrain to the summit cap. We descended the east face on snow by a new route. We made two new routes on the Gorra de Hielo (5700 meters, 19,701 feet). Michel Drapier and Mesili climbed the southwest ridge while Gaby Pellicot, Chaux and I ascended the west couloir, 1350 feet high and up to 60°. I descended on skis, belayed in parts.

Georges Bettembourg, *Club Alpin Français*

The Pupusani-Dasiri Group. The new highway from La Paz to the Yungas gives access to the impressive Pupusani-Kasiri group in forty minutes from the city limits. (Kasiri sometimes is called Rodolfo Gutiérrez.) These peaks are in the low 5000-meter class and are composed of steeply tilted hard grey sedimentary rock. There are small glaciers on the south sides. The prinicipal summits have been reached via scrambles on their back (north) sides, but all other exposures offer superb rock climbing and some ice. I did the south face of Pupusani on a Sunday last June by following the central ice sheet into a hidden fault-plane chimney or gully, starting in double boots and crampons and finishing in EBs and self-belays on iced and rime-coated rock. Lightning buzzed me off short of the summit, so I backed down an easier line to the west in a couple of rappels and some tedious downclimbing. I came back later with Oscar Fernández, owner of a pair of EBs and my only reliable climbing partner, this time to do Pupusani's long west ridge, a great climb as far as we got, because after three hours of speed-climbing third- to easy fifth-class rock, the weather dumped on us again as if we were in Patagonia and not sunny Bolivia. We bailed out to the north, thoroughly soaked.

STANLEY S. SHEPARD

Sancayuni West Face. Look up the Río Chekapa lobe of the Linco Valley and you will see Sancayuni (c. 5400 meters, 17,717 feet) with a west face half hanging glacier and half rock. On a Sunday last summer, Dave Bishop, Frank Zafran and I did the hanging glacier, a good line, direct but easy. Uncertain of whether the north or south peak was the higher, we selected the north. Of course the south was higher, by a couple of meters. On the same day, Len and Mireille Marks repeated my south ridge of Ventanani.

STANLEY S. SHEPARD

Useful information: To oversimplify, the biggest climbs in the Cordillera Real, as well as the best new material, will be found on the eastern side. This is inconvenient because most approaches are from the west; too, east-side weather is not as good, although still not very violent. Bolivian rock is underrated; there is an enormous amount of unexplored rock and mixed climbing. *Campesinos* attacked at least three parties, robbing one of everything, including boots and outer clothing, and attacking the other two with stones, resulting in one head injury. Although this is not common behavior in Bolivia, climbers should be alert, especially in the areas below Chearoco and Chachacomani and near the town of Achacachi, where civil strife is frequent. Campsite thefts have increased sharply, a result of desperate poverty and social problems. The very low prices current in Bolivia probably are temporary, the result of exchange-rate imbalances.

STANLEY S. SHEPARD

Chearoco west face, south and north summits. Rodolfo Grispo and I climbed the west face of Chearoco (6157 meters, 20,200 feet) in June. The face consisted of 55° frozen firn of excellent quality above a large icefall. We bivouacked at the base of the face at about 5200 meters. Our climb topped out near the south summit, which may have been unclimbed, and then we traversed to the higher north peak. A note about the approach: We entered via the towns of Kerani, Corpapacu and Chachacomani, typical indian villages. The road, which requires a sturdy vehicle, ends here, but you can easily hire pack llamas. Above the last village, we unfortunately encountered problems with a group of *campesinos.*

DANIEL BURRIEZA, *Club Andinista Mendoza, Argentina*

Rock routes near Huayna Potosí, 1981. Yves Astier and Olivier Mandrènes climbed four rock routes in the Huayna Potosí region from June 30 to July 7, 1981. Two of the climbs were on the south side of *Khala Cruz* (5240 meters, 17,192 feet), sometimes called "Ayallaco," south of the Zongo Pass. A third was the southeast ridge of Peak 5485 (17,995 feet), west of the Zongo Pass. The fourth was the north-central pillar on the west side of "Cerro Milluni," (5720 meters, 18,767 feet), the peak south of Huayna Potosí and prominent from the Milluni mine. The Zongo Pass area offers the best rock climbing near La Paz, on generally sound granite.

Nevado de Atoroma, Jachacunocollo or Jacha Collo, Gigante Chico, Cordillera Quimsa Cruz, and Other Peaks. Our expedition was made up of Heiko Metz, the Bolivian Jorge Morato, my wife Ria and me. We drove from La Paz via Patacamayo, Panduro and Caxata to the Atoroma Mine at 15,750 feet. From there we made the following ascents: Nevado de Atoroma (5600 meters, 18,373 feet) north of the mine via the southwest snow ridge on August 5; P 5600 (18,373 feet) via the northwest snow ridge on August 6 and "Pirámide de Atoroma" (5650 meters, 18,537 feet) via the western snow slope on August 8 (These two peaks are the second and third peaks on the ridge that runs southeast from Nevado de Atoroma to Gigante Grande. There was another summit between Pirámide de Atoroma and Gigante Grande, which we did not climb.); and Apacheta (5250 meters, 17,225 feet) south of the mine via the north rock ridge on August 7. From the Chojñacota Mine we climbed Jacha Collo as the locals call it or Jachacunocollo (5800 meters, 19,029 feet) via the west snow ridge and then traversed to the south over the neighboring P 5750 (18,865 feet) and P 5680 (18,635 feet) on August 9. On August 10 we climbed Gigante Grande (5750 meters, 18,865 feet) via its southwest snow ridge.

ANTON PUTZ, *Deutscher Alpenverein*

Argentina—Northern Andes

Nevado San Miguel and Other Peaks. In April 1979, an expedition of the Club Amigos de la Montaña, Salta, climbed San Miguel (c. 5400 meters, 17,717 feet), located south of Nevado del Acay. As expected, archeological remains were located on the summit. Its steep scree slopes are crowned by ice ridges above 17,300 feet. The ascent was repeated by N. and María-Alejandra Chocobar, A. Cruz and A. Choque (January 1980), by N. and J. Chocobar (February 1982) and by L. Aguilar, F. Lisi and A. Gómez, (April 1982). Also in the Acay area, Cerro San Jerónimo (5370 meters, 17,618 feet) and Cerro Verde (5490 meters, 18,012 feet) were ascended by E. Moretti and C. Vitry in December 1979. Both peaks are located southwest of the town of San Antonio de los Cobres, Salta and both ascents are believed to the first in modern times. The highest peak in the Nevados de Palermo received its first ascent on August 1979 by J. Echenique and E. Moretti. Identification of this peak is not clear. Official height is 6300 meters (20,670 feet), but other maps show the highest peak to be Cerro Quemado (6130 meters, 20,112 feet). Chilean maps closely agree with this height, registering a Cerro de las Honduras (6140 meters, 20,145 feet) as the highest in this range, located west of Poma summer resort, in Salta. Members of the Club Amigos de la Montaña also made several repeat but important ascents of Llullaillaco, Acay, Cachi, Piedra Sonada, Galán, Morado, etc.

EVELIO ECHEVARRÍA

Argentina—Central Andes

Aconcagua, South Buttress of South Summit. In January, a Slovene expedition of 15 members first spent ten days acclimatizing by climbing Mirador (5500 meters, 18,045 feet). They then split into three groups. The first, including a woman member, Tamara Likar, tackled the Polish east-face route and reached the summit on January 23. The second, Bogdan Biščak, Milan Črnilogar, Slavko Svetličič and Igor Škamperle, started up the south face to the left of Messner's route, joined the French route and finished the uppermost part on Messner's variant. They reached the summit on January 22 after four days of climbing. The third group, Zlatko Gantar, Pavel Podgornik, Peter Podgornik and Ivan Rejc, started on a new route, the south buttress of the south summit, well left of the usual south-face route, on January 20. Bad weather bothered them on the whole climb. For the first 3000 feet they could climb only at night when running water and rockfall were reduced by freezing. Only after three days did they reach the first good bivouac site. Because of the very rotten rock, they climbed on ice wherever possible. After passing séracs and climbing 55° ice to the base of the rock buttress, they traversed right on crumbling rock (UIAA V +) to reach steep ice. They next climbed a snow ridge to a red-rock barrier, which they found broken by a narrow, steep ice couloir. This gave access to the snowfield below the overhanging rock band which traverses the whole buttress. The seventh day was spent climbing some 65 feet of UIAA V,

A3 difficulty. They bivouacked twice at the foot of this section. All got over the barrier and the nearly vertical ice above on the eighth day. They climbed steep snow to the base of the final rock barrier where they had their eighth and last bivouac. On January 28 they climbed the rock barrier and snow summit ridge to reach the south summit. They descended the normal route.

FRANCI SAVENC, *Planinska Zveza Slovenije, Yugoslavia*

Vallecitos, East Face. Members of the Club Andinista Mendoza opened several new routes on peaks located in Mendoza province: Cerro Sosneado Sur (4800 meters, 15,748 feet) via southeast face by A. Randis in January; Cerro Laguna, (5034 meters, 16,515 feet) via southeast face, ice, by A. Randis, C. Santili, J. Vega in January; Cerro Vallecitos (c. 5550 meters, 18,209 feet) via east face, "Great Buttress" (*Gran Pilar*) by A. Randis, D. Rodríguez, E. Tarditti on January 31. This last route, graded as MD Sup., involved some 3400 feet of actual climbing on unstable rock and was accomplished in 11 hours from the base of the *pilar*. In the area east of Puente del Inca in the Relichos valley, D. Alto and D. Alvarez made the first ascent of Cerro Relincho (5150 meters, 16,897 feet) in January.

EVELIO ECHEVARRÍA

Chile—Central Andes

Marmolejo, North Face. Juan Pardo, Dagoberto Peña, Nelson Rivera, Cristián Peña and I made the first ascent of the 7000-foot-high north face of Marmolejo (6100 meters, 20,013 feet), which had resisted four previous attempts. On February 1 we climbed a spur of loose 50° rock and across *nieves penitentes* to camp at 15,750 feet. We then climbed a hanging glacier to camp a second night at 17,050 feet. On February 3 in twelve hours we climbed to the summit, ascending the 40° to 55° ice slope and a final 1250-foot rotten-rock face. We descended the same route.

IVÁN VIGOUROUX, *Federación de Andinismo de Chile*

Peaks in El Brujo Group. Two peaks belonging to El Brujo group, located at the head of the Maitenes valley, north of Tinguiririca river (Colchagua province) were ascended in early January by Chilean climbers. Besides other repeat ascents, F. Arias, J. Barrera, J. Rivera and F. Rodríguez reached the summit of a rock tower northeast of El Brujo, probably about 4700 meters (15,420 feet) high, or perhaps lower. Cerro Mirador de los Volcanes (c. 4400 meters, 14,436 feet) was ascended by J. Contreras, E. Lagos and L. Miranda. Both are believed to be first ascents.

EVELIO ECHEVARRÍA

Photo by Gino Buscaini
FITZ ROY's Super Couloir.

Chilean-Argentinian Patagonia

El Tronador and Catedral Group, New Routes above Bariloche. During January a climbing instruction and certification course was carried out on the Argentine-Chilean frontier. The course, organized by the Argentine Federación de Ski y Andinismo, was directed by me, who am a Spanish high-mountain guide. Thirteen of the best Argentine climbers took part. The skill of the group, the good weather and a camp on the glaciers of the Cerro Tronador facilitated a number of new routes, four on el Tronador and six in the Catedral group. We did the following on el Tronador: northeast ridge of the Argentine summit, mixed climbing, by Paul Cottescu, Daniel Horecky, Jerónimo López; variant of normal route via southeast face of International summit, ice, by Alejandro Randis, Alberto Tarditti; another variant of the same, ice, by Antonio Arko, Ariel Murtagh, all three on January 5; northwest face of Chilean summit, ice, by Jorge Arias, López, Randis, on January 6. The following were done on rock in the Catedral group: west face of the Torre Principal, by Pedro Friedrich, Randis; northwest face of the Torre Principal, by López, Tarditti, both on January 11; east face of Punta Philip Heron, by Randis, Tarditti; west face of Aguja Frey, by Arias, Cottescu, southeast spur of el Abuelo, by Friedrich, Horecky, Jorge Jasson, all three on January 13; wall below the Astilla, by Horecky, Randis on January 14. Before the course we did another new route in the Catedral group: the north spur of el Abuelo, by Alicia Barba, Jasson, López. Nearly all climbs are rated very difficult.

JERÓNIMO LÓPEZ, *Federación Española de Montañismo*

Interim Report on Patagonian Climbing in the 1982-3 Climbing Season. My husband Gino Buscaini and I were in Patagonia from the middle of November to the middle of January 1983. We attempted Fitz Roy three times, once by the Chouinard route and twice by the Super Couloir, but bad weather drove us back each time. While we were there, Slovaks climbed some 6500 feet up a difficult new route on the west face but had not got to the summit before we left, but they had joined the Chouinard route. On Fitz Roy there were Argentines, Yugoslavs, Japanese and Spaniards. On Cerro Torre there were French, Spanish and Swiss. A Spanish group led by Paco Aguado was trying a very daring route: a new ascent of Cerro Adela and then from there the traverse of Cerro Torre.

SILVIA METZELTIN BUSCAINI, *Club Alpino Italiano*

Fitz Roy and San Lorenzo, 1983. On January 15, 1983 the constant bad weather cleared, allowing two ascents of some importance. Slovaks led by Tibor Surka and including Michal Orolin, Vladimir Petrik, Zdenek Brabec and Robert Gálfy completed the first ascent of the 7000-foot-high west face of Fitz Roy, which they had attempted a year ago. (See below.) Climbers from Bariloche climbed San Lorenzo by the de Agostini route from the west. Tulio

Calderón, Oscar Orizzi, Guillermo Zampieri, Alex Scheuer, Jorge Rivera and Mario Gutiérrez Burzaco set out. Gutiérrez, who is 60 years old, waited on the foresummit while the rest continued along the summit ridge to the top. I don't have news of the other expeditions today (February 3, 1983). There are Japanese and two Slovenes on Fitz Roy and climbers from the Centro Andino Buenos Aires on the steep ice east face of San Lorenzo. [We hope to complete the accounts of climbs in the 1982-3 season in *A.A.J.*, *1984.—Editor.*]

VOJSLAV ARKO, *Club Andino Bariloche, Argentina*

Fitz Roy, West Face Attempt, 1981-2. From December 27 to February 17, 1982 we operated in the Fitz Roy area. We were Michal Orolin, leader, Daniel Bakoš, Zdeno Brabec, Vlado Petrik, Dušan Kovač and me. A month later Ivan Fiala, Juraj Weincziller and Vinco Dubeč, who had been on Aconcagua, joined us and assisted us in one of our attempts. On December 30, 1981 we erected Base Camp on the lake, Laguna Torre. We hoped to make a new route on the western face of Fitz Roy, continuing the unsuccessful attempt of English climbers in 1977. On January 1, five of us set off for the face. We climbed the lower 2300-feet in a day, despite carrying overloaded packs and hauling two more. We bivouacked on a large shelf under the prominent tower in the face. The rock sections had been very rotten and threatened with falling rocks. At night strong winds and rain rushed in. The next morning we descended in this appalling weather. It was dangerous to abseil down the western side amid the rockfall and so we rappelled down to the east, beneath the Super Couloir. We had to go for 40 kilometers around Fitz Roy from there, losing much strength on such a descent; during the time we were in the region, we repeated it three times. The bad weather we spent in Base Camp, relaxing. On January 9 it cleared. We set out immediately up the face but strong winds forced us to descend to Base Camp the next day. On January 21 the weather was better again. In one day we reached the high point of our last attempt and climbed higher. We bivouacked on a large ledge under the top of the prominent tower in the ridge leading to the face. The next day I climbed brittle flakes with Bakoš. We bivouacked under the huge rock corner, but already in the evening saw the storm over Cerro Torre, driven by a strong wind. While we arranged the bivouac, the wind grew stronger and we were not even able to draw out our sleeping bags. We slept in our clothes, covered only by thin bivouac sacks. In the morning the face was covered with a glaze of ice. We abseiled on frozen ropes down under the Super Couloir. In our next attempt from February 2 to 4 Orolin and Petrik climbed a rotten, overhanging corner, taking all day to make it. We hauled up packs. The last one was hauled up in the dark at two A.M. The next morning dawned windy and snowy. Angry and desperate, we abseiled off again. It was February 6 and we knew that we had time for only one more attempt. On February 12 it cleared suddenly. The next day we were above the corner. I climbed two pitches in the overhanging chimney. Its top was covered with ice. Then followed an icy groove and we were on shelves on the rim of huge flakes. I alternated leads with Brabec. He climbed five pitches in a long rising traverse. The last pitch was under the huge overhang.

It was late and so we rappelled to our companions, who had already prepared the bivouac. In the evening we saw heavy clouds over Cerro Torre. The wind did not calm down all night. Snow started to fall. In the morning strong winds and new snow forced us to descend. Billows of powdery snow were pouring over us while we abseiled. After many unpleasant incidents we were on the glacier under the west face. We found the tent on the pinnacle on the ridge completely destroyed; only the poles remained. We continued the descent from the ridge. On February 17 we left for home. The west face remains unclimbed.

ROBERT GÁLFY, *Iames, Slovak Mountaineering Association,*
Czechoslovakia

Aguja Guillaumet, East Face, Cerro Eléctrico Principal, Cerro 30° Aniversario Traverse and Attempt on Fitz Roy. My husband Gino Buscaini and I had our Base Camp at the Piedra del Fraile on the Río Eléctrico from December 13, 1981 to February 9. The weather in December was unsettled with a few good days, but from January to February 9 it was nearly constantly bad. On December 27, 1981, in good weather, we made a difficult (UIAA V, A2) route, 1500 feet in height, on the east face of the Aguja Guillaumet (2593 meters, 8507 feet). The route* ascended the middle of the face and ended up the edge of the snow summit triangle. On January 2 we were driven back from Fitz Roy's Supercanaleta (Super Couloir), first climbed in 1965 by Fonrouge and Comesaña. In rather poor weather we then on January 8 climbed the long, easy west ridge of Cerro Eléctrico Principal (2182 meters, 7269 feet). In cloudy weather on January 25 we again set out up the Supercanaleta and reached the first 1965 bivouac. On the 26th we climbed the couloir to about 650 feet from the summit of Fitz Roy but were stopped by hurricane-strength winds. On January 27 the continued violence of the wind forced us to descend the couloir under dangerous conditions. From February 2 to 4 we made the following trip: from the Piedra del Fraile up the Marconi Glacier to el Morro, across the Gorra Blanca Glacier up the south ridge of Cerro Neumayer, down to a tributary glacier of the Laguna del Diablo, traverse of the Cerro del 30° Anniversario from west to east to a col before the east foresummit, down the south face and back through the forest to the Piedra del Fraile.

SILVIA METZELTIN BUSCAINI, *Club Alpino Italiano*

Aguja Guillaumet. In checking ascents on the Aguja Guillaumet, we find several ascents which have not been mentioned in the *A.A.J.* Two routes near the Italian one were made by French climbers in 1968 which were reported in the *Annales du Groupe de Haute Montagne, 1969.* J. Coqueigniot and F. Guillot ascended the left-hand couloir on the right part of the east face which led to the north ridge, while Bernard Amy and P. Vidailhet climbed the right-hand couloir and also finished via the north ridge. In 1978 Argentines G.

---

*It seems likely that this was the route taken in 1979 by Jim Jennings and Robert Beager. See *A.A.J.*, 1980, page 598.—Editor.

Maioli and P. Castiarena climbed the northwest spur, the normal route. The Buscainis found a slip of paper on the summit which told of their ascent. Aside from the American 1979 ascent mentioned above, there are the following in the *American Alpine Journal: A.A.J.,* 1966, pages 76-7; *A.A.J.,* 1978, page 581; *A.A.J.,* 1980, page 599; *A.A.J.,* 1982, page 195.

Fitz Roy. West German Reinhard Karl (killed later in the spring of 1982 on the south face of Cho Oyu) and Spaniard Luis Fraga were plagued by the usual bad weather in Patagonia in late 1981 and early 1982. Over a period of two months, using the best of the weather, they made several attempts on the Super Couloir, one which brought them up some 3500 feet and the last of which took them to within 1000 feet of the summit at the top of the Couloir. There they encountered frightful weather. After three bivouacs and a severe slip, they had to admit defeat and rappelled down the couloir. Karl then joined with two Swiss, Peter Spiri and Toni Lüthi, on the American route. On February 14 they climbed from the Collado de la Silla to Karl's previous high point. The next morning they reached the summit.

Aleta del Tiburón, La Hoja, La Máscara and Other Peaks, Paine Group. Our joint expedition from the Universities of Grenoble and Santiago consisted of nine Frenchmen and seven Chileans. Our achievements were greater than our expectations. Patagonian weather has a bad reputation, but we were able to climb on part of most days. We made eight ascents and everyone made at least one ascent. We made the following climbs: *Aleta del Tiburón* (1800 meters, 5906 feet)* first ascent of the south ridge by Gilbert Banneville, Miguel Ignat and Denis Ravaine (French) on January 2; by west face (normal route) by Eduardo Párvex and Nelson Rivera (Chileans) on January 9; *Punta Catalina* (2100 meters, 6890 feet; west of Cabeza del Indio) first ascent of peak by west ridge by Gastón Oyarzún, Iván Ybaceta and Patricio Keller (Chileans) on January 2; *Cuerno Principal del Paine* (2600 meters, 8530 feet) by Rivera, Francisco Medina, Párvex and Iván Vigouroux (Chileans; see separate account below) on January 1 and 2; *la Hoja* (2200 meters, 7218 feet) first ascent of west face and south ridge (TD+) by Didier Boyrie, Denis Charron, Jacques Comparat, Jean Pilon and Alain Rebreyrend (French) on January 1, 2 and 5 (the climbers descended each night and had a two-day delay.); *Punta Quirquincho* (1800 meters, 5906 feet; north of Catedral) first ascent of peak by east couloir and north ridge by Ignat, Banneville and Ravaine on January 5; *la Máscara* (2300 meters, 7546 feet) second ascent of south face (ED+ with 1650 feet of artificial aid) by Boyrie, Charron, Comparat, Pilon and Rebreyrend on January

---

*The editors feel that these altitudes may be inexact. The altitudes here are those given by the French. There are no official altitudes to our knowledge for most of them. Cuerno Principal del Paine has been given officially as only 2110 meters or 6922 feet.

7 to 10; *"Pointe des Eboulis"* (1750 meters, 5742 feet; peak just east of la Espada) first ascent of the north face on January 10.

JACQUES COMPARAT, *Club Alpin Français*

Cuerno Principal del Paine. Nelson Rivera, Francisco Medina, Eduardo Párvex and I made the second ascent of the Chilean route and third ascent of the mountain on the Cuerno Principal (Main Horn) del Paine. On January 1 we climbed for four hours to bivouac amid huge granite blocks next to the peak. On January 2 we climbed a granite buttress which left us at the foot of the black rock final section. We went around the summit block to the north and rappelled onto the northeast face. The black rock was very rotten at first but got better as we ascended. There were eight rope-lengths of UIAA V and one of VI difficulty. This part of the climb took us six hours. On the summit we found a carabiner, apparently left by the American-South African second-ascent party in 1976.

IVÁN VIGOUROUX, *Federación de Andinismo de Chile*

ANTARCTICA

Monte Francés and Other Peaks, Grahamland. Sponsored by the Instituto Antártico Chileno an expedition of 19 climbers and scientists participated in the 18th Antarctic campaign that this institute carried out in the southern summer of 1981-2. The Osterrieth Mountains of Anvers Island were chosen as a suitable goal. Base Camp was established on Point Biscoe, where scientific work by glaciologists and geodesists (including two German engineers from Hannover University) was carried out with the support of the climbers. The mountaineering objectives were accomplished with the aid of two high camps on the ice, at 450 meters (1476 feet) and 750 meters (2460 feet) above sea level. After an approach march of 15 kilometers on skis, Gino Casassa and Dagoberto Delgado made the first ascent of the south summit of Monte Francés (2630 meters, 8630 feet) on January 27, by way of its northwest ridge. On February 5, Eduardo García, Félix Quiroz, and Jorge Quinteros climbed the main, northeast summit (2822 meters, 9259 feet), believed to be a second ascent (first ascent by an Argentinian party; *A.A.J.* 1968, page 231). On February 7, in a near blizzard Alejandro Izquierdo, Patricio Toro and Abelardo Velásquez climbed the imposing peak of Monte Egregio (1300 meters, 4265 feet). Monte Williams (c. 2000 meters, 6561 feet), the most attractive peak in the Osterrieth, was next. On February 15, Delgado, Izquierdo, Toro and Velásquez, plus Andrés and Cedomir Marangunić climbed it by its northeast ridge. Two days later, leader Quinteros and Casassa climbed the steep southwest wall and ridge, which was occasionally crowned by snow mushrooms. A bivouac had to be placed at 1750 meters (5740 feet).

HUMBERTO BARRERA, *Club Andino de Chile, Santiago*

EUROPE

International Meet, La Bérarde, France. Seven countries were represented at the meet, Great Britain, Netherlands, Yugoslavia, Sweden, Turkey, Spain and the United States. The hospitality of the French Alpine Club was excellent, providing us with as much help, information, food and wine as we could possibly need. La Bérarde is a beautiful, remote town nestled in the Dauphiné Alps. Being an abnormally warm, dry summer prior to our arrival, the ice climbs were out of condition but the rock climbs were in reasonable shape. Although the weather consistently deteriorated during our stay, Kurt Winkler and I, representing the American Alpine Club, did two climbs. Our first was the northwest Pillar of the Dôme de Neige des Ecrins (TD, 1000 meters). In the last few days we did the Davis-Gervasutti route on the north face of the Ailefroide (D, 1050 meters). Referred to as the Walker Spur of the Dauphiné, technically easier though more serious, it has to rank as one of the finest climbs I have ever done.

STEVEN LARSON

International Women's Climbing Meet, Britain. The Women's International Rock Climbing Meet, sponsored by the British Mountaineering Council, took place in Britain between June 12 and 26. Representatives from Denmark (1), Norway (2), Sweden (1), France (3), Italy (2), the United States (2) and Ireland (1) participated in the meet, and were accompanied by about 20 British women climbers who served as hosts for varying lengths of time. The meet assembled in London, where we spent most of the first two days. June 12 was consumed by the task of collecting all the representatives in one place; by evening we were all located and had dinner together. Day 2 we visited a climbing wall and a sandstone top-roping site south of London called Harrison's Rocks. We left London on the morning of June 14 to spend four days in the Peak District, four days in Wales, and three days in the Lake District. The general format of the meet was quite informal. Generally we visited a different crag or cliff each day and a visitor would pair off with one of the British women to climb for the day. These partnerships were formed on the basis of climbing ability and a generally shared desire to meet and climb with a variety of the participants. Transportation, food and lodging were provided by the BMC. We travelled in two vans and whatever cars were available at a given time. We stayed in climbing club huts, which were very comfortable accommodations. Mark Hutchinson did all the food shopping while we climbed, but participants shared in the food preparation tasks. Generally breakfast and lunch were informal, with dinners being a shared, sit-down meal. We did eat in restaurants on a number of occasions, including an elegant dinner provided for us by Karrimor at a Victorian-style dining establishment (for which we were perhaps a little scruffy). My overall impression of the meet was very favorable. It provided me with a unique opportunity to meet other women climbers, to visit a new place and make important contacts. I feel it is a trip which will continue to be a part of my life for a long time to come. I am already making plans to climb with women I met on the meet. Catherine Freer and I appeared to be doing the hardest climbs of any of the visitors; the British women were most closely matched with us of the other participants. Catherine and I apparently did some first female ascents during our visit, although this was never firmly established. I would have preferred for there to be less of a gap in ability among the participants, so that I could have climbed with more of the women and still tried the climbs that interested me. This type of meet seems a really worthwhile undertaking. My major recommendations would be to limit group size to 12 to 15 participants and strive for a narrower range of ability among the participants. Otherwise, it was a memorable experience that I am pleased to have shared with others.

Rosie Andrews

British Mountaineering Council Meet. Mark Hutchinson, our British Mountaineering Council host, has a most enjoyable and charismatic personality and did an unsurpassable job of organizing the meet and in particular of arranging an itinerary which allowed us a sampling of a wealth of crags in a relatively short time. The BMC reserved a hut in Capel Curig for our week in North Wales and a hut near Matlock for our week in the Peak District, a complex area of hills and valleys near Sheffield. The latter has limestone in the valleys and gritstone on the ridges of the hills. We took day excursions from these huts and returned each night. Meals were prepared as a group, using the hut facilities, Especially enjoyable were the several evening meals we had at fish-and-chips shops, Indian Tandoori restaurants and other typically British eating places. Transport was via a rented van combined with several private cars belonging to British participants. This allowed us to split up when consensus dictated and visit several crags simultaneously. Climbing with many of Britain's top climbers, I feel we all developed an appreciation not only of the distinctly bold style and high standard of climbing but also of the intense social scene in British climbing, due in part to the great number of active climbers combined with the limited size of the country. Climbers frequently travel to all parts of the country and are very much aware of and keenly interested in what others are accomplishing. This fosters a strong sense of competition among British climbers which is lacking in the United States. I personally was able to do 34 different routes of high standard, from 5.10a to 5.12b. The BMC graciously treated us to several evenings in the pubs, allowing us to appreciate these social gathering spots as well as to taste the legendary beer! Those representing the American Alpine Club were Douglas Madara, Randy Vogel, Maria Cranor, Kjell Swedin, Dan Lepeska and I.

Alex Lowe

AFRICA

Kilimanjaro, Western Breach. On September 16, Harold Knutson and I ascended and descended this route next to the Arrow Glacier. Beginning at the rarely used 12,500-foot roadhead on the Shira Plateau (only four parties signed in at the national park gate in the previous six months), we reached the main summit of the mountain, 19,340-foot Uhuru Point, in seven hours, then regained the roadhead in four-and-a-half hours. Local climbers later told us that this was the first one-day round-trip up and down Kilimanjaro. A major contributing factor was our footgear. The use of new Nike trail shoes enabled us to wear the same footgear for crossing glaciers up high and for running trails down low. Also, neither of us had the slightest sign of headache or altitude sickness, which we attribute to rapid descent and minimal time up high. We left Moshe at 3500 feet one afternoon, slept at 12,500 feet, and returned to 3500 feet just 15 hours after the start of the climb.

GALEN A. ROWELL

Batian, Mount Kenya. Our group consisted of Juan Carlos Robla, Pilar Fernández, Teresa Marchán, Luis Suárez, Nando Marné, Luisa Alonso, César de Prado, Angeles García, Angeles Navarro, Paco Gómiz and me. After several ascents of Lenana by the normal route and Point Peter by the difficult east face, on July 12 Suárez, de Prado, Marné and I made a new route on Batian on the north face. Our route was between the west ridge and the north glacier. On July 14 Marné, de Prado, Gómiz and I climbed the Firmin-Hicks route on Batian.

ISIDRO RODRÍGUEZ CUBILLAS, *León, Spain*

ASIA

India-Sikkim

Kabru Dome, Sikkim. The Indian Mountaineering Foundation sponsored an expedition to Kabru Dome (6600 meters, 21,654 feet) through the Himalayan Mountaineering Institute of Darjeeling. It was one of the selection camps for the members, both men and women, to be chosen for the Indian Everest Expedition in 1984. Kabru Dome had been attempted three times in the past: by two British expeditions, the first led by N.A. Tombazi in 1925 from the Alukthang Glacier and the second led by C.R. Cooke in 1935; and by an Indian expedition led by B. Biswas in 1964 whose claim of ascent is not accepted as valid. The 30-member IMF expedition, under the leadership of Colonel D.K. Khullar, Principal of the HMI, set up Base Camp near the snout of the East Rathong Glacier on September 14 at 14,500 feet. Advance Base was established on the true left medial moraine, where the Kabru Dome icefall meets the glacier at 15,800 feet. The icefall was the biggest obstacle. Up to Camp I at 18,000 feet, we skirted the icefall mostly via a rock gully to the true right of it. Three days were spent finding a route through the upper icefall above Camp I. We were finally divided into three groups. The first group worked on the route while the other two stocked Advance Base and Camp I. The first group occupied Camp II at 20,000 feet above the icefall on September 20. Unfortunately due to whiteout and weather, they were unable the following day to make the summit. The second group occupied Camp II on September 23. Climbing on the southwestern flanks and finally gaining the south ridge, Mahabir Thakur, T. Lobsang, K.N. Singh, Gautam Dutta, Umeshwari Devi (the only woman) and P. Bhotia reached the summit at 12:30 on September 24. The third summit party managed to put Captains R.S. Sandhu and B.S. Rai, Manik Banerjee, P.P. Gautam and Ki Kami Sherpa on the peak on September 26.

YOUSUF ZAHEER, *St. Stephen's College, Delhi, India*

Nepal

Kanchenjunga. Reinhold Messner, Friedl Mutschlechner and Sherpa Ang Dorje reached the summit of Kanchenjunga on May 6 without the use of artificial oxygen. They climbed the north face and north ridge, partially on the Japanese route, partially new. They had two camps and above them, two bivouacs. In making this ascent, Messner reached the summit on his seventh different 8000er. On the descent, Mutschlechner suffered a frozen right hand and left foot and had to be flown back to Austria for treatment.

MICHAEL J. CHENEY, *Himalayan Club,* and ELIZABETH HAWLEY

Kanchenjunga, Normal Route. Our expedition was composed of Franco Garda. climbing leader, Lelio Granier, Oscar Tayola, Riccardo Borney, Abele Blanc, Giuliano Sciandra, Oreste and Arturo Squinobal, Pietro Ferraris, Vittorio Mangili, Sergio Mezzanzanica, Giuliano Trucco, Luigi Pession, Innocenzo Menabreaz, Eliseo Cheney and me as expedition leader. We had hoped to climb the main peak by the previously unattempted southwest face, along the center buttress starting at the end of the great sickle. Unfortunately heavy snowfall and bad weather during the first part of the ascent prevented this. We therefore decided to repeat the normal route, first climbed by the English in 1955. We left Dharan with 300 porters on March 10 for the 17-day approach march to Ramser. After some days in Ramser because of heavy snowfalls, we started up to the Yalung Glacier, placing three intermediate camps: Glacier Camp at 15,750 feet, Kuna Camp at 15,825 feet and Intermediate Base Camp at 17,050 feet. We set up Base Camp on April 2 at the foot of Kanchenjunga's south face. For the first few days we explored the area and then followed the route of previous expeditions. Camp I was installed at 20,850 feet at the top of the first ridge on April 8. The approach to Camp II was more complicated; we had to descend for 650 feet into a very steep and dangerous gully, then cross a crevassed glacier and ascend a second ice wall. Camp II was made at 22,650 feet on April 20. Camp III was placed at the beginning of the sickle at 23,950 feet on April 26. Camp IV at 24,950 feet at the end of the long snow ramp was composed of three small bivouac tents, set up on April 28. Cheney, Menabreaz, O. Squinobal, Ang Chopal and Nga Temba set out for the summit on May 2. At 26,900 feet Cheney and Ang Chopal gave up, while the other three reached the summit (8598 meters, 28,208 feet) at four P.M. Nga Temba and Squinobal did not use artificial oxygen. They were back in Camp IV at nine P.M., while the other two descended to Camp II. Two days later the weather turned bad with heavy snowfalls and we gave up all further attempts.

RENATO MORO, *Club Alpino Italiano*

Omi Kangri. Our joint Japanese-Nepalese expedition was composed of Kotaro Nakajima, Yoshinori Suzuki, Shinichi Kohara, Michio Maki, Jun Goto, Ms. Michiko Suzuki, Hideichi Gomi, Dr. Junichi Shioda and me as leader, *Japanese,* and Nawang Khroklang, Ang Temba and Ang Kalden, *Nepalese.* Omi Kangri is located on the border between Nepal and Tibet, northwest of Kanchenjunga, at the head of the Yangma Khola, from which the Tamur River springs. One finds no report of climbing there. There are many virgin peaks over 6500 meters in the Yangma Khola. On April 3 we set up Base Camp at 16,400 feet on the right bank of the Pandra Glacier after 17 days of approach from Dharan Bazar. Since it was impossible to climb the glaciers on either side of the south ridge because of 1000-foot icefalls in the lower parts and crevasses higher, we climbed the south ridge itself. There were slabby rock cliffs low and bad snow conditions higher. On April 9 we set up Camp I at 18,875 feet on the south ridge. Above Camp I we fixed 1500 feet of rope on the steep ice face and narrow snow ridge to reach the foot of the buttress. We traversed around the foot of the buttress and climbed a snow gully to set up Camp II at 20,000 feet on the snow ridge on April 18. Camp III at 20,850 feet was placed on April 27 on the snow plateau after climbing past crevasses and a snow wall. The ridge continued to the summits. There are three summits: east, central and west. The central summit is 100 feet higher than the other two. On April 29 Nakajima, Gomi, Nawang Khroklang and I reached the east peak as the first summit party. However, fierce winds and snow prevented our going to the central summit. On May 1 the second bid was made by Y. Suzuki, Kohara and Ang Temba. They reached the central peak in four hours from the east peak. The Nepalese Ministry of Tourism reports Omi Kangri as being 7922 meters (25,991 feet) high. Other maps give it as 7028 (23,059 feet). Our altimeter broke before we got to Camp III (and we feel that Camp III may be higher than we recorded it). We can infer the height of Omi Kangri by comparisons with other peaks. It is lower than Jannu (7710 meters). It seems as high or a little higher than the Twins (7380 meters). It is nearly as high as

Jongsang Peak (7473 meters). It is much higher than the Outlier (7090 meters). Our opinion is that Omi Kangri is about 7400 meters (24,279 feet).

Toshio Kaneko, *Tokyo Metropolitan Government Alpine Club*

Jannu, North Face Attempt. Unfortunately we did not succeed on the north face of Jannu (Kumbhakarna) in spite of eight weeks on the mountain. We stopped at 23,300 feet, still three days from the summit as we calculate it. It was the most moving experience I have ever had in the Himalaya because of the harshness of the wall. None of us had ever seen such a cold, steep face. In October there was no sun at all except for three to four hours a day at Camp I. The last 3000 feet were like the Cima Ovest's north face in the Dolomites with much overhanging in the last 1500 feet. When we discovered how smooth this part of the face was, we headed for the northeast ridge, which we would have reached at 24,000 feet. We were unlucky. First, Patrick Benhault left us at the beginning, judging the face too harsh. Our two Sherpas couldn't carry beyond 21,000 feet and we five remaining climbers had to carry everything. This year the weather in October was very bad. A meter of snow fell on Camp I on October 20. All camps were destroyed. I tried to solo to the ridge on October 26. Because there were no more camps on the mountain at that time, the liaison officer forbade the expedition to continue and I had to come down.

Pierre Beghin, *Groupe de Haute Montagne*

Makalu, Solo Winter Attempt. Frenchman Ivan Ghirardini attempted first the very difficult west buttress of Makalu in winter. After a first sortie, on January 7 he bivouacked at 19,350 feet and on January 8 at 22,000 feet. On January 9 he reached 23,000 feet, but the wind and cold were so severe that he had to give up, despite good climbing conditions. He estimated winds to be up to 125 mph and temperatures down to $-50°$. He then turned to the normal route before being turned back again at 23,000 feet by the severity of the weather.

Makalu, Southeast Ridge to East Face. Our sixteen-member expedition, which included scientists and three reporters, made a new route variation on Makalu. The leader was Ham Tak-Young. Because of customs delays in Calcutta, we did not set out from Tumlingtar until March 16. The advance party reached Base Camp on March 30. On April 2 they set off preparing the route up the icefall and established Camp I at 17,725 feet on the 5th and Camp II at 19,350 feet on the 8th. The main party got to Base Camp on April 10. Camp III was established at 21,925 feet on April 15. We pitched Camp IV at 23,625 feet. Just below the Black Gendarme was a steep, avalanche-prone slope but we managed to set up Camp V at 24,275 feet there. We left the Japanese route there and went out onto the east face. On May 19 we established Camp VI at 25,250 feet on the upper part of the east glacier, chiseled out of the steep ice. Young Ho-Huh and Sherpas Pasang Norbu and Ang Phurba set out at 4:30

A.M. on May 20 and reached the summit (8481 meters, 27,825 feet) at two P.M. They found a plastic toy on top which had been left there in October 1981 by the solo Polish climber Kukuczka. They had climbed the very steep east face directly toward the summit onto mixed terrain and then onto the sharp rocky east ridge. There was a needlelike summit just before the real summit. Young and Ang Phurba used artificial oxygen on the ascent only. On the descent one of the Sherpas slipped and they all fell 350 feet but fortunately no one was injured. Our route was shorter and quicker than the Japanese route. A second summit attempt had to be called off because of bad weather.

Seung Mo Shin, Korean Alpine Club

Makalu, West Face. A Polish-Brazilian expedition climbed the 8000-foot-high virgin west face of Makalu. Since Wojciech Kurtyka and Alex MacIntyre had twice attempted it, all eyes have been on this face. The team, led by Adam Bilczewski, consisted of 17 Poles and three Brazilians. The only Sherpa was sirdar Ang Kami. The team climbed the prominent left buttress of the face, which was difficult but free from rockfall and avalanches. Base Camp was established from August 28 to 31 at 17,700 feet. On September 2 Camp I was placed at 19,700 feet above the dangerous icefall. There the steep face began, involving mixed ice-and-rock climbing. Two camps were set up on the buttress: Camps II and III at 21,650 and 23,300 feet on September 11 and 19. The section above Camp III was very hard (UIAA V +, AO), but the crux of the route was at 24,600 feet. A vertical, and in places overhanging, rock band of some 350 feet was most difficult. Tragedy struck when Tadeusz Szulz was fixing ropes and suddenly died of a heart attack. Having completed the greatest difficulties, the members decided to continue. On October 7 Janusz Skorek and Andrzej Czok reached the north ridge, on which the Polish route had been pioneered in 1981 by Jerzy Kukuczka solo. Camp IV at 26,250 feet was established. They slept using artificial oxygen. The following day this pair made the first summit attempt, but extreme cold and winds made the climbing impossible. Skorek's fingers were frozen and the next day he descended with Andrzej Machnik in doubtful weather. Czok remained at Camp IV waiting for better weather. He was without artificial oxygen. Base Camp tried to persuade him to turn back, but he insisted on a summit try. He spent the day and a third night at Camp IV. On October 10 the weather was suitable and Czok set out alone and, without oxygen, followed Kukuczka's north ridge route. At 12:45 P.M. he reached the highest point of Makalu (8481 meters, 27,825 feet). The weather was fine and he sat for 40 minutes on top. He returned that same day to Camp III, having been over 8000 meters for three days and nights, using supplemental oxygen only during the first night. The weather was now favorable, but Bilczewski did not agree to further ascents because of the difficulty of the route. Ang Kami reached Camp I and the three Brazilians Camp II. This was the 19th ascent of Makalu and the second Polish one. The west face *direttissima,* pioneered by Kurtyka and MacIntyre remains for future expeditions, but the Polish climbers consider the route possible.

JÓZEF NYKA, *Editor, Taternik, Poland*

Makalu Attempt and Baruntse. Our expedition reached Base Camp at 16,075 feet on September 8 after a 10-day approach. We placed Advance Base at 17,400 feet on September 17. The Makalu group, Jean Troillet, Yves Rausis and I, had hoped to climb the difficult west-buttress route of the French in alpine style, while Claudio Righeschi, Rudolf Homberger, Marie Hiroz, Patrizia Barbuiani, Patrizia Riva and Vreni Kull climbed Baruntse. We worked our route on Makalu's west buttress up to 24,275 feet, where the greatest difficulties begin. On October 4 we three set out from Base Camp for a final push on the route, but on the 6th Rausis' health made him decide to give up the attempt. With only two climbers, one leading without a pack and the other hauling everything, it was obvious that we could not continue. Troillet and I decided to try a new route on Makalu's west face on the left edge, both being well acclimatized. On October 13 we left Base Camp for Advance Base. From there, with three bivouacs, we reached the north ridge where we bivouacked at 25,425 feet on the night of October 16. On the 17th we continued along the north ridge in bad weather to 26,250 feet, where we joined Kukuczka's route. Troillet waited there while I kept on alone to 26,900 feet, some 900 feet below the summit. We descended to 25,250 feet to bivouac. The weather on October 18 was worse and we descended Kukuczka's route to 21,000 feet. We reached Base Camp on the 19th. Meanwhile the group on Baruntse had been successful. Homberger reached the summit (7220 meters, 23,688 feet) on October 2 alpine style. The route on the south ridge was mostly without notable difficulties except for a traverse of 650 feet at 22,650 feet, which had 60° ice. On October 9 Marie Hiroz and Claudio Righeschi also reached the summit.

ROMOLO NOTTARIS, *Club Alpino Svizzero*

Makalu. Japanese climbed Makalu from the north with four high camps. The route was more direct to the northwest ridge than the standard route. On September 30 leader Kazuo Yuda, Makoto Ishibashi and Dr. Yukihiro Michikawa climbed to the summit without artificial oxygen.

MICHAEL J. CHENEY, *Himalayan Club,* and ELIZABETH HAWLEY

Kangchungtse (Makalu II) Attempt. A Spanish Basque expedition was led by Carlos Ochoa and composed of Iñigo Barandiaran, Imanol Ollaguindía, Juan Oyárzabal and Atxo Apellaniz. They attempted the south ridge of Kangchungtse (7640 meters, 25,066 feet), placing two camps at 17,400 and 20,350 feet above Base Camp before continuing alpine-style with two more bivouacs at 21,650 and 23,000 feet. They reached 24,125 feet on April 21 but quit because of snowfall, wind and exhausted food supplies. They brought too little money and bought insufficient food in Nepal because of a shortage of funds.

MICHAEL J. CHENEY, *Himalayan Club,* and ELIZABETH HAWLEY

Ama Dablam, Winter Attempt. Our expedition sought to make an alpine-style winter ascent of Ama Dablam. We were Kurt Krueger, Steve Risse, Steve Jorgenson, Dan Murphy and me with Mark Knaebe as Base Camp manager. After troubles recruiting enough porters for the approach, we finally on December 3 established Base Camp at 15,800 feet. Relatively easy ground led to Camp I at 19,000 feet on the south ridge. Without Sherpa support, each team member had to make several carries before Camp I was occupied on December 9. Unexpectedly Murphy left the expedition on the 11th. Above Camp I interesting and varied rock climbing up to 5.7 along the ridge led to Camp II, established on top of the Red Tower at 19,700 feet on December 15. A mixture of rock (up to 5.8) and snow (50° to 60°) took us to Camp III at 20,700 feet. On December 22, Camp III was made on a snow plateau near the base of the summit pyramid, but because of high winds it was moved the next day 200 feet lower. The first summit bid was made on December 24 by Risse, Jorgenson, Krueger and me. Low temperatures and high winds made the 60° snow climbing miserably exciting. We continued to 21,500 feet before retreating to Camp III. Krueger and I made a second summit try on December 26 but were again turned back by cold and high winds.

ROBERT SIEGRIST, *Wisconsin Hoofers*

Kwangde, North Face Winter Ascent. From November 28 to December 3 David Breashears and I made the first ascent of the north face of Kwangde (6194 meters, 20,323 feet) above the village of Hungo. The face is 4500 feet high and comprised of tongues and smears of thin white ice over boiler-plate granite slabs. The average angle (taken from the Schneider map) is 65°, exceptionally steep for an ice route. In the morning we'd peek out of our Bat tents to see the sun rise over Makalu's pink granite. During the day we could trace the trade route over the Nangpa La into Tibet. In the afternoon fingers of clouds crept up the valleys toward Cho Oyu, Everest and Lhotse. Supper was accompanied by alpine glow on the tip of Ama Dablam. We spent the fourth night hacking a cave from hard ice of an old cornice just below the summit. Inside the coffin-sized hole, we wondered if the wind would rip our home off the mountain, but we arrived on the summit early the next morning, convinced that we had completed what will become a hard modern classic climb. We descended in two days via the south face, over a notch in the southeast ridge, down its east face and finally around the toe of the northeast ridge to Hungo.

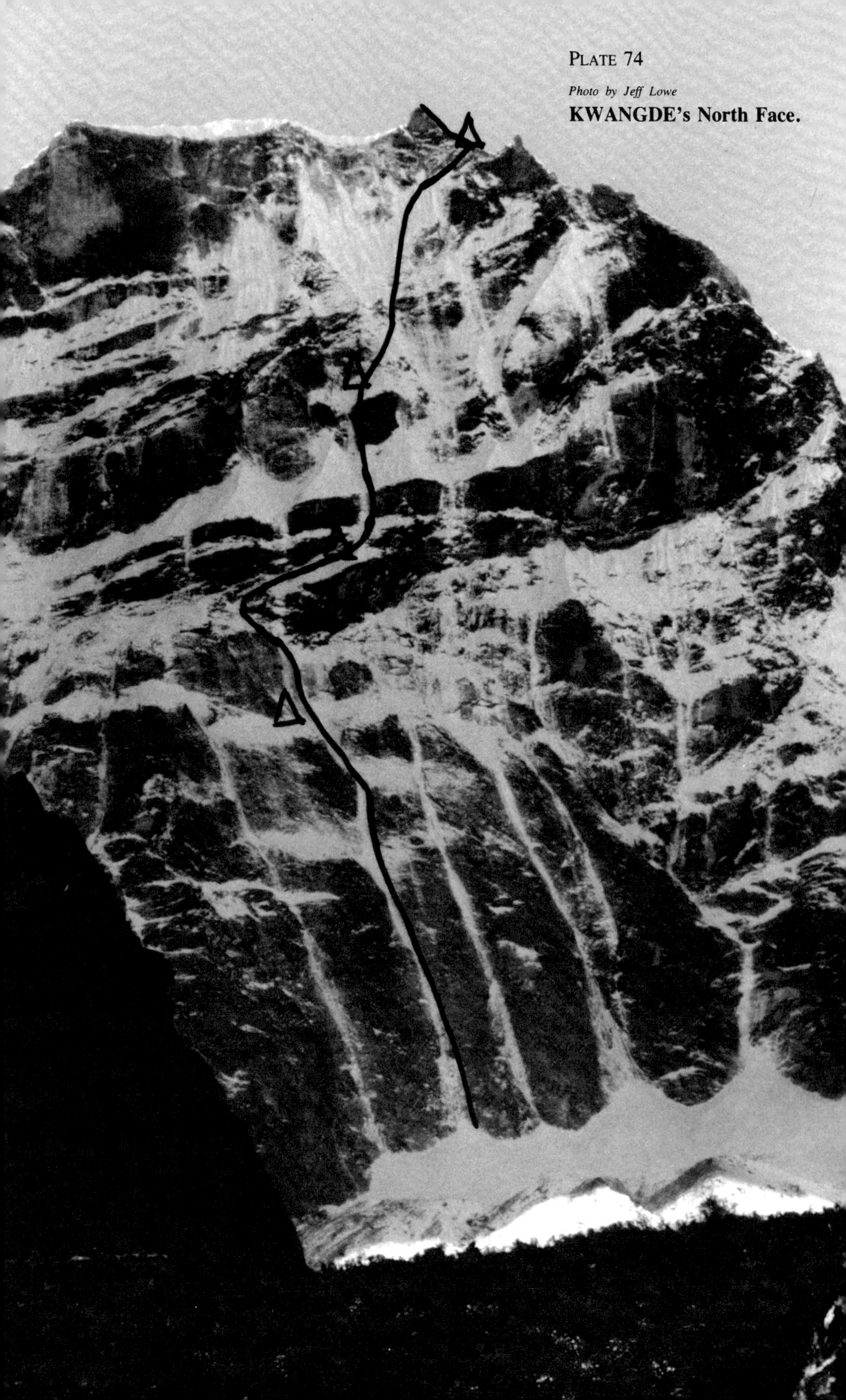

PLATE 74
Photo by Jeff Lowe
KWANGDE's North Face.

The weather was good during the climb with daytime temperatures of 15°F and nighttime ones of −5° to −10°F. Moderately high winds and spindrift early in the climb made us feel like salmon swimming upstream.

JEFF LOWE

Lhotse Shar Attempt. In the pre-monsoon period Hans Berger led a Swiss expedition that attempted Lhotse Shar (8383 meters, 27,504 feet) by its southeast ridge, the Swiss route of the autumn of 1981. Only the four-man team carried loads above Camp II (21,825 feet) since the Sherpas were unwilling to carry higher. They could get only to Camp III (24,450 feet) because of continuous deep snow and avalanche danger.

MICHAEL J. CHENEY, *Himalayan Club,* and ELIZABETH HAWLEY

Lhotse Attempt. Peter Hillary (New Zealand), Fred From (Australia), Paul Moores (U.K.) and I attempted Lhotse by the normal west-face route. We were sharing the route through the Khumbu Icefall with a large Canadian expedition intent on climbing the South Pillar of Everest. The Canadians fixed the route through the icefall and we were under contract not to enter this section until they had reached Camp I at 19,200 feet. On August 31 and September 2, two separate accidents took the lives of three Sherpas and one Canadian. This threw them into turmoil and they asked permission to change to the South-Col route. Our routes were to be common until 25,600 feet. Our light-weight expedition was to be swamped beneath fixed ropes and Sherpas. Continuing bad weather in early September prevented any progress. On September 16 Camp I was established and Camp II was placed in the Western Cwm at 21,500 feet on the 20th. Camp III was lower than normal at 23,300 feet but we used it rarely because we usually went from Camp II onto the Lhotse Face in order to fix rope. On October 7 we moved up to 26,000 feet and established Camp IV. Our summit try was on October 8. A long traverse rightwards led to the summit gully. At 27,000 feet we were hit by a sudden snowstorm and strong winds. The increasing bad weather forced us to stop and descend. Our expedition did not use oxygen and cost $15,000.

ADRIAN BURGESS, *Alpine Climbing Group*

Nuptse and Thamserku Attempts. Three Scots led by Malcolm Duff attempted the west ridges of both of these peaks in the post-monsoon but reached only 20,175 feet on Thamserku and 22,000 feet on Nuptse. One climber failed to acclimatize and technical difficulties on both peaks meant slow progress for the other two.

MICHAEL J. CHENEY, *Himalayan Club,* and ELIZABETH HAWLEY

Nuptse Attempt. Hans-Burkhard Nix led an unsuccessful German attempt on the north face of Nuptse; they had hoped to repeat the Doug Scott route. They arrived late in the post-monsoon season and gave up after twelve days at 21,325 feet before reaching the face because of worsening conditions in the Khumbu Icefall.

MICHAEL J. CHENEY, *Himalayan Club,* and ELIZABETH HAWLEY

Mount Everest, New Route on Southwest Face. The objective of the expedition was to climb Mount Everest by a new route on the southwest face to the left of the Bonington Couloir. The expedition consisted of 25 members: 17 climbers, camera crew, a doctor, a radio man. The leader was the well known Soviet climber, Evgeny Tamm. Base Camp was established by an advance group on March 16 at the traditional place, the Khumbu Glacier. By March 21 when the main party arrived at Base Camp, the route through the Khumbu Icefall had been prepared by the same group of five members led by the senior coach of the expedition, A. Ovchinnikov. Camps I (at the foot of the face), II, III, and IV were established at 21,325, 23,800, 25,750 and 27,050 feet on March 25, April 1, 10 and 22 respectively. Placing camps and preparing the route were carried out by the climbers. Ten high-altitude Sherpas led by Sirdar Pemba Norbu managed to carry loads to Camp II. Camp III was reached by only two of them. The strongest, Nawang, made an attempt to join the advanced group of climbers but had to give up because of the technical complications of the route. The route between Camps II and V is rated at 5 difficulty (Soviet classification). The most difficult stretch was the approach to Camp IV. Having established Camp IV, all climbers descended for rest to the Thyangboche Monastery. On April 27 Eduard Myslovsky and Vladimir Balyberdin set out from Base Camp to prepare the route above Camp IV. On May 3 they placed Camp V at 27,900 feet, 150 feet below the west ridge. On May 4 these two set out from Camp V and reached the summit at 2:35 P.M. Balyberdin did not use oxygen while climbing. While descending from the top, they were met by Sergei Bershov and Mikhail Turkevich, who were waiting for them with spare oxygen cylinders. Having left the oxygen, Bershov and Turkevich went on and reached the summit at 10:25 P.M. As they descended, they caught up with Myslovsky and Balyberdin and helped them to reach Camp V, which they all reached at six A.M. on May 5. On May 5 Valentin Ivanov and Sergei Ephimov got to the summit. On May 7 Kazbek Valiev and V. Khrishchaty attempted to reach the top from Camp V but were turned back by violent wind. Their second attempt was made in the evening when the weather seemed to be improving. They reached the summit on May 8 at 1:45 A.M. The last group of climbers consisted of Yuri Golodov, Vladimir

PLATE 75

Photo by USSR Sports Committee

The Soviet route on the Southwest Face of MOUNT EVEREST.

Puchkov and Valery Khomutov, who got to the summit on May 9 at 11:30 A.M. Thus a total of eleven Soviet mountaineers climbed Mount Everest by the most difficult route ever ascended by Everest climbers.

USSR Sports Committee

Mount Everest. Our team members were Lloyd Gallagher, John Amatt, Tim Auger, Robert Baillie, Alan Burgess, James Blench, Dwayne Congdon, Jim Elzinga, Roger Marshall, Dave McNab, Pat Morrow, Dave Read, Gordon Smith, Laurie Skreslet, Don Serl and I as leader, supported by Dr. Steve Bezruchka, Dr. David Jones, Kurt Fuhrlich, Blair Griffiths, Bruce Patterson and Peter Spear. We left on July 26 for the walk to Base Camp. Most of the food and equipment had been sent in ahead in the pre-monsoon and was stored at Namche and Periche. Two members went ahead to set up Base Camp and by August 15 the team arrived at a fully established Base Camp. The Nepalese authorities had given permission to prepare the icefall and to carry to Camp I between August 20 and the start of the official season on September 1. We used the time well and by August 30 we had 120 loads at the site of Camp I. At 5:30 A.M. on August 31 an avalanche from the west shoulder swept away three Sherpas and four members. The Sherpas were buried and killed whilst the members survived with minor bruises apart from Spear who was completely buried and was dug out suffering from a wrenched back. Two days later tragedy struck again. Griffiths, the cameraman, was killed by a falling sérac in the icefall. The expedition reeled under these heavy blows and it was decided that everyone reconsider his commitment to the climb in view of the high level of danger in the icefall. Auger, Baillie, Blench, McNab, Elzinga and Serl decided to leave. Dave Jones also left as he was not acclimatizing. The remaining climbers were held up by bad weather for a week. Permission was granted to change from the South Pillar to the South Col and the New Zealand expedition on the Lhotse face agreed to cooperate with us between Camps II and IV. On September 16 Camp I was reoccupied at 19,600 feet. Conditions were good and progress was rapid, with Camp II occupied at 21,400 feet on September 22 and Camp III at 23,400 feet on the 28th. On October 4 Skreslet, Read and Sherpas Sundare and Lakpa Dorje occupied Camp IV on the South Col. The following day Skreslet and the two Sherpas climbed to the summit, returning to Camp II the same day. Two days later, Morrow, Pema Dorje and Lakpa Tsering also made the summit. Two climbers, Gallagher on the first attempt and Burgess on the second, were thwarted by faulty oxygen; the latter reached 27,500 feet without artificial oxygen. All climbers returned to Base Camp by October 8.

WILLIAM MARCH, *University of Calgary Outdoor Pursuits*

Everest West Ridge Attempt. Our expedition was composed of Lluis Belvis, leader, Emili Civis, Manuel Mateu, Jordi Pons, Jaume Altadill, Oscar Cadiach, Narcis Serrat, Alfons Valls, Jordi Sugranyes, Xáxier Pérez Gil, Lluis Hortala, Josep Vidal Ponce, Antoni Llasera, Josep Casanovas, Francesc Sabat, Joan Ribas and me. The first group got to Base Camp on August 11. We reconnoitered and fixed ropes up the spur leading to the Lho La, following the Yugoslav route of 1979. We built an aerial tramway with a 5mm carrying cable, a 4mm traction cable, a 3-meter tower and a winch. This served between 19,000 feet and the Lho La at 19,850 feet and raised in all five tons to the Lho La. Early on September 7 we heard a terrific avalanche. A huge rock tower had crumbled and destroyed the final 650 feet of ropes and ladders of the route to the Lho La. The aerial tramway was not damaged. We found a new and easier route right of the Yugoslav one. On September 17 we established Camp II at 22,150 feet. The beginning of the route above Camp I was steep and we fixed ladders on an iced wall. On September 21 we placed Camp III at 23,450 feet near the top of the west shoulder. On September 27 we received word that Sherpa Lhakpa Tsering had died from a stomach perforation. This stopped progress while his body was evacuated and cremated. Camp IV was 1½ miles from, but only 1150 feet above, Camp III. Finally on October 6 four members slept there at 24,600 feet. Camp V was occupied at 26,575 feet on October 13 by Cadiach, Gil and Sherpa Nima Dorje. It was so cold (− 45°C) that on the 14th their headlamps would not work and they had to wait until four A.M. to set out with oxygen in a cruel wind. At midday they reached 27,900 feet but realized they could not reach the summit that day. While Cadiach and Gil made a snow hole to leave their oxygen cylinders, Nima Dorje started the descent. While out of sight of our two top climbers but in the sight of members in Camp I, Nima Dorje slipped and fell down the north side to his death on the Rongbuk Glacier. With continuing strong winds, it was decided to abandon the attempt.

Josep Manuel Anglada, *Centre Excursionista de Catalunya, Spain*

Mount Everest, Winter Attempt. Our expedition was led by Michel Metzger and composed of Marc Batard, Alain de Blanchaud, René Ghilini, Yves Laulan, Michel Mabilon, Michel Piola, Jean Bourgeois, Pierre-Alain Steiner, Emmanuel Schmutz and me. We got to Base Camp on November 21 and acclimatized until December 1. After eight days' work in the Khumbu Icefall, we got to 21,325 feet in the Western Cwm, but the icefall was in such bad shape that we asked for and were granted permission to change to the west ridge. Following the Yugoslavian route, we climbed to the Lho La in one day. We hauled loads with the Catalan winch, which was still in place. Camp I was in the col at 19,500 feet and Camp II at 23,000 feet. The winds were so strong that Batard and I could not get over 25,000 feet. Others wanted to make a final attempt. The Belgian Jean Bourgeois was accompanying four climbers on December 27 from the Lho La to Camp II. Fearing a headache and dizziness were signs of an oncoming cerebral edema, he chose to descend alone. Wanting to lose altitude as quickly as possible and not daring to rappel from the Lho La, he descended on the Tibetan side, reaching finally the deserted, ruined Rongbuk Monastery and after several days the first village. Eventually he was taken to Shigatse, where he was interrogated. The authorities allowed him to proceed on January 11 and drove him to the Tibetan-Nepalese frontier at Kodari. Although winter floods had washed out a part of the road, he walked across this and caught a bus for Kathmandu. My companions had feared him dead in a crevasse and searched six days for him. After they had returned to Kathmandu, he finally turned up "from the dead."

Louis Audoubert, Club Alpine Français

Everest Winter Ascent and Tragedy. Yasuo Kato, 33, was lost on Everest after becoming the first climber to reach the summit in a winter, solo attempt. His partner, Toshiaki Kobayashi, 34, who was following with bivouac supplies and met Kato just below the South Summit, also failed to return. This was Kato's third ascent of Everest. Kobayashi had been on expeditions to Dhaulagiri, K2 and Everest. The 7-man Japanese expedition accomplished its ascent in a very rapid 25 days. After establishing Base Camp on December 2, Kato reached the base of the South Col on December 22. In winter the main enemy is the frigid high-altitude jet stream which drops down to blast the mountain with force enough to send loose rocks sailing. Kato counted on the belief that the jet stream rises clear of the mountain every few weeks for two or three days. His plan was to launch an alpine-style attempt in that brief, calm period, with Kobayashi following in support. His first attempt on December 23 took him to 8100 meters before he was turned back by 50 to 60 kph wind and $-40°C$ temperature. Kato could hardly keep upright, and the batteries of his radio froze within 15 minutes. Kato's next chance came on the 27th. Using oxygen, Kato and Kobayashi left Camp IV at five A.M. At ten A.M. climber Yoshimasa Sasaki caught Kato's transmission reporting they had reached 8400 meters and discovered the body of a climber (Frau Schmatz?). At 7:30 P.M. Kato reported the following: He had reached the South Summit at 1:50 P.M. and the summit at 3:55 P.M., at which time it was almost dark. On his descent he had met Kobayashi, who carried 27 kilos (60 pounds) of bivouac supplies to the agreed upon campsite just below the south summit. By then it was already pitch dark and very cold. Kobayashi was slightly frostbitten. Sasaki asked if Sherpas should be sent up to the South Col in preparation for a possible rescue. "No, that won't be necessary," Kato replied. "Both of us are well, and we've got a good bivouac. I'll call you tomorrow at seven A.M." Kato's voice sounded confident and in good spirits. In each of his other two Everest ascents he had bivouacked above 8000 meters without equipment. Now being fully prepared, he expected no difficulties. That night a terrific storm and cold wave blew in. The Indian Mountaineering Foundation forecast winds of 150 to 200 kph (!) at Everest altitude, and a temperature of $-43°C$. The resulting cold wave caused the deaths of over 200 people in northern India. The jet stream dipped down enough to strip Camp II at 6600 meters off the mountain. The next day, in spite of terrific wind, Sherpa Noan Yonden was able to climb to the South Col in hope of helping the stranded climbers to descend. He saw no sign of them, nor any the following day. On December 30 the search was abandoned. Dr. Yasuo Sasa, the President of the Japanese Alpine Club, flew to Kathmandu with Kato's sister to attend the funeral of the two lost climbers. The Japanese speculate that because there was too little snow on the southeast ridge to dig a snow cave, the climbers were probably forced to seek shelter in the tent carried up by Kobayashi. The extreme force of the jet stream wind, they believe, had blown the tent and occupants down the mountain. Other Japanese Everesters expressed the opinion that no one would be able to climb the southeast ridge in the wind storms typical of the post-Christmas season. (This information was sent by the Japanese Alpine Club.)

THOMAS HOLZEL

Articles Resulting from the American Medical Research Expedition to Everest. Only two scientific articles have so far (February 1983) been published. They are:

West, J.B. "Man at Extreme Altitude." *Journal of Applied Physiology,* 52: 1393-1399, 1982.
West, J.B. "American Medical Research Expedition to Everest, 1981." *The Physiologist,* 25: 36-38, 1982.

Many articles are in the process of publication and the book *High Altitude and Men* edited by J.B. West and S. Lahiri should be published late this year or early next. An update will appear in the *American Alpine Journal,* 1984.

JOHN B. WEST, M.D.

Pumori. The four members of our expedition were Pierre Faivre, Jean-François Lemoine, Guy Mevellec and I, all mountain guides. We made an alpine-style ascent of the south ridge (French route of 1972) and descended the east ridge, the normal route. We left Kathmandu on September 14 and with 17 porters arrived at Base Camp after a 14-day walk from Kirantichhap. We spent eight days acclimatizing and reconnoitering the lower section of the normal route. On October 5 we placed a camp on the south ridge at 20,350 feet and then waited a full week for good weather. We all left Base Camp on October 14 and camped at 23,000 feet on October 17 at the head of the south ridge, which had been mainly a mixed climb with very sustained difficulties. We fixed the rock sections. On October 18 Lemoine and I reached the summit in a storm. Bad weather obliged us to spend another night at 23,000 feet. On the 19th the weather cleared and Faivre and I got to the top. All four of us descended the normal route in one day to Base Camp.

ERIK DECAMP, *Club Alpin Français*

Pumori, Winter Ascent. A three-man South Korean expedition made the second winter ascent of Pumori via the south ridge. The expedition leader Nam Sun-Woo and Sherpa Lhakpa Gyalgen left Camp II at 21,150 feet, bivouacked at 22,300 feet and reached the summit on December 11.

Cholatse Ascent, Taboche Attempt. A Swiss expedition was led by Dr. Heidi Lüdi. They climbed a new route, the southeast ridge, on Cholatse (6440 meters, 21,130 feet). They established three high camps. They reached the summit twice: on October 18 by Heidi Lüdi, Niklaus Alpiger and Kancha Tamang and on October 29 by Alpiger again and Werner Zäher. For the attempt on Taboche (6542 meters, 21,463 feet), they used the first two Cholatse camps and had no fixed camp higher. They reached 19,350 feet but then were forced to retreat because of deep snow.

MICHAEL J. CHENEY, *Himalayan Club,* and ELIZABETH HAWLEY

Numbur. A New Zealand expedition led by Peter McInally climbed Numbur (6954 meters, 22,815 feet) via the southwest ridge, the route of the French in 1981. They had an advance base and two high camps. On March 29 McInally, Rob Hall, Bill King, Steve Lassche and Gavin Tweedie reached the summit.

MICHAEL J. CHENEY, *Himalayan Club,* and ELIZABETH HAWLEY

Karyolung. A joint Nepalese Police-Japanese expedition was led by Yoshiyuki Inoue and Yogendra Thapa. After a brief try at the west ridge, they climbed the northeast face, where they placed two camps. On October 31 Inoue, Hiroshi Nishi, Masatoshi Isawa, *Japanese,* and Thapa and Baburam Tan, *Nepalese,* reached the summit (6681 meters, 21,920 feet). Later in the same day two Japanese and Nepalese Gorey Tamang, Gita Bahadur Joshi and Sherpa Pemba Tsering got to the top. On November 1, a third group including two Japanese women summited: Sohei Fuji, Yasuhiko Nakao, Kozuko Mainasaki, Makao Nishimara, Makio Nakahara and a Nepalese. This previously unclimbed peak is now open to foreign expeditions.

KAMAL K. GUHA, *Himalayan Club*

Karyolung, Winter Ascent. Another Japanese-Nepalese expedition climbed Karyolung, also by the northeast face, but this was done in the winter. Two Japanese, Akira Yamada and Katsuichi Tanaka, and two Nepalese members, Sherpas Ang Kami and Pemba Tshering, reached the summit on December 24. The leader was Hajime Nagatoshi.

MICHAEL J. CHENEY, *Himalayan Club,* and ELIZABETH HAWLEY

Ngozumba Kang Attempt. A joint expedition of four Frenchmen, two Belgians and three Sherpas led by Guy Cousteix attempted the south face of Ngozumba Kang (7806 meters, 25,610 feet). After establishing three camps, they abandoned the climb because of deep snow, reaching 23,000 feet on October 13.

MICHAEL J. CHENEY, *Himalayan Club*, and ELIZABETH HAWLEY

Ngozumba Kang. A South Korean-Nepalese expedition led by Park Dong-Gyo made the first ascent of Ngozumba Kang (7806 meters, 25,610 feet). They climbed the south face direct with four high camps. On November 2 Sherpas Ang Tsering and Dorje and South Korean Kim Yong-Han got to the summit.

MICHAEL J. CHENEY, *Himalayan Club* and ELIZABETH HAWLEY

Cho Oyu, South Face Attempt. Our expedition intended to climb the south face of Cho Oyu (8153 meters, 26,750 feet) which had first been climbed by Koblmüller's party in 1978. We had four members, the Austrians Wolfgang Nairz, leader, Rudi Mayr and me, and our German friend Reinhard Karl. We also had three Sherpa members and three high-altitude Sherpas. We flew to Lukla on April 12, and established Base Camp at 16,575 feet on April 18. On the following day I suffered from a slight form of pulmonary edema and tried an experimental treatment (nitroglycerin and positive end expiratory pressure). Subsequently my lungs cleared, but I fell into deep unconsciousness due to high-altitude cerebral edema. I was brought down by my friends and evacuated by helicopter to Kathmandu. Due to a subsequent pulmonary embolus I had to return to Europe. Between April 24 and May 6 Karl, Mayr and Nairz established Camp I at 19,350 feet and Camp II at 21,325 feet in the lower part of the face. It was very difficult to find a more-or-less secure route and the climbing involved long pitches of steep and sometimes vertical ice. Progress was slowed by repeated snowfall. The final summit attempt was started on May 17. Nairz and Karl spent the night of May 18 in Camp II, which was located underneath an almost vertical ice face with no séracs. The Sherpas occupied a tent 10 meters apart from my friends. On May 19 at five A.M. an ice avalanche, which originated roughly 2000 feet above the camp, buried the tent of Nairz and Karl. The Sherpas' tent was spared. The Sherpas started to dig immediately and found Reinhard Karl after 20 minutes. He was dead due to head injuries. Subsequently they found Nairz who was unconscious and had a broken leg. He regained consciousness within an hour and managed to climb down the face with the help of Rudi Mayr and the Sherpas. Reinhard Karl was an outstanding mountaineer (both physically and mentally) and a very close friend. He certainly was the most successful German all-round climber of recent years. He had climbed many of the most difficult routes in the Alps and he had done some big walls in Yosemite and elsewhere. We had climbed Mount Everest together in May 1978 and he had subsequently reached the summit of Gasherbrum II. Just before our start to Cho Oyu he had climbed Cerro Fitz Roy.

OSWALD ÖLZ, *Österreichischer Alpenverein*

Cho Oyu, South Face Winter Attempt. Reinhold Messner, Friedl Mutschlechner, Paul Hanny, Hans Kammerlander and Peter Eisendle, *South Tirolean Italians*, Wojciech Kurtyka, *Polish*, and I, *Austrian*, were accompanied to Base Camp by four women, a writer and a painter. We flew to Lukla on November 8 and acclimatized on trekking peaks. On November 27 we set up Base Camp at 16,750 feet above Gokyo. We had four experienced Sherpas. We started up Cho Oyu's south face on December 1, the official opening of the winter season. From 17,400 to 19,700 feet, we climbed the broken icefall on the right of the face. We were helped by the Korean fixed ropes, which they had used to climb Ngozumba Kang. We placed Camp I at 20,000 feet at the top of the icefall on December 2. Camp II was established on December 6 at 21,825 feet at the beginning of the second upswing. Between Camps I and II was a wind-swept, crevassed ice plateau. From December 10 to 18 we climbed the often dangerous and extremely difficult ice face, which rises from Camp II to 24,600 feet. The chief problem was a 70° to 80° ice buttress in the last 1000 feet. We found fixed ropes from the Koblmüller-Furtner first ascent of the face in 1978. The ice was extraordinarily hard, making the placement of ice screws difficult; it was covered by rotten snow. Messner, Kammerlander and Sherpa Ang Dorje on December 18 reached the top of this ice pillar. The plateau would have been easy up to the final 250 feet, but it was covered by hip- and chest-deep powder snow. They could not advance and also feared avalanches. By December 21 all climbers and equipment were back in Base Camp.

OSWALD ÖLZ, *Österreichischer Alpenverein*

Khatang, Rolwaling Himal. This mountain was opened to climbers only in 1981 and we were the first to try it. We climbed the northeast ridge. We established the following camps: Base Camp at 15,700 feet on October 8 and Camps I, II and III at 17,825, 19,325 and 20,700 feet on October 12, 26 and 30 respectively. The northeast ridge is very steep, knife-edged and with unstable snow. The most difficult climbing was between Camps II and III. The following reached the summit (6853 meters, 22,484 feet): Tastumi Kawamura, Yoshimi Kitayama, Dorje Sherpa on November 1; Koji Kimura, Hideaki Sato, Chiharu Watanabe on November 2; and Kenji Koyama, Shigenori Sawada, Takehiko Ono on November 2 from Camp II.

MASARU OTANI, *Japan Workers' Federation Hokkaido*

Phurbi Chhyachu, Jugal Himal. Our joint expedition made the first ascent of Phurbi Chhyachu (6658 meters, 21,844 feet) by its southwest ridge. We were three Nepalese and sixteen Japanese. We left on March 25 and got to the Jugal Base Camp at 13,625 feet in the Balephi Khola on April 2. On April 7 we set up Camp I at 14,275 feet on the Phurbi Chhaychunbu Glacier after an easy three or four hours from Base Camp. We took six hours to Camp II at 17,050 feet, established on April 12. In this part we had to climb a 135-foot rock step and 30° to 65° snow with three more 65-foot rock steps. We placed Camp III at 19,025 feet on April 22, first climbing a snow ridge to 17,875 feet, a treacherous rock ridge for another 1000 feet and finally a 150-foot ridge of 60° ice to camp. We prepared the route above to reach the edge of the summit icecap at 20,500 feet on April 30. This part of the route was up 40° to 75° ice and was particularly steep for the last 135 feet. The icecap, which rose to the summit, was a wide snowfield. On May 1, Nepalese Ang Phuri and Pemba Lama and Japanese Hajime Takigami, Shintaro Kurokawa, Hiromitu Oka-moto, Humihito Ogawa and Takashi Singaki left Camp III at 7:45 A.M. and got to the top at 1:45 P.M. On May 3, Sakurahiko Fujikawa, Isao Hatori, Miss Junko Khono, Hiroyasu Ihara, Kazunoli Takezawa, Takashi Nishioka, Hisanobu Shimizu, Miss Chizuko Ohoi and I left Camp III at 5:20 and reached the summit at 9:45. We fixed 6500 feet of rope and placed 60 ice screws, 60 rock pitons and 120 snow pickets.

ICHIRO YASUDA, *Osaka Workers' Alpine Federation*

Longpo Gang or Big White Peak. A joint Japanese-Nepalese expedition made the second ascent of this peak (7083 meters, 23,238 feet) via the east ridge, the same route taken by the Japanese in 1962. They set up Camps I, II and III at 15,425, 17,625 and 21,650 feet on April 5, 12 and 25 respectively. On May 3, leader Koji Kato and Sherpa Norbu Jangbu reached the summit. Takashi Kurokawa, Hiroshi Zamaguchi and Yoshitsugu Deriha also got to the top on May 7.

KAMAL K. GUHA, *Himalayan Club*

Dorje Lhakpa. An expedition of eight Japanese and three Nepalese first tried the northeast ridge of Dorje Lhakpa, which they found too difficult, and then switched to the west ridge to complete the second ascent. The summit (6990 meters, 22,933 feet) was reached on April 26 by Tazunori Tanaka, leader, Keisuke Shibata, Migushi Ishihara, Yuzi Katsuhiro, Ikunori Nurotani, Kotaro Takahashi and Hiroshi Honjuhu on April 26 and by Yutaka Saito and Sherpa Chhewang Karma on April 29 from Camp III.

KAMAL K. GUHA, *Himalayan Club*

Langshisha Ri. A five-man Japanese expedition led by Hiroshi Inoue, made the first ascent of Langshisha Ri (6300 meters, 20,670 feet). They had two high camps. They climbed the south face, finding difficult climbing that required fixing 4500 feet of rope between Camp I and the summit. On April 23 Takuya Kujimoto and Sherpa Pasang Norbu got to the top, followed the next day by Inoue, two Japanese and another Sherpa.

MICHAEL J. CHENEY, *Himalayan Club,* and ELIZABETH HAWLEY

Langshisha Ri. A nine-man, two-woman Japanese expedition made the second ascent of Langshisha Ri (6300 meters, 20,670 feet), using the same route, the south face, climbed by other Japanese in the spring. On October 6 the leader Shozo Terakawa and five others left Camp II at 18,700 feet and got to the top. The next day two women, Kumiko Imamura and Akiko Sakamoto and two Sherpas reached the summit, followed on October 9 by three other members. (Information from *Iwa To Yuki,* N° 93.)

Langtang Lirung, Ascent and Tragedy. The Trieste expedition was composed of Bruno Toscan, leader, Bruno Crepaz, Mauro Contento, Mauro Petronio, Giuliano Ravagnan, Adriano Tavernaro and Dr. Luisa Mestroni. Unfortunately my husband and I found at the last moment that we could not join the expedition. The objective was to climb the southwest ridge, which had been climbed only once before, by Japanese in 1981. The summit (7246 meters, 23,764 feet) was reached on October 17 by Petronio and Sherpa Nga Temba. The ascent had been tiring and dangerous because of bad weather. Some 3250 feet of rope were fixed. On October 18 Crepaz disappeared during the descent at about 20,000 feet, apparently having made a false move on the fixed ropes. He was one of the best climbers in the Dolomites, where he had made over 100 new routes.

SILVIA METZELTIN BUSCAINI, *Club Alpino Italiano*

Langtang Liring Attempt. French climbers led by Denis Chatrefou reached only 16,400 feet on the east ridge of Langtang Lirung when after three days of climbing in the post-monsoon season an avalanche buried men in Camp I; they got out after a struggle.

MICHAEL J. CHENEY, *Himalayan Club,* and ELIZABETH HAWLEY

Ganesh IV. A South Korean expedition led by Joo Si-Jeong climbed Ganesh IV (7102 meters, 23,300 feet) via the south face, establishing three high camps. Korean Lee Sung-Ryul and Sherpas Dorje and Ajiwa reached the summit on October 5. They completed the climb despite many avalanches, one of which took out fixed ropes and led to a fall by a Sherpa, who, climbing without a fixed rope, fell 100 feet into a crevasse and broke his leg.

MICHAEL J. CHENEY, *Himalayan Club,* and ELIZABETH HAWLEY

Ganesh IV (Pabil) Attempt. A Japanese expedition led by Shigeru Nakada had hoped to climb Ganesh III and IV from a col between them. They were plagued by illness which kept four of the seven members unable to climb. They established two camps and reached the site of Camp III at 20,350 feet on October 18 on Ganesh IV's northeast ridge.

MICHAEL J. CHENEY, *Himalayan Club,* and ELIZABETH HAWLEY

Peak 29 Attempt. A badly equipped and badly funded British Army expedition led by James Green failed on Peak 29. They reached 19,400 feet on October 23 on the southeast ridge.

MICHAEL J. CHENEY, *Himalayan Club,* and ELIZABETH HAWLEY

Manaslu Tragedy. A Catalan expedition from Spain attempted to climb Manaslu (8156 meters, 26,760 feet) via the standard northeast face but varying the route above 23,000 feet to follow a more direct line to the summit. The expedition's leader, Enric Font and deputy leader, Pere Aymerich, attempted to reach the summit on May 10 from Camp V (24,275 feet) but got only to 24,900 feet when snowfall drove them back to camp. That evening on the walkie-talkie radio they reported to the other four members that they would descend the next day if weather permitted because they were not feeling well and because they had no more food. They did not respond to the next morning's radio contact and were never seen or heard from again. When the weather cleared on the morning of May 12, those in Camp II could see where a huge slab avalanche had come down the mountain, sweeping the site of Camp V, which had completely disappeared. Those below were unable to mount any rescue and the two are presumed to have died in the avalanche, probably during the night of May 10 to 11. The expedition had spread itself very thin on the mountain: no one in any camps except II and V on May 10, no food in these or other camps except rice at Base Camp. Some food had been lost in earlier avalanches. The survivors left Base on May 15 but were unable to buy food at Sama because it was under snow and its potato crop ruined. The first food they could buy was not found until May 18.

MICHAEL J. CHENEY, *Himalayan Club,* and ELIZABETH HAWLEY

Manaslu. We were Aldo Bonino, Christine Chapoutot, Marc Ferrari, Jacques Granjean, Jacques Sananes, Monique Vidaillac, Jacques Vuillemin, my wife Gilberte and I as leader. We were on the mountain from September 24 to October 14. We had camps at 17,050, 19,700 and 21,150 feet on the standard northeast-face route. In the dangerous zone between Camps I and II we found a safer route to the right of the séracs. Heavy snowfalls hampered us. On October 9 I left Camp III with the excellent Sherpa Ang Tensing (of

Tibetan origin) and we bivouacked at 24,275 feet. On October 10 we set out at seven A.M. in high winds and cold. It was snowing above 23,950 feet. We reached the summit at noon and descended to Camp III in the afternoon.

Louis Audoubert, *Club Alpin Français*

Manaslu East Ridge Attempt. Hervé Thivierge, Gilles Claret Tournier, Jean Franck Charlet, Dr. François Dantoine and I arrived at Base Camp at 14,450 feet on September 10, where we had four days of bad weather. After establishing Camp I at 18,050 feet, we climbed to 20,000 feet but bad weather and dangerous snow conditions made us decide to abandon the east ridge. We carried our supplies to Naike Col on the normal route, where a French-Italian expedition agreed to have us join them. However, the liaison officer refused us permission and did not pass on to higher authority their leader Audoubert's letter agreeing to have us join his expedition.

Jean-Paul Balmat, *Club Alpin Français*

Manaslu Tragedy. A Japanese expedition led by Noboru Yamada attempting a winter ascent of the normal route, the northeast face, of Manaslu was given up when Takashi Sakuma fell some 650 feet to his death from an altitude of 24,600 feet. Sakuma, Fuji Tsunoda and Hiroshi Aota had left Camp III at 23,450 feet on December 18 and had reached 25,100 feet before being turned back by high winds and cold. Sakuma slipped during the descent.

Himlung Himal Attempt. An 11-man Japanese-Nepalese team was led by Masatoshi Sato. Three full members were Sherpas and there were also three Sherpa high-altitude porters. They attempted the northeast ridge from the southeast of Himlung (7126 meters, 23,380 feet), which had never been successfully climbed. Two Japanese and a Sherpa got to 22,000 feet on May 16 from Camp IV before the expedition gave up. Heavy snowfall and winds had broken several tents and made climbing difficult.

Michael J. Cheney, *Himalayan Club*, and Elizabeth Hawley

Kang Guru. A seven-man Japanese team was led by Haruo Kanbe. They established Camp I at 17,225 feet on April 9 and Camp II at 19,700 feet on April 16. Ikuo Yoshita and Sherpas Ang Temba and Tsering on May 2 reached the summit (6981 meters, 22,904 feet) via the west face. On May 3 Keiichi Sudo and Sherpa Lhakpa also made it to the top from Camp III.

Kamal K. Guha, *Himalayan Club*

Kang Guru. Our expedition was composed of Dr. Borislav Aleraj, Stipe Božić, Marijan Čepelak, Mladen Briški, Nenad Pivac, Branimir Predović, Borislav Starčević, Branko Šeparović, Boris Vrbek and me as leader. The main party having left Dumre on September 22, we met our southeast-face reconnaissance group on September 27 at Dharapani. Due to great difficulties on the approach from Karche to the mountain, we changed to the west face, the German route of 1954. We established Base Camp on September 30 at 11,800 feet. Camp I was at 15,750 feet. We fixed 125 feet of rope on a rock step at 15,900 feet and another 125 feet on an ice step at 18,050 feet. Camp II was established at 19,000 feet on October 5 and Camp III at 20,675 feet on October 11. On October 12 Božić, Šeparović and I climbed to the summit (6981 meters, 22,904 feet). Šeparović skied from 22,300 feet and Božić from 20,350 feet to the end of the snow at 16,000 feet.

VLADIMIR MESARIĆ, *Planinarski Savez Jugoslavije*

Lamjung Himal, Southeast Ridge. Our women's expedition was composed of Key Hyoung-Hee, Youn Hyun-Ok, Lee Won-Haeng, So You-Mee, Manager Kim Kyung-Bae and me as leader. Our difficult route on the southeast ridge starting from Chame had been previously untried. We set up Base Camp at 12,500 feet on April 8, Camp I at 16,250 feet on April 15 and Camp II at 17,725 feet on April 20. Between Camps II and III, which was established on May 2 at 20,675 feet, the steep ridge is knife-edged. In honor of Korean Children's Day, May 5, Key Hyoung-Hee, the Sherpani sirdar Ang Riti and Sherpas Nima Wangchu and Dawa Wangchu started for the summit, late because of strong winds, and had to bivouac at 22,650 feet. On May 6 they met blue ice close to the summit. They stepped onto the top (6986 meters, 22,920 feet) at 12:20. A second party, Youn Hyun-Ok and Sherpas Ang Phurba and Pemba Tshering, reached the summit at 2:30 P.M. On top they met the Japanese expedition, which had taken a different route.

CHUNG KEEL-SOON, *Sunkyong Women's Alpine Club, Korea*

Lamjung. This three-person Japanese expedition was composed of Kazuki Yoshino, the lone man, and two women, Tomoko Takasu and Keiko Kido. Base Camp was established on the Kamba Khola at 12,650 feet on April 11. Camps I, II, III and IV at 15,100, 17,550, 19,200 and 21,325 feet were placed on the north ridge on April 11, 21 and 28 and May 5 respectively. All three Japanese and Sherpas Pemba Tshering and Phurba Tenzing on May 6 reached the summit (6986 meters, 22,920 feet), where they met the Koreans who had ascended the southeast ridge. The Japanese made the fifth ascent of the peak and the second of the north ridge.

Annapurna II Attempt. A Japanese group led by Kazuhiko Yamada reached 24,125 feet on the unclimbed south face of Annapurna II on October 5 but had to give up because of bad weather. They had established two high camps.

MICHAEL J. CHENEY, *Himalayan Club*, and ELIZABETH HAWLEY

Annapurna IV. Our expedition, organized by Auslandsbergfahrten of Graz, Austria, had five Austrians, eight Yugoslavs, two Swiss, a sirdar and two Sherpas. After an eight-day approach from Dumre to Omgre in the Marsiyandi valley in the last days of September, we established Base Camp at 15,425 feet under the northern slopes of Annapurna IV. We ascended the northern slopes to the northwest ridge, placing Camps I, II and III at 17,400, 19,700 and 22,300 feet. We fixed 600 feet of rope below Camp I and 200 feet below Camp II. On October 15 Jean Luc Amstutz, *Swiss,* and Willi Wehinger and Walter Bell, *Austrians,* reached the Dome, the 7450-meter (24,443-foot) foresummit. On October 17 Sirdar Pemba Lama, Sherpa Ang Nima, Mario Bago, Edin Alikalfic, *Yugoslavs,* and I, *Austrian* got to the summit (7525 meters, 24,688 feet). That same day the Dome was reached by Theo Kubicka, Herbert Kaltenegger, *Austrians,* and Zelco Gobec, *Yugoslav.*

WOLFGANG STEFAN, *Österreichischer Alpenverein*

Annapurna III Tragedy. A Japanese expedition of eleven was led by Tsukasa Nakase. They attempted the north face of Annapurna III (7555 meters, 24,787 feet), hoping to repeat the Indian route of 1961. On April 24 Masayoshi Okabe was killed by an avalanche at 22,000 feet while carrying a load to Camp V; two other members and a Sherpa were buried. Camp V at 22,650 feet was entirely swept away. All climbing ceased. They were well aware of the avalanche danger, but they said there was no route which would not take them under the fatal séracs.

MICHAEL J. CHENEY, *Himalayan Club*, and ELIZABETH HAWLEY

Annapurna III, Southwest Face Attempt. Our expedition was made up of Guillem Arías, leader, Manuel Benavent, Josep Fuste, Joan Oliva, Dr. Anton Rañe and me. We left Pokhara on September 17. We prepared the route with fixed rope beyond Machapuchare Base Camp up the Modi Khola gorge on September 22 and moved up to our Base Camp on the 23rd. The fixed rope was needed for the porters in this section. We established Camp I at 14,600 feet on September 25 on the true right bank of the Modi Khola. We placed Camp II at 15,750 feet just below the rock buttress on the true right side of the glacier that descends from the Gangapurna-Annapurna III col on September 27. On

October 3 we sited Camp III at 18,175 feet on the snow ridge above the rock buttress. This part of the route had difficult rock climbing. We climbed the lower part of the glacier close to the buttress wall to where the glacier became heavily crevassed. Unlike the Japanese women in 1970 and the Italians in 1977, who kept up the glacier, a dangerous route, we climbed the buttress, fixing rope and climbing rock of UIAA IV to V+ difficulty. We found some of the rope of the 1978 American expedition. Camp III was above a steep couloir that led to the snow ridge. Camp IV was placed at 19,900 feet on October 6, some 1250 feet below the bergschrund of the Gangapurna-Annapurna III col. Rising from 18,700 feet we saw the great unclimbed central couloir of the southwest face, which leads directly to the summit and would be an ideal climb. On October 7 we climbed to the col. The snow was in bad condition and we eventually reached 21,325 feet. The snow was so bad that we realized we could not reach the summit in less than ten days. We had to give up the ascent for lack of time.

XAVIER NOGUER, *Catalonia, Spain*

Glacier Dome Attempt. A French group led by Michel Richard attempted the north face of Glacier Dome (Tarke Kang), the route of the Italians in 1981. They placed four camps. They were defeated by arriving too late; Base Camp was established on October 22. They had daily new snow and high winds. They reached 22,800 feet on November 4.

MICHAEL J. CHENEY, *Himalayan Club,* and ELIZABETH HAWLEY

Annapurna Ascent and Tragedy. An expedition of Austrians, Swiss and one Czechoslovakian was led by Hanns Schell. They were on the mountain at the same time as the West German expedition described below. After abandoning the Dutch route because of avalanche danger, they turned to the Spanish route of 1975, which they climbed up to a ramp which let them traverse back westwards toward the main summit. On May 4 Austrian Wastl Worgötter, Swiss Werner Bürkli and Thomas Hägler and Sherpa Dawa Tenzing climbed to the summit. On their return to the high camp, Bürkli suddenly collapsed and died, apparently from a heart attack. A high-altitude porter, Shanti Rai, was lost on May 12 while clearing the mountain. He left Camp III for Camp II but never arrived. He must have slipped on the descent.

MICHAEL J. CHENEY, *Himalayan Club,* and ELIZABETH HAWLEY

Annapurna I Attempt. For ten weeks from mid-March to the end of May we were on Annapurna. We were Siegfried Siebauer, leader, Günther Schnait, Erwin Beyerlein, Dr. Bernhard Einzinger, Heinz Herbert Güntner, Gerhard Kern, Karl Heinz Kirner, Jürgen Kühn, Alfred Lechleitner, Heinz Riess,

Dieter Sause, Jürgen Schenk, Otto Umlauft and I. We cooperated with Hanns Schell's Austrian group. We planned to climb without oxygen and without Sherpas. At first we hoped to climb the Dutch Rib but avalanches urged us to look for a safer route and we turned to a route on the séracs of the northeast buttress, up the 1975 route of the Spaniards who climbed Annapurna East. This led to a ramp on the north slope and to the summit of Annapurna I. We fixed 3500 feet of rope between the séracs. Camp III was placed at 20,675 feet below the ramp in a crevasse. Camp IV was established up the ramp at 22,475 feet in a snow cave and Camp V at 23,800 feet. On May 6 Beyerlein, Lechleitner, Kirner and Güntner were at Camp V, hoping for the summit. Five more of us were at Camp IV. The top four struggled to 25,925 feet after a late start, delayed by the weather, but had to turn back. We all spent three more days waiting, but the weather stayed bad and we had to give up.

HERBERT ZIEGENHARDT, *Deutscher Alpenverein*

Annapurna, South Face Tragedy. Alex MacIntyre, René Ghilini and I climbed in the Annapurna Sanctuary in the post-monsoon season. Our main objective was a new route on Annapurna's south face to the right of the Polish buttress. The expedition ended in tragedy when Alex was killed when descending from 23,625 feet on the face. The expedition was low-cost and light-weight, with a total budget of only $5500. We had only 29 porters to carry to Base Camp, which was established at 14,000 feet on September 15, just at the end of the monsoon. We immediately began what Alex described as a "heavy-duty" acclimatization program. During September 18 to 20, while Alex was tent-bound with an infected toe, René and I climbed to the bottom of the proposed route on the south face. We followed the Polish ridge initially and then turned right above the glacier to bivouac at 20,000 feet. The hot afternoon sun brought a continuous deluge of water down the entire five-mile-wide face, accompanied by the eerie rumble and whine of rockfall. We consoled ourselves with thoughts of colder weather and shorter days when we should return to the face in mid-October. Alex's toe had healed when we returned to Base. We three then made a number of sorties, climbing high but reaching no summits on peaks on both sides of the Sanctuary. We completed the acclimatization program, and although I did not realize it immediately, I was finished off as well. Perhaps being ten years older than the other two or perhaps dysentery contributed, but four days later when the time came to leave for the face, I was not well enough to be confident of climbing the face in the planned three days and then of descending the north side. Alex and René waited for one more day, but I was still unwell when they left on October 10. The next day the second major storm of the trip forced them to descend to Base. On the 13th they set out again in clear, cold weather. A line of vicious snow plumes blew from the summits. The winter jet stream had descended to 26,000 feet. There was no sign of them during the stormy day that followed. During the afternoon of the 15th two tiny dots appeared beyond the ramp at half height on the face in a spectacular position between overhanging walls above and below. The next morning was clear and I watched as they moved up to a 100-foot rock band that separated the steep lower wall from the massive icefields that led to the final buttress beneath the east peak. With growing concern, I saw them try one, then another and then a third route through the rock with no success. What appeared a minor obstacle from Base Camp was a vertical, compact wall. The ice runnels were too thin to climb and they had only two rock pitons. They descended to the top of the ramp and bivouacked for the last time on the face. I began my search at 9:30 the next morning at the point where they would have to cross the couloir at the bottom of the ramp. At ten they appeared and crossed the couloir, doubtless the end of the major dangers. I felt happy that I would be given a second chance to join them on the face. They moved to the crest of a small spur. When I looked again, there was only one dot, seemingly frozen on the slope. I knew immediately that there was only one explanation. When the remaining climber had descended out of sight, I ran back to Base, packed emergency gear and with Sherpa Pinjoo set out toward the face. Halfway up the ridge we spotted René descending alone. Alex had been killed instantly when a single stone that fell from high on the face hit him on the back of the head. He fell 1500 feet to below the bergschrund, where René buried him as best he could. Bad weather set in during the next few days and we could not return to the site. The loss of Alex MacIntyre in the same year as Joe Tasker and Pete Boardman has been a terrible blow to their friends and relatives and to the whole concept of alpine-style climbing. Alex was an especially accessible person. He was willing to help and advise climbers of any standard, an attribute which made him an effective National Officer during his days with the British Mountaineering Council. His climbing record was outstanding. He was a dedicated, inventive, composed mountaineer.

JOHN PORTER

Annapurna Tragedy. A three-man Japanese expedition was attempting Annapurna via the Dutch rib when on October 18 Camp II was buried by an avalanche. Susumu Akimatsu and Miko Ono died but Takashi Ozaki escaped.

MICHAEL J. CHENEY, *Himalayan Club*, and ELIZABETH HAWLEY

Fang (Varaha Shikhar) Attempt. Although the Fang (7647 meters, 25,088 feet) is the third highest summit in the Annapurna group, it has had less attention from climbers, possibly because its name does not have "Annapurna" in it. It lies southwest of Annapurna I. Our expedition wanted to make a new route by climbing the east side of the south ridge and continuing along the ridge. This was completely different from the only ascent yet made; the Austrians in 1980 passed Moditse on the other side from us, on the west, climbed from the southwest and finished on the west ridge. Unfortunately, due to very bad weather and huge avalanche danger, we did not reach the south ridge. Base Camp was in the Annapurna Sanctuary. Camp I was on a moraine beside the east glacier. The route on the glacier to Camp II was treacherous because of hidden crevasses and unstable séracs, rendered worse by warm weather. We placed Camp III at the foot of the east slope of the south ridge at 20,850 feet. We got to a high point of 22,300 feet on May 6 on the very steep snow slope, which was about 70° near the top and was very dangerous after heavy snowfall. We realized that if we kept on, we would be carried away by avalanches. The members were Sylvain Sarthou, leader, Patrice de Belfon, Pierre Viorrain, Pierre Ravier and I.

HENRI SIGAYRET, *Club Alpin Français*

Annapurna South Attempt. A French expedition led by Patrick Jacquenot failed to climb Annapurna South by the east ridge. Despite eleven members and two Sherpas above Base Camp, they reached only 21,325 feet on October 21 and abandoned the climb because of heavy snowfall which brought avalanche danger. They had no time to wait for better weather.

MICHAEL J. CHENEY, *Himalayan Club,* and ELIZABETH HAWLEY

Tilicho, Sherpa Winter Ascent. On January 24 the first all-Sherpa expedition climbed Tilicho. We were only three climbers: Dawa Gyalzen Sherpa, leader; Gyalzen Sherpa and I. This expedition we arranged as an individual test and to change the Sherpa attitude toward mountaineering, which we approached more as sport. We left Kathmandu on January 4, accompanied by a liaison officer, B.B. Rana. We walked up the Kali Gandaki valley until we reached Jomosom on the 14th. There we met our advance party of nine porters, a Base Camp cook and a mail runner. Base Camp was established on January 17 above Lamphu Dome at 14,450 feet. On the 18th we three carried two days' food and climbing gear to Camp I on the flat above Tilicho Lake at 16,825 feet and returned to Base Camp for one day's rest. We departed from Camp I on January 22 at 7:30 A.M. We carried only five days' food and five coils of rope. We fixed about 1000 feet on the rocky ridge which we climbed most of the day. We spent the night at 18,475 feet. Leaving some food at the rocks, we set off for another day's climbing at 7:45 on the 23rd and had some difficulties on the rocky ridge. We also had snowfall during the afternoon but managed to reach 21,175 feet for the night. The wind was so strong that we felt we were in a helicopter about to take off. We overcame our nervousness by teasing each other. The next morning we faced a steep 1000-foot slope which we climbed, arriving at the summit at 1:45. Visibility was poor. We could stay for a mere ten minutes after placing a picture of our King and Queen in the snow, pitching a Nepalese flag and taking photographs. Hampered by snowfall, we reached

Camp III at six P.M. We descended on January 25 to near Camp I but could not find it. Due to heavy snowfall, it seemed as if our camp had moved to somewhere else. We spent the night without food or tent. That night Dawa joked while Gyalzen complained of dying from hunger and myself of cold. Three feet of fresh snow fell. We established communication with our party when we found Base Camp at 9:30 on the morning of January 26. The weather did not permit us to fly from Jomosom and so we walked, arriving at Pokhara on February 3.

SARKEY TSHERING SHERPA, *Sherpa Cooperative*

Tilicho. A Nepalese Royal Army expedition led by Lieutenant Colonel Gopal Singh Bhora climbed Tilicho (7132 meters, 23,400 feet) via the northeast ridge. They pitched Camp I at 17,975 feet on April 21. Seven members reached the summit on April 30 from Camp II. Six others reached the top on May 2. Details are not yet available.

KAMAL K. GUHA, *Himalayan Club*

Tilicho. A 14-person expedition sponsored by the German Alpine Club's Mountain and Ski School was led by Günther Härter. They approached in 14 days from Dumre up the Marsyandi valley to Base Camp on the west shore of Tilicho Lake at 16,050 feet, reaching there on October 11. Camps I and II were established at 19,000 and 20,675 feet on October 13 and 15 respectively. The summit (7132 meters, 23,400 feet) was reached on October 17 by Härter, Josef Hirtreiter, Adi Welsch and Sherpas Ang Dorje and Ang Pasang. Two later summit teams were driven back by strong winds and snowfall. The route was the northeast spur and north slope, the same as the Swiss route of 1980. The summit slope was in part threatened by windslabs. They fixed 4250 feet of rope.

GÜNTER STURM, *Deutscher Alpenverein*

Nilgiri North. A six-man and one-woman Japanese expedition led by Kenji Sugishita climbed Nilgiri North by a new route from the Miristi Khola: the southeast ridge of P 6706 and the east ridge of the mountain itself. Base Camp was at 13,300 feet. Camps II, III and IV at 18,050, 18,700 and 20,670 feet were established on April 8 and 17 and May 2 respectively. The summit (7061 meters, 23,166 feet) was gained on May 4 by Sugishita, Keiji Yamaguchi, Miss Kayo Ikeuchi and Sherpas Dawa Norbu and Pangma.

KAMAL K. GUHA, *Himalayan Club*

Nilgiri North Attempt. Scots Michael Fowkes and Gunson failed on Nilgiri North's southeast ridge. Fowkes developed high-altitude sickness and Gunson got to 20,200 feet alone on September 28.

MICHAEL J. CHENEY, *Himalayan Club,* and ELIZABETH HAWLEY

Nilgiri Central. On March 30 Shim Sang-Don, Lim Byung-Gil and I as leader set out for Base Camp at 13,625 feet, where we arrived on April 11, having crossed the Thulobugin Pass. On April 14 we set up Camp I at 16,075 feet two miles up the Nilgiri Glacier. On April 17 we placed Camp II at 17,725 feet up the steep southeast face in the icefall zone. We pitched Camp III at 20,000 feet on April 21 above the icefall. We then fixed 800 feet of rope on the southeast ridge. After that, we three Koreans and Sherpas Ang Tshering and Dorje spent two days at Camp III to adapt ourselves to the altitude. At 4:40 A.M. on April 25 all five left for the top along the knife-edged snow ridge and reached the summit (6940 meters, 22,770 feet) at three P.M. Our route was the same as the Japanese in 1979. We had difficulties on the summit climb. We broke crampons. We were short of fixed rope. Lacking enough snow pickets, we substituted ice axes and had to descend with only ice hammers. The descent was difficult and we did not get back to Camp III until 11:15 P.M. with the aid of head lamps.

KIM KI-HEYG, *Korean Alpine Club*

Bhrikuti, Damodar Himal. This peak is situated north of Kagbeni (and north of the Annapurna and Dhaulagiri massifs). The area was opened for expeditions only in 1982. The first to obtain a permit to enter the restricted area was an 11-man Japanese group led by Kaoru Kikuchi. They were joined by three Nepalese of the Tribhuvan University Hamalayan Club; co-leader Kishore Bhattarai, Tashi Jangbo Sherpa and Kapil Shrestha. A reconnaissance group, earlier in 1982, had found that an approach via Manang was not feasible and so they trekked along the south bank of the Chhiley Khola and not in Mustang proper. The western approach was previously unexplored. The expedition left Pokhara on April 24 and reached Jomosom on May 1. The area east of Kagbeni and Chuchang was unknown even to officials. The terrain beyond Chuchang is difficult for porters. They got to Base Camp on May 10. Camp I was occupied on the glacier on May 15 and Camp II on the west ridge at 19,800 feet on May 17. On May 19 Tashi Jangbo Sherpa, Takashi Sakuma and Masanobu Tsuchiya reached the virgin summit (6720 meters, 22,047 feet). On May 20 Sakatashi Yamagata and Kijuro Endo got to the top, followed on May 21 by leader Kikuchi, Sutemi Terada, Isao Niitsuma, Akie Asami, co-leader Kishore Bhattarai and for a second time Tsuchiya.

KAMAL K. GUHA, *Himalayan Club*

Bhrikuti, North Summit, Tehachang and P 6300. Damodar Himal. Seldom-visited Mustang is separated from Tibet by the Mustang Himal and the Damodar Himal. Though most applications have been refused, the Österreichische Himalaya Gesellschaft (Austrian Himalaya Society) was, as an exception, granted permission to climb 6720-meter (22,047-foot) Bhrikuti. I traveled from Austria on August 28 with much of the equipment, followed a week later by expedition leader, Christian Unger, and the other 16 members. We had a 125-mile approach from Pokhara, up the Kali Gandaki, through Jomosom and Muktinath, where we turned north and followed high paths to the head of the Tehachang valley. In the last four days we did not pass a village. We set up Base Camp on a flowery meadow beside a small lake at 15,000 feet. Reconnaissance showed that we had ascended the wrong valley and that the main summit could not be reached from there. After placing two high camps, we were able to make the first ascent of two easy peaks, Tehachang Peak (6250 meters, 20,506 feet) and P 6300 (20,670 feet). I made a solo attempt on Bhrikuti and reached the north peak (6600 meters, 21,654 feet). To have reached the main peak, I should have had to descend into another valley, which lay in Tibet. That seemed risky and time was short.

WOLFGANG AXT, *Österreichische Himalaya Gesellschaft*

Dhaulagiri I. The first Belgian expedition to the Himalaya, led by Eduard Apts, climbed Dhaulagiri by the standard northeast ridge. They set up Camps I, II, III and IV at 16,900, 18,700, 21,325 and 23,625 feet on April 9, 12, 17 and 23 respectively. Rudy van Snick, Philip Cornelissen and the Sherpa Ang Rita reached the summit on May 5. Jan van Hees, Lutgaarde Vivijs, Marnix Lefever and Sherpa Ang Jangbo summited on May 6. Ang Rita has now climbed to the summit of Dhaulagiri a total of four times. Lutgaarde Vivijs made the first ascent of the mountain by a woman.

KAMAL K. GUHA, *Himalayan Club*

Dhaulagiri. A five-man Japanese expedition led by Ken Kanazawa climbed Dhaulagiri by the standard northeast ridge. On October 17 Toichiro Mitani and Jun'ichi Tanaka got to the summit. They had three camps above Base Camp.

MICHAEL J. CHENEY, *Himalayan Club*, and ELIZABETH HAWLEY

Dhaulagiri, Pear Route. After many tries, the Pear Route on Dhaulagiri has finally been climbed. An 18-man Japanese expedition was led by Norio Sasaki. They established six camps, the highest at 26,100 feet. On October 18 Noboru Yamada, Kozu Komatsu and Yasuhira Saito reached the summit. They slept with oxygen at the high camp and used it on the final climb along the northwest ridge.

MICHAEL J. CHENEY, *Himalayan Club*, and ELIZABETH HAWLEY

Dhaulagiri, Winter Ascent. A Japanese expedition led by So Anma made a successful winter ascent of Dhaulagiri on December 13 by the normal northeast ridge when Akio Koizumi and Sherpa Wangdu reached the summit. They bivouacked on the descent in a snow hole at 26,000 feet. Three other members made a summit attempt three days later but were thwarted by strong winds.

Dhaulagiri II Attempt. French climbers led by François Imbert attempted Dhaulagiri II by a new route, the south ridge. They established four high camps. They reached 22,300 feet on October 19 but gave up because of too much snow which threatened avalanches and slowed progress. One member had hoped to use a hang glider, but this was irreparably broken during the approach march. Two Sherpas suffered frostbite, one seriously, whilst carrying supplies over the French Col from the Kali Gandaki valley.

MICHAEL J. CHENEY, *Himalayan Club,* and ELIZABETH HAWLEY

Churen Himal Attempt. A French expedition led by Gérard Grossan attempted Churen Himal (7371 meters, 24,184 feet) by the southeast face to the east ridge, hoping to reach the east peak. After establishing five camps, they reached 23,450 feet on November 3, but they gave up defeated by a very long route, no Sherpas, few remaining supplies and frequent snowfalls.

MICHAEL J. CHENEY, *Himalayan Club,* and ELIZABETH HAWLEY

Putha Hiunchuli. An expedition led by Nicolaas van Lookern Campagne climbed Putha Hiunchuli (7246 meters, 23,775 feet) by the south ridge to the south face, much the same route as that climbed in 1972, 1978 and 1979. Netherlander Dr. Rinus Lamers, Luxemburger Roland Zeyen and Sherpa Ang Temba reached the summit on October 18. A second party was turned back some 250 feet below the summit by fierce winds.

MICHAEL J. CHENEY, *Himalayan Club,* and ELIZABETH HAWLEY

First Across the Roof of the World, Traverse of the Himalaya. Graeme Dingle, Chewang Tashi and I formed the traverse party with other Indian and New Zealand members as a support team with which we rendezvoused every three or four weeks. Far more than a ten-month, 3000-mile trek from Kanchenjunga in Sikkim to K2 in Pakistan, we crossed dozens of high, glaciated passes, two over 20,000 feet in the Makalu-Everest region, and mixed with isolated and forgotten communities. Our life-style was of unexpected simplicity as we lived like nomadic cavemen, eating *tsampa* and *solja* (barley flour and Tibetan tea), sleeping under the stars or under bivouac rocks or within the dark, sooty confines of a villager's house. Starting in Sikkim during the late winter of 1981, in February, we crossed Sikkim to the pass, the Ratong La, and descended the Singalila ridge to where we could cross into Nepal. From there, we climbed back into the Himalaya via the Milke ridge, traversing into the Makalu region and over to the Khumbu via the Far East Col, West Col and the difficult Amu Laptsa pass. After a rest in Kunde village (above Namche), we continued west across the Rolwaling, Langtang and Ganesh Himals, to the Buri Gandaki valley. Here we trekked north to pass Manaslu on its northern side on the Tibetan border. Descending into the Manang valley, we moved west via frozen Tilicho lake and Jomosom, past Dhaulagiri, making an inadvertent visit to the forbidden district of Dolpa. After extricating ourselves, we trekked to Jumla and Rara Lake and finally Jolaghat, where we crossed into India. The monsoon caught us and for three months we slogged along muddy tracks beneath umbrellas with leeches hanging from our legs. We failed to cross into the Nanda Devi Sanctuary by an uncrossed pass to the south and so we circumvented it to Joshimath, Kedarnath, Uttarkashi, Gangotri and via the upper Sutlej Gorge to Manali. Turning north, we marched over the Bara Lapcha Pass to the desolate Zanskar valley with its Tibetan communities, and hence to Lamayuru Gompa in Ladakh, the westernmost point of our trek in India. We had to take a circumlocutory route via New Delhi and Islamabad in Pakistan to reach Skardu on the far side of the Indo-Pakistani cease-fire line. Up the Braldu valley, we reached the Baltoro Glacier. We walked up the chaotic moraines of the glacier to Concordia, where the pyramidal form of K2 stood above us. It was early winter and extremely cold. It had been an extraordinary experience, the most multi-faceted adventure of my life.

PETER HILLARY, *New Zealand Alpine Club*

Renamed Nepalese Peaks. On January 1, 1983 the Nepalese government considered renaming a number of peaks and geographical features, but this is not yet official.

Past Name	Present Name	Past Name	Present Name
Cross Peak	Taple Shikhar	Lady's Peak	Gumba Chuli
Jannu	Kumbhakarna	Madiya Peak	Bhairab Takura
Pyramid Peak	Pathibhara	Morimoto	Bhemdang Ri
Sphinx	Pathibhara Purba	Peak 29	Ngadi Chuli
Tent Peak	Kirat Chuli	Fluted Peak	Singu Chuli
Twin Peak	Gimmigela Chuli	Fang	Varaha Shikhar
Wedge Peak	Tamthan Chang	Gabelhorn	Gandharva Chuli
White Wave Peak	Anidesh Chuli	Glacier Dome	Tarke Kang
Outlier	Janak Chuli	Roc Noir	Khangsar Kang
Island Peak	Imja Tse	Tent Peak	Tharpu Chuli
Mehra	Kongma Tse	Hanging Glacier Peak	Tripura Hiun Chuli
Peak 38	Shar Tse II	Junction Peak	Shey Shikhar
Peak 43	Kyashar	Milchberg	Palta Thumba
Pyramid	Hongku Chuli	Wedge Peak	Phunphun Chuli
Pig Pherage	Likhu Chuli	Annapurna Sanctuary	Annapurna Deuthali
Big White Peak	Longpo Gang	Hidden Valley	Patale Chhango

India-Garhwal

Kalabaland Glacier Region. The pre-monsoon expedition to the Kalabaland Glacier commemorated the tenth anniversary of the Mountaineering Club of the Students' Gymkhana, Indian Institute of Technology, Bombay. The glacier lies in the remote northeastern corner of the Kumaon Himalaya on the borders of Tibet and Nepal. The glacier descends from the northwest. Towards the south, it meets the Yanchar Glacier and both swing southwest to form a smaller glacier called Sankalpa. The highest peak is Chiring We (6559 meters, 21,520 feet; 30°26′N, 80°18′E). There is a major icefall toward the head of the glacier, about 1.5 kms in length and from 16,000 to 19,000 feet. At the head of the glacier above the icefall, there is an amphitheater of peaks. Going from left to right the peaks are Unnamed I, Sankalpa, Unnamed II, Kalabaland Dhura, Unnamed III, Bamba Dhura and Chiring We. Below the icefall on the west flank is Burphu Dhura and on the east flank is Suli-Top. On the west face of Suli-Top, a rock tower projects. We started the approach from Bageshwar on May 7 and reached Ralam (12,000 feet) on the 11th. We hired 38 porters and 40 goats for the approach. The weather was bad from May 11 to 16 and we stayed at Ralam. Base Camp was established at 13,500 feet on May 19 just below the junction of the Kalabaland and Yanchar Glaciers. Advance Base Camp was set up at 15,500 feet on May 20 about 1.5 kms below the icefall. Camp I at 16,200 feet was placed on May 22 near the eastern base of the icefall, Camp II at 17,400 feet on May 25 below Unnamed I and Camp III at 19,200 feet on May 27 towards the eastern side of the top snowfield. We made the following climbs: *Sankalpa* (5928 meters, 19,450 feet) from Camp II via northeast face by Ajit Shelat, Ajei Gopal on May 26 and by Mahesh Bapaye, Dr. Vinay Kulkarni, porter Premsung Rawat on May 30; *Rock Tower* (5599 meters, 18,370 feet) from Advance Base via northwest ridge to a steep gully on the north and up west slope by Shrikrishna Karkare, Nitin Valame on May 25 and 26; *Bamba Dhura* (6334 meters, 20,780 feet) from Camp III via 19,500-foot col between Bamba Dhura and Chiring We and up southeast ridge by Gopal, Allwyn Carvalho, Sherpas Kami and Migma on June 4; *Kalabaland Dhura* (6105 meters, 20,030 feet) from Camp III via east ridge by Ashish Desphande, Shelat on June 6; *Unnamed II* (19,685 feet, 6000 meters), named by us *Khadga Dhura*, first ascent, from Camp III via east ridge by Gopal, Carvalho on June 6 and by Nitin Anturkar, Amit Bhargava, Premsing on June 7; *Unnamed I* (18,865 feet, 5750 meters), named by us *Tridhar*, first ascent, from Camp II via east-face gully by Rahul Vora and me on June 7 and by Karkare, porter Jagveersing Negi on June 8; and *Unnamed III* (19,685 feet, 6000 meters), named by us *Uttar Dhura*, first ascent, from Camp III via 19,500-foot Kalabaland Dhura-Utter Dhura col and southwest ridge by Desphande, Nitin Dhond on June 7. We attempted Chiring We, climbing through the Chiring We-Bamba Dhura col and to 20,300 feet on the west ridge, where equipment was dumped for the next day's attempt. The attempt was postponed due to bad weather. Later the route was found to have been swept by an avalanche and the attempt was abandoned.

VASANT LIMAYE, *Indian Institute of Technology*

Nanda Devi Attempt. Our Australian expedition to Nanda Devi was unsuccessful. The team comprised Tom Miller, Gary Wills, Ed Neve, Hugh Foxcroft, Keith Egerton and me as leader. With 28 porters and 65 goats we departed Joshimath on August 23. Further five days of delay was caused by heavy rain at Lata Kharak and we finally reached Base Camp via the Dharansi Pass route on September 3. On September 7 Camp I was established on the 1981 Indian site at 18,500 feet. The position was relatively dangerous and at three A.M. on September 9 Neve was injured by rockfall while asleep in his tent. With difficulty we evacuated the concussed Neve to Base Camp and to Sarson Patal on September 16 to meet a helicopter. Tom Miller became unexpectedly ill and it was necessary to evacuate him too from Sarson Patal. Climbing resumed on September 18. Camp II at 20,500 feet was established on September 19 and, after heavy snow, Camp III below the rock face on September 25 at 21,750 feet. Egerton was suspecting retinal haemorrhaging while Foxcroft had not acclimatized well. Wills and I therefore prepared to establish Camp IV above the rock band. On September 27 throughout the day the weather worsened with increasing wind. We could not erect a tent and spent an open bivouac at 24,000 feet. On the 28th we dropped back to Camp III, where we discovered frostbitten fingers. We rejoined Foxcroft and Egerton on September 29 at Camp II and determined to give up the climb.

MICHAEL RHEINBERGER, *New Zealand Alpine Club,*
Southern Australian Section

Kalanka. We set out from Lata on September 11 and six days later reached Base Camp on a moraine lake north of the Uttari Rishi Gal. For three days we reconnoitered the approaches to Kalanka over the Uttari Rishi Gal but found it would have taken two days more up dangerous moraines, a tiring glacier and a difficult icefall. Moreover, the northeast face seemed too dangerous. The 4500-foot-high face has perpendicular rock sections and is overall very steep. The top ridge was guarded by giant cornices. We then set up an Advance Base below the south face at 16,750 feet. A first summit attempt on September 23 was stopped by bad weather. On September 26, Dr. Bernhard Lukas, Peter Färbiger, Manfred Hesse and Gerry Besl left Advance Base and climbed the steep hanging glacier of the south face directly up toward the summit. They bivouacked below the final summit wall at 20,350 feet, then they climbed the 55° to 65° wall, much of it bare, hard ice, and reached the summit (6931 meters, 22,740 feet) at five P.M. They descended the west ridge to the

Changabang-Kalanka col to bivouac. On the third day they traversed back to their first bivouac and descended. On September 27 Erwin Praxenthaler and I climbed the 3500-foot-high glacier to the right of the summit which leads to a col in the east ridge. The slope was 60° to 65° and the ice bare and hard. To save time we climbed the first 1000 feet unroped and above, the second man jümared. We reached the ridge at four P.M. in time to hack out a bivouac in the ice. The next day we climbed the ridge on difficult mixed terrain, reaching the main ridge at 21,500 feet. In deteriorating weather we got to the summit at 4:30 P.M. and descended the west ridge to bivouac in the col at six P.M. On September 29 we descended the south face in four hours.

KARL SCHRAG, *Deutscher Alpenverein*

Changabang. Our group consisted of Elke Rudolf of West Germany, Brigitte Koch of Belgium, and Mark Moorhead, Rod Mackenzie, Jon Muir and me of Australia. At Lata we hired Dharam Singh, nine other porters and some 70 goats for the approach. We were delayed for four days at Lata Kharak due to heavy rain and arrived at Base Camp near the Ramani Glacier at 15,000 feet on August 31. For the next 18 days we climbed Hanuman (6075 meters, 19,931 feet) and other minor peaks for acclimatization. We four Australians began our first attempt on Changabang on September 20, leaving our Advance Base at 17,000 feet. We started up the snow slope on the left of the southwest ridge and just before the slope finished, we joined the ridge proper. We spent our first night at the first Japanese bivouac site at 19,250 feet. The next day we climbed difficult aid and mixed pitches to the second Japanese bivouac site at 19,800 feet. From there we traversed to reach the Italian south-buttress route. We climbed a few more pitches of this route before tossing for the night on a miserable little ledge halfway up the conspicuous triangular snowpatch on the Italian route at 20,000 feet. Following two days of snowfall, we abseiled down the Italian route until we reached the col where the Italian route ascends from the Changabang Glacier. Below the col on the Ramani side is an 800-foot wall. On the lower 650 feet we left our four climbing ropes for a second attempt. The descent below the band to the glacier was interesting without ropes! We began out second attempt on October 2 and after reascending our ropes and climbing a few other pitches, we reached the col that night. The next day we reached our previous high point on the Italian route at 21,000 feet and left rope on the two pitches above it in the afternoon. On the 4th we reached the top of the snow dome at midday and spent the night about a third of the way along the gendarmed ridge to the summit. On October 5 we reached the summit and bivouacked there. It took us two days to descend to the Changabang Glacier via the east ridge , which was so covered with hard water ice that we abseiled 1000 feet down its southern side. From the Changabang Glacier we had planned to cross to the Ramani via Shipton's Col but because of snowy slabs and the likelihood of bad weather, we chose to walk back to Base Camp via the Rishi Gorge. This took four days and brought on new dimensions of fatigue. Of the two routes, I prefer the Italian. It had some fine rock and interesting mixed pitches, nearly all of which could be climbed free. The hardest climbing we did was on the Italian route.

CRAIG NOTTLE, *Australia*

Hanuman and Rishi Kot, North Face. Our expedition was composed of Mario Blasevich, *Canadian*, Rafael Fernández, Dr. Juan Bejarano and me as leader, *Spaniards*. We were in Garhwal from July 29 to August 29. We had hoped to climb the south face of Dunagiri, but monsoon weather and bad snow conditions prevented this. On August 15 Blasevich and I climbed Hanuman (6075 meters, 19,931 feet) by the normal route, followed the next day by Fernández solo. On August 18 and 19 Blasevich soloed a new route on Rishi Kot (6236 meters, 20,460 feet), the 4000-foot-high, 55° to 75° north face.

ANTONIO LUNA, *Federación Andaluza de Montañismo, Córdoba, Spain*

Dunagiri. Our members were Jordi Anglí, Manuel Broch, Josep Fontcuberta, Francesc Pañella, Manuel Quevado, Martí Vall and I as leader. We left Lata with 31 porters and in four days got to Base Camp on the Ramani Glacier on August 20. We placed Camp I at 17,000 feet, Camp II in the west col at 19,200 feet and Camp III on the top of the spur on the northwest ridge at 21,650 feet. On September 6 Fontcuberta and Pañella left Camp III and after a bivouac in a snow cave they dug got to the summit (7066 meters, 23,183 feet) at midday of September 7. Time prevented further attempts.

MIQUEL CASTELLSAGUÉ, *Centre Excursionista Badolana, Spain*

Trisul. Trisul (7120 meters, 23,360 feet) is now being climbed frequently. Two commercial groups were successful, one Italian led by Alberto Re and a German one led by Günter Kampf. An Indian expedition under the leadership of Samir Kumar Guha also reached the summit. A Spanish and another German group were less successful.

Kamet and Abi Gamin. In 1982 the Indian Military Academy completed fifty years of its existence. As a part of the Golden Jubilee, a commemorative expedition, led by me and consisting of its alumni past and present, was organized to scale Kamet and Abi Gamin. After establishing Base Camp at 15,500 feet on June 3, we made steady progress and were poised for the final assault on June 18, when exceptionally bad weather thwarted our attempts. When the weather improved four days later, Abi Gamin (7355 meters, 24,130 feet) was scaled from Camp IV at 22,000 feet by Major Pushkar Chand,

Captain Bhupinder Singh, Gentlemen Cadets Gautam Shaunik and R.S. Mann, along with support members Sonam, Tashi and Shiv Singh. The next day, June 23, Tsering Norbu made an exciting solo ascent from Camp V in Meade's Col at 23,030 feet. The Kamet team consisted of Captain D.B. Thapa, Second Lieutenants Pankaj Awasthy and Prem Prakash, Gentlemen Cadets H.S. Rawat and R.S. Bakshi and support members Gill, Liqdon, Nima and Tsering Tashi. Leaving Camp V at 4:30 on June 23, they reached the summit (7756 meters, 25,447 feet) in deteriorating weather after a gruelling twelve-hour climb.

JAGJIT SINGH, *Brigadier, Indian Army*

Gangotri Region. There were a number of successful expeditions in the Gangotri region. Japanese Masaki Ohashi and Kaoru Totani climbed Satopanth (7075 meters, 23,212 feet) on September 30 by the north ridge. Another Japanese expedition led by Makoto Segiura climbed Bhagirathi II (6512 meters, 21,365 feet). Two Indian groups led by A.G. Vaidya and Dr. D.P. Roy climbed Jogin III (6166 meters, 20,065 feet). Another Indian team led by Bharat S. Mahghre climbed Gangotri III (6577 meters, 21,578 feet).

Bhagirathi II North Face, Ascent and Tragedy, 1981. In the autumn of 1981, Dawson Stelfox, Tommy Maguire and I visited the Gangotri region. From the usual Base Camp beside the Gangotri Glacier, we made exploratory trips to study the west faces of Bhagirathi I, II and III and the north face of Bhagirathi II. The west faces of Bhagirathi II and III were superb rock faces, but we were underequipped for such formidable undertakings. The west face of Bhagirathi I was aesthetically unappealing. We decided on the north face of Bhagirathi II (6512 meters, 21,365 feet), a beautiful ice face, which we easily reached in six hours from Base Camp. After a night on the moraine at the base of the face, we spent the first day on the route crossing a long but easy glacier which led to the bergschrund at the foot of the steep upper slopes. From here it was 35 pitches to the summit. On the second day we climbed 14 pitches to find a small but adequate ledge for our two-man dome. Weariness on the third day forced us to bivouac on a ledge chipped out of the slope, seven pitches from the summit ridge. On the fourth day we got to within 200 feet of the top, electing to visit it the next morning. This we did, unladen, on September 10, 1981. On the descent of the rotten east slope, Tommy Maguire slipped and fell 500 feet onto steep scree. Despite attempts from below at rescue, he died from his injuries on September 12. We buried him high on the mountain.

IAN REA, *Dalriada Climbing Club, North Ireland*

PLATE 76

Photo by Allen Fyffe

The Southwest Buttress of
Bhagirathi III. Brown Tower is at
base of line. Bivouacs are marked.

PLATE 77
Photo by Robert Barton
BHAGIRATHI II, III, and I.

Bhagirathi III, Southwest Buttress. Bob Barton and I established Base Camp on the meadows at Tapovan at 14,750 feet on September 11 after a day-and-a-half walk-in from the roadhead at Gangotri. In three days more we stocked and occupied Advanced Base across the Gangotri Glacier and below the southwest buttress of Bhagirathi III (6454 meters, 21,175 feet). Above this an unpleasant slope of shale scree and loose rock led to a bivouac at the Brown Tower, below the route proper. The first section of the route was on immaculate granite (5.8, A2) with some soloing on the more broken ground. Once we had fixed our seven ropes, we retired to Base to rest and restock. Our return was delayed by heavy snowfall, but on September 27 we were again at the Brown Tower. We worked our way up the granite in a self-contained manner, fixing rope between the rare bivy ledges. Hauling was tiring and so we usually did two trips instead on the lower part. In general the climbing was excellent, up fine cracks, although ice was a problem particularly on the obvious flake-pillar, which didn't get the sun till noon. Evening snowfall on most days called for more aid, but did alleviate the water shortage. At the top of the granite we jettisoned all excess gear and climbed the upper third alpine style. This started with very rotten shale but soon changed to hard black ice covered by a foot of fresh powder. We reached the summit on October 8 and descended the north ridge in a minor storm, with poor snow and a lack of protection. After the col, we found the east face even worse with awful rock, poor anchors, difficult route-finding and abseils that were either nearly horizontal or overhanging. We reached the glacier on the evening of the 9th and Base the day after. The 4500-foot-high route had 30 pitches on granite, 2 on shale and 12 on ice. The main problems were lack of good ledges, snow cover on the granite and poor belays higher up. Rockfall was minimal and mainly to our right. This was a superb route which offered something of everything.

ALLEN FYFFE, *Scottish Mountaineering Club*

Shivling Northwest Face Attempt. Tony Bedel, Dominique Julien and I had hoped to climb the 4000-foot-high northwest face of Shivling. We placed our tent at 17,725 feet above the bergschrund from which we thought we could make the climb in three days with good weather. The difficulties seemed essentially those of ice and to be greatest in the upper 2000 feet: 1000 feet of ice drapery on very steep slabs, followed by an icefall, and finally a wide couloir and chimney that leads to the summit. The weather, however, was atrocious. We did not have two successive good days in the whole month. Avalanches of heavy snow were frequent. We could make no serious attempt.

BERNARD DOMENECH, *Club Alpin Français*

Shivling Photo Correction. Plate 75 on page 250 of *A.A.J.*, 1982 is apparently incorrectly labeled. Monsieur Domenech suggests that we should have the following: "North faces of Shivling. On the left is the east ridge, 'Ganesh's Trunk.' The ridge between sun and shade is the north ridge, dividing the northeast and the shadowed northwest faces."

Shivling Tragedy. After delays, Richard Cox and I reached Gangotri on August 31. The walk-in with seven porters to Base Camp at 14,600 feet at Tapovan was from September 1 to 3. We acclimatized until September 17. Advance Base Camp was established at 16,750 feet below a rock buttress descending from the north ridge. From there we made a reasonably safe approach onto the northeast face of Shivling to fix the initial snow slope and made carries to Advance Base and to the top of the fixed ropes at 17,225 feet. We set off for the face on the 18th with food for 12 days and much climbing equipment to bivouac at 17,725 feet below the first rock band. The band proved difficult (UIAA V, A1) but on good rock. On September 19 we bivouacked below the second rock band at 18,375 feet and then carried up equipment and fixed the remaining rope to that height. The second rock band involved ice of 70° to 80° and mixed climbing (V and VI). On September 22 we started to climb the main icefield, not as difficult as the 60° angle suggested but with some hindering soft snow. We reached the top of the icefield at five P.M. Cox led through the first pitch on the upper rocks. An anchor failed while he was hauling sacks, causing him to fall some 65 feet, injuring his ankle and possibly giving him a concussion. By nightfall I had managed to get him back up to the belay for a make-shift bivouac. That evening the weather deteriorated and the next day we were pinned there at 20,000 feet by heavy snow. By the morning of the 26th the weather had cleared but Richard Cox's condition was so bad that it was imperative to descend. He was unable to stand and had to be lowered down the face. At eight P.M. that evening an accident occurred in which it is believed that he became detached from his Jümars and was killed in the resultant fall. On September 27, I managed to descend by rappel to Base Camp.

NICHOLAS KEKUS, *England*

Meru North Attempt. Fifteen members of the Mountaineers' Youth Ring of Calcutta led by Kamal K. Guha attempted to climb Meru North. They had worked their way to the head of the Meru Glacier and to the Meru-Shivling col by September 19. They worked for four days to climb the 800-foot-high rock wall above the col and got up to 19,250 feet (5920 meters) but had to give it up.

Kirti Stambh Ascent and Kharchakund Attempt, Gangotri Region. Our expedition consisted of Rick Allen, Ernie McGlashan, Malcolm McCullough, Beverley Hurwood and me as leader. We hoped to make the second ascent of Kharchakund (6612 meters, 21,693 feet) by the unclimbed north ridge. We also planned to acclimatize by climbing the northeast face of unclimbed Kirti Stambh (6270 meters, 20,570 feet), which lies between Bhartekunta and Thalay Sagar. We reached Base Camp at Tapovan on October 1. Kirti Stambh was a more elusive summit than we expected. Not until the third attempt was it successfully climbed. It involved ice of Scottish grade IV and rock of Alpine IV. The slabby rock was not an ideal base for holding snow. On one occasion we noted that the northeast face had suffered five major windslab avalanches. Despite this, McGlashan and Allen found an inherently safe route on October 4 and 5, climbing to 19,800 feet from a 17,000-foot bivouac. A second attempt was mounted by McCullough and me on October 7 and 8. We reached 17,800 feet for a bivouac. Unfortunately on October 8 McCullough was suffering from altitude sickness and a return to lower altitude was necessary. It was not until after the Kharchakund attempt that on October 18 we returned to Kirti Stambh. McCullough still suffered from the altitude. We three other climbers bivouacked at 17,800 feet. The next morning, having traversed out from the shelter of the cliff and ascended a snow ramp to join a gully at 18,000 feet, we were nearly struck by tragedy. I was hit by an avalanche, funneled down the chute from snow slopes above. I extricated myself from the snow before it poured over an ice slope and onto boulders 300 feet below, but I had to retreat, accompanied by McGlashan. Allen, after some deliberation, continued on alone, confident of safely negotiating the rock traverse and steep ice pitches solo, having previously climbed these difficulties with McGlashan. He reached the col between P 6254 (east of the peak) and the summit on the evening of October 19. October 20 dawned fine and he reached the summit of Kirti Stambh at 9:20 A.M. Meanwhile, two camps had been established up the Gangotri Glacier, the higher at 15,800 feet at the foot of the north ridge of Kharchakund. From the foot of the ridge, McGlashan and Allen set out on October 13. They had on the 12th reconnoitered the ridge from its northeast aspect and espied a gully leading onto the ridge. By the evening of the 13th, after slow progress in the unconsolidated snow of the gully and some tricky climbing above, they bivouacked. On October 14 their progress was even slower and they gained only 600 vertical feet. On the third day they crossed left over the shoulder on the ridge and into a snow couloir, which they climbed in two pitches. A rock wall now barred their way, but it was surmounted by a difficult slabby rib, which involved an extremely difficult pitch. The third day's climbing took them only 600 feet above their previous night's bivouac. They had completed 2200 feet of the 5900-foot ridge in three days. In view of the climbing difficulties and hampered by unconsolidated snow lying on slabby rock, they anticipated three further days of climbing to reach the col behind the great north tower and another day for the summit snowfield with its icefalls and bergschrund. The two climbers quit and abseiled down the ridge, not reaching Advance Base until October 16.

Roy F. Lindsay, *Scottish Mountaineering Club*

Thalay Sagar Attempt. "Third time lucky" didn't work in 1982 on Thalay Sagar's north flank. We got to within 350 feet of the summit on June 26 but had to retreat because of a slight mishap. In excellent conditions we reached our previous high point in eight days and on June 17, Joe Brown and I completed three extremely difficult pitches and found a splendid bivouac site. After a few days of bad weather we two, plus Bill Barker, Malcolm Howells and Clive Rowland, climbed to the bivouac and on June 25 set out for the summit. We were soon held up by a holdless slab in which Brown placed his first ever direct-aid bolts. He managed to fall from the second one and was left suspended from a sling by his left ankle in a most undignified manner. The pitch took three hours to complete but proved to be the last really difficult one before the summit cone. While looking for a higher bivouac site, Brown and Howells dropped Howells' rucksack, which apart from containing his bivouac gear, carried the cooking pots and stove. We all retreated to the previous bivouac site and decided to rush the summit the next day. On the 26th, Brown, Barker, Howells and Rowland left early with no bivouac equipment while I retreated down the face to find the dropped rucksack. They quickly reached their previous high point and completed two more comparatively easy pitches to the base of the summit cone. The first pitch of very loose, steep black rock defeated the others and Brown had to be used to find a solution. He was faced with a similar pitch and 250 feet of easy snow, but it was five P.M. Retreat was decided on and the attempt was abandoned at about 22,550 feet (6875 meters). Maybe the adage should read, "Fourth time lucky."

J.V. Anthoine, *Alpine Climbing Group*

Bhrigupanth. A Japanese expedition led by Koji Yamakura climbed Bhrigupanth, repeating the route first climbed in 1980 by Penny Brothers, Susan Coons and Nancey Goforth. Base Camp was established at 15,350 feet on September 3. Advance Base, Camps I and II were placed at 15,950, 18,050 and 19,525 feet on September 6, 9 and 16 respectively. They placed fixed ropes up the final south face to 21,325 feet. On September 21 Yamakura, Toshiharu Iwagaki and Sai Kimura reached the summit (6772 meters, 22,218 feet), followed on the 22nd by the other members of the expedition, Mitsuru Nakano, Yoshihiro Matsumoto and Takaharu Sasaki.

Manda. Our members were Masatosi Sasaki, Tomoyuki Sogabe, Takanori Sasaki, Hiroyuki Kawaguchi and I. We set up Base Camp on May 29 at 13,775 feet at Kedarganga Kharak. We set up Camp I on June 2 on the Manda Glacier at 16,400 feet and Camp II on June 9 at 18,375 feet where we reached the north ridge. On June 18 Sogabe, T. Sasaki and Kawaguchi left Camp II at 5:50 A.M. and reached the summit (6510 meters, 21,360 feet) at 1:30 P.M. The route was the same as that of the Indian expedition led by Dr. Minoo Mehta, which climbed the peak on June 7, 1981. (See *A.A.J.*, 1982, pages 256-7.)

TSUNENORI OKADA, *Ehime University Alpine Club, Japan*

P 6568 ("Manda South") and Jogin I. From Bheronghoti it took Peter Athans, Maggie Fox, Peter O'Neil, Rachel Cox and me three days to march up the precipitous Kedar Ganga to reach Base Camp at 15,500 feet on the slopes west of the Kedar Tal (lake) on September 26. For the next week we turned our attention to the Jogin group. After establishing camps at 16,800 and 18,600 feet, O'Neil, Fox and I reached the summit of Jogin I (6465 meters, 21,211 feet) at four P.M. on October 2 after arduously postholing up the main glacier to the col between Jogin III and I. The summit ridge provided exposed, moderately difficult cramponing on ice and névé. On October 6 O'Neil, Athans and I crossed the main Kedar Glacier and camped at 17,000 feet in the cirque below the 3500-foot ice-and-snow ramp which led to the notch between "Manda South" and P 6529. [*Editor's Note:* Permission had been given for Manda, the next peak to the north. The climbers apparently mistook P 6568, which is slightly higher, for Manda. P 6568, unlike Manda, had never been climbed.] On October 7 we climbed most of the ramp in 13 hours. On the lower 2000 feet we climbed unroped. The ramp, which began at 35°, steadily steepend to 60° or 65°. We began belaying after 2000 feet. After three 60° ice pitches we bivouacked in an ice-hole. On October 8 Athans was feeling ill. O'Neil and I climbed the remaining 400 feet to the ridge and returned to the bivouac after fixing our two ropes. With a five A.M. start, all three of us ascended the two ropes and a third pitch to the ridge. We followed north along the ridge on frozen dirt, loose shale and snow for half a mile. We ascended a moderate snow-and-ice slope of 800 feet to the south summit ridge of "Manda South" and followed the ridge to the summit (6568 meters, 21,550 feet).

MARK UDALL, *Colorado Outward Bound School*

Jogin I and III. Our team was Shrikant Oka, Anil Kumar, Ashok Rajderkar, Sanjay Borole, Suhas Risbud and I as leader. From Gangotri we went up the Kedar Ganga Gorge to Base Camp at 15,200 feet at Akhari Bhuj-Kedar Kharak. We set up Camps I, II and III at 16,500, 17,500 and 19,100 feet respectively. Camp III was in the col from which Jogin I and III were climbed.

Borole and the high-altitude porter Datta climbed Jogin III (6116 meters, 20,065 feet) on June 10. Oka, Risbud and porter Nar set out at 2:30 A.M. on June 11 and reached the summit of Jogin III at 4:30 A.M. Oka and Risbud continued on and up the very steep southeast ice face to the summit of Jogin I (6465 meters, 21,210 feet) at nine A.M. The ridge was heavily corniced.

(MISS) NEETA BHOIR, *Girivihar, Bombay, India*

Gangotri I and Rudugaira. A second Indian Mountaineering Foundation Pre-Everest Expedition climbed Gangotri I (6672 meters, 21,890 feet) on October 15, 16, and 17, when eleven men and three women reached the summit. Eleven members also climbed Rudugaira (5819 meters, 19,420 feet) on October 9. Gangotri II was attempted on October 21, but deteriorating weather drove them back.

HARI C. SARIN, *Indian Mountaineering Foundation*

India—Himachal Pradesh

Leo Pargial. A ten-man Indian expedition led by Paritosh Das Gupta climbed Leo Pargial. Base Camp at 14,500 feet was set up on May 14 and Advance Base at 16,200 feet on May 16. Camp I was placed beside the Leo Pargial Glacier at 18,200 feet on May 18. They switched from the south face to the direct route via the northwest ridge. Camp II at 19,500 feet was higher than originally planned and eliminated the need for Camp III. On May 24 Jadu Gopal Acharya, Badal Datta, Utpalendu Das and Sherpas Marma and Sona set out from Camp II. The last 650 feet were steep and the gradient worsened as they went up. After a struggle of 10½ hours, they were on the summit (6791 meters, 22,280 feet). Another Indian expedition led by Usha Bhide Sathe also ascended the mountain later in the year.

KAMAL K. GUHA, *Himalayan Club*

Ninjeri, Chango Glacier, Spiti. The Chango Glacier lies at the northeastern end of the Kinnaur District of Himachal Pradesh on the Indo-Tibetan border. The glacier is surrounded by snowy peaks and Chamonix-type aiguilles, which had been viewed from Leo Pargial in 1933 by Marco Pallis but had remained unexplored. In June 1981 I was a member of the expedition which charted a route to the glacier, but we made no attempt to climb peaks. On May 27 our seven-member team of present and former members of St. Stephen's College, Delhi University, left Delhi for the village of Chango, our roadhead. The journey by road took two days via the Sutlej and Spiti valleys on the Hindustan-

Tibet road. Being behind the Inner Line, no foreign expeditions are allowed. The journey through the awesome granite walls of the Sutlej valley to the dry, barren Spiti valley is a fantastic experience. The people of Chango were friendly and honest. Porterage was ridiculously inexpensive and nine porters and eight mules ferried our food and equipment to the snout of the glacier in a two-day march from the village up the Chango gorge. With more snow than in 1981, members and porters ferried loads in three days from our approach camp at the glacial snout at 14,500 feet and established Base Camp on the medial moraine at 16,500 feet on June 7. There are ten major peaks above 20,000 feet. Except for Leo Pargial (6791 meters, 22,280 feet), the highest, at the head of the southern branch of the glacier, all others were unclimbed and unnamed. We chose P 21,800 (6645 meters), the second highest, at the head of the northern branch of the glacier. Advance Base was established at 18,000 feet at the base of the south ridge. The first 1500 feet of the ridge over steep rock and hard snow led to easier ground. After a gradual ascent of another 500 feet, we placed our high camp at 20,000 feet. At five A.M. on June 13 Sanjiv Saith, Rahul Sharma, Chering Namgyal, Deepak Chandnani and I left camp. We soon veered off the south ridge and were climbing on the west face. The last very steep 500 feet were on a wind-slab. Frightfully cold, we reached the summit at 9:40. The peak we climbed, though the second highest, was not the most difficult. We named the peak "Ninjeri." Ninje is Ladakhi for pure and Ri means mountain.

Yousuf Zaheer, St. Stephen's College, Delhi, India

Peaks in Himachal Pradesh. Dharamsura (White Sail; 6445 meters, 21,145 feet) was climbed by Scots led by A.N. Ridley. A peak in Bara Shigri (6225 meters, 20,424 feet), whose name was given by the Indian Mountaineering Foundation both as "Snow Cone" and "Snow Cave," was climbed by Indians led by Asit Kumar Moitra. The following Chandra Bhaya peaks were climbed: CB 10 (Tra Pahar; 6227 meters, 20,430 feet) by Japanese led by Takao Shimio by a new route on the snow northeast ridge; CB 13 (6264 meters, 20,560 feet) by Indian women led by Miss Arati De and by Japanese led by Osamu Sakiguchi; and CB 31 (6096 meters, 20,000 feet) by Japanese led by Yukio Munemori. Indians led by Debabratra Bhattacharya climbed Gangstang (6162 meters, 20,218 feet).

CB 14. A Japanese party made the first ascent of CB 14, climbing the east ridge. They climbed an icefall to reach a col on the east ridge at 17,500 feet. On September 10, after a bivouac on the col, Akira Yoshitomi and Toshio Kurihara reached the summit (6079 meters, 19,945 feet), followed the next day by leader Tadao Ito and Kurihara. More details and a photograph appear in *Iwa To Yuki*, N° 93.

Koa Rong IV. Our expedition comprised Lieutenant Colonel Richard Hardie, John James Farquharson, Graham Hall, Corporals Jeffrey Schuneman and Ian Clegg, Lieutenant Tom Beese, Sergeant Gareth Davies, Lance Corporal Anthony Dean and Troopers Ian Allcroft, Stuart Ward and Moray Orr. We reached the roadhead at Darcha by bus on August 27. Base Camp was finally established on September 3 at 16,000 feet north of Koa Rong IV. On September 5 Camp I was established at 16,500 feet at the foot of the icefall leading to the summit ramp. Hardie and Davies found a route through the icefall which led into a snow bowl, where Camp II was placed at 19,500 feet on September 7. From there the steep north ice face with a rock ridge on the left led directly to the summit. Hardie and Davies completed the first ascent of Koa Rong IV (6340 meters, 20,800 feet) on September 8. During the next three days we managed to get a further five people to the summit.

CHARLES A. HOOKEY, *Captain, British Army*

India—Ladakh-Kashmir

P 6392 (Janam), Kishtwar Himal, Second Ascent. P 6392 (20,970 feet), locally called Janam, is located north of the Kiar Nalla. The first ascent was reported in *A.A.J.*, 1978, page 612. Base Camp at the Sarbal meadows at 11,800 feet was reached on July 28 after a five-day march from Kishtwar. Advance Base was pitched after crossing the Kiar Nalla twice to avoid a gorge on the right bank. On the mountain we generally followed the south ridge. Camp I was placed at 15,425 feet on August 3. The route to Camp II led from a basin up a couloir. A ridge was then followed over a short distance to a rock tower of loose rock which was avoided by skirting on the left, following a fixed rope of the 1977 party. On August 6 we all moved to Camp II at 18,050 feet on a snow plateau just behind the rock shoulder. Firm rock led to a corniced ridge which we followed through an icefield on the west side. Late in the afternoon, after climbing in fog all day, we got to a level icefield and a col just below the summit. On August 8 all climbing members, Hans van den Berg, Rudolf de Koning, Jan Spit and I, reached the summit in excellent weather. A slightly higher peak was seen a kilometer to the northwest.

JAAP BARENDREGT, *Koninklijke Nederlandse Alpen Vereniging*

Nun, Kun, White Needle and Pinnacle Peak. These peaks are now being frequently climbed. Aside from ascents noted elsewhere, Nun (7135 meters, 23,410 feet) was climbed by French led by O. Pierre, Swiss led by Michel Roch and Japanese led by Masaki Matsumoto. Unfortunately Japanese Junichi Keino froze to death while descending alone to Camp III. Kun (7077 meters, 23,220 feet) was climbed by two German groups, one led by Günter Schulz and

West Face of NUN. Route ascended right of west face to right fork of rock ridge and then skyline.

the other from Hauser International. A large but unsuccessful Japanese expedition lost Novitaka Katsuyama in rockfall. The White Needle (6600 meters, 21,654 feet) was climbed by Indians led by Daljit Singh, French led by Robert Fargeas and Taiwanese led by Wu Hsia Hsung. Pinnacle Peak (6930 meters, 22,737 feet) was climbed by Germans led by Walter Spindler on July 20.

Nun, Direct West Ridge Variant. Heavy late-winter snows and the closed Zoji La created logistical problems but Indian Airlines solved the Zoji Pass problem as we converged on Leh on April 26. We were Gary Ball, Andrew Dennison, Peter Lev, Paul Stettner and I. Our friendly and efficient liaison officer, Flight Lieutenant T. Shridhar, arranged passage by bus to Kargil and then by truck to "as close to Tongol as he could take us." A few kilometers north of Panikhar we stopped just short of a muddy bog. From there it was the muscle power of beast and man. The local pony driver knew he had a sellers' market: double overcharge for four days even though it took only two half days to get to Tongol! The Tongol porters knew the rig too. They used the spring snow just above town to charge double the normal rate. Despite these delays, Base Camp was established on May 4 a kilometer beyond the col of the most prominent gully south of town, not by the normal route because the more direct route led over dangerous snow slopes. Now carrying our own loads, Camp I was placed on a dramatic 16,000-foot pass in full view of Nun. Much of our carrying was done on skis while pulling our loads on light-weight plastic sleds. The move to Camp II dropped 500 feet into the valley leading to the main icefall. There a four-day storm dumped over a meter of snow. It was not until May 13 that we could start moving supplies to Camp III below the plateau headwall. The recent heavy snow caused us to use great caution on the headwall. Hugging ridges and ice bulges without fixed ropes, a safe route was established to a cache on the great plateau itself. By May 17 the entire cache was sledded to within a kilometer of the west face. From Plateau Camp we spied the face with binoculars and debated which route on the face was best. Large ice streaks appeared to grow with each sunny day. Despite an early start on May 19, Ball, Stettner and I were not near the actual face until noon. There we were stopped by a vertical ice ledge bottoming out into an ice chute that drained anything loose that wished to come off the west face. We gave up the idea of the face and headed up the vast slopes of the Czech route. Ball turned back with cold feet. Stettner and I traversed up to the north ridge and bivouacked in a storm-whipped snow cave. We returned to the plateau the next day. Earlier Lev had suggested we gain the west ridge directly from the plateau up the extreme right side of the west face. Climbing alpine style, we began this venture on May 21, camping beneath the bergschrund that evening. The next day was a long one. Six rope-lengths took us over the 45° snow face with touches of underlying ice. Above that we wound our way through rock outcrops and snow gullies ending with a sudden finish over the ice headwall which guarded the upper bowl between the west ridge and the French route. There, at 22,100 feet, we pitched High Camp and shivered at −35° C. May 23 dawned with ominous clouds but then cleared. With dispatch Lev led the last difficult 30-meter rock pitch just below the start of the summit snow ridge, but one pitch later he elected to turn back with Ball, who again was suffering cold feet in his too small boots. Also, Lev did not like the hollow sound of the snow and the snowy look of the Zanskars behind us. Stettner and I pressed on. The knife-edged summit ridge rose relatively gently for twelve rope-lengths, but on either side it dropped steeply. I had to decide on which side to step. Some of the way we belayed, some we climbed simultaneously, but near the summit there was a kind of Hillary Step for the last two exhausting leads. On the top (7135 meters, 23,410 feet) the storm seemed imminent and unconsolidated snow seemed ready to collapse at any moment. Less than an hour later we were off the difficult rock pitch just as the edge of the storm hit. By 6:15 P.M. we were back at High camp. By May 28 Base Camp was cleared.

JOCK GLIDDEN

Kun. Our expedition made the difficult crossing of the Suru river on August 16. Fortunately we had a small pneumatic boat. We climbed the northeast ridge, the normal route. We placed Base Camp at 14,750 feet on the 18th, Camp I at 17,725 feet on the 20th (the glacier was easy but dangerously crevassed), Camp II at 19,700 feet on the 22nd (two steep walls and an easy glacier) and Camp III at 20,675 feet on the 26th (after a long but easy crossing of the plateau). On August 28 Michel Vincent, Marie Guislaine Jessenne, André Berthet, Pascal Jouenne, Léonard LaLoy, Jean Pierre Gadel, Robert Geay and Christian Deronce made a 14-hour round-trip summit climb up the difficult summit ridge. On the 29th Guy Lemoine and Christian Meynier reached the summit. An injured ankle kept me from the climb. The weather was generally bad except for August 27 and 28. We registered − 25° C at Camp III on August 29 and some climbers suffered frostbite. Bears came to Base Camp on several nights. They destroyed six unoccupied tents but did not bother the occupied ones.

CLAUDE JACCOUX, *Club Alpin Français*

Nun, North Ridge. A ten-man Indian Army team from the Dogra Regiment, led by Major Prem Chand, set up Base Camp on June 10. After establishing four more camps, on June 19 Harnam Singh, Thakur Dass, Lalit Kumar and Mohammad Amin reached the summit of Nun*(7135 meters, 23,410 feet) by way of the unclimbed north ridge.

KAMAL K. GUHA, *Himalayan Club*

---

*Because of the large number of people ascending such high peaks as Nun, Kun, Trisul and others, we can no longer try to give accounts of all of the more commonly climbed peaks, except for new routes, interesting ascents, etc.—*Editor.*

Z3 and P 5750, Zanskar. Our objective had been to climb P 6550 at the head of the Durung Drum Glacier. We ascended the glacier for about ten miles and placed Base Camp at 14,775 feet. However bad weather and intestinal infections caused us to change our program. Domenico Bidese, Giancarlo Contalbrigo, Paolo Ghitti and Franco Brunello on August 14 climbed Z3 (6280 meters, 20,604 feet) from a camp at 17,725 feet, which was not easy to reach and where we fixed rope on the approach. This beautiful snow peak was one of the few in the group which had been previously climbed. That same day Giuseppe Pierantoni and I climbed lovely P 5750 (18,865 feet), which lies just north of Z3. We ascended the north ridge and face from Base Camp and had notable rock-and-ice difficulties. At the same time Alberto Campanile soloed the same peak by a steeper and more difficult route on the north face.

Ostilio Campese, Club Alpino Italiano

P 5854, P 6025, P 5895 and Z2, Zanskar Range. Our expedition was composed of Gianni Calcagno, leader, Giustino Crescimbeni, Mario Pelizzaro, Stefano De Benedetti and me. From the Kargil-Padum road, we ascended the Rundum valley to Base Camp at 13,300 feet at the tongue of the Rundum Glacier. We climbed four unclimbed summits and made two first ski ascents and descents. We placed a high camp ten miles up the glacier at 14,275 feet. Calcagno, Pelizzaro, Crescimbeni and I climbed P 5854 (19,206 feet) on June 21 by the northeast spur and descended the easy southwest ridge. On June 26 Calcagno and I ascended P 6025 (19,767 feet) by the 70° ice northeast face and rappelled down the east face. Calcagno, Pelizzaro and I climbed P 5895 (19,340 feet) by the north face on June 28. Calcagno, Pelizzaro and I unsuccessfully attempted for three days to reach the unclimbed lower summit (6080 meters, 19,948 feet) of twin-peaked Z2 along the south ridge, but we could not get by a 35-foot completely smooth red-granite slab 1000 feet below the summit. We rappelled and then climbed the southeast face, which was a difficult mixed climb. De Benedetti made two solo ski ascents and descents: the higher of Z2's twin summits (6175 meters, 20,260 feet) by the south face on July 9 and the north spur of P 5854 on July 12.

Tullio Vidoni, Club Alpino Accademico Italiano

Kang Yisay. An Indian expedition set up Base Camp at 17,000 feet on August 20 and Camp I at 18,600 feet the following day. Naseer Ahmed Mir, Fayez Ahmed Bala and Showkat Hussain Mir left Camp I at 5:30 A.M. on August 22. They started up the northeast face but found it heavily crevassed. They switched to the southwest face and trudged up it to reach the summit (6300 meters, 20,670 feet) at 2:30 P.M. A team from the United Kingdom or Ireland had climbed the peak in early August but details are lacking.

Kamal K. Guha, Himalayan Club

Pakistan

K7 Attempt. Japanese led by Masayuki Hoshina made an attempt on K7 (6934 meters, 22,750 feet) by way of the 17,000-foot west col. They approached from Hushe via the Charakusa Glacier, where they established Base Camp on May 27. They fixed some 5000 feet of rope. The expedition reached a little higher than 20,000 feet.

Hidden Peak (Gasherbrum I), North Face Attempt. Granger Banks, Richard Soaper, Lyle Dean and I arrived at Gasherbrum I Base Camp on May 19 after eleven days on the Baltoro approach with 23 porters. After placing a food cache at 21,325 feet in the Gasherbrum La Icefall, we descended to recuperate. On June 3 we returned up the West Gasherbrum Glacier icefall to the cache in two days. The next day we climbed the right side of the north face in twelve hours unroped. The face consisted of wind-blown ice on the bottom, mixed climbing on a rotten rock arête in the middle and a final third of "funky" névé up to 80°. We carried four days' food. We were on the north face itself, well left of Messner's route. On the top of the north face, on the northwest shoulder of Hidden Peak, we placed our high camp at 23,300 feet next to Messner's and Habeler's destroyed tent. On June 6 we rested, hoping to join Messner's route the next day and climb to the summit. We were wrong. The next three days were spent battling gale winds. Supplies dwindled. Granger Banks and I descended the north face. Dean and Soaper waited in hope of a calming of the winds. That evening they thought there was a chance and started off that night. Soaper reconsidered and returned to the high camp. At 24,600 feet Dean found the conditions worse and decided to come back down too. We felt that the ice and snow conditions might be better later in the season.

GORDON BANKS, *Unaffiliated*

Hidden Peak, Ski Descent. After arriving at Base Camp at 17,050 feet on May 15, four French and Swiss climbers, Sylvain Saudain, Jean Pierre Ollagnier, Daniel Semblanet and Marie José Valençot, and high-altitude porter Mohammad Ali climbed Hidden Peak after 32 days. On the summit day, the Swiss skier and leader of the group, Saudan, skied down for two hours and bivouacked. Laurent Chevalier and a Swedish photographer stayed at 25,600 feet to film the run. The next day he descended to Base Camp in nine hours, completing the descent of over 9000 feet with 3000 turns. Between 21,325 and 19,700 feet the corniced ridge was difficult. We presume they followed the first-ascent route.

Hidden Peak (Gasherbrum I), North Face. We made the seventh ascent of Hidden Peak by a partially new route, the north face, when Michel Dacher, Sigi Hupfauer and I got to the summit (8068 meters, 26,470 feet) on July 22. Base Camp was established on June 18 and Camp I on June 21. We had placed

Camp II at 21,000 feet on the Gasherbrum La on June 26 before nearly a month of bad weather set in. We could not start on the summit push until July 18. The most difficult part of the route was rotten rock (UIAA IV and V) between Camps II and III, which we established at 23,300 feet. At Camp III we joined the Habeler-Messner route of 1975, which had been well to the right of ours. On the summit day we went too far to the left, to a rib in the north face, had to retrace our steps a considerable distance and so got to the summit very late, at 6:20 P.M. We could not find Camp III in the dark and had to bivouac 350 feet above it. Dr. Gerhard Schmatz, Dr. Wolfgang Shaffert and Peter Vogler had to give up their attempt at 23,000 feet because of frightful weather. (This was Dacher's fifth 8000er and Sturm's and Hupfauer's fourth.—*Editor.*)

GÜNTER STURM, *Deutscher Alpenverein*

Gasherbrum II. It took 13 days to get from Dassu to our temporary Base Camp at 16,000 feet on the Abruzzi Glacier, including two rest days, one caused by heavy snowfall at Concordia. We arrived on May 14. We had started with 60 porters but arrived with 40 since many who had carried food could be discharged. Because of cold, fog and snow, the porters could not carry the last two or three hours to Base Camp. Expedition members made the carry in five days. We followed the first-ascent route and used no fixed ropes. We set up Camp I at 19,700 feet on May 21 and Camp II on the southwest spur at 21,650 feet on May 25. Bad weather and stomach troubles defeated the first summit try. On June 8 Georg Kaser and Gerhard Markl set up Camp III at 24,275 feet and climbed to the summit on June 9. Michel Grüner and Robert Renzler ascended from Base Camp to Camp II on June 7 and in the next two days to 23,000 and 24,275 feet to reach the summit on June 10. On June 9 Christine Miller, Josef Trattner and I reached Camp III and headed for the summit on June 11. Christine Miller fell ill and I descended with her while Trattner made the summit. On the descent on the 12th she suffered third-degree frostbite on three toes and Grüner had minor frostbite. We had picked up stomach and intestinal infections in Rawalpindi, which bothered us throughout the expedition.

HELMUT ROTT, *Akademischer Alpiner Verein, Innsbruck, Austria*

Gasherbrum II Tragedy. After arriving at Dassu by jeep, Glenn Brindeiro, Steven Casebolt, Donald Goodman, David Hambly, Dr. Brack Hattler, David McClung, Dr. Thomas Vaughan and I as leader on May 15 started our trek to Base Camp (16,500 feet), which we reached on May 27. Thanks to the trail blazing by the Austrian expedition, we found the fierce-looking South Gasherbrum icefall relatively easy. Camp I was at 18,000 feet just above the first icefall. One night we were nearly blown away by an ice avalanche from Hidden Peak. From Camp I to Camp II (19,700 feet), the South Gasherbrum Glacier was horribly crevassed and both we and members of other expeditions took falls into hidden crevasses. Our route, the Austrian southwest ridge route of 1956, was straightforward but steep. Up to Camp III (21,150 feet) Casebolt and Goodman fixed rope most of the way. During the second part of June the weather was often bad. Despite heavy snowfalls, Casebolt and Goodman forced the way up to Camp IV (23,000 feet). Finally, on June 28, Brindeiro, Casebolt, Goodman and Hambly moved up to Camp III and the following day they continued on to Camp IV. Goodman, not feeling well, returned to Camp III. Camp IV was very exposed and buffeted by strong winds until July 1. On that evening an enormous avalanche swept the south face of Gasherbrum II. July 2 dawned fine, clear, cold and calm. Brindeiro, Casebolt and Hambly tried to establish Camp V at 24,500 feet. They climbed unroped as had other expeditions. On the ridge the snow was knee-deep and the slope increased to 45° by the time they reached the rock section at 23,500 feet. While they discussed the snow conditions, the snow slope to their right avalanched. Hambly, the highest, was knocked over, Casebolt, some 30 feet below, was carried down about 50 feet, but of Brindeiro, who was 30 feet below Casebolt, there was no sign. The ridge fell off to the right as a 30° slope for 50 to 100 yards before dropping off in a series of ice cliffs. An immediate search from the top and side of the ice cliffs revealed nothing. Because of avalanche danger, no attempt was made to enter the ice cliffs for a further search. They descended to Camp III in very poor snow conditions and increasingly bad visibility. Further examination of the ice cliffs during the descent from Camp III to Camp II was also unsuccessful.

MICHAEL D. CLARKE

Gasherbrum II Attempt. Our expedition was composed of Dr. Jean Pierre Becquemin, Thierry Cazenave, Thierry Gallouët, Marc Souchal and me. We left Skardu on June 9 and reached Base Camp on June 19. After carrying two loads to Camp I at 20,000 feet, an alpine-style attempt for the summit via the normal south ridge was made by Cazenave and Gallouët who reached 25,425 feet after a bivouac at 22,000 feet. They had to turn back on June 30. After June 28 the weather had become worse and worse.

JEAN MICHEL GOSSELIN, *Club Alpin Français*

Gasherbrum II, Husband-and-Wife Ascent. My wife Liliane, her brother Alain Bontemps and I reached the summit of Gasherbrum II on June 12. We were accompanied to Base Camp by Louis Thiberge, thus complying with the Pakistani regulation of having four members. We reached Base Camp at 16,250 feet in nine days on June 1. We followed the Austrian route on the mountain. From Base Camp, to reach the beginning of the southeast ridge at 19,500 feet, one must climb a contorted icefall to 17,725 feet and then ascend the upper part of the less crevassed and gentler glacier. We used cross-country skis on this part. At 19,700 feet one starts up a 55° to 60° snow slope and then follows a more moderate snow ridge to 21,650 feet. At 22,300 feet there are three sérac barriers. We had hoped to make a new variant by following straight up the whole southeast ridge from 23,950 feet, rather than by traversing right, but there was too much snow on mediocre rocks. We placed a camp at 19,500 feet on June 3 and 4 and by June 7 had reconnoitered to 21,650 feet. On June 9 we left Base Camp, bivouacking at 19,500, 21,650 and 23,950 feet. We got to the summit on the fourth day after leaving Base Camp. Liliane and I made two more attempts on the direct route. When we got to 21,650 feet on June 21, we found that ravens had destroyed the food we had left there. It also snowed a foot. From June 24 to 29 we two climbed to 24,600 feet but were stopped by deep snow and bad weather.

MAURICE BARRARD, *Groupe de Haute Montagne*

Gasherbrum II and Broad Peak. Reinhold Messner turned to Pakistan after his successful climb of Kanchenjunga. On July 24 he climbed Gasherbrum II and on August 2 reached the summit of Broad Peak. He was accompanied by Pakistanis Nazir Sabir and Major Sher Khan. Broad Peak was Messner's eleventh ascent of an 8000er. He has now ascended nine of the fourteen 8000ers and has climbed Everest and Nanga Parbat twice. Nazir Sabir climbed K2 from the west in 1981.

Deaths on Broad Peak and Gasherbrum II. The leaders of two expeditions died in the unusually bad weather in the Karakoram this year. Both expeditions were then called off. Austrian-born Canadian Hans G. Frick died in an avalanche on Broad Peak on May 16. On July 10 West German Dr. Gerd Brunner and Austrian Dr. Norbert Wolf were last seen from far below as they were climbing at 25,200 feet on Gasherbrum II. Dr. Wolf was later found at 25,600 feet by Reinhold Messner and his companions frozen to death in his bivouac sack. The expedition leader, Dr. Brunner, was not found although some of his clothing and equipment was further down the slope. He is presumed to have fallen.

Gasherbrum IV Attempt. An eight-man Japanese expedition led by Yukio Katsumi failed to climb Gasherbrum IV by its west face. Base Camp was established on June 9. They placed four camps on the mountain, Camp IV at 20,350 feet. On July 29 a high point of 21,325 feet was reached. Attempts by British in 1979 and Japanese in 1981 also failed. Further information and a photo of the route appear in *Iwa To Yuki,* N° 92.

Broad Peak, West Ridge Attempt. Our expedition was made up of Paul Briggs, Steve Strain, Bob McIntosh and me as leader, but McIntosh injured his knee near the tongue of the Baltoro Glacier and had to leave the expedition. We arrived in Skardu on June 19. We walked to Base Camp at 15,750 feet from June 22 to July 2. We acclimatized until July 8 around Base Camp and on July 9 we climbed to 18,500 feet up the same couloir used by previous expeditions and spent the night, during which there was an earthquake. We descended to Base Camp on the 10th. From July 11 to 17 it snowed every night; the new snow melted off by mid-afternoon but much snow accumulated high on the mountain. We had hoped for a four-day period of settled weather to make a summit bid. On July 17 Briggs and Strain climbed to Camp I at 20,600 feet, but bad weather set in and they descended. We walked out to Skardu from July 20 to 27.

HOWARD A. WEAVER

Broad Peak. We started from Dassu with 52 porters on June 24 and got to Base Camp at 16,400 feet, west of Broad Peak, eight days later with 42 porters, having been able to send ten back who had been carrying food. We had no high-altitude porters and used no artificial oxygen. We established camps at 21,000 and 23,300 feet. For the first three weeks the weather was never good enough to go above 21,325 feet. Then it turned fine until our departure. The route started up a steep gully with mostly bare ice in the upper part, where we fixed 500 feet of rope. The rest of the way to the upper camp was steep ribs and slopes, generally free from avalanches and almost no crevasses. Up to 23,000 feet there was hardly a flat spot for a tent. The last part below the col between the middle and main peaks is a basin, usually filled with much snow. From the col to the foresummit the ridge is exposed and corniced. From there to the summit it is nearly flat. By previous arrangement, we were joined on the summit climb by three Austrians: Georg Bachler, Werner Sucher and Walter Lösch. With them, Hans Kirchberger, Konrad Lewanskowski, Ralph Bärtle and I climbed to the summit (8047 meters, 26,400 feet) on July 23. The other members of our expedition were Sepp Ölker, Walter Janner and Otto Parzhuber.

PETER GLOGGNER, *Deutscher Alpenverein*

Broad Peak North, Solo Attempt. Solo I attempted the north buttress of Broad Peak North (7600 meters, 24,935 feet) during June and July but I had to give up because of bad weather. I was on the wall for 24 days, but had to stop at 23,000 feet because with the bad weather the avalanche danger became too great.

RENATO CASAROTTO, *Club Alpino Italiano*

K2 Attempt and Broad Peak. Our expedition arrived at Base Camp on June 2. From June 13 until July 20 we spent most of the five weeks in uninterrupted bad weather. We could not climb higher than Camp II at 22,650 feet on the Abruzzi spur. Continuous wind even chewed through our fixed rope. When Wanda Rutkiewicz-Scharfetter and her Polish women's expedition arrived, they finally brought some good weather with them. Walter Lösch, Georg Bachler and Werner Sucher for a time joined the German expedition led by Peter Gloggner and on July 23 with them reached the summit of Broad Peak. At that same time our Pakistani liaison officer Major Fayyaz Hussain and I prepared the route from Camp II to the site of Camp III on K2, at the top of the Black Pyramid at 25,000 feet. On July 27 all five of us were ready for our final attempt. I climbed for the fifth time to Camp II. On the 29th we were again held up by storm at Camps I and II, but we were all at Camp II on July 30. That afternoon the Poles Halina Krüger-Syrokomska and Anna Okopińska arrived at Camp II. We helped them prepare their tent site. At five P.M. Anna summoned us. Halina had suddenly fallen deathly ill. Oxygen, mouth-to-mouth resuscitation, nothing availed. In a few minutes she died, apparently from a cerebral hemorrhage. We evacuated her body on July 31 with great difficulty. After a memorial service for her, we had neither the physical nor moral strength for a further attempt.

ALOIS FURTNER, *Österreichischer Alpenverein*

K2 Women's Expedition Tragedy. The expedition organized by Wanda Rutkiewicz-Scharfetter was further composed of Alicja Bednarz, Frenchwoman Christine de Colombel, Anna Czerwińska, Halina Krüger-Syrokomska, Aniela Łukaszewska, Dr. Jolanta Maciuch, Anna Okopińska, Ewa Pankiewicz, Marianna Stolarek, Krystyna Palmowska and Danuta Wach. After an 11-day approach, they arrived at Base Camp at 16,400 feet on July 19. Advance Base was placed at 17,725 feet at the foot of the Abruzzi Ridge on July 21. On the same day Camp I was pitched at 20,000 feet by Czerwińska and Palmowska. Camp II at 22,000 feet was established on July 27. On July 30 Halina Krüger-Syrokomska reached Camp II with Anna Okopińska. After supper she called Base Camp by radio. The talk was good-humored and did not signal anything wrong. resting in the tent with Anna, she suddenly died either from a heart attack or a stroke. Efforts to revive her by Anna and the Austrians failed. An art historian, at 44 years she was also one of the outstanding women climbers. She had made remarkable ascents in Europe and Asia. Perhaps the most notable was the ascent of Gasherbrum in 1975 with Anna Okopińska, the first ladies-only ascent of an 8000-meter peak. After some days action resumed. Czerwińska, Palmowska and de Colombel reached 23,300 feet on August 7, the expedition's high point. More tries were made in doubtful weather. During August there were only two good days. Between September

15 and 26 the camps were brought back to Base Camp. The women's party was accompanied by Wojciech Kurtyka and Jerzy Kukuczka.

JÓZEF NYKA, *Editor, Taternik, Poland*

K2, Northwest Ridge Attempt. Our joint Polish-Mexican expedition was composed of Lucio Cárdenas, Manuel Casanueva, Antonio Cortés, Hugo Delgado, Enrique Miranda and Eduardo Mosqueda, *Mexicans,* and Roman Bebak, Dr. Grzegorz Benke, Eugeniusz Chrobak, Leszek Cichy, Zbigniew Dudrak, Marek Grochowski, Jan Holnicki-Szulc, Tadeusz Karolczak, Aleksander Lwow, Krzysztof Pankiewicz, Bogumił Słama, Ryszard Urbanik, Krzysztof Wielicki, Wojciech Wróż and me as leader, *Poles.* We left Skardu on June 26. Base Camp was established on July 8 at 17,400 feet on the Savoia Glacier. We placed Camp I at 19,500 feet a short distance from the wall descending from our goal, the northwest ridge, on July 10. Two days later we attacked the 2300-foot-high face. The slope was very steep and more dangerous than we had expected. After eight hard days in bad weather, we climbed the wall and on July 19 established Camp II at 22,000 feet on the northwest ridge. In this way we hit the ridge beyond the pinnacled section which stopped the Americans in 1975. Cárdenas had a lucky escape when he was hurled by an avalanche and fell 700 feet. He suffered only a fracture of the forearm. The ridge above Camp II was rocky and presented considerable difficulties. We traversed obliquely to the left. It was very difficult to find a place for Camp III. On July 26 we set up the tents at 23,300 feet in two separate small platforms 150 feet apart. From there the rock face was steeper and presented continuous difficulties. Camp IV was established on August 5 at 24,900 feet on the big spur where we found the fixed ropes of the Japanese expedition that was at the same time attacking K2 from the north. The Japanese turned up to the left of the spur. We attacked the depression on the right side. On August 7 Chrobak, Cichy, Pankiewicz and Wielicki established the depot of equipment at 26,100 feet near the top of the pinnacle uniting the northwest ridge and the north buttress. After August 9 the weather deteriorated. On only two days, August 14 and 15, was there an opportunity for the summit. (It was then that the Japanese climbed to the summit.) But we were not yet ready. The first summit party was moving from the lower camps and was stopped by bad weather (strong winds and snowfall) in camp IV on August 16. After this date, we made several attempts to climb to the summit, but all parties were stopped for the same reason, very strong winds. The last group, Chrobak, Cichy, Wielicki and Wróż, established Camp V at 26,500 feet on September 5. The next day Cichy and Wróż set out for the summit without oxygen, but they were forced back by strong winds and frostbite. They had reached 27,000 feet.

JANUSZ KURCZAB, *Polski Zwiazek Alpinizmu*

PLATE 79
Photo by Janusz Kurczab
K2 from the West. The ridge
attempted is on the left.

Savoia Kangri Attempt. Our expedition was composed of Jan Tichý, Jiří Ulrych, my brother Zdeněk Lukeš and me. All but my brother are Czechs in exile. We set up Base Camp on June 6 at the junction of the Godwin Austen and Savoia Glaciers at 16,400 feet. We had only 23 days left for the climb. From then until June 19 bad weather prevented our occupying Advance Base at 17,725 feet on the Savoia Glacier at the foot of Savoia Kangri I (7263 meters, 23,830 feet). The 6000-foot-high east face seemed best, as the rest of the mountain was avalanche-threatened. Without Ulrych, on June 20 we started up the prominent ridge. We were stopped on June 22 by strong winds and snowfall 2000-feet-up. On June 24 we came to where the ridge abutted the true face. The link was a very delicate, thin ice ridge. We just did not have enough time or equipment to cross this. We had reached 21,500 feet. After our descent, the weather deteriorated again, confirming we had made the right decision.

ČESTMÍR LUKEŠ, *Czech living in Switzerland*

Various Unsuccessful Expeditions to the Karakoram. Bad weather drove back a number of expeditions. Frenchmen under the leadership of Hubert Odier got to 23,950 feet on Gasherbrum II before being turned back. Germans led by Dr. Volker Stallbohm failed on Masherbrum. Japanese under Kenichiro Tsujiyama could not climb Saraghrar. There were two unsuccessful expeditions to Kunyang Chhish: Japanese led by Isao Nakamura on the east ridge and French under Pierre Pujot on the north ridge. Guillermo Lateo's Spanish group failed on Latok II (the official Latok II, not the Italian designated one).

Latok I Attempt. (The officially designated Latok I, called Latok II by the Italians.) The mountain was everything we expected: superb rock, good line, good sustained climbing. Unfortunately Martin Boysen, Choe Brooks, John Yates and I could not finish the job. We attempted the north ridge tried by the Americans in 1978. (See *A.A.J.*, 1979, pages 24 to 28 for text and photos.) In July we placed Base Camp at the junction of the Panmah and Choktoi Glaciers and Advance Base up the Choktoi. There was more snow than usual around. Our first 2½-day sortie was to leave equipment and a tent a third of the way up the ridge. The second attempt took place several days later. We reached our high point in a day and continued up for two more. On the fourth day one of the team decided it was too dangerous. A single person could not retreat safely or stay in the tent alone and so we had to retreat. Afterwards we had no food, equipment or inclination to return.

RAB CARRINGTON, *Alpine Climbing Group*

Baintha Brakk II (Ogre II) Attempt. Brian Hall, Alan Rouse, Andrew Parkin and I attempted unclimbed Baintha Brakk II or Ogre II (6960 meters, 22,835 feet). It promised to be at least as difficult as Baintha Brakk (Ogre). A British party tried it in 1979 and large Japanese and Korean expeditions

SAVOIA KANGRI. The route attempted rises up the rock ridge on the right.

subsequently. None scored much success, and one Korean died when ice swept him away in "Death Valley," the dangerous corridor between the Ogre peaks. Baintha Brakk II is a difficult and complex peak. The west summit is a gigantic Matterhorn-like spire. The east peak is an icy ridge, and between is the central and highest summit, approachable only by devious routes through the lower walls and an extremely long and difficult summit ridge protected by steep towers. The lower reaches were obviously dangerous, making alpine style seem best. Thirty-three porters took our equipment to Base Camp in six days from Dassu. By July 16 we were installed at 15,500 feet. For acclimatization, we attempted Uzun Brakk Spire, a challenging rock spire of about 19,500 feet on the west side of the Uzun Brakk Glacier. A new route was pioneered on July 23 and 24 and we bivouacked within a day of the top. A storm ended the attempt and enforced a dangerous descent by a different unknown route. On July 28 we climbed the ice slopes towards the northwest ridge of the west peak of Baintha Brakk II. After a bivouac, we reached 20,000 feet early in the day after crossing an extremely hazardous hanging glacier, to bivouac in an ice cave we excavated. The next day we proceeded up difficult rock to 20,850 feet, but no bivouac position could be established. This enforced a retreat to the ice cave. The labour on this buttress caused damage to half our supply of rope either through stonefall or razor-edged flakes of rock. Our supplies were too limited to continue, and so on July 31 we retreated, traversing the northwest face and abseiling into the top of Death Valley down steep rock and ice. In this fast descent we were mightily impressed by the immense amount of debris and danger on this route; all wished if possible to avoid it in the future. On August 2 and 3 we investigated the south face but decided that the only possibility was far too steep and threatened by falling ice. The south ridge of the west peak did have some appeal though it was technically of the highest standard. This attempt was delayed when Hall injured a shoulder in a fall near Base Camp; for him further climbing was impossible. On August 6 and 7 we three remaining climbers tried the south ridge of the west peak. Unfortunately the gully leading to it was extremely long and very dangerous. The Japanese had tried this route in expedition style. It took us twelve hours of extremely threatened climbing to reach the ridge and we bivouacked in an exposed position on the corniced ridge. The next day we set off but turned back when one of my crampons disintegrated. With four or five days of difficult climbing ahead, retreat was inevitable. On August 8 we made a dangerous retreat to Base Camp. The only really feasible fast route now seemed to be the north ridge of the central summit, which involved taking our life into our hands in Death Valley. When the weather cleared on August 16, we bivouacked below it and set off in fine conditions early on the 17th. We climbed the corridor quickly before dawn and by six A.M. were almost clear of the dangerous area. Just then, an ice cliff 1000 feet higher collapsed and swept the gully, crashing past within thirty feet. Much chastened, we climbed fast into the safer area ahead. Yet to reach the ridge, we had to climb under ice cliffs with the risk of falls.

BAINTHA BRAKK II's Northwest Face.

We decided to retreat. Base Camp was reached that day and vacated on August 21.

PAUL NUNN, *Alpine Climbing Group*

Distaghil Sar, Second Ascent. After arriving on June 23 at Nagar, we spent two days haggling with the porter chiefs. We finally contracted for 37 porters and a sirdar. We ascended the Hispar valley and glacier and on July 1 got to Bularung on the Kunyang Glacier. With the help of other porters from Hunza, we moved supplies to Base Camp at 14,600 feet on the true right lateral moraine from July 3 to 8. Our liaison officer and cook stayed at Bularung and then returned to Hunza. We placed Camp I at the foot of the southeast face of Distaghil Sar at 16,400 feet on July 8. Camps II and III were established on the face at 19,350 and 21,650 feet on July 19 and 22. We fixed 2600 feet of rope between Camps I and II and 1000 feet between Camps II and III. We were entirely on snow and ice. We followed the route of the only other ascent, that of Wolfgang Stefan's Austrian expedition of 1960 except between Camps I and II, where we were well to the right. From July 19 on, we finally had good weather. The summit attack began on July 26. Five climbers ascended to Camp III on July 28. Three carried to Camp IV the next day, fixing 500 more feet of rope, and established it on July 30 at 23,800 feet on the west ridge. On July 31 Ramón Biosca, Jaume Matas and Toni Bros set out. Bros was too tired to climb the last 150 feet, but the other two arrived on the summit (7885 meters, 25,868 feet) at 2:50 P.M. They were back at Camp IV at seven P.M. Soft snow made the descent to Base Camp take two days more. Other members were Dr. Josep Aced, Josep Paytubi and I as leader.

JOAQUIM PRUNÉS, *Club Muntanyenc de Terrassa, Spain*

Bojohaghur Duan Asir I. Six Japanese climbers led by Muneo Uyeda failed to climb Bojohaghur Duan Asir I (7329 meters, 24,046 feet). They approached the mountain up the Ultar Glacier from Hunza and attempted the south side. Base Camp at 12,950 feet was established on June 9 and Camps I and II at 14,450 and 16,750 feet. Then the weather went bad. Camp III was placed on the southwest col at 19,525 feet only on July 19. The high point of the expedition was not much higher. The route was threatened by rockfall and three members were hit.

Bubuli-Mo-Tin, Ultar Group. Jacques Maurin and I made the first ascent of a 6000-meter (19,685-foot) tower, a satellite of the Ultar group on May 22. It lies southwest of Bojohaghur Duan Asir between the Ultar and Hasanabad Glaciers. We ascended north from Karimabad, a village just east of Baltit. We reached the summit in three days from Karimabad. The climb was mixed ice and rock and at times was very difficult. The approach was threatened by avalanches. We climbed to the east col and up the east ridge. The final granite tooth rises some 2500 to 3000 feet.

PATRICK CORDIER, *Groupe de Haute Montagne*

Hachindar Chhish, East Face. The march-in with 110 porters to the foot of Hachindar Chhish from Aliabad in Hunza took us four days. On May 30 we established Base Camp on the Muchichul Glacier at 12,000 feet. We used no high-altitude porters. Our route was in three parts: the lower face of 4000 feet to Advance Base Camp, the steep upper wall of 3000 feet to the forepeak and the knife-edge ridge to the summit. We climbed a wide couloir above Base Camp to Advance Base Camp, which was occupied on June 19 at 15,950 feet on a broad snow ridge leading to the upper wall. This part was troubled with occasional rockfall and snow avalanches and a vertical aid pitch. Camp I was placed at 17,950 feet on the snow slope immediately below the east face of the forepeak. The route above Camp I started with a steep snow slope, then a smooth snow ridge and higher up, the steep icy rock wall of the forepeak with many aid pitches. On July 4 Camp II was set up on an ice band on the face at 19,150 feet. On July 12 we placed an uncomfortable Camp III at 19,650 feet on a small ledge. Camp IV, right below the forepeak, was established at 21,000 feet on the corniced ridge leading to the summit on July 21. We followed the tricky, heavily corniced ridge leading to the summit over some pinnacles. After ropes were fixed over the forepeak to the foot of the final summit ridge, all descended to Advance Base Camp to rest. On August 3 four members pitched Camp V at 21,325 feet just below the third pinnacle on the summit ridge. On August 4, seven members headed for the summit from Camps IV and V. We found a final icy gully running up to the summit cornice. Breaking through the cornice, leader Yasuyuki Higashi, Kenji Yoshida, Toshikazu Saito, Kensaku Sakai, Tatsuya Takinami, Kenichi Kimura and I stood on the summit of Hachindar Chhish (7163 meters, 23,500 feet) at two P.M.

KIYOSHI HAYAMI, *Kanazawa University Alpine Club, Japan*

Passu Peak Attempt. Our expedition consisted of Mamoru Shimizu, Norihide Taniuchi, Makihiro Wakao, Kazuhisa Ikegami, Hitoshi Mitsuishi, Kanichi Ichikawa and me as leader. We placed Base Camp at 13,300 feet on May 22 after a three-day approach from Passu village. From 13,950 to 16,250 feet there was a dangerous icefall; we prepared the route there from May 28 to June 3. Camps I, II and III were established at 16,250, 18,875 and 21,000 feet on June 4, 7 and 13 respectively. We skied between Camps II and III. Bad weather kept us from establishing Camp IV at 21,650 feet until June 20. Wakao and I started for a summit try on skis but at 22,950 feet we had a radio message

PLATE 82
Photo by Kuyoshi Hayami
HACHINDAR CHHISH's East Face.

that Ichikawa was suffering from high-altitude sickness in Camp III and we descended. On June 23 we carried him to Camp I but he died of pulmonary edema on the 24th. Our expedition was over.

TOSHIO NARITA, *Japanese Alpine Club*

Kuksar, Batura Karakoram. This previously unattempted peak, which lies at the head of the Batura Glacier in the northwestern Karakoram, was climbed in July. Success was marred by a fatal accident which during the descent befell the two members who reached the summit. The expedition members were Tim Hurrel, leader, Steve Brodrick, Martin Gledhill and me. Following extensive reconnaissance, we attempted the peak alpine style from Advance Base at 17,725 feet by a broad couloir in its southwest flank, followed by the short ridge. An attempt by Gledhill and me was aborted at 21,000 feet. On July 19 Brodrick and Hurrell reached the summit (6934 meters, 22,750 feet) after two bivouacs. On July 20, on their descent, they were swept to their deaths by an avalanche in the couloir. We found their bodies on July 22 and buried them in a crevasse. A diary and films were found, which authenticated the ascent. Poor snow conditions and unsettled weather prevailed throughout the expedition. The area, despite a tedious glacier approach, offers a number of attractive, unclimbed peaks of 21,325 to 23,625 feet.

MARTIN HORE, *England*

Saraghrar Northwest II. Our expedition was composed of Enrique Lucas, Ricardo Herrero, Nil Bohigas, Néstor Bohigas, Antonio García, Joan Martí and me as leader. We climbed the southwest buttress of Saraghrar Northwest II without oxygen, without high-altitude porters, without high camps nor tents. We established Base Camp on July 13 at 14,100 feet at the junction of the Rosh Gol Glacier and a tributary glacier southwest of the Saraghrar group. After depositing supplies at 15,900 feet on July 14, we started on the face at 16,100 feet on July 15 and had placed Advanced Base at 17,225 feet by July 19. By August 2 we had fixed rope to 19,700 feet. From August 4 to 8 we moved up the buttress, bivouacking at 19,000, 20,850, 21,325, 22,475 and 23,000 feet. The climbing was difficult. On August 9 Enrique Lucas, Nil Bohigas and I climbed to the summit of Sargahrar Northwest II (7200 meters, 23,622 feet), which we reached at ten A.M. The peak we climbed is the fourth one west of the highest summit. The third and fourth are Saraghrar Northwest, which has two tops. The more easterly one, which we did not climb, is about 100 meters higher than our top.

JUAN LÓPEZ DÍAZ, *Cataluña, Spain*

Nanga Parbat, Northwest Ridge Attempt and Tragedy. Our expedition, sponsored by the Swiss Foundation for Alpine Research, was international. The members were Harald Nevé, leader, and Richard Franzl, *Austrians,* Albrecht Baumgartner, Dr. Peter Forrer, Fredy Graf, Hans Howald and Marcel

Rüedi, *Swiss,* Oswald Duba, *Czech,* and Sepp Brantner, Alice Zebrowski and I, deputy leader, *Germans.* Our objective was to climb the northwest ridge, the 1976 Hanns Schell route. We were in Base Camp in the Rupal valley on May 7. Like other expeditions, we suffered unusually miserable weather and heavy snowfall during the whole month of May. Despite this, we established camps and had Camp III at 22,300 feet by the end of May. While heading for Camp IV on June 4, Dr. Peter Forrer was swept by an avalanche to his death down the Rupal face. After this sad event, we gave up the expedition. Dr. Forrer who was so preeminent in mountain rescues fell victim to Nanga Parbat.

HANS ZEBROWSKI, *German living in Switzerland*

Nanga Parbat, Rupal Buttress Attempt. Our expedition was composed of Yannick Seigneur, leader, Jean Afanassieff, Bernard Prud'homme, *French,* Bernd Neubaur, Michael Hoffmann, Rainier Pickl, Siegfried Wirth, Thomas Nuber, *Germans* and me, *Swiss.* We took two days from Rampur to Base Camp at the foot of the east face of Nanga Parbat, aided by 120 porters. On May 9 Seigneur and I placed Base Camp at 13,775 feet at the very foot of the Rupal buttress. We placed Camp I at 17,400 feet above a zone of rock and snow slopes, made more difficult because of the enormous amount of snow and avalanches. Camp II at 19,525 feet was above a great sérac barrier, which increased the danger of this difficult route. A big 1650-foot-high ice gully of 50° to 60° led to Camp III at 21,000 feet. On June 12 we lost Sheikh Ali, one of our two high-altitude porters who was killed while carrying a load and apparently slipped off a fixed rope; this caused the other one to withdraw. On June 13 Seigneur and I reached 23,300 feet, having overcome great difficulties. As we descended, a windslab broke and carried away seven lengths of fixed rope. After some bad weather, on June 20 two rope pairs left for a summit attempt. We replaced the fixed rope. Just as we finished this, a snow-and-ice avalanche struck Seigneur. He had several broken ribs, a cracked pelvis and many bruises, but he was still alive! It took three days to get him down. This ended our attempt. A month later the Herrligkoffer expedition was able to use our ropes from 19,000 feet up.

STÉFANE SCHAFFTER, *Club Alpin Suisse*

Nanga Parbat South Summit, East Buttress. The east buttress, which rises from the upper Bazhin Glacier, had long attracted my attention since I had first reconnoitered the Rupal Face with Toni Kinshofer in 1963. We got to Base Camp on the left moraine of the Bazhin Glacier on July 8. We were Schorsch Ritter, Valentin Demmel, Hartmut Münchenbach, Doris Kunstermann, Dr. Joaquin Zietz and me, *Germans;* Andrzej Bielun and Tadeusz Piotrowski, *Poles;* and Ueli Bühler, *Swiss.* We chose the right side of the buttress, which faces the Bazhin Glacier. We had reconnoitered the left side in 1975 and found

PLATE 83

Photo by Yannick Seigneur

**Rupal Buttress, NANGA PARBAT.
Camps are marked. X = Accidents.**

it threatened by avalanches. Yannick Seigneur had been shortly before us on the middle of the buttress and had reached 23,000 feet. Our route rose from the Bazhin Glacier at 12,500 feet in a bold line to the south summit. It first climbed a rock spur which protected us from ice avalanches on the way to Camp I at 15,100 feet. The camp was at the foot of a 6500-foot-long couloir, which we climbed on the left side. Camp II was halfway up at 16,750 feet in the only possible spot. The exit from the couloir was 70° and threatened by rockfall, and so our Hunza porters carried only once to Camp III at 19,350 feet on the central icefield above the couloir. This was the first camp not subject to falling rock and ice. It was there that we joined the route attempted by Seigneur. On July 31 Ritter and Bühler first climbed the 65° ice face above. On August 9 Camp IV was set up at 21,325 feet among séracs. On August 14 Ritter, supported by Piotrowski, climbed the "First Icefield" on the right side of which Camp IV was pitched at 23,950 feet. The next day they ascended the "Second Icefield" and crossed a small rock band to the "Third Icefield," which led to the south col. They were forced back by deep powder snow. That same day Münchenbach and Bühler climbed to Camp V. The four spent a crowded night in one tent. On August 16 the four set off. A nearly vertical 150-foot section took over an hour to lead. The warm sun had melted the snow so that they were soaked and did not dare to bivouac. All but Bühler descended to Camp V. Though the others expected him to follow them down, Bühler kept on without adequate bivouac gear to spend the night out below the south col in frigid weather. On August 17, around noon, Bühler reached the south summit (8042 meters, 26,384 feet), the top of the east buttress. He got back at six P.M. with seriously frozen hands and feet to Camp V, where Ritter and Piotrowski were waiting for him.

Karl Maria Herrligkoffer, *Deutsches Institut für Auslandsforschung*

Nanga Parbat, Southwest Ridge, Tragedy and Ascent. Our expedition, made up of Stefan Wörner, leader, Dr. Alex Berger, Martin Braun, Peter Hiltbrand, Norbert Joss, Hansruedi Staub and me, arrived on May 9 at Base Camp below the Diamir Face. On the second day Peter Hiltbrand was evacuated by the porters to the last village because of cerebral edema. The weather was bad. Finally, on May 14, we headed in the direction of Ganalo Peak and placed Camp I at 17,050 feet. On the 15th we continued toward the Diama Glacier, but the objective danger was so great that we gave up the idea of making a new route and decided on the Kinshofer route on the southwest ridge (first climbed by Austrians Hanns Schell, Hilmar Sturm, Robert Schauer and Siegfried Gimpel on August 11, 1976). On May 18 we set up Camp I at 16,400 feet and on May 22 Camp II at 20,000 feet. On May 23 Joos and I made a supply dump at 21,325 feet but had to descend because of bad weather, which lasted for ten days. Meanwhile Hiltbrand returned to Base Camp. On June 3 Berger, Braun, Joos and I regained Camp I, which was deep in snow. On the 4th we plowed our way to Camp II, digging out our fixed ropes. Dr. Berger

PLATE 84

Photo by Herrligkoffer Expedition

NANGA PARBAT. Camps IV and V are marked. Route ended on South Peak.

had to descend, sick, to Base Camp on June 5 but we other three climbed the Kinshofer couloir to our dump and from there traversed towards the Bazhin col on windslab which luckily held to let us reach a rocky island, where we placed Camp III at 22,800 feet. On June 6 we broke trail to 23,625 feet and descended to Camp II as planned. On the way down, we met Wörner, Staub and Hiltbrand, who hoped to establish Camp IV the next day and climb to the summit the day after. We tried to discourage them since none of them had yet been above 20,000 feet and they were not acclimatized. On June 7 Braun, Joos and I climbed back to Camp III while the other three advanced to establish Camp IV at 24,275 feet. Wörner and Staub got there in good time, but Hiltbrand lagged; he was definitely sick. At two A.M. on June 8 Wörner got to our tent at Camp III to say that Peter Hiltbrand was in very bad shape. Joos and I hurried upwards, soon joined by the other two. At eight A.M. we began to drag Hiltbrand down in a cloth sack. After 50 feet or so we were exhausted and realized it would take two days to get him down to Camp III. At 8:15 he went to sleep for ever. We closed his eyes and slipped him into a crevasse. Should we continue or give up? To quit would serve no purpose; we'd climb the mountain for Peter. Braun had to go down because of hemorrhoids, accompanied by Wörner. Joos, Staub and I went back up to Camp IV on June 9. In the afternoon Joos and I broke trail to 24,600 feet. On June 10 we set out at five A.M. A half an hour later I struck my cold feet with my ice axe and to my horror my plastic boots split! Could I continue? I took off boot and socks, rubbed my feet and after replacing my footgear, put on my crampons to hold it all together. Despite the wind, cold and the wind slabs, we continued. My foot stayed warm. After 650 feet, the couloir split. The right branch had normally been taken, but because of avalanche danger we kept left. We skirted two rock steps (UIAA IV+ to V) unroped and got to a rather delicate ridge that led to a north summit at 8035 meters (26,362 feet). In a violent wind we continued toward the main summit. I was going well and got to the summit (8125 meters, 26,660 feet) at 1:30 P.M., the tenth party and the first Swiss to reach it. Joos joined me at two P.M. We found that Staub was content to reach the north summit. But was this "victory" worth the price? Nanga Parbat has had 42 victims for its ten "victories."

ERHARD LORETAN, *Schweizer Alpen Club*

Nanga Parbat, Diamir Face. A Franco-German-Austrian expedition was led by Pierre Mazaud and composed of Michel Afanassief, Michel Berruex, Raymond Despiau, Kurt Diemberger, Hans Engl, Walter Cecchinel, Hubert Hillmaier and others. They climbed the Kinshofer route on the Diamir face of Nanga Parbat. On July 12 Berruex, Engl and Hillmaier set out with five Hunza porters to establish Camp IV at 23,950 feet. The next morning Hillmaier felt sick and he and Berruex returned, but Engl kept on, reconnoitering on the 13th and reaching the summit, despite miserable weather, on the 14th. He descended safely, still in very bad weather.

Ganalo Peak Attempt. Ganalo Peak (6606 meters, 21,664 feet) flanks Nanga Parbat on the northwest. We had access to it from the Diamir side, placing Base Camp at 13,775 feet on the moraine of the Diamir Glacier. We were Emilio Hernando, Jesús Gómez, Mikel Martínez and I. The climb was planned as a reconnaissance for our forthcoming Nanga Parbat expedition to the Diamir face rather than as an ascent in itself. Leaving Rawalpindi on August 1, we drove on the Karakoram Highway and to Bunar Sard. Four days later we were with eleven porters at Base Camp, 10,000 feet higher than where we left the road. We spent five days acclimatizing, which included going to Camp I on the Kinshofer route. We then headed for the virgin summit of Ganalo. After climbing scree, we placed a tent at snow line on the south side at 17,000 feet. At dawn the next day we headed along a sharp but not difficult ridge for what we thought was the summit. When we got to the western foresummit (6400 meters, 21,000 feet), we could see the real summit 650 feet higher, separated from us by a 1 1/4-mile difficult ridge. We gave up hopes of climbing Ganalo, having accomplished the reconnaissance.

ANGEL LANDA, *Spain*

Tirich Mir. Our expedition consisted of Anton Knecht, Eric Marchand, Paul Beyeler, Ernst Hunziker, Heinz Fahrer, Pierre Galland, Daniel Chevallier and me as leader. We climbed the Czech route of 1968. After a four-day approach, we reached Base Camp on the north side of Tirich Mir at 14,750 feet on June 21. We had no high-altitude porters. Because of bad weather and nearly daily snowfall, we had to set up six camps instead of the planned four. We set up camps at 17,050, 18,700, 19,350, 20,675, 21,650 and 23,625 feet on June 22, 25, 28, July 5, 8 and 11 respectively. On July 11 five members were at Camp V and three at Camp VI, but bad weather set in. On July 13 four climbers went to Camp VI but three returned to Camp V. On July 14 Knecht went solo to the summit (7708 meters, 25,284 feet). Further ascents were prevented by bad weather. We left Base Camp on July 19.

MARKUS ITTEN, *Schweizer Alpen Club*

Tirich Mir. On August 10 Jon Dasler, Dennis Olmstead, John Smolich and Allen Webb reached the summit of Tirich Mir (7708 meters, 25,260 feet) via the Upper Tirich Glacier and west saddle. They were supported by Lath Flanagan, Tom Gordon, Terry Jones, liaison officer Hamid Rao and me as leader. We were the first expedition to an Asian peak to arise within and be sponsored by the Mazama Climbing Club of Portland, Oregon. The jeep road from Chitral up the Mastuj River has been extended to Lunku in the Tirich Gol and will eventually reach Shagram. Until then, expeditions are advised to continue using the route from Drasan over the Zani An despite the 5400-foot rise, so as to avoid porter troubles arising from fierce and rigid territoriality. We paid Rs. 900 per jeep to Lunku, 73 miles, were forced by strikes and threat of violence to change porters at Zundangram and Shagram and upon reaching the traditional Base Camp at Qulish Zom. In four days we paid Rs. 575 per porter in total. Following the 1967 route of the Czechs, we placed camps at 17,300, 19,300, 21,500 feet and on the west saddle. Previous snowfall made route-finding through crevassed fields interesting but surface conditions were good. Only one day of marginal weather was experienced from July 14 to August 18. The "overhanging chimney" (see *A.J.,* v. 73 (1968) page 250), consisted of 140 feet of easy to moderate 5th-class climbing with an odd off-balance move. The rock was sound but with some overlying ice. Snow slopes of 55° led to the west saddle. We set 1200 feet of line between Camp III and the col. The route to the summit is mixed snow and shattered rock, not difficult. A ski pole with a Pakistani flag was found on the summit, presumably left by the earlier Swiss party. Costs in the Tirich Gol are out of control because a representative of the Ministry of Tourism is not posted to that area and no such system of "porter's book" documentation exists in contrast to the Baltoro. Previous expeditions had paid exorbitant wages, setting new standards of expectation.

ROBERT A. WILSON

Tirich Mir West I. Our expedition was made up of Salvador Boix, Joan Hugas, Pere Planas, Josep Aliu and me as leader. After a four-day approach from Lunku, we placed Base Camp on July 18 at 15,425 feet on the moraine on the right bank of the Upper Tirich Glacier. We placed Camps I, II and III at 18,050, 19,850 and 21,325 feet on July 20, 26 and 30 respectively. On August 4 Boix and I climbed to the col between Tirich Mir and Tirich Mir West I, where we installed Camp IV at 23,625 feet. On August 5 we two ascended the ridge to the summit of Tirich Mir West I (7487 meters, 24,564 feet). We had fixed rope on the difficult spots between Camps III and IV. Aliu had to descend to 10,000 feet with pulmonary edema, but he was later able to rejoin the expedition.

RAMÓN ESTIU, *Unió Excursionista de Catalunya*

China

Another Gongga Shan Tragedy. A horror story comes from another Japanese attempt on Gongga Shan. The five-man, two-woman expedition was led by Hideaki Saito. They reached Base Camp at 11,500 feet on the Hailoko Glacier on March 19, hoping to complete the new route on the northeast ridge, so disastrously attempted by other Japanese in 1981. (See *A.A.J.,* 1982, pages 284-5.) After skirting the icefalls, they established Temporary Camp I, Camps I, II, III (on the northeast ridge col) and IV on March 28, April 4, 9, 21 and

26 at 13,450, 16,075, 17,050, 19,000 and 20,350 feet respectively. The entire route from Camps II to IV was fixed with rope. S. Suzuki slipped and having damaged his back, had to return. Hironari Matsuda and Makoto Sugawara established Camp V at 22,300 feet on April 28. On the 29th their summit attempt took them to a bivouac close to the summit, but bad weather on the 30th precluded going higher. In their last radio transmission, they reported difficulty in finding the descent route. Leader Saito had had to return to Japan for personal reasons and Deputy Leader Yoshio Takeda and the two women moved up to Camp II on May 2. On the 4th they made a half-hearted attempt to climb up the fixed ropes from Camp II but were technically incapable of doing so! They assumed the others were dead and on May 6 descended to Base Camp, which they evacuated on May 9. It is difficult to know what progress Matsuda and Sugawara made, but eventually they reached Camp I. Sugawara could descend no farther but Matsuda kept on going down. He was found at 9500 feet on May 21 by local herb gatherers. A massive rescue was carried out, involving 200 Chinese, but Matsuda could be saved only with the loss of both frozen feet above the ankles and all ten fingers. (More details appear in Iwa To Yuki, N° 90, pages 99-100.) In September Japanese returned and unsuccessfully tried to retrieve Sugawara's body. On September 27 Takeshi Nakatani died from cerebral and pulmonary edema during the attempt and the effort was called off.

Gongga Shan, North Face and Northwest Ridge Ascent and Tragedy. Our expedition was composed of Ruedi Alder, Guido Bumann, Claus Coester, Andreas Eschmann, Georges Herren, Thomas Hess, Kurt Weibel and me as leader. We had planned to climb the mountain by the route attempted by the tragic Japanese expedition of 1981, from the Yan-Tsöko valley and over the Sun-Yat-Sen col. The approach under the north face was so threatened by avalanches that we gave up the plan and climbed through a steep snow basin up the north face to reach the northwest ridge, the first-ascent route, just beyond the "Hump." On April 28 we reached Chengtu, where we were joined by our liaison officer, Xiao Mong. We got to the last village, Sin-Sin at 6000 feet on April 29. On May 1 we started to our 13,600-foot Base Camp, which we reached in three days. The 15 porters made four relays to there. On May 8 we got for the first time to Advance Base at 17,000 feet in the snow basin. From Base Camp we first followed a lateral moraine and bypassed an icefall on the eastern edge of the glacier to the basin. Good weather favored our establishing Camp I three-quarters of the way up the couloir beside the north face. I suffered a broken arm while returning to Base Camp and had to spend the rest of the expedition there. On May 16 the northwest ridge was reached and on the 17th Camp II stood at 21,325 feet on the northwest ridge. On May 23 we placed Camp III on an ice bulge at 22,800 feet. The first summit bid by Coester and Weibel failed in high winds on May 24. On May 25 Alder, Eschmann and Georges Herren set off for the summit at six A.M. and got there at two P.M. The last part of the ridge was of difficult ice and rock and steeper than we had expected. About a quarter of an hour below the summit on the descent Eschmann broke the sharp edge of the ridge and plunged down the north face to his death. We gave up thoughts of a further ascent. The weather had a nearly daily pattern. Each morning thick clouds rose from the lower parts of Sichuan up the valleys until they formed a sea of clouds with an upper level from 11,000 to 16,500 feet. While Base Camp was under heavy clouds and for days in heavy rain, lovely sunny weather reigned above. In the afternoon the clouds rose and the weather deteriorated in the evening, often with snowfall, but by morning the weather up high was lovely again.

ERWIN HERREN, *Schweizer Alpen Club*

Gongga Shan Attempt. Canadians led by Roger Griffiths attempted the first-ascent route on Gongga Shan in the spring. They were plagued by bad weather, avalanches and an accident and did not reach the ridge. Details are lacking.

Anyemaqen, First Ascent by Japanese, 1981. Details previously lacking of the first ascent of Anyemaqen have appeared in *Iwa To Yuki* N° 88. An expedition of eleven men and two women was led by Yuzo Tada. From Base Camp at 14,750 feet east of the mountain, Camp I was placed at 17,000 feet on May 7, 1981 and Camp II was established at 18,700 feet May 19 after a week of heavy snowfall. On May 22 Giichiro Watanabe, Yoshio Yamamoto and Katsumi Miyake reached the summit. Five others got to the top on May 25.

Anyemaqen, 1981, Third Ascent. [On page 285 of *A.A.J.*, 1982, details were lacking about two ascents of Anyemaqen. We are grateful for further details sent us by Herr Hupfauer, which arrived too late to be published last year.—*Editor.*] Our Austro-German party of seven took two days from Shie San Shang to get to Base Camp at 14,750 feet on the Quheershaoma Glacier on June 2, 1981. We were held up by bad weather until June 7 when we established Camp I at 16,250 feet. Camp II was placed at 18,600 feet on June 9. That day we watched the American group reach the summit! We followed the route of the Japanese first-ascent party, which definitely climbed the peak in May 22, 1981. This led over the Quheershaoma Glacier and the east-northeast ridge to the summit of P 6000, over P 6090 and P 6127 to the main summit (6282 meters, 20,610 feet). We found some 3000 feet of Japanese fixed rope. On June 10, 1981 Hans Gaschbauer, Franz Lämmerhofer, Dr. Gerhard Schmatz, Peter Vogler and I climbed to the summit for the third ascent and the second by our route.

SIEGFRIED HUPFAUER, *Deutscher Alpenverein*

Mount Everest Attempt. Our expedition had as members Jan van Banning, Willem ten Barge, Eelco Dijk, Geert Geuskens, Gerard Jansen, Ronald Naar, Mathieu van Rijswick, Gerard van Sprang, Johan Taks, Han Timmers, Bart Vos, Robert Weijdert and me as leader. Local transport and all further arrangements were in the hands of the Chinese Mountaineering Association. Their fees are stiff in comparison with those in other countries such as Nepal and also some of their services will have to improve, but their spirit of cooperation was excellent and we were, on the whole, very satisfied. We planned to climb the traditional route of the pre-World War II expeditions. We made the following Camps: Base Camp (4 miles south of the Rongbuk Monastery), I, II, III, IV (on the North Col) and V at 17,000, 18,375, 19,700, 21,325, 23,000 and 24,950 feet on August 16, 18, 22, 25 September 16 and October 5 respectively. The delay in establishing Camp V was due to a serious avalanche accident on September 29. One member escaped with bruised ribs, but Dijk broke eight ribs, suffered a punctured lung and was dramatically saved after a bivouac at 22,300 feet, thanks to all expedition members available and the strong support of Tibetan "high-altitude assistant climbers." He has now recovered. Our high point of 25,750 feet was reached on October 7. In August the mountain was whiter than we had seen in any photograph published before. The conditions leading to the North Col were correspondingly dangerous and led to the accident and a number of narrow escapes later. The traditional approach lines were rejected and a moderately steep (45° to 55°) line was fixed to the left of the sérac zone of the normal way. In the middle of September the monsoon ended, but instead of the usual northerly circulation, fierce southwest winds established themselves. The snow was blown off the mountain in less than a week, leaving no scope for alternative routes. When the winds and temperature of $-35°$C continued, the expedition was broken off on October 10. The mountain was absolutely free of cloud most of the time and looked harmless from Base Camp, but above the North Col the wind made life downright dangerous.

Alexander Verrijn Stuart, Koninklijke Nederlandse
Alpen-Vereniging

Mallory and Irvine Second-Step Clues. When honorary member, Shi Zhan Chun, of the Chinese Mountaineering Association spoke at the Annual Meeting of the American Alpine Club in Los Angeles in December 1981, he revealed that the Chinese Everest Expedition of 1960 had discovered much evidence of the British pre-World War II north-face attempts. During an interview of Mr. Shi, many people in the audience understood his interpreter to say that a hank of manila rope and a short pole were discovered *above* the Second Step (28,480 feet). This evidence would prove that Mallory and Irvine had indeed surmounted this severe obstacle. If true, it advances dramatically the possibility that the pair actually reached the summit in 1924. Yet, Mr. Shi gave altitudes of those 1960 discoveries and they were all below the First Step near or at the site of the 1933 Camp VI. Many attempts to ascertain the exact location of the find were made. Finally Chris Bonington met with Mr. Shi. He writes that he asked Mr. Shi about this find and had its location pointed out to him on a photograph. The location was *below* the *First* Step in line with the altitudes Mr. Shi originally gave. The working oxygen system the Chinese found with 20 atmospheres of gas remaining was also not that of Mallory and Irvine (as reported in *Outside Magazine*) but the set abandoned by Peter Lloyd during his descent from 27,300 feet in the British expedition of 1938.

THOMAS HOLZEL

Changtse. Our members were Dr. Hansjürgen Tauscher, co-leader, Paul Braun, Thomas Dünsser, Martin Engler, Walter Ernst, Rudolf Frick, Andreas Heckmair, Jr., Ludwig Hösle, Peter Lechart, Udo Zehetleitner, Dr. Wilfried Zink and I, co-leader. We drove from Lhasa over increasingly bad roads to Base Camp at the terminal moraine of the Rongbuk Glacier at 16,750 feet. We continued on the historic route up the East Rongbuk Glacier toward Mount Everest and Changtse. Camps I and II were set up on October 2 and 4 at 18,375 and 20,000 feet, the latter at the foot of the long northeast ridge of Changtse. We had no porters but used six yaks and our own backs to there. We first had to climb a 2000-foot snow-and-ice slope with some rock. Camp III was at 21,000 feet sheltered by a rock spur. Above, we fixed some rope on a steep snow-and-ice slope on a wide ridge that led first north and then east. Camp IV was set up on the ridge at 22,650 feet on October 13. On October 14 Zehetleitner and on October 16 Braun, Frick, Hösle and Engler completed the first ascent of Changtse (7550 meters, 24,771 feet).

EDUARD GEYER, *Deutscher Alpenverein*

Shishapangma, 1981. In *A.A.J.*, 1982 we mentioned the ascent of Reinhold Messner and Friedl Mutschlechner but we lacked details. The pair got to the summit on May 27, 1981 by a route which lies to the right of the normal route. An article with a sketch of the northern routes appears in *Alpin* of May 1982.

Shishapangma. Dr. Makoto Hara led another Nagoya High-Mountain Research Institute expedition, this time to Shishapangma. All members reached the summit by the normal route. One of the members, Masaaki Tomita, made an amazingly fast ascent from Advance Base at 18,700 feet to the 26,291-foot summit, which he reached on October 12, in only 50 hours. Three summit attempts in early October failed. Dr. Hara, Hiroo Komamiya and Hirofumi Konishi got to the summit on October 10. Takayoshi Chiba and Motomu Omiya also reached the top on October 12.

Gang Ben Chen. We left Lhasa on March 22 and established Base Camp at 15,250 feet on March 27 and Advance Base at 18,700 feet on April 4, both on the Boron Plain. Camp I was on the small glacier north of Gang Ben Chen at 20,450 feet. We placed Camp II at 22,000 feet on the snow face above the icefall. Camp III was pitched at 23,300 feet on April 20. On April 21 Riyuko Morimoto, Kozo Matsubayashi, Kazunari Ushida, Shiro Koshima, Takao Morito, Goro Hitomi, Kiyoshi Nakagawa and Hiroshi Kondo climbed to the summit (7281 meters, 23,888 feet) in 2½ hours. The weather was fine and the route not difficult. The next day Shoichiro Ueo, Takashi Nishiyama and Rikuyo Morimoto stood on the summit too.

YOSHIO KONDO, *Academic Alpine Club of Kyoto, Japan*

Porong Ri, First Ascent and Tragedy. A 14-man Japanese expedition led by Toru Ito made the first ascent of Porong Ri (7294 meters, 23,898 feet), which is connected to Shishapangma by a ridge and lies some five miles to the northwest. Base Camp was established at 17,000 feet on April 15. Minoru Wada and Yukio Eto got to the summit via the north ridge on May 14, but Wada fell to his death during the descent.

K2, North Ridge. The Japanese Mountaineering Association led by Isao Shinkai and Masatsugu Konishi was composed of 14 climbers and 29 Japanese support people, since no high-altitude local porters were available. "Base Home" was established on May 5 at 12,650 feet on the Shaksgam River. Climbers and support personnel had carried four tons ten miles to Base Camp at 16,075 feet on the K2 Glacier by May 29. The support party withdrew on June 5 and climbing started on June 9. Camp I was placed at 19,000 feet on June 13 but bad weather for 22 of the next 34 days slowed progress. The route was on the north ridge at the edge of the northwest face. Camps II, III and IV were established at 21,650, 24,775 and 25,750 feet on July 17 and 24 and August 1 respectively. The last camp was on a north col. After rope was fixed to 26,250 feet, they all returned to rest at Base Camp. The summit push started on August 9. On August 14 Naoe Sakashita (an American Alpine Club member), Hiroshi Yoshino, Yukihiro Yanagisawa and Takashi Ozaki set out for the summit without oxygen, but Ozaki had to return from 26,900 feet. They climbed unroped above the end of the fixed rope with little equipment and mostly separate from each other. They turned left and climbed the big snowfield in the upper center of the north face. After climbing for some 12 hours, Sakashita reached the summit, soon followed by Yanagisawa. Yoshino arrived an hour later. On the descent Yoshino bivouacked at 27,550 feet and Sakashita and Yanagisawa at 27,400 feet. Yanagisawa had no down jacket and Sakashita hugged him all night long to keep him warm. In the morning Yoshino joined them. While Sakashita descended, the other two waited for the second summit team to bring them a climbing rope and hot tea. When the pair reached the fixed rope, Yoshino untied to straighten out the fixed rope. When he looked up, Yanagisawa had disappeared. On August 16 his jacket was sighted on the north face at 16,750 feet, but avalanche danger prevented a search. On August 15 Kazushige Takami, Haruichi Kawamura, Tatsuji Shigeno and Hironobu Kamuro reached the summit after having carried supplies to the descending climbers. After the mountain had been evacuated, Dr. Toshitaka Sakano on August 29 strolled up a small peak behind "Base Home." He did not return. His body was found on the 31st. He had apparently fallen from a rock on the top and hurt himself. He had frozen to death while attempting to return. Details, photographs, maps, etc. appear in *Iwa To Yuki*, Numbers 85, 87, 91, and 92.

A Note on the Chinese Name for K2, "Qogir." The Chinese use "Qogir" for the name of the world's second highest peak. The Editor and other experts deplore this name. It would be written "Chogir" in our usual orthography. This is obviously a corruption of "Chogori," a synthetic name made up by Western explorers early in this century from two Balti words: *chhogo* = big and *ri* = mountain. It has no local usage. The mountain was not prominently visible from places where local inhabitants ventured and so had no local name. Years ago, the Survey of India assigned the peak a survey number, K(arakoram)2. This still is its official name in Pakistan. Most Pakistanis I know object strenuously to "Chogori" and insist on the use of the official name, K2. In my experience, the Baltis use no other name for the peak than K2, which they pronounce "Ketu." I strongly recommend *against* the use of the name *Chogori* in any of its forms.

H. Adams Carter

Kongur Attempt, Xinjiang. The first American expedition to Kongur (7719 meters, 25,325 feet) arrived at Base Camp on July 20. The climbing party consisted of Gil Anderson, Rob Leitz, Art Porter, Andy Shidner, Ed Stachon and me as leader. Our goal was to repeat the first-ascent route of the 1981 British Expedition. High temperatures and consequent abysmal snow conditions severely hampered our progress. Even at 18,000 feet the temperature did not drop below freezing on some nights. Snow conditions practical for travel would exist for only four or five hours a day at best. We reached our Camp III at the approximate location of the British Advanced Base in the upper basin of the Koksel Glacier on August 1. Camp V at 22,000 feet was established on August 8, and a reconnaissance to the Kongur-Kongur Tiubie col at 22,300 feet showed that even there the snow conditions were not better. Since we were running out of both food and enthusiasm for wallowing in slush, a retreat began on August 10. We may have encountered an exceptionally hot summer, or perhaps it was just a mistake to attempt a south-facing route in early August. Skis, which we did not have, would have been a great help. We acknowledge with thanks the assistance of the Chinese Mountaineering Association. Our liaison officer, Chen Shangren, and our interpreter, Guo Jin-Wei, executed their duties with consummate skill. This expedition was sponsored by the Colorado Mountain Club Foundation.

Richard Dietz, *Colorado Mountain Club*

P 20,700 and P 21,750, near Kongur. I led twelve schoolboys on a mountaineering expedition to the very west of China, also accompanied by six recently left "Old Boys" of the school and one woman, Fiona Blake. Base

Camp was established at 13,000 feet beside the Karakoram Highway, the new road linking China with Pakistan. We undertook mountaineering, ornithological and botanical projects. First Marc Heading, Dominic Vincent, Robert Taylor and I and then Malcolm Harrison, Giles Hammersley and Mike Logsdon made separate ascents of P 20,700. Both groups climbed the main glacier flowing west to get onto the north ridge, which took us to the summit. The mountain was first ascended by Chris Bonington and Alan Rouse during their reconnaissance expedition in 1980 prior to climbing Kongur in 1981. P 21,750 was ascended by Harrison, Vincent and Guy Smith. They climbed the west ridge setting up a camp at 17,000 feet and a snow hole at 19,400 feet. Both mountains were climbed from an advance base camp at 15,000 feet.

JONATHAN LEE, *Oundle School, England*

Mustagh Ata. A five-man Japanese party led by Keizo Yabuki climbed Mustagh Ata in the autumn. Yukata Takagi and Shohei Suzuki arrived at the summit.

Mustagh Ata. Englishman Norman Croucher was a member of a Mountain Travel expedition to Mustagh Ata led by John Cleare. Croucher reached the summit on two artificial legs.

Mustagh Ata. Our group of eleven rode with jeep and truck south from Kashgar. On July 4 we reached a Kirghiz settlement, Jambukuk, at 12,500 feet, west of Mustagh Ata. Five camels carried our loads to 14,750 feet below the Chal Tumak Glacier on July 6. We climbed alpine style on the part of the mountain between the Chal Tumak and the Tergen Bulak Glaciers, a different route from five of the previous climbs, but the same as the American-Canadian group of September 1981. One climber at our first high camp had high-altitude mountain sickness and had to return to Kashgar, where he recovered. We camped at 17,050, 20,000 and 22,000 feet. The chief difficulty was breaking trail. On July 17 Erich Hofwimmer, Gottfried Heinzel, Baltasar Kendler, Helmut Wagner and I reached the summit (7546 meters, 24,757 feet).

MARCUS SCHUCK, *Österreichischer Alpenverein*

U.S.S.R.

Pik Lenin, Pik Kommunizma and Other Peaks on Skis, Pamir Mountains. Our best skier of the extreme, Pavol Rajtar, made several first ski descents in the Pamir Mountains. After several acclimatization climbs, on July 20 he climbed Pik Shatayeva (5700 meters, 18,701 feet) solo and made the first ski descent. The next day he was helicoptered to the Moskvin and Walter Glaciers along with Milan Hoholík, Oleg Štulrajter and Robert Gálfy. They bivouacked at 13,125, 16,400, 19,000 and 23,000 feet and on July 25 climbed the Tzetlin (southwest) Ridge of Pik Korzhenevska (7105 meters, 23,310 feet). Rajtar and

Gálfy made the first ski descent, skiing down the same ridge to the end of the glacier at 16,400 feet in three hours. The next day they climbed back up to 19,000 feet to help evacuate a sick climber. They were then helicoptered to the Fontambek Glacier at 13,125 feet. On July 30 Rajtar and František Compel climbed some 7000 feet up the Burevestnik Buttress to bivouac at 20,000 feet. The next day they skied eight miles across the Pamir Plateau to bivouac at 20,000 feet below Pik Dushanbe, which they climbed on August 1 to bivouac on the summit at 22,650 feet. From there Rajtar soloed Pik Kommunizma (7495 meters, 24,590 feet) and skied down to 20,000 feet. On the 3rd they crossed the plateau, descended the buttress and returned to Fontambek Base Camp. Rajtar was helicoptered to 13,450 feet on the Achik Tash Glacier, which he ascended to Pik Razdelna, where he bivouacked on August 5. He then soloed Pik Lenin (7134 meters, 23,406 feet) in four hours. He skied down the northwest ridge to 22,800 feet and turned north onto the face. He completed the ski of 10,000 vertical feet in two hours and 25 minutes. The slopes were up to 48°.

OTO CHUDÝ, *Czechoslovakia*

Fanskiye Gory, Western End of Pamir-Alai Chain. A strong 10-man expedition of the Czechoslovak Mountaineering Federation was led by Petr Schnábl. They made eleven ascents, six of them firsts. The new routes follow. Jiří Martiš and Petr Valovičon from July 22 to 26 made a new 6500-foot route on the northwest face of Chapdara (5157 meters, 16,919 feet; UIAA VI, A2). It was similar to the south face of the Marmolada. Josef Rakoncaj and Miroslav Šmíd climbed the left side of the west face of Bodkhona (5304 meters, 17,402 feet; VI +, A2) from July 23 to 26. This 5000-foot-high rock face is vertical or overhanging for 3250 feet. Igor Koller and Radovan Velísek climbed the Great Groove on this face (VI +, A1) from July 25 to 28. On July 27 Karel Jakeš and Bohuslav Mrozek climbed the 3000-foot-high north face of Soan (4750 meters, 15,584 feet), which was 60° ice with pitches of 80°. Šmíd soloed two new routes. On July 31 he made a new route on the right of the north face of Maria (5000 meters, 16,404 feet; V), 3525 feet of ice up to 80°. On August 5 and 6 he climbed the great couloir on the left of the north face of Miraly (5170 meters, 16,962 feet; VI with ice up to 80°). The Fanskiye Gory Mountains are a small but spectacular group of inaccessible-looking summits and pinnacles. They offer many climbing problems of high standard on both rock and ice.

JÓZEF NYKA, *Editor, Taternik, Poland*

Belukha, Katun Range, Altai Mountains, Siberia. Nine Austrian and two Czechoslovakian mountaineers were invited to see this marvelous mountain region. Base Camp was installed by the Soviet Sports Committee at Lake Ak-Kem at 6650 feet. We were there from July 17 to August 15. On July 26 all members reached the top of Belukha (4506 meters, 14,783 feet), the heavily

PLATE 85

Photo by Leo Graf

**East and West Peaks of BELUKHA
from Pik Delone.**

glaciated highest point in the Soviet Altai Mountains. We climbed over Delone (4200 meters, 13,780 feet) and then ascended the northeast ridge. We had two high camps and took seven days in all. This was the first visit by foreigners. We also climbed other summits and enjoyed the very beautiful scenery and especially the warm hospitality of Soviet mountaineers. The good experiences of this experimental expedition will probably lead to the installation of another International Mountain Camp—Altai '83 in the Katun and the Chuiski Mountains. Inquiries should be directed to Director M. Monastyrski, USSR Sports Committee, Skaterynyi per. 4, 121069 Moscow, USSR.

FRIDEBERT WIDDER, *Österreichischer Alpenverein*

Caucasus, International Mountaineering Camp, July session. After a week of travel from Helsinki to Tallinn, Leningrad and Moscow, Bill Sumner and I were joined by Americans Dick and Louise McGowan and 52 climbers from six other countries to participate in the July Session of the Soviet-sponsored International Mountaineering Camp in the Caucasus. In Moscow we met and were given a hearty send-off by famed Soviet climber-scientist, Eugene Gippenreiter. Our already emotional Soviet experience continued for three more weeks, based in the resort town of Cheget in the Baksan Valley nestled between Asia and Europe. A well-organized staff made every effort to make our experience safe and fulfilling. Although July brought unsettled weather, we spent our first week on a trek over Mestia Pass (3980 meters) into the heart of Soviet alpinism, the land of Svanetia. We survived hearty Georgian hospitality with the McGowans and two Russian companions. After a couple of days we left the medieval town of Mestia and returned to Cheget over Donguz Arun Pass (3060 meters). During our second week, we ascended to the Priute Hut (4200 meters) on Elbrus, and after two days of waiting for better weather and undergoing "passive" acclimatization, we climbed the west summit (5642 meters) of this popular peak (the highest in Europe) with Czechs Pavel and Hana Danihelka and Soviets Vasily Elagin and Sergei Penzov. For our last week we set our sights on the jewel of the Caucasus, Ushba (4710 meters). We were left alone to seek out this statuesque, double-spired granite peak. We awaited better weather while camped on the Ushba Plateau and on the third day had a lucky weather break. We ascended the classic ice faces and long corniced ridge of the northern summit of Ushba in what was felt by the Soviets to be the first American ascent. As happens so often, the freedom to travel to the mountains of the world had afforded us the opportunity to experience far greater events and to be with peoples whose common interest in the mountains had bared similar hopes and desires for peace with each other. As Dr. Gippenreiter had so aptly stated, "if only our leaders could meet on such summits and share such feelings."

ROBERT B. SCHOENE

PLATE 86
Photo by Hans Wagner
BELUKHA's North Face.

Book Reviews

EDITED BY JOHN THACKRAY

Everest: A Mountaineering History. Walt Unsworth. Houghton Mifflin Company, Boston, 1981. 578 pages, black-and-white and color photographs, maps, appendices, summary of expeditions, glossary, bibliography. $30.00.

For the past several decades, we have been subjected to a plethora of Himalayan expedition accounts. In this genre, even today Maurice Herzog's *Annapurna* has not been surpassed. Only rarely, as with Kenneth Mason's *Abode of Snow,* has an author provided the historical perspective that is so necessary to illuminate, beyond the merely immediate, the activities of those climbers who have sought the challenges of the world's highest peaks. Walt Unsworth fills this vacuum with his *Everest: A Mountaineering History,* a book that will surely be regarded as the definitive treatment of Mount Everest.

Transcending Mason's classic work on the Himalaya as a whole, Unsworth has assembled a voluminous, but highly readable and cohesive chronicle of the events on Everest from the first close assessment by Captain C. G. Rawling during the Younghusband mission to Lhasa in 1905 to the difficult new routes done in the 1970s—anticipating Reinhold Messner's astounding solo, oxygenless climb from the north in 1980 (after press time).

In his preface, Unsworth sets his task as follows:

> As any mountaineer will tell you, Everest is not technically the hardest climb in the world, and certainly not the best. It is, however, the *highest*— and that's what makes it so special, what sets it apart from all other mountains and makes its story much more than a catalogue of daring feats by brave men. It has the power to arouse both the best and worst in human nature; a theme which previous writers have tended to ignore.

"To have simply recounted yet again the climbing annals of the mountain," Unsworth goes on, "would have served no useful purpose except that of bringing the story more up to date." Most important is his effort, successful for the most part, of taking the Everest story away from preoccupation with pure climbing exploits. Not only does Unsworth disclose the frequent obstacles of "bumbling officialdom, international rivalry and plain double dealing," but he weaves perceptive character sketches of the main actors into the Everest drama.

Unsworth spends ample space in tracing the initial attempts to reach Everest, let alone climb it. For most, the climbing history of Everest commences with the famous reconnaissance of 1921. Yet, we learn of much effort from the start of this century on. His account of the political complexities of entering

Tibet in those days strikes a common chord with modern-day experiences in piercing the bureaucratic veils of the host countries that guard access to Everest and the other giants of the Himalaya.

The author's treatment of the 1921 reconnaissance and the two expeditions that closely followed is fascinating for its intricate weave of the mountain events with what transpired in the hallowed halls of the Alpine Club before, during and between the expeditions. George Mallory, who with Hillary and Tenzing, is one of the most famous names in mountaineering history, does not emerge untarnished. According to Unsworth, Mallory had greatness thrust upon him, but had little actual talent. The most telling comment comes from Longstaff who described Mallory as a "very good stout-hearted baby, but quite unfit to be placed in charge of anything, including himself." Unsworth submits the Mallory-Irvine disappearance to exhaustive analysis. Other than Odell's sighting of them on the First or Second Step, their failure to return to Camp VI, and the finding of one of their ice axes nine years later near the crest of the Northeast Ridge, there still are no hard facts to answer the question whether they reached the summit. After the book went to press (1979), there have been unconfirmed rumors that Chinese climbers sighted a body high on the Northeast Ridge clad in nonmodern climbing garb. Even the discovery of the remains of Mallory or Irvine would not necessarily end the speculation; their disappearance undoubtedly will continue as one of the most tantalizing mysteries of mountaineering.

I have always wondered why it took the British so long to return to Everest after the 1924 attempt. Unsworth provides the answer in the person of Major F. M. Bailey, who served as political officer in Sikkim during the 1920s. Bailey, who had earlier solved one of the great riddles of exploration in tracing the course of the Tsangpo River around Namcha Barwa to prove that the river was the same as the Brahmaputra, unaccountably acted to frustrate subsequent attempts to enter Tibet. Among Bailey's papers found at the time of his death was a note providing a strong clue: "[Everest] must be climbed one day and I hope I will be one of the men to do it."

The British made four more attempts on Everest in the 1930s, but Norton's 1924 altitude record of 28,126 feet was not surpassed. What is interesting about these expeditions is the sharp contrast between the large, heavy approach of the 1933 and 1936 attempts and the lightweight tactics of Tilman and Shipton in 1935 and 1938. As Unsworth correctly observes, had Shipton converted the 1935 reconnaissance into an actual attempt and succeeded, the whole concept of Himalayan mountaineering would have been tipped in favor of small, highly mobile teams instead of the usual massive expeditions of the next thirty years. Aside from a few exceptions, such as the ascent of Nanda Devi in 1936 and the attempts on K2 in 1938 and 1953, led by Charles Houston, this practice did not wane irrevocably until the Messner-Habeler two-person ascent of Hidden Peak in 1975. Tilman's 1938 team was even better positioned to succeed with the "small is beautiful" approach but was unlucky enough to face an exceptionally early monsoon that kept the climbers from going above 27,500 feet.

Although we are familiar with the bizarre activities of Maurice Wilson and Earl Denman, the would-be adventurers who tried to climb Everest alone, Unsworth breaks new ground with his account of Klavs Becker-Larsen's amazing sorties to Everest. In 1951, Larsen, a strong, young Dane with no climbing experience, journeyed up the Khumbu glacier with a small contingent of Sherpas to the site of the present-day Everest Base Camp. Only Tilman and Houston had been there ahead of him. Ignoring the Khumbu Icefall, Larsen tried to reach the North Col by climbing up the steep and dangerous slopes of the Lho La. He made it halfway up before retreating. Undaunted, Larsen next crossed the Nangpa La into Tibet. Making his way up the traditional British prewar route to the base of the North Col, he nearly succeeded in reaching the col itself before his Sherpa companions compelled him to descend after experiencing rockfall off the flanks of Changtse. He barely escaped the clutches of Chinese soldiers before re-entering Nepal.

The story of the final events leading to the history-making ascent by Hillary and Tenzing in 1953, though familiar, is well told. What is not widely known, however, is the backroom maneuvering that led to Eric Shipton's dismissal as leader. With Tilman, Shipton stands as the finest mountain explorer of all time. Yet, as Unsworth points out, Shipton was not well suited to the demands of leading large expeditions. What counted for Shipton was "his unbounded curiosity to see what lay over the next ridge," but as the author notes, "the minutiae of a mountain ascent held no interest for him."

Sandwiched between the 1953 British ascent and later events on the Nepalese side is Unsworth's account of the north side of the mountain. This is, perhaps, his most interesting chapter, mainly for its new material. He discusses a rumored 1952 Russian post-monsoon attempt that ended in disaster when six climbers, including the leader, disappeared near the highest camp at 26,800 feet. A planned joint Russian-Chinese expedition in 1960 resulted in the Chinese going it alone when the political split between the two communist regimes erupted.

Until quite recently, the nighttime ascent by two Chinese climbers and a Tibetan companion has never been fully accepted in Western countries because of a lack of summit photos and a sketchy account. Unsworth, however, flatly states: "There seems little doubt now that the Chinese did climb Everest in 1960." Along with several other climbers, I recently had the opportunity to talk with two of the summit climbers, Wang Fu-chou and Qu Yin-hua, about their ascent. Although such personal contacts are hardly conclusive, one had the distinct feeling that these men had been where they said they had.

Of the 1975 Chinese ascent, there can be no doubt with the undisputed proof of the survey marker being left on the summit. Puzzling, though, was the need for the Chinese News Agency to proclaim that three Chinese surveyors had climbed to the summit in 1969, each in separate solo dashes! This episode only serves to undermine the credibility of the earlier ascent. As for the Russians, they made up for past lapses and absences with their outstanding achievement of putting twelve climbers on the summit last spring via a difficult, new route on the Southwest Face.

Dominating the post-1953 events are the American West Ridge climb and traverse in 1963 and the seven separate expeditions to the Southwest Face in the early 1970s that tackled the mountain "the hard way." Of all the Everest climbers mentioned, Unsworth appears to have the most admiration for Tom Hornbein, whose tenacity and single-minded drive were chiefly responsible for the remarkable West Ridge climb and traverse that stands as one of the major achievements of Himalayan mountaineering history. Chris Bonington, whose expedition to Annapurna's South Face in 1970 pioneered the breakthrough to the difficult face climbs, also comes in for high praise. Despite a hailstorm of criticism from some quarters about the tremendous cost and publicity that attended Bonington's Southwest Face endeavors, in 1975 his team brilliantly succeeded in climbing the face to the summit. Only Mick Burke's disappearance on a solo excursion to the summit marred the outcome of an expedition that Unsworth contrasts markedly with the ill-starred 1971 International Expedition, also ably chronicled.

Unsworth concludes his book with an account of what most thought impossible at the time: climbing the mountain without the benefit of supplementary oxygen. During the British prewar attempts, the issue of oxygen use was hotly debated. As with the heavy versus lightweight expedition issue, had Norton, Smythe or some of the others reached the summit without oxygen, the almost total reliance on oxygen for climbing the highest peaks in the so-called "golden age" of Himalayan mountaineering would have been avoided. It remained for Reinhold Messner and his Hidden Peak companion, Peter Habeler, to surmount this last great physiological challenge, to climb the mountain by "fair means."

The account of the historic Messner-Habeler climb in 1978 is greatly enhanced by the use of lengthy comments from Habeler obtained in an interview with the author. Unlike the sanitized version in Habeler's published account, Habeler here gives a graphic rendition of their summit climb, not altogether favorable to Messner, but one that has the ring of truth.

Unsworth's book also contains an extensive bibliography as well as a useful summary of all the expeditions. The color plates are one of the few shortcomings. For Everest buffs, or for that matter anyone interested in the climbing history of the world's highest peak, this book is a must.

JAMES WICKWIRE

Everest the Cruel Way. Joe Tasker. Eyre Methuen, London, 1981. 166 pages, black and white photographs. £6.95.

This book by Joe Tasker describes the British 1981-82 winter attempt on the west ridge of Mount Everest. It is a grim story of eight comrades, with slender resources—crack mountaineers all—undertaking a cruel task with high resolve, but who are worn down by the unremitting, bitter cold, by their decision not to use oxygen equipment and, finally, by their formless organization which the group labels "democracy."

Reaching Everest Base Camp on the Khumbu Glacier on December 6, 1981, the British group contrasted their spartan digs with the lavish tent-city laid out by the Japanese who were also attempting a winter ascent of the mountain, via the South Col. They lacked for nothing material. "I have a contract to go to 200 metres from the summit," one member of the Japanese expedition confides to Tasker. "After that, only Mr. (Naomi) Uemura goes alone."

Tasker's group climbed up the 3000-foot steep, exposed rock face to the left of the Lho La that partially breaches the ridge connecting Mount Everest to Khumbutse. This pass is subject to constant avalanches, one of which wiped out six members of the Chamonix Guides' West Ridge Expedition of 1974.

The true west ridge of Mount Everest has been climbed only once, by the Yugoslavs in the spring of 1979. And the mountain has been climbed only once in winter, by the Poles along the South Col route. Both of these large expeditions used oxygen equipment which climbers, such as Haston and Messner, experienced in oxygenless ascents, believe the paralyzing cold of a winter ascent of Everest requires. So this attempt by Tasker's group was more than a little ambitious.

After shuttling equipment up to higher camps, they left the selection of what to shuttle up to democractic principles. The reader comes to realize that this form of democracy—the climbers' misnomer for a complete lack of formal leadership—while certainly the preferred way to run an alpine-sized assault, turns out to be woefully inadequate to accomplish a difficult climb with a larger group. Every five pages of *Everest the Cruel Way* contains a bitter reproach against the inefficiency of their anarchic organization, or recriminations against the selfishness of others who were perceived to be working less hard, or hogging the lead, etc. It all sounds like ten-year old kids playing unsupervised baseball: two minutes of play, ten minutes of argument.

The end of the game for this group came while Tasker and Ade Burgess lay holed up in a wretched snow cave at their highest camp—Camp III at 23,200 feet. Exhausted by their efforts to place a higher camp on the West Buttress, short on supplies, numb with cold, they were cut off from below by comrades who, also desperately weakened, would no longer come to their aid but, being democratic, would not say they would not come. A final, fruitless argument ensued on their walkie-talkies. Without hope of further reinforcements, the stranded climbers retreated.

There are no maps or route diagrams in the book, so following the climbers' progress becomes confusing. The twelve pages of photographs suffer in two respects: they are all murky, contrast-flat conversions of color slides—a cost reduction strategem that this publisher has not yet mastered. One picture required 15 minutes of intense scrutiny to discover the climber, so expertly does this conversion process camouflage his bright uniform against the gray rocks. And secondly, one has become so spoiled by the visual artistry of

Rowell, Messner, et al, that the lackluster point-and-shoot photographs of this book are disappointing.

Yet it would be a disservice to the reader to end this review on the same sour note as did the British expedition. Joe Tasker disappeared in 1982 with Peter Boardman while the two were boldly attempting another first route on Mount Everest without oxygen, in an even smaller—this time truly democratic—expedition. Joe Tasker deserves a better epitaph.

In his splendid book, *The Shining Mountain,* which describes a brilliant two-man ascent of Changabang with Tasker, Boardman paints a far more sympathetic picture of Tasker than comes through in the cool, distant writing of *The Cruel Way.* Tasker himself wrote a second book *Savage Arena.* Printed in an edition of only 5000 copies, it was impossible to obtain in time for this review. Scheduled for reissue, this book, I have heard, is probably one of the finer mountaineering works to have come out in a long time. It, not *Everest the Cruel Way,* is what we should remember Joe Tasker by.

Tom Holzel

A Walk in the Sky: Climbing Hidden Peak. Nicholas Clinch. The Mountaineers, Seattle and The American Alpine Club, New York, 1982. xii + 214 pages, black and white and color photographs, map. $18.95.

Millions of years ago, a mighty and inexorable clash of drifting continental plates pushed against one another and created a group of huge peaks on what is now the eastern border of Pakistan. Five of these summits are higher than the magic number of 8,000 meters, which is 26,247 feet (not 26,268 feet, as stated on page xi or 26,240 feet, as stated on the book's dust jacket). One of them, Hidden Peak (26,470 feet) is the highest of the Gasherbrum group and was the only eight-thousander whose first ascent was made by Americans. Author Nick Clinch was the driving force behind the expedition and now his book, written in 1959, has finally been published.

Nick's friends, myself included, know him as an outstanding mountaineer-politician, who has been both the friend and the protégé of the elders of our tribe, the bridger of generation gaps. He is a cajoler of the recalcitrant and, of course, a fine mountain climber with strong powers of endurance. Combine these qualities and you have what it took to organize and mount a successful assault on Hidden Peak, on a marginal budget, by a small party of enthusiasts, who learned as they went along.

The expedition was first conceived in 1954, on a climbing trip in British Columbia. From then on, Nick pulled strings, wheedled, improvised and recruited, as described in Chapters One to Three. He says that without Laurence Coveney, the expedition "would never have been more than a pile of papers inside a manila folder." One of Nick's most important achievements was to persuade, by repeated pressure ("I bombarded him with special-delivery letters and long-distance phone calls") the redoubtable Pete Schoening to join the group; he was the only one of its members with "eight-thousand-meter experience."

Chapters Four through Nine describe, with many hilarious anecdotes, the journey from Skardu to Base Camp. The delights of Balti buttered tea are chronicled on page 57:

". . . the lambardar's son brought out a brackish mixture of thoroughly boiled tea, ghee, salt and other ingredients that remained unknown. 'But this isn't regular tea, Tas,' I protested. 'Oh, no. From here on all we'll have is Balti tea,' he smilingly replied. I took a whiff and warned Pete not to smell it. Making a mental note to avoid all further invitations for tea, I watched with horror as Schoening gulped down the contents of his cup. Now everyone was looking at me. The United States' reputation in Baltistan seemed to depend upon my drinking that tea. 'How did you do it, Pete?' I whispered. 'Simple. I followed your advice and didn't smell it,' he whispered back.

"I remembered how General G. O. Bruce, leader of the 1922 British Everest Expedition, had adroitly extricated himself from a similar situation involving yak butter tea by informing his lama host that he was on a pilgrimage and had to forego the things he enjoyed most, which unfortunately included buttered tea. Lacking both the gall and the skill to use that ruse successfully, I kept placing the cup to my lips but was unable to take the fatal step. It was just about time for us to leave and my cup was still conspicuously full, when suddenly our porter train came into the village and the men began to disperse among the trees."

Chapters Ten to Thirteen are about Camp II and the big push upwards to establish the higher camps, with the help of high-altitude porters. (I wonder do high-altitude porters still receive cigarette rations as part of their compensation?) Finally, Camp V was set up at about 24,000 feet.

Chapter Fourteen, "The Summit," is by Pete Schoening. He and Andy Kaufmann left Camp V, where they had been alone overnight, at five A.M. and made the climb, with the aid of oxygen, by three P.M. The weather was clear. They got back to camp by 7:30 P.M. on July 5.

Chapters Fifteen and Sixteen describe the return. The epilogue tells what has happened to members of the expedition—and to climbing—since 1959.

There are several unusual things about this thoroughly enjoyable book. It was written in 1959 and, except for a short preface and an epilogue, has been published unchanged twenty-three years later. On the dust jacket, there is a photograph of the Free Hungarian flag that was taken to the summit "in memory of some very courageous people" (page 176): a people who were ruthlessly suppressed by the man who now heads the government of the Soviet Union.

One year after the trip, the author's photographic memory enabled him to recall many conversations and minute details. His style is easy, garrulous and humorous. He says in the Introduction, "I am not the same person that I was in 1959." But the publication of *A Walk in the Sky* brings to us a vivid account of those days, twenty-four years ago, when eight young Americans and two Pakistanis decided that they could do without the elaborate financial and political support that was customary for most expeditions, and succeed they did.

Time and again, from start to finish, the enterprise barely surmounted a long series of hurdles that might have stopped it. As member, Bob Swift, said, the expedition was "at the precise limits of the equipment, finances, physical endurance and imagination we then possessed." After all, to reach such limits, but not to exceed them, is why people climb.

Thomas H. Jukes

Kongur: China's Elusive Summit. Chris Bonington. Hodder and Stoughton, London, 1982. 224 pages, black and white and color photographs, maps, bibliography. £14.95

In an age when mountaineering is concerned primarily with approaching old problems in a different style—a new route, a harsher season, a smaller party, sans oxygen—it is stimulating when an expedition sets time back, undertaking real exploration before challenging a virgin summit. This was the mission of a team led by Michael Ward (overall expedition and scientific leader) and Chris Bonington (climbing leader) in getting to and climbing Mount Kongur and recounted in *Kongur: China's Elusive Summit.*

What a delicious opportunity this must have been, a kind almost overlooked in the contemporary scramble to raise the purely technical standards of climbing. The team was the first to visit a remote, long-closed and culturally exotic region (western Xinjiang) at a historic time when China was turning away from the traumatic path it had followed since 1949 and opening its doors to foreign mountaineers. During the 1980 reconnaissance, they were given virtual carte blanche to roam at will in fascinating high country, picking off a few satellite peaks. Then, in 1981, in clean style, with a four-man climbing team, they made the first ascent of a 7,719-meter mountain that refused to fall until the waning moments of the battle. Thanks to the efforts of a four-man scientific team, much valuable data on the effects of high altitude was also contributed.

Given these colorful and dramatic experiences, Bonington should have had a field day in the literary presentation of the venture. By almost any standard, the book is very good. But, I suppose, as is true with any well known and respected figure, we expect continued excellence. As I read, I couldn't shake the feeling that Chris had perhaps written one too many expedition books; his heart may well not have been totally in it. Even so, it is very good.

His books on Annapurna and Everest's Southwest Face have a vitality which the Kongur book lacks. The nuggets of quotable quotes are missing. I mention this because, after all, we buy books as much to get close to the author as to the subject. Books were a frequent and cheerful conversational subject around the Rongbuk Base Camp which I shared in June 1982 with Bonington whose team had no less than four climber-writers. As on previous trips, Chris had his trusty home computer with him. A great deal of writing had been done on it. Rival author-climbers claimed the machine was programmed for every standard expedition subject. Hit the right keys and the sunset passage would zip forth; hit other keys and the incoming storm would print out.

There is a bit of truth in the jest. The book is a chronology, a reporting of a series of events. There is a lot of information on the life and scenes of Peking and Kashgar and on the Kirgiz—semi-nomads of the high Pamir. Although discerned with a keen eye, they are reported with a certain detachment, in long paragraphs that are little more than a sightseer's lists. I would have preferred that he be more personal and intimate, as in his previous books.

When Bonington does shine forth, it is fun. For instance, the passages relating the frustrations endured while trying to organize portage in remote areas through intermediaries, complicated by ignorance of the local language, were magnificent. So, too, his honesty about his own shortcomings. I liked the description of a high, miserable bivouac on Kongur.

Peter Boardman's diary selections are gently poignant. And the book teaches a lot about the world's best climbers in action: notably their midnight action (wrenched from warm sleeping bags) to evacuate tents that were situated on an avalanche slope, in favor of snow caves dug in the dark discomfort of frigid night.

The book is impressive in format. There are lots of lucid maps and sharp, four-color photographs, the most memorable being of Bonington himself, "a study in outrage," immediately after Boardman stepped through the roof of his snow coffin. The appendices are informative: team members, diary of events, medical science research, history of the Kongur area, fauna and flora, geology, equipment, food, photography, medical kit and a delightful description of that most anarchic of games, buzkashi. Best of all, the book is about a resourceful, stylish and quite happy expedition.

NED GILLETTE

When Men and Mountains Meet: The Explorers of the Western Himalayas 1820-75. John Keay. Archon Books, Hamden, Connecticut, 1982. 277 pages, black and white photographs, illustrations, maps, bibliography. $17.50.

This is a book of the men who mapped, whore'd, botanized, ran guns, out-maneuvered kings and plumbed the rivers of the Himalaya from 1820 to 1875. These are engrossing tales of adventure, easily more enthralling than modern, microcosmic accounts of Himalayan climbs. The mountains were unknown then, unmapped and unsafe. The attrition rate for the early explorers easily outweighs recent climbing fatalities in the Himalaya. Back then, in addition to the frostbite, avalanches and river crossings, there were other hazards like the knives of suspicious Sikhs.

Perhaps one drawback of these excerpts from Victorian adventurers' journals is their style which tends to be personal with superficial observations. The reader can only imagine the voluminous research the author must have done to present us with introductory gems such as: "After the enthusiasms of Moorcroft, the affectations of Jacquemont and the ravings of Wolff, one shakes his (Vigne's) outstretched hand with a sigh of relief . . . his charm is neither florid nor demanding but a quiet and genial affability."

Despite Keay's polished presentation, the reader still must wade through empty, shallow travelogues of a time that demanded reticence of its heroes.

The photographs cleverly show the reader more of the itinerant Himalayan wanderers' personalities than their own journals. There is Gardiner bedecked in a tartan turban with a fierce mustache, clutching a weapon. Or Robert Shaw's assumed air of British regality, a sort of well-suited appearance of pomposity. Then there is the image of Hayward, "possessed with an insane desire to try the effects of cold steel across my throat." The intensity of Hayward's furrowed brow while holding a spear is unmistakably powerful.

The map illustrations are simply sketeches, covering vast topographical complexities with a quick sweep of the pen. It is possible that these modern map drawings are intentionally vague, so that the reader can identify with an adventurer's frustration at the rudimentary maps of the 1800's. Nonetheless, the maps' vagaries lost me.

When Men and Mountains Meet won't make any climber's best seller list. Yet it reveals a richness that has, perhaps, been lost nowadays. If you are willing to wade or skim through the digressions of olden-day pioneers, you'll find that these early Himalayan explorations have more excitement, scope and inspiration than most modern-day state-of-the-art accounts of a climber searching for a fingertip handhold.

JON WATERMAN

K2: Mountain of Mountains. Reinhold Messner and Alessandro Gogna. Kaye & Ward, London and Oxford University Press, New York, 1981. 177 pages, 31 black and white photographs, 109 color photographs, 6 sketches, 4 maps. $35.00

This is principally a photographic essay for a small coffee table—ninety-six pages of color photographs and sixty-eight pages of text, of which one-third covers previous climbs and explorations of K2. The text presents personalized but limited views of the 1979 Italian-German ascent, with most of the writing by Gogna and the introduction and account of the summit ascent by Messner. Joachim Hoelsgen, a journalist-turned-climber contributes a worthwhile summary of the history of the peak.

The photographs are first rate and include grouped views of the approach march, reconnoiterings and establishment of camps on the Abruzzi Ridge and the summit climb. Broad panoramic views obtained with an extreme wide-angle lens provide a better aspect of the ridge and surrounding countryside. In many cases, however, the fine photography suffers from inadequate captions with respect to locales and personnel; some of them are erroneous as well and others are not always applicable to the adjacent text.

With text and photo groups isolated from each other, the book provides a rambling, uncoordinated story which causes the reader to jump back and forth to ascertain his whereabouts (and whenabouts) on the peak and in time. Shifting authors creates even more confusion; only in the table of contents are we informed as to who authored what. Apart from the introspective writings of Messner and Gogna, we learn little about the other members of the team who end up simply as colorless names in the text.

It does not seem to have been a happy expedition, at least for Gogna whose account is overly subjective. One wonders why he signed on, unless it was to ascertain whether he could measure up to his companions in ability and determination. In fairness to Gogna, perhaps this is an unspoken characteristic of many climbers who challenge the big ones. However, he seldom expresses delight in his surroundings and the experience. At one point he writes: "When will this accursed expedition come to an end, so I don't continually have to be faced with these people?" He shows only a superficial, detached interest in the village people en route to the mountain and is depressed by their culture, poverty and illnesses. He does have his good days; after having scouted part of the route and established a high camp, he enjoys the congratulations he receives on having completed this important task. He makes note of the effect (probably not uncommon) on his tentmate: "Glowing from their praise, I glance at Renato who is very discouraged, hardly eating and not drinking much either. Every success, it seems, is at the psychological cost of someone else!"

There are some interesting comparisons to be made between the techniques used during the early exploratory climbs and those done alpine style in recent years. Ski poles seemed to be much more in evidence as hiking aids but short-shafted axes were only occasionally used. However, the fixed-rope, jümaring style of ascent lacks the camaraderie that formerly characterized roped teams. Once the fixed rope is placed, each climber is on his (her) own while ascending during carries between camps. Gogna reveals the isolation of the modern climber, caught in his own world of introspection as he mechanically moves along the fixed line. (Willi Unsoeld described the same feeling of isolation from the group during a solo Jümar climb to the 24,000-foot level on Nanda Devi in 1976.)

Messner's account of the summit day, with deep, soft snow much of the way, reveals how alone in spirit the unroped high-altitude climber can be, even when with a companion. There is much inward observation of oneself, as in a dream world, and only infrequent, unspeaking, nodding acknowledgements of another's presence. Messner notes that during the brief radio contact with

Base Camp from the summit, fellow climber Michl Dacher ordered flowers for his wife.

A few last nit-pickings: poor grammar and an inaccurate summary of some of the peak's climbing history. Some of the maps contain notable errors—on page 105, the Abruzzi Ridge and route are placed too far to the east.

DEE MOLENAAR

Filming the Impossible. Leo Dickinson. Jonathan Cape, London, 1982. 250 pages, color photographs. £12.50.

Rarely does one find in a single person both top-level climbing ability and top-level film-making skills. Leo Dickinson is such a person. His new book, *Filming the Impossible,* recounts his experiences making eleven different outdoor adventure films; with subject matter spanning climbing, ballooning, sky diving, and canoeing.

Dickinson's first documentary film, for Yorkshire Television, was no less than a climber's-eye-view of the north face of the Eiger. Not for Dickinson the long-distance perspective of the Kleine Scheidegg telescopes, or the hovering platform of the helicopter. Dickinson the film maker was also Dickinson the climber, feeling the crunch of his crampons into the brittle surface of the second icefield, and craning his neck worriedly upwards as the high-pitched whine of yet another falling stone narrowly missed Dickinson, the target.

To climb the Eiger Nordwand by any means, under the best of conditions, travelling as lightly as possible, is an achievement that has eluded some of the best mountaineers in the world. Don Whillans, for example, spent many fruitless years in this quest, and did not succeed. Others who have tried, too many, are now only crosses on a route diagram. Dickinson made it, carrying the weighty paraphernalia of the film maker, and brought back a superb documentary.

As with the Eiger, Dickinson's account of the north face of the Matterhorn blends the story of a gripping climb with technical details of filming in the most difficult of terrain.

Everest Unmasked, Dickinson's film of the Messner/Habeler oxygenless Everest ascent, rightfully won the Golden Gentian Award at the Trento Film Festival.

Among the other accounts, filming Eric Jones' solo ascent of the north face of the Eiger; the drama of Cerro Torre; and ski exploration of the Patagonian Icecap hold the most interest for climbing readers. However, descent by kayak of the Dudh Kosi, the river that flows from Everest Base Camp, together with accounts of hot-air ballooning and sky diving, provide diverse elements held together by a common thread.

This is a well-written, interesting, albeit somewhat specialized book, written by a person who is unquestionably the world's leading adventure film maker. Anyone who carries a camera in the mountains, whether still or movie, will profit from the tips to be gleaned from its pages. The ascents themselves, household names in the main, are different when viewed by Dickinson's perceptive eye behind the lens.

BOB GODFREY

Man at High Altitude. Donald Heath and David Reid Williams. Churchill Livingstone, New York and London, Second edition, 1981. 347 pages, many illustrations. $65.

High Altitude Physiology. Edited by John B. West. Hutchinson Ross, Pennsylvania, 1982. 462 pages. $55.

High Altitude Physiology and Medicine. Edited by Walter Brendel and Roman A. Zink. Springer Verlag, New York and Berlin, 1982. 316 pages. $65.

Hypoxia; Man at High Altitude. Edited by John Sutton, Norman Jones, and Charles Houston. Thieme-Stratton, New York, 1982. 210 pages. Many illustrations. $35.

Oxygen Transport to Human Tissues. Edited by Jack A. Loeppky and Marvin L. Riedesel. Elzevier Medical, New York, 1982. 374 pages. Illustrations. $45.

In the last two years more books have been written about high altitude and our accomodation to lack of oxygen than in the last quarter century. And a good thing too, what with the great increase in high-altitude mountaineering and accompanying increase in death and disability from avoidable, preventable illnesses. Climbers by nature are risk-takers perhaps, but there are risks and risks, and some may be taken to test oneself, but others seem a futile, foolish macho exercise. There's a middle ground—testing our physiological limits. How high, how fast can the human climb? How much cold, wind, privation can one endure? These are legitimate expansions of human capability—much like running an ever-faster marathon, or rowing alone around the world. We have to admire, even applaud such efforts, always bearing in mind Mallory's question about climbing: "Whom have we conquered? None but ourselves."

At any rate, he who wishes to challenge the effects of high altitude should understand the risks and these books will help, although unfortunately these particular ones, the best and most up-to-date, are written in medi-speak and much of their contents hard for the nonprofessional to grasp.

Man at High Altitude is a second, extensively revised edition of a major book, probably the single most authoritative book on high altitude today. It is well written and put together, extensively illustrated with photographs, charts, and diagrams which for the most part are easy to understand. It covers the entire field of high-altitude lack of oxygen thoroughly as the title promises, but does not deal with cold, heat, cosmic radiation, or illness and trauma. If one wishes a single volume about lack of oxygen at altitude, this is the one, even though the price is almost double that of the 1979 first edition. It has two shortcomings, unfortunately. First, the extensive bibliography contains no references later than 1979, which means that the information in these articles dates back to 1978 because of the long lag between submission and publication. With knowledge advancing so precipitately, this is a serious flaw. Secondly, the authors being pathologists, it is understandable that their emphasis should be on that discipline, and the book is weak, and in places wrong, about clinical aspects. (One small but important example is their statement that climbers who have had retinal hemorrhages should be advised not to go above 10,000 feet again! Such a patently unjustified statement might encourage destructive litigation and absurd bureaucratic regulation.) Thirdly, their discussion of safe rates of ascent has been out-dated by the demonstration by many world-class climbers that ascending 1000 feet a day is too fast for some but much too slow for others. But these are trivial faults in a first-class book. If you want an encyclopedic medically oriented text about altitude, get this one.

High Altitude Physiology. Coleridge wrote "the lessons of the past illuminate the future" and the more one studies, the more one comes to respect the successes or failures of our predecessors. West's book (one of the Benchmark collection) is an indispensable reference for anyone curious about how we got where we are today in our knowledge of altitude physiology. He has managed to collect—and even better to edit skillfully—the most valuable materials of the last several centuries, and it is exciting to read, in their own words, what our brilliant forerunners wrote. One misses some: for example excerpts of Hurtado's 1937 paper might have been translated and included to enlighten the many who quote without having read him, and Longstaff's privately printed thesis, one of the first comprehensive treatments of altitude illness would be a valuable addition. But every one would have a different list, and West has made a splendid selection. If you wish to know some of the classics in this field, there is no better—in fact no other single source.

High Altitude Physiology and Medicine is a collection of forty-nine papers presented at a symposium on high altitude held in Germany in 1980 and sponsored by the Volkswagen Foundation. The majority of the articles are by Europeans, with significant contributions from South America and Asia. Although most are written in medical terms, primarily for health professionals, sixteen sections relate directly to mountaineering and illnesses attributable to high altitude. Not surprisingly some of the statements are at variance with what we accept as gospel in this country—and such variants are stimulating and welcome. Many of the papers have been given elsewhere, but as a collection this is a refreshing and valuable book.

Hypoxia; Man at Altitude, like the preceding book, is a collection of papers given at the Second Hypoxia Symposium in Banff in 1981 and also contains many papers directly related to high-altitude mountaineering. Unlike the others, discussion follows each paper, which gives additional insight. Especially interesting are the case reports, recounted by victims of high-altitude edema, sickle cell crisis, thrombo-embolism and in the words of non-medical people these stories are impressive. Since the Symposium was planned to be comprehensive, the coverage is broader and a reader will get a more complete, less fragmented picture of what hypoxia does or can do to the human body and how to ward off the effects. This book is probably of more interest to the non-doctor climber than most of the others reviewed here.

Oxygen Transport to Human Tissues is another collection of papers given at a symposium. This one was held in Albuquerque in the spring of 1981 in honor of Dr. Ulrich Luft, a distinguished leader in high-altitude medicine. Virtually all the leaders in altitude research participated and their papers record the cutting edge of research at the time. Not surprisingly they are sophisticated and complex and few have any direct bearing on mountaineering. A number of speakers from abroad gave the symposium and this book an international flavor, and most of the material is new, prepared especially for this meeting. For the non-scientific climber this book is a bit much, but for a physiologist or physician interested in the latest advances, the book is a must.

CHARLES S. HOUSTON, M.D.

Ascent. The Spiritual and Physical Quest of Willi Unsoeld, by Laurence Leamer. New York: Simon and Schuster, 1982. 392 pages, eight plates of black-and-white photographs, and N.G.S. pictorial drawing of Mount Everest. $17.50.

This biography of a great mountaineer of outstanding character is a shallow book written by a man who shows no understanding of the sport of mountaineering or the joy of climbing; or in my opinion of the man he writes about, for I knew Willi Unsoeld well. To Leamer, Unsoeld is a man obsessed with risk, who drives himself, his daughter and others to danger and death. Perhaps this approach sells books or movie rights, but it does not do justice to a man of extraordinary humanity and unselfishness who set high standards for himself and always had time to help others with their problems. Yes, Willi believed in risk as a confidence-and-character builder, so long as the risk was justifiable and the risk-taker was aware of the consequences of failure. Joining the Peace Corps is a risk. Marriage is a risk—but who wants to live in a risk-free world?

This book leaves a bad taste in the mouth, for it contorts an outgoing, outspoken, generous man into an egoist with a sick mind whose thoughts focus only on Everest and a death-wish so strong that he doesn't care who dies with him. In similar manner, Unsoeld's devotion to his close-knit family is questioned and his home life is treated with smug contempt. The well known stories of Willi's climbs are the best part of the book. They shadow closely the original published versions familiar to climbers, but the often lengthy imaginary dialogues in the book are "based on recollections" only, yet read as if they were fact. Also some statements obviously made in jest are misinterpreted. Ignorance and carelessness result in numerous small errors too. Anyone who calls a glacial *moraine* "a long tongue of ice licking its way down the valley" or writes of the "ore-like rock of Everest's *summit*" should not write about mountains or mountaineers. Willi deserves better.

ROBERT H. BATES

High Adventure: A Biography of Reinhold Messner. Ronald Faux. Victor Gollancz, North Pomfret, Vermont, 1982. 180 pages, 45 black and white photographs, 2 maps. $22.50.

For many years, I have been a Reinhold Messner buff. I think that I have read almost everything he has written, including a delightful and perhaps not so well-known guidebook to the celebrated *vie ferrate*—the so-called 'iron routes'—that have been nailed into the Dolomitic faces to give adventurous tourists a sense of what climbing in the Dolomites is like. In fact, I once helped to lash together some unpublished material of Messner's to make an article about him which appeared in one of the previous incarnations of *Geo Magazine*. I have never met Messner, so I really do not have much of an idea of what makes him tick. One has the impression that he has, or could earn, as much money as he needs to live as well as he would like to, without having to drive himself the way he does. He seems persuaded that he can be the first person to climb *all* the eight-thousand-meter mountains. And perhaps he can. But then what?

In any case, given all of this, I was extremely eager to read Ronald Faux's book. Faux is a British journalist who works for the *Times* of London and who specializes in reporting about mountaineering for that newspaper. He was in Base Camp when Messner and Peter Habeler returned from their oxygenless climb of Everest in 1978. The book, he claims, is based on "extensive interviews" with Messner. In short, on the face of it, Faux would seem to be splendidly positioned to produce a really first-rate book about the man who is, arguably, the best active mountaineer in the world today. The only problem is that Faux can't write or, at least, write well enough.

Faux belongs to the "It was a modest smile but a significant one for the future." school of literature. (This ghastly sentence is the terminal one of Chapter Three.) Take this sentence: "Whatever darker subconscious motives were now driving him, if indeed there were such egocentric forces pushing him along, it was too late now to turn back. Climbing was dyed deeply into his nature and he was as committed to going forward as he would have been after starting an irreversible pitch." The "dyed deeply into his nature" is really the *je ne sais quoi* that gives that sentence its peculiar charm. Perhaps I will use it in *my* next book.

Faux is also a sensitive observer of the human scene. Of the Sherpas who accompanied Messner on his unsuccessful attempt on Makalu—one of the few times that Messner failed to climb something he started out on—Faux reflects:

"Seventy-five pence a day for dangerous work. They enjoyed it. The pay was high by Nepalese standards. The price of an average Mercedes would make a villager in Nepal an extremely rich man, comfortable for the rest of his days." There is much food for thought in this perceptive observation. If Ang Dorje did not actually want to *sell* his Mercedes, he could drive it down from Namche to the Dudh Kosi and take a swim. Or take Faux's comments on the apparently endless stream of women who make the trip to St. Magdalena in the Villnöss in the South Tyrol where Messner lives. "From women," he notes, although how, one wonders, does he know, "the reaction was usually an inquisitive stare. Was there something darkly attractive about a man who lived constantly in the shadow of such danger, who thought perceptively about the motives for his adventures and wrote about them with great frankness?" This weighty question is, needless to say, never answered by Faux and the reader is left, in a manner of speaking, hanging to a vertical wall of suspense by his merest pitons. In fact, the real trouble with Faux's book is that, after reading it, one does not have the feeling that one knows much more about Messner than before, especially if one has read Messner. While, for my taste, Messner may carry on a little too much about "the Death Zone" and the like, at least he writes with simplicity and clarity about both his life and his feelings about the mountains. There is no indication from Faux's book that he spoke to any of the other people, such as Messner's family or his former wife, Uschi, or Peter Habeler, with whom, it seems, Messner will no longer climb, who have played an important part in his life. All one has by way of external comment are some singularly vapid observations by Messner's current girl friend, one Nena Holguin, such as "Sometimes I feel so squelched by this man, but then I know that is what I want anyway—a strong man, a single separate identity." Who cares what *she* wants. Let her write her own book. It is to read about Messner that we are going to pay our $22.50—*yes, $22.50*—for a 180-page book with mediocre black-and-white pictures. Alas, Faux seems incapable of telling us anything about Messner that is not obvious. When I finished his book, apart from a great sense of relief that I did not actually have to buy it, I was reminded of a review that one of the New York food critics gave of a pretentious and over-priced French restaurant in Princeton. The critic wrote, "Princeton has long needed a truly first-rate restaurant. It still does." Someday, someone may write a decent biography of Messner but this ain't it.

JEREMY BERNSTEIN

Total Alpinism. René Desmaison. Granada, London, 1982. 202 pages, black and white photographs. £12.50.

Total Alpinism is certainly a book to read. It is like sitting down with one's best pal and listening to him tell about his latest wild climb. This book is a combined translation of *La Montagne à Mains Nues* and *342 Heures dans les Grandes Jorasses* which René wrote at the peak of his climbing career in the early seventies, when he was around forty. This account of dramatic alpine climbing over twenty years, the unglossed version of a climber who realized early on in life that he was not a literary genius or a profound philosopher but an exceptional climber of the highest degree, mercifully spares us self-indulgent, weird ideas about why he and the rest of us climb.

The first section of the book describes his early new routes and exploits: the Direct on Olan, the first winter ascent of the Dru's West Face, the direct of the Cima Ovest, the first ascent of Jannu, the Walker in winter, the first ascent and first winter ascent of the Frêney Pillar and the first ascent of the Shroud. Of special interest to me is his account of the 1966 rescue on the West Face of the Dru where René gives his version of a most controversial affair that starred his friend Gary Hemming.

The last section of the book deals with his tragic first attempt on the Walker Direct in winter and his eventual success. For those unfamiliar with the story, here are the highlights: René and Serge Gousseault, a younger (23) but accomplished climber, went up on a new route on the Walker Spur in the winter. After seven days of climbing, Serge froze his fingers and started to slow down, unable to retrieve a lot of the gear as well as dropping some. Then they had to spend the next two days battling for a few feet in a blizzard. Two hundred feet from the top, and hanging from slings after the ninth bivouac, Serge was unable to move. With no more food, in miserable weather, and still hanging from the slings, Serge managed to endure two more bivouacs but finally died. As a rescue was being organized by Simone, his wife, René waited through four more bivouacs (losing his sleeping bag in the second to last) before finally being rescued and hospitalized. He concluded with his description of his successful ascent the following winter, eloquently letting go his feelings at the top. "We had won. I had won, but what had I won? Glory? Material success? If glory, it would not last; if material success, it was too dearly bought. I could have had both so much more easily, so much less hazardously elsewhere. And yet it is for such moments of triumph and success that the mountains exact their toll. Logic asks why, but the question is meaningless. Only the passion and agony are real. . . ."

After reading *Total Alpinism,* one is left with the feeling that Desmaison made climbing his life simply because he liked to climb—not as obvious a statement as it seems. I put it down thinking "Wow! I would have loved to have climbed with this guy." And that's unusual.

JOHN BOUCHARD

On Edge: The Life & Climbs of Henry Barber. Chip Lee, with David Roberts and Kenneth Andrasko. Appalachian Mountain Club, Boston, 1982. 291 pages, black and white photographs. $14.95.

At age 28, Henry Barber makes a problematic subject for the biographer. Many of his achievements are difficult to dramatize: short rock problems rather than the evolving alpine adventures that books are more often made of. His most arresting climbs have been solo efforts that place a burden on Barber's own powers of narration. And at the center is Barber himself: can he be as interesting as his accomplishments? The preface to *On Edge* terms him a "fascinating character"; the book unfortunately fails to substantiate this claim.

The coolly competitive, businesslike Henry Barber is a familiar figure. But according to this book he also has "a deep-seated fascination with animals and all that is animated and irrational," "seeks solace" in relations with women and, in his own words, thinks "a lot" about dying. He simultaneously craves and resents attention, a complexity embodied in a scary moment during a solo on a Welsh sea cliff. Performing for a film, he is nearly shocked off the face when the cameraman, a "foreign presence," makes a sudden movement. Such complications of character are little explored; we can only guess at their depth. David Roberts' preface acknowledges that some readers will find Chip Lee "too close, too uncritical" for accuracy. The problem is that he is indeed too uncritical, despite serious efforts not to be, yet finally not close (or penetrating) enough to illuminate Barber's nature, which emerges as opaque rather than mysterious.

Lee provides some lively characterizations, such as Dresden's Bernd Arnold and the late British wildman, Al Harris. Henry Barber is one of the less vivid people in the book. Whether because of reticence—Lee's or Barber's own?—or literary misjudgment, a number of areas of interest are merely touched upon. Barber's conservative upbringing, reflected in attitudes that troubled many a climbing partner, is not analyzed. His failure to climb with his "hero," Royal Robbins, is attributed in part to "personality differences," but we are given no hint of their nature. In the Shawangunks, a reckless hiker takes a fatal fall. Barber, in whose arms the man dies, calls the episode "very sobering, something to think about." But, Lee adds, "the implications were never pursued."

To his credit, Lee addresses the 1978 Kilimanjaro issue directly. While *The Breach* was apparently published too late for his consideration, he does quote from Rob Taylor's earlier article in *Climbing,* which embodies many of the charges elaborated in that book. Lee establishes his most nearly critical stance in the Kilimanjaro chapter, his longest and last. Some light is thrown on such questions as the reasons for the length of Taylor's fall, Barber's lack of participation at the end of the rescue, his choice of route off the mountain and failure to remain in Africa long enough to visit Taylor in the hospital. Both participants have allowed that Barber was "caught unaware" by the accident, yet Barber's remarks here give a contrary impression as well: "I was concerned about him. . . . After he got his first screw in, I just stopped taking pictures. I knew something was wrong." Taylor's larger assault was upon Barber's whole character, which he portrayed as shallow and harsh. Barber's own words at times only intensify that view: immediately after the accident "I just smiled at him and said something like, 'Just like everything else on this trip, isn't it?' What could I say? He was in incredible pain and was apologizing to me. I just told him to stop his sniveling or I'd leave him there." Barber's great resourcefulness during the difficult descent is manifest, but not all readers will be persuaded by his ascription of his "seeming lack of compassion" to a "defense mechanism to deal with what was happening."

The narrative has an obstructed energy. Block quotations, mostly from Barber, appear frequently, not always well integrated with Lee's text. More editing would have eliminated irritating repetitions. The volume provides a publisher's preface and a glossary for the lay reader, a nonpublisher's preface describing how the account came to be written and a prologue that seems designed to humanize the book's subject. Many photographs are interspersed; they range from the murky to the striking.

Although afflicted with many shortcomings, *On Edge* recounts some stunning achievements from Yosemite to England, Dresden, Australia and Turkestan. I failed David Roberts' sweaty-palms test ("I doubt that there is a climber in the world who can read some of the episodes in Chip's book . . . without having to pause to wipe his sweating palms on his trousers."), but other hands may respond more readily. The book is of importance for those who follow the frontiers of hard climbing. It establishes or confirms Barber's significance in several areas: his insistence on good style, ability to lead on sight climbs that had stymied locals, and his extraordinary solo ascents.

STEVEN JERVIS

50 Years of Alpinism. Riccardo Cassin. Diadem Books Ltd., London and The Mountaineers, Seattle, 1982. 207 pages, black and white photographs, diagrams, maps. $17.50.

Riccardo Cassin has written a masterpiece of an autobiography—possibly the most important mountaineering book to be published in the last twenty-five years! It's all here—a scintillating record of a half century of high-standard Alpine endeavor: his first climbs in the Grigna, the Dolomites, the north face of the Cima Ovest, the north face of the Piz Badile, the Walker Spur of the Grandes Jorasses, the Cassin Ridge of McKinley, Jirishanca, Gasherbrum IV and Lhotse. Perhaps the world's best climbs done by one its best climbers. What more could one ask for?

But Cassin does deliver more. Recorded in these pages are tales usually ignored by his predecessors—tales of the roles of patriotism and nationalism within the framework of mountaineering. The joy expressed at making the first "Italian" ascent of a Dolomite north wall was clearly a source of great satisfaction to the young Cassin. It was also a significant step in overcoming the territorial constraints of a twentieth century Europe about to go to war. Neglected by most authors as taboo subjects, nationalistic feelings are discussed quite openly by Cassin—to his great credit. It may prove very surprising to the modern climbing generation to discover how profound these feelings actually were during the prewar period and how much psychological pressure each leading superstar of his day felt due to outside political forces beyond his control. Not free to luxuriate in the endless expanses of the North American landscape of space and liberty, the leading European climbers were thrust into the midst of political currents which were as difficult to navigate as were the outstanding routes they pioneered.

Cassin's views on the continuing search for and overcoming of difficulties in the mountains are presented in one very interesting chapter. Cassin was one of the first to adopt artificial means to overcome impossible routes where his predecessors had decided to retreat rather than use aid. He notes that progress has and always will occur in mountaineering. The search for greater difficulty gives its just rewards and satisfaction. But he ends this section with an appeal to all to seek also the aesthetic and ethical sensations which the mountains offer. Here, finally, is a glimpse of Cassin's personality and he is not shy about telling it as he believes it is.

The translation from Italian to English is excellent and faithfully records Cassin's style. The only obvious defect is the lack of color photographs which were present in the original Italian edition. Nonetheless, ninety photographs—some of them never before published—record the climb, the climbers and the action.

It is rare when one man has such an outstanding record and career. Even rarer is the ability to write about climbing in a logical and flowing fashion. This book is surely destined to become one of the great classics of modern mountaineering literature.

Roy Kligfield

Great Expedition Hoaxes. David Roberts. Sierra Club Books, San Francisco, 1982. 182 pages, 14 black and white photographs, 8 maps, bibliographies. $12.95.

Dave Roberts has here produced another one of his very readable books. He has chosen what he regards as ten great historic exploration deceptions and psychoanalyzed the leading actors in each. The book begins with Sebastian Cabot who, in 1508-9, reported he had discovered a Northwest Passage to Cathay and that he had also explored the North American coast down to the tip of Florida; Roberts thinks that this Cabot never left England and may simply have been seeking to appropriate and expand the actual explorations of his father, John Cabot.

Undoubtedly, the most curious story in this collection is the case of James "Abyssinian" Bruce, 1769-73, who was regarded as a complete fake almost immediately upon his return to England and was mocked and scorned through the remainder of his life. Not until years after his death, in 1796, was it discovered by subsequent travelers to Abyssinia that Bruce had indeed done essentially what he claimed—thus providing us with a sort of mirror image of the frauds in Dave Roberts' other tales, this time of why people refused to believe what, in fact, was true.

Our most famous old faker, Dr. Frederick A. Cook, is in the collection, with his bogus 1906 "Summit of Mount McKinley" picture—perhaps the most controversial single photograph in the history of exploration. Roberts offers essentially the same interpretation as most of us who have climbed to the top of McKinley and examined the outrageous 1906 claim.

Other hoaxes include the slyly faked "first ascent" of Cerro Torre in Patagonia and the most recent world-class fraud, the 1968 London *Sunday Times* round-the-world race for solo sailors. During seven months at sea, Donald Crowhurst, sent back periodic radio reports of his progress, supposedly all the way around, though in fact he never got farther than cruising about in the South Atlantic!

The character analyses are necessarily based upon secondary sources throughout and may, therefore, be questionable; they are, nevertheless, fascinating.

TERRIS MOORE

To Stand at the Pole—The Dr. Cook-Admiral Peary North Pole Controversy. William R. Hunt. Stein and Day, New York, 1981. 288 pages. 21 photographs. $19.95.

To Stand at the Pole is an extremely interesting discussion of the Dr. Cook-Admiral Peary controversy. Both were charter members of the American Alpine Club. An early AAC investigation led to Dr. Cook's dismissal from the Club. Subsequent investigations have done little or nothing to vindicate Dr. Cook. His blatantly fraudulent claims of having made the first ascent of Mount McKinley have further cut the ground out from under his credibility. Hunt gives us a fascinating and complete history of this intriguing character.

Hunt also presents us with a summary of earlier polar exploration by such Americans as Elisha Kent Kane, Charles Francis Hall, George Washington De Long, George Melville and Adolphus W. Greeley. Much of the rest of the book is dedicated to the still continuing Cook-Peary controversy. Hunt is clearly on the side of Admiral Peary. Much of this material has been aired before as may be seen from his extensive bibliography. One bit of new evidence, in print I believe for the first time, is definitely in favor of Admiral Peary's having reached the North Pole, a fact disputed by some who also discredit Dr. Cook. This evidence is a letter from Peter Freuchen to Vilhjamur Stefansson, dated November 16, 1934. In the letter, which fills seven pages of text, Freuchen tells of his conversations with Eskimos who had been with Dr. Cook and claimed that they had never strayed from regions they were familiar with. He also knew well Peary's Eskimos and the story of the Polar dash. "They have told me time after time about it," he states. Their statements would seem to vindicate Peary.

The book is a valuable addition to those written about this fascinating controversy.

A.C.

Mountains of North America. Fred Beckey. Sierra Club Books, San Francisco in association with The American Alpine Club, 1982. 256 pages, 140 color photographs, map. $35.00.

Shore up your coffee tables: here comes another three-and-a-half pounds of lavish illustration in a large format. Somewhere between *The Mountains of America,* by Franklin Russell, and *Climbing in North America,* by Chris Jones, Fred Beckey has perceived a gap; this book is his attempt to fill it.

Mountains of North America is not a mountaineer's atlas, as its name implies; nor is it a climber's route book, for which we should be grateful. Neither is it a geology text, a history, a photo-essay, or a catalogue of the author's climbs, although it partakes of all these things. It is hard to say just what it is. Perhaps it most resembles the Combination Plate at a Mexican restaurant: you get a bit of each item, and after a while, with enough salsa, they all taste the same.

Each of the thirty-five chapters of the book concentrates on a single peak, chosen either for its unique qualities or as representative of an area. Though not necessarily the highest, the most difficult, or the most well-known mountains in North America, the features they do share are Fred Beckey's footprints and his love. Whether that is sufficient adhesive to hold a book together the reader will have to determine.

For each of the mountains selected, we are treated to a basic geology lesson, a bit of history, the story of the first ascent, a brief rundown on the local flora and fauna and, perhaps, a firsthand description of a climb on the peak. The book is evidently not meant to be read from cover to cover, as much of the information is repeated from chapter to chapter; taken one chapter at a time, it may prove less insulting to a reader's intelligence. I think that if I had had a copy as a teenager, I would have found it inspiring: there are a lot of little tidbits of information to pique one's interest and the scent of adventure is definitely in the air. Youth would have kept me from noticing all the clichés.

Be especially careful not to spill your coffee on any of the 140 color photographs, as they are the most painstaking reproductions ever to appear between hard covers. The color is brilliant, the detail perfect and the layout tasteful. At least two of the pictures have appeared before, in Russell's similarly named book, but this time around it is like remembering to put your glasses on: they might as well be new.

I am personally familiar with only about a third of the peaks selected for inclusion but found little to squabble with among the meticulously researched facts of their chapters. The real core of the book, though, is not the factual content but the attempt to evoke the feeling peculiar to each place. It is the photographs, not the text, that do most of that work; they do it by small revelations, with details of plant life or lighting that say much more than the often ponderous narrative.

With such a vague program giving it form, it is not surprising that this book should be so difficult to describe. The gap it attempts to fill would not even be perceptible to many of us, yet Beckey pours a lot of his soul into it. The climber might disdain it for its insistence on the nobility of the walk-up peaks; the ecologist might skip over it for its superficiality; the historian might pick at its inaccuracies; but the simple lover of mountains will probably pick it out from under his accumulation of *Time* magazines and junk mail to read a chapter now and then and wish he were there. If he had been as peripatetic as Fred Beckey, he wouldn't need the book.

RON MATOUS

Yosemite Climbs. George Meyers. Chockstone Press, Denver, 1982. 260 pages, black and white photographs, route diagrams, maps. $16.95.

Friends of Yosemite Valley relax! No longer do you have to guard your worn and torn topos against thieves or grudgingly lend your copy to a desperate soul who then pleads to use the Park Service's Xerox machine. George Meyers has published a concise, artistic and, indeed, beautiful update of *Yosemite Climbs,* which has been tragically out of print for yea these many years.

As with the previous version, it is sparse and lean—what little language there is comes in an introduction by the usually laconic Jim Bridwell. It does have a few things that the earlier volume lacked: like a bouldering guide, a list of recommended classics and better information on descent routes. Its dayglow yellow cover is a dubious improvement on the old green one but the material is more resistant to wear and tear.

What would a review of a guidebook be without a little cavil or two? So, for the sake of form, I offer that the Mountaineers route on the northwest face of Half Dome is mixed up with Arcturus in one picture caption and that Australia is misspelled once. But these are nothing compared with the book's comprehensiveness and thoroughness.

I expect it will sell fast and that all too soon it will go out of print. The climbing public will then be back to its old mooching and scrounging, wheedling and pilfering of these indispensable maps to Valley pleasure.

R.D. CAUGHRON

Rock Climbs in the White Mountains of New Hampshire. Ed Webster. Mountain Imagery, Conway, New Hampshire, 1982. 294 pages, black and white photographs, route diagrams, bibliography. $14.95.

"Have you seen the new guide to the Valley, man? Like it's *really* awesome!"
"What? Did you say a *new* guide to the Valley?"

"Yea, it's like really radical. Lots of pics, new cliffs, and like a totally awesome format."

"What sort of format, man? You mean *big,* with lots of photos and topos?"

"No way, Jay, like it's *really* well laid out—cross references, like cosmic cliff pics . . . you know, like from outer space or somethin'. And to top that all off, it's uh, you know, filled with new routes that are even starred to tell you the good ones fer sure."

"Wow, I was, you know, getting' like kinda bummed to have to repeat all those old climbs again. Now I can go get pumped on some new lines."

"Yea, but I did find a couple problems in Webster's book, but they're no biggies. Like, it would have been real nice to have cliff photos of Mount Willard and Frankenstein, and some of the starred routes out on the K Highway like gagged me out."

"Whatdoyameanman? Why'd they gag you out? Like *too* wild?"

"Naw, *too* groady man. You know, loose rock, bushes, that kinda stuff. So if you go out to the Painted Walls or Far Out Sundown, like beware of some of the starred routes."

"Man, it's great Webster got his act together to, like, do a new guidebook. Did Roper help out?"

"Roper who man?"

"Like you got brain drain or somethin'? *Steve* Roper, he wrote the last guide to the Valley—you know the *green* one."

"Like this is *really wild!* I'm like rapping to you about the Mount Washington Valley, and you're thinkin' about Yosemite! This is *too* much!"

"Whatdoyameanman—Mount Washington Valley? Where's that?"

"Ever hear of New Hampshire, man?"

"Nope. Whereisit?"

"Buy the guide and find out, man. It's worth it."

TODD SWAIN

An Ice Climber's Guide to Northern New England. Rick Wilcox. International Mountain Equipment, Inc., North Conway, New Hampshire, 1982. 225 pages, 35 black and white photographs, 33 diagrams and photodiagrams, 4 maps. $15.00.

New ice routes have been created so rapidly in Northern New England during the past decade that even if more ice-climbing guides had been published, they would have been out of date by the time they traveled from the printer to your favorite climbing shop. Rick Wilcox has accomplished a formidable task by getting most of the routes, both new and old, between two very photogenic covers.

Descriptions start in the Smuggler's Notch and Lake Willoughby areas of Vermont, continue through the major (and minor) areas of the White Mountains of New Hampshire and proceed to the Camden area on the Maine coast, culminating in the far reaches of Mount Katahdin.

In the acknowledgements, Wilcox's sources of information read like a "Who's Who of Eastern Hardmen"—impeccable references. The approach information will enable the climber to find his way to the bottom of a climb with little difficulty (or as little difficulty as one may have in New England in the woods in the winter). The route descriptions, along with the photographs and their accompanying route lines, should leave little doubt as to where one is to go. Also, almost all of the photographs and their route lines contain the respective route names, their overall grade, the NEI (Northeast Ice) technical grade and the page of the text on which the route description can be found. Two indices are included: one lists the climbs by area and difficulty and the other alphabetically.

However, as with most guidebooks, there are bound to be a few problems. Unfortunately, there are no photographs or diagrams of the Baker River Valley near Plymouth, New Hampshire. This and smaller omissions—such as Grafton Notch in the vicinity of Bethel, Maine or the Blue Room ice flow in Smuggler's Notch—are minimal. The reader should also be aware that in order for some of the descriptions of mixed rock-and-ice routes to be complete, one must occasionally turn to the earlier works of Cote, Ross or Webster to fill in gaps.

The book's convenient pocket size (6¼″ x 4¾″ x ½″) and durable construction are certainly assets. The printing and binding by the Nimrod Press is also commendable.

PHILIP J. OSTROSKI

The Trekker's Guide to the Himalaya and Karakoram. Hugh Swift. Sierra Club Books, San Francisco, 1982. 342 pages, black and white photographs, maps, bibliography. $10.95.

This book covers a large geographic area, so naturally the descriptions of individual routes are not as detailed as one would expect in a book limited to a single country, such as Nepal. The author has trekked extensively in Asia and his descriptions are accurate and complete, reflecting his personal experience, observations, and respect for local cultures and customs. He was not able to personally inspect every route included in the book. Therefore, those which are based on secondary information are less detailed.

This is one of the first guidebooks to cover the entire Himalaya-Karakoram area. Swift does an admirable job of providing an overview of a vast and complex region. Readers who seek more detailed information on specific areas can consult the maps and other guidebooks to which he refers. A glossary of Tibetan, Nepali, Hindi-Urdu and Burushaski terms is a helpful feature.

This volume should be particularly useful to mountaineers and trekkers who want to consider all geographical options before deciding upon their destination. It is pleasing to find that many of my favorite trekking areas in Pakistan are presented as alternatives to trekking in Nepal.

GENE F. WHITE

Trekking in the Himalayas. Stan Armington. Third Revised Edition. Lonely Planet Publications, South Yarra, Australia, 1982. 218 pages, black and white illustrations, maps, bibliography. $6.95.

Contrary to the implication of the title, this book is a guide to trekking in Nepal, with two pages devoted to trekking in China. The author describes various approaches to trekking but is biased towards the use of an agency which will make all arrangements in advance. In view of the fact that many visitors to Nepal successfully follow a more informal or spur-of-the-moment approach, this is surprising. In contrast to Hugh Swift's descriptive *The Trekker's Guide to the Himalaya and Karakoram,* this is essentially a "how-to" book on trekking. The route descriptions are detailed and complete but they cover only five or six of the most frequented areas. There is less background information on the culture and the characteristics of the areas visited than in the Swift book. The route descriptions are divided in terms of trekking days, whereas several other guidebooks to Nepal, such as Stephen Bezruchka's *A Guide to Trekking in Nepal,* describe routes in terms of hours of walking between given points, permitting more flexibility in the length of each trekking day and selection of alternative camping sites.

This book is certainly useful for planning a first trip to Nepal. The traveller who prefers to adventure more independently will want to consult other guidebooks, including Swift and Bezruchka, as well as several from Japan and Europe.

GENE F. WHITE

Alpine Club Library Catalogue. Volume One. Heinemann Educational Books, Ltd., London, 1982. viii + 350, x + 230 pages. Paper. $95.00 (Available in the United States from: Jenny Watson, PO Box 915, Exeter, New Hampshire 03833.)

This volume is the result of a major undertaking on the part of the Alpine Club and is the first catalogue of the library's holdings to be published since 1899. As the Alpine Club began to collect books soon after its founding in 1857, and has continued to do so over the years, its holdings are now considerable: 40,000 items at time of publication.

The catalogue covers both books and periodicals. There is an author listing of all titles followed by a classified listing. There is a separate classified listing for guidebooks as well as an index to the major mountain areas of the world. As access to the material can be gained both through author and by subject, the catalogue is, thus, doubly useful.

The entries range from Abadie, A., *Itinéraire topographique et historique des Hautes-Pyrénées* to Zwickh, Nepomuk, *Geschichte der Alpenvereinssektion München.* Many of the books are familiar, indeed, almost friends: Maurice Herzog's *Annapurna premier 8000* in both French and English; Leslie Stephen's *The Playground of Europe,* in French, English and

German; and some thirty titles by that indefatigable author, Frank S. Smythe, including a Japanese translation of his *Edward Whymper*. Other titles are more obscure: i.e., *The snow-storm; or An account of the nature, properties, dangers, and uses of snow, in various parts of the world* [Charles Tomlinson], Society for Promoting Christian Knowledge, 1845.

As might be expected, there is a great deal of material relating to and editions from the British Isles and the continent. North America and the polar regions are, however, less well represented. The literature of the Himalaya is extensive, covering many aspects of the area: geography, description, travel, climbing history and reminiscences and expedition accounts. Appropriately, there are over one hundred entries under Everest, many of which reflect the British efforts that culminated in Hillary's 1953 ascent of the mountain.

Whatever one's interest, there is something here. For the casual browser, there are entries under an amazing range of headings: alpine gardens, flying, military mountaineering and natural history to name but a few. For the bibliographically inclined, there is a wealth of information as well. This catalogue is both a source of endless fascination and an invaluable research tool. The Alpine Club is to be commended for its efforts and for adding significantly to the literature of mountaineering.

PATRICIA A. FLETCHER

Traprock. Ken Nichols: The American Alpine Club. 1983, 479 pages, black-and-white photographs, sketches, maps. $19.25.

In the beginning there were no guidebooks. And lo this was good. Wind and rock and sky and man were free with one another. And later when man first came to the hills with his ropes and jangling iron, there were still no guidebooks. And this also was good. Then little guides appeared across the land. And this was bad, but we got used to the badness. Nowadays the jangling iron echoes in all the secret places, and guidebooks will plague us forever . . . and if you accept this inevitability, then Ken Nichols' *Traprock* must be reckoned a monumental achievement, the result of a magnificent obsession.

Traprock compares to the run-of-the-mill guidebooks as *Moby Dick* to pulp fiction. It is encyclopedic. It is finely crafted. It is the apotheosis of the urban climbing guidebook which exists not so much for the qualities of rock or setting but because of modern man's confinement to the territories of industrialization. *Traprock* is also a harbinger of where guidebooks are heading. We can anticipate—with dread or excitement—a decade or two hence when Yosemite will have been as intensely climbed and documented as *Traprock's* central Connecticut region. The result, applying the relative scale of Traprock's 1318 climbs, would fill whole library shelves: and still, as with *Traprock*, while the presses rolled new routes would be created.

Because knowledge of these 14 crags cannot be fitted into a pocket guide, Nichols has produced a one-and-a-half pound volume suitable for reading in bed or in the car. As much as an actual guide, it is about a love affair between Nichols and the local dolerite. The historical and geological material is lovingly presented; even the broken glass, used prophylactics, beer cans and butt ends at the base of cliffs he treats with sympathetic understanding. The quality of sketches by Nichols and Clint Cummins, who spent many hours tied into tree-tops drawing, is first class. And there is even an occasional flash of wit and humor—qualities that seem to be getting rarer these days, as guidebooks too often read like computer print-outs.

One ancient game played by guidebook reviewers is to catch and parade a handful of inaccuracies. There might be contentions about interpretation, but on matters of fact I'm so confident of Nichols' steel-trap mind that I promise to donate $50.00 to the American Alpine Club Endowment for each one sent in.

There is one small point of criticism that I'll raise, though I don't know that there's a better alternative. In *Traprock*, Nichols uses a three-, two- and one-star quality rating system, much praised in Jim Erickson's *Rocky Heights* about the Boulder region. Ostensibly this is to help the visiting climber who is scarce on time. The trouble is that one- and no-star climbs become pariahs, and when these are no more than 50 or 60 feet long—extended boulder problems almost—one wonders if they are worth the paper they're printed on.

JOHN THACKRAY

Surviving Denali: A Study of Accidents on Mount McKinley, 1910-1982. Jonathan Waterman. The American Alpine Club, 1983. 160 pages. Black and white photographs, map, charts, appendices. Estimated $10.00.

McKinley is a paradoxical mountain. Windswept and devoid of life for the greater part of the year, the peak suffers an onslaught of brightly-clad bipeds each spring and summer, a short-lived migration accompanied most often by flocks of noisy metallic birds, glacial snow-sculpture reminiscent of Stonehenge, and odd pagan rituals involving the carrying of huge weights to great heights, with the subsequent sacrifice of various items of food and equipment to the bowels of the mountain. On occasion, one or several of the pilgrims is sacrificed as well. Mount McKinley is the highest point in North America, as well as the most easily reached Himalayan-scale peak in the world, making it a justifiably popular goal for mountaineers from many countries. It is also one of the coldest, and precisely *because* of its accessibility, one of the most serious peaks available to large numbers of climbers. On the standard West Buttress route, it is entirely possible to fly into the Kahiltna Glacier at 7500 feet and reach the 20,320-foot summit three or four days later. *If* one doesn't succumb to one of the more serious forms of altitude sickness, *if* one isn't too befuddled by the cold and the wind, *if* one doesn't fall into a crevasse, *if* one doesn't get caught in an avalanche. . . . From the searing heat of its lower glaciers on a sunny midday to its windswept, below-zero upper plateau, McKinley is always fickle, contradictory, friendly at one turn and deadly at the other. A McKinley climb can be a cruise or an epic, or anything in between.

Surviving Denali is also a paradoxical book. In an era when the West Buttress often seems as crowded as the regular route on Mont Blanc, many would argue that anything which makes the mountain more accessible to the masses is unnecessary and probably undesirable. At the same time, McKinley's rising popularity over the past decade (slightly over 100 climbers in 1970 and nearly 700 in 1982) has created a demand for ever more information. Will the publication of this climbing guide *cum* accident report result in still more traffic on what some consider an already crowded peak? Or will the information thus disseminated lead to better prepared, more responsible climbing parties and a consequent reduction in the accident and fatality rate on McKinley?

It's a real chicken-and-egg question. *Surviving Denali* certainly isn't a Chamber-of-Commerce style guidebook; if anything, it would discourage most normal folk with its tales of avalanches, frostbite, crevasses and altitude sickness: a gruesome collection of the mountaineer's worst nightmares. Most of the book is devoted to case histories and analyses of accidents on McKinley, with chapters on pulmonary and cerebral edema, crevasse and climbing falls, prior medical history and exhaustion, and avalanches. These span the years 1968–1982, while a separate chapter ("The Self-Sufficient Pioneers 1910–1967") covers McKinley's golden (and less populous) age.

Although Waterman presents the incidents in a refreshingly straight-forward, largely nonjudgmental tone, all of this makes for grim and upsetting reading. He occasionally offers suggestions as to preventive measures that could have been taken but mainly lets the accidents speak for themselves. The lessons we learn are clear: go slowly and with a clear head, take care of yourself *and* the mountain and, if things get bad, turn back before it's too late—the mountain will be there another year. These are all things that we've heard before, made more convincing by the framework within which they are stated.

By far the most immediately useful section of the book is an "appendix, How to Prepare For Denali." Drawing liberally from Boyd Everett's classic *Organization of an Alaskan Expedition,* Waterman offers a cohesive and informative primer on climbing in the Arctic environment. As most of his suggestions can be applied to other Alaskan peaks, to winter climbing in the Lower 48 and Canada and to climbing in the Himalaya, the value of this section is not limited just to McKinley. The comments on clean climbing are especially pertinent considering the increase in traffic on the peak in recent years, as well as the relative permanence of trash and excreta discarded high on the peak.

The author is well qualified for his task, having made ascents of McKinley by several routes both on his own and as a guide, as well as climbing other peaks in the Alaska Range and Mount Logan. More importantly, Waterman is no stranger to pulmonary edema or frostbite and readily admits the mistakes and miscalculations that very nearly led to his own demise on the Cassin Ridge in the winter of 1982. Bravo to an author (and a book) which is *not* holier-than-thou!

MICHAEL KENNEDY

In Memoriam

FRANZ MOHLING

1930-1982

Franz Mohling died in an avalanche on Mount Logan last summer. With him perished two friends, Stephen Jensen and Turan Barut.

His daughter Shanti said at his memorial below the Boulder Flatirons, "Franz gave to me a sense of the frontier." Indeed, her dad had the ability to see much of his life as an unspoiled frontier even though he was making the second or the sixteenth ascent of a mountain. His family and friends must have been infected by Franz's way of making the traversed seem untraversed, an alpine meadow undiscovered, a folk dance never quite danced as he did.

Born in Jersey City, N.J. in 1930, Franz took his undergraduate degree at Renssalaer Polytechnic Institute. He completed his doctorate in theoretical physics at the University of Washington in Seattle in 1958. It was in the Pacific Northwest that he began his serious climbing career and contributed a chapter to a classic Seattle publication, *Freedom of the Hills*.

He continued post-doctoral research at Tata Institute in Bombay in 1963 and 1964. There Franz helped pioneer the first ascent of a 21,500-foot peak, which he named "Kulu Pumori."

During his twenty years as a physics professor at the University of Colorado at Boulder, Franz authored more than thirty scientific papers and had just completed writing an advanced physics textbook.

I would guess that Franz's favorite climb was the second ascent of the north face of Mount Robson, done just before the advent of high-tech ice-climbing equipment. Franz also distinguished himself on Mount Logan, in the Cordillera Blanca and on Mount Waddington.

Beyond these accomplishments, Franz's heart was always with social and environmental issues. By his generosity in both time and money, he promoted humanitarian justice and land preservation. He was also a leading figure in the Colorado Mountain Club, where he helped establish and direct the mountaineering school. He played an equally strong role in the Boulder Folk Dance Group.

I do not think that he was always at peace with himself. Sometimes, while the rest of us were passing some oh-be-joyful around the fire, Franz would work out his day in a journal by a lone candle in the tent.

Franz had also made two previous attempts on Mount Logan before his fatal, third bid. Was this compulsion a method he had worked out for himself so that he could live with others and continue with such sustained energy?

333

Perhaps it makes no difference what the answer is. It is enough for his wife Judith, daughter Shanti, son Tor and those of us whose lives have touched his to know we have been lucky simply to have known this total man.

JOCK GLIDDEN

STEPHEN WAYNE JENSEN
1952-1982

Although he considered himself an amateur climber, mountaineering was playing an increasingly large role in Stephen Jensen's life. His hobby had taken him to McKinley in Alaska, to Athabasca, Eisenhower, Assiniboine and many others in Canada, and to Chopikalki among the giants in the Peruvian Cordillera Blanca. He had dreams of many more and was working to make those dreams come true. His recent move to Colorado was a step on that path.

Stephen's life was marked with vigor and excellence in everything he did. At age 23 he received a PhD in Physics from the University of California at Riverside. Shortly afterwards, he worked as a physicist at the National Bureau of Standards in Gaithersburg, Maryland and finally in Boulder, Colorado with the Bureau there. He was the author of numerous technical papers and an internationally recognized authority on high-resolution-beam lithography. Many a volleyball team he played on vied for a championship place.

His caring and giving attitude is well remembered. A saving grace of his many business trips was the opportunity they afforded him to visit friends throughout the country. His home was always open. The magnificent view from his newly-finished backyard deck that he built was a further reason that his home was always crowded. Stephen spent four years with the Riverside Mountain Rescue Group in California taking many a step to aid others. He was planning on becoming a leader for the Colorado Mountain Club, of which he was a member. He showed his concern for family and friends by staying in touch no matter where he travelled.

Stephen had a perpetual smile on his face, always radiating his love of life, people and God. Though his life was short, his drive, caring and total joy in living will be long remembered.

Stephen's friends were not surprised to learn that his strength and drive had been key ingredients in what seemed to be a successful new route on the north side of Mount Logan. These hopes, the climb, and Stephen's life were abruptly ended by an avalanche high on the mountain. He will be missed.

KEN NOLAN *and* JUDY KING

CLINTON M. KELLEY
1913-1982

Clint Kelley, 69, fell to his death June 20, 1982 while climbing with friends on Mount Shuskan. Clint had first climbed Shuskan in 1938 while working on his Ph.D. at the University of Washington. He had started climbing in 1937 and in 1939 was in the first-ascent party of Sinister Peak, a classic climb near Dome Peak in the North Cascades. His love of mountains, his enthusiasm and his energy were legend and seemed only to grow through the years.

Clint had retired in 1973 as chairman of the chemistry department at the University of Denver, probably to have more time for mountaineering. Wherever his academic sojourns took him, he had found time for the mountains. While at M.I.T. in 1946, he was active with the Appalachian Mountain Club; while at Denver, he climbed with the Colorado Mountain Club and from 1950 to 1962, while at the Stanford Research Institute, he participated with the Sierra Club's climbing and conservation activities. In 1968 he was elected to the American Alpine Club.

In addition to being an active climber, Clint was an effective conservationist. He and his wife, Virginia (Jinks), whom he had first met on a climb in Colorado, worked tirelessly on significant conservation issues in the Pacific Northwest. Clint's effectiveness in whatever endeavor he was about was always enhanced by the calm, patient reasoning he would bring to any matter. It was, perhaps, this trait that made him an outstanding teacher of neophyte mountaineers. His fondness for working with students must have rivaled his love of the mountains and of climbing.

For many years Clint was active with The Mountaineers in Seattle, serving on their climbing committee first in 1939. He was a member of numerous committees and served as club secretary in 1980 and 1981. In 1981 he was voted The Mountaineers' Service Award, the highest honor that organization can bestow.

Clint Kelley climbed American mountains. He climbed many and he climbed well. It is perhaps a strange stroke of irony that one of the most considerate and careful climbers should die in a fall on a mountain he loved perhaps most of all, but Clint would have understood that.

JAMES S. SANFORD

GEORGE EVANS
1935-1982

I knew George for thirty years as a friend, a fellow engineer at Perkin Elmer and climbing companion. He attended M.I.T. and University of New Hampshire.

In climbing, George was conservative, careful and confident. He thought out climbing problems before attempting them. These were attributes which made him such a good partner. You could depend on him, and in mountaineering that is everything. He understood and accepted that in spite of all precautions, careful planning and training there were objective dangers. He accepted that, as did his family.

Most people wonder why perfectly sensible individuals will risk their lives to climb a mountain. For those of us who climb, the beauty found in the mountains is not matched anywhere. The acceptance of a challenge, the meeting of a self-set goal, the reliance on one's strength and knowledge and on the complete support of one's companions combine to make climbing unique in a world where most of us carry out someone else's dictates. The body's movement is always in harmony with its environment, shifting the weight to adapt to changing needs, while the rope serves as the life line tying you to your companions. As one climbs, little is disturbed; there is almost no trace of one's passage. The mountains were there long before us. For us the memories of sharing and understanding the unique beauty with George will last a lifetime.

George made major climbs in Europe, Canada, Mexico and this country. He was a member of the American Alpine Club, the Alpine Club of Canada and the Appalchian Mountain Club. The last mountain I climbed with him was one of the classic climbs in the Swiss Alps—the Biancograt, the white route, on the Piz Bernina. George, Bill Smith and I climbed the long, steep, knife-edged snow ridge on a blue-sky day. It was the perfect climb and that is how I will always remember George, climbing that snow ridge into the deep blue sky.

George E. Evans of Ridgefield, Connecticut was killed in an accident on the east ridge of Mount Whitney, California on July 14, 1982.

ROBERT JONES

RICHARD C. HOUSTON
1922-1982

A phrase used by Dick Houston over his many years climbing and trekking points to the essence of the man. It would be under adverse conditions—say, three-fog-bound in a two-man mountain tent with hostile elements closing in. At the very moment when despair seemed to be gaining the upper hand, invariably Dick would counter with a lusty bellow. "This group is having *fun*!"

Teacher, climber, runner, friend. Even the most casual association would lead a perceptive man or woman to guess that his profession was teaching. Graduate of the University of California with a Master's Degree from San Francisco State University, Dick taught high school science in San Francisco for 32 years, the last 18 as science-department chairman.

He was drawn to Yosemite's granite in his late teens through the influence of the Sierra Club Rock Climbing Section, by then the dominant organization of rockcraft on the West Coast. But World War II intervened. As a navigator in the Army Air Force, Dick flew many combat missions over Germany, strengthening a bond with fellow Air Force officers, Robin Hansen and Fritz Lippmann, two who had been at the cutting edge among the Yosemite climbers before their enlistment.

After the war Dick resumed climbing with the RCS, often in exploratory probes of Yosemite's uncharted walls. Perhaps Hansen best summarized those years in his words at the Houston Memorial gathering. "Dick, together with the climbers of his era, provided experience that enabled the next generation to improve equipment, climbing techniques, and to set their sights on ever more difficult climbs as those who went before him gave him a shoulder-stand."

In 1947 he joined an RCS expedition to the Mount Waddington region, accomplishing new ascents on various summits surrounding the Upper Tellot Glacier. Three years later he returned, a member of the summit team on a first ascent of the Southeast Chimney, third for Waddington itself, and sharing in the many first ascents made on satellite peaks ringing the Tiedemann. After a warmup ascent of Robson in 1953, expedition climbing for Dick culminated the next year in a first attempt of Makalu where he was regularly among those thrusting higher on the mountain. In later years Dick's mountain interest shifted toward climbing treks, with a focus on the Bella Coola region of British Columbia where in the late 50s and early 60s he joined friends on a number of ventures, pioneering new routes and making occasional first ascents. His last big climb was Kilimanjaro in 1972, although he continued treks in the Sierra Nevada with family and friends for several more years.

Dick served several terms on the executive committee for the parent chapter of the Sierra Club as well as on that club's mountaineering committee. An AAC member since 1948, he was the first chairman of the newly formed Sierra Nevada Section in 1956 and also was Acting Editor of the *American Alpine Journal* that year.

With a lifelong interest in track and field, he blossomed as a serious distance runner, completing a Boston Marathon at age 54 on the hottest Patriot's Day on record; shortly thereafter, he knew he was afflicted with cancer and underwent surgery. Yet within months Dick was again in training, often with his wife Lola, daughter Cheryl, or son Jeff. Soon he was running marathons and longer distance races, later setting national records for his age group. He kept it up until his last year.

A gentle, unpretentious man has passed, one who cared for mountains as he cared for people and who had the rare capacity to make the rest of us smile when winds blew ill.

WILLIAM W. DUNMIRE

RICHARD M. EMERSON
1925-1982

Dick Emerson and I met almost forty years ago and shared the U.S. Mountain Trooper's war. Thirteen years his senior, I am unprepared to write the inclusive dates after his name and to face his leaving before I did. I had rather counted on the reverse.

Dick's high points in mountaineering I shared only vicariously. His high point on Masherbrum was the highest camp, where his stomach rebelled and forced him to stay there alone while others spent the day and an entire night reaching the summit and struggling back down to camp. On his approach to Everest's West Ridge his stomach again lowered his expectations, but this time not out where he could spend a day overlooking the world at its highest, but rather within that world, bivouacking by secret plan, secure and snug within a crevasse, safely out of the tempest of one of the wildest Himalayan storms on record. He climbed back out of his fortress when the night and the winds relented, astonishing the friends who had not expected to see him alive again.

Lesser highs, in altitude if not in achievement, were in the post-war Tetons, where as a National Park Service climbing ranger he participated in rescues so scary you'd rather not hear about them, and in climbs that it was a delight to read about.

It was the skill of his writing and telling that let me share his postwar climbing world, in which he carried on far beyond where I left off—at the bergschrund under the north face of the Grand in 1956, which he and Phil Berry thereupon ascended. His other world I shared through an unbroken friendship; this let me be on hand for his wedding in Wyoming, watch his postwar winning of his Ph.D., witness his skill as a parent with Pat of their two delightful children, and enjoy the excellence of his photography. Out of everyone's twelve thousand slides, one hundred made it into the Sierra Club book, *Everest: The West Ridge*; seventeen were Dick's, and they are revealing of what mountains and mountain people meant to him. His camera and he got along very well together, and I am anxious to try to find out what he had in mind in the mixing of photographs, research, and prose to explain what Professor Emerson, social anthropologist, wanted to interpret for us about the Inhabited Wilderness of the western end of the Himalayan chain. He and Pat went to Baltistan again and again. At the year's beginning, the material to be interpreted was awaiting the organizer, there on the desk to which he was not to return.

A cardiac arrest as he slept, perhaps triggered by the stress of a malignancy I had always thought Dick was far too rugged to incur or put up with, took away the years that ought to have remained for him, just before Christmas and the wedding planned for his daughter, Leslie, and Randy Udall. On January 2, for his part in the eulogy, Randy selected some words of Dick's that were some of his finest, of special meaning to me, and good medicine, I think, for anyone who cares about mountains. Back in 1960 I had asked Dick to write about the Masherbrum expedition for the *Sierra Club Bulletin,* and he did a craftsman's job. I had one useful editorial suggestion to make. When Nick Clinch and Jawed Akbar headed for the top, and Willi Unsoeld and George Bell were far below and out of sight, there Dick was, alone. "What was all that solitude like?" I asked him. "Could you add a paragraph or a page and tell us about it?" He did, and the *Bulletin*'s passage also occupies a page of the Everest book. Randy found it there and excerpted it:

It did not come all at once, that sense of consuming solitude. At first it was just a matter of resting passively, amidst spectacular scenery, but this steadily changed into a peculiarly mixed sensation of aroused relaxation: poised and attentive, infinitely at ease. After so much effort, to sit there, totally alone at 25,000 feet, surrounded by a still and motionless world of rock and ice and blue-black sky, was satisfying in a very special way. It was not the euphoria of altitude. It was the exhilaration of wilderness. . . . I raised my goggles for an unobstructed view of Beauty.

And I remembered a few poignant words borrowed from a tombstone in England to grace a plaque on Olaus and Mardy Murie's mantel, seven thousand feet below one of Dick's favorite summits, the Grand Teton:

THE WONDER OF THE WORLD

THE BEAUTY AND POWER

THE SHAPE OF THINGS

THEIR COLORS, LIGHTS AND SHADES

THESE I SAW

LOOK YE ALSO WHILE LIFE LASTS

Dick looked and saw very well, far more sensitively than his detached manner would ever let you think. He also heard the sound and caught the aroma and the flavor. He felt the mountain, underfoot and at his fingertips, respected it, and moved there with an assurance that I have never seen surpassed. "We never grow tired of each other, the mountain and I," Li Po wrote long ago. I think that Dick, twelve centuries later had some Li Po in him and, given enough time, would have seen the mountain tire first. Many people knew how much he loved and was loved. I am grateful to be one of them.

DAVID BROWER

GUNNAR NASLUND
1950-1982

On August 4, 1982, Gunnar Naslund, a four-year member of the American Alpine Club, lost his life when he was struck by a collapsing cornice as he led a rope attempting the first ascent of Needle Mountain in Alaska's remote Granite Range.

Gunnar located in Anchorage after his 1975 graduation from Marquette Law School in Milwaukee, Wisconsin. His attraction to Alaska's mountain wilderness quickly turned to unfailing devotion when the climbing bug bit and he became an inveterate mountaineer and explorer almost from the start. After several years of sporadic legal employment punctuated by longer and longer mountaineering sabbaticals, he largely abandoned the law for the mountains. He organized Wrangell-St. Elias Mountaineering, a mountain guiding business, and taught mountaineering courses both privately and through a local university.

Whether teaching, guiding, or just climbing, Gunnar's star always shone brightest in the mountains of Alaska. We shared a 68-day Denali epic in 1977. That same year, we were unsuccessful in attempting a winter attempt of Mount Sanford (Gunnar returned twice more in later years before finally reaching that 16,000-foot summit), and were "earthquaked" off the very top of Bashful Peak in the Chugach Range. Subsequently, Gunnar guided four successful Denali expeditions by three different and progressively more difficult routes. He also climbed on Hunter and Foraker in the Alaska Range, Bona, Churchill, Drum, Blackburn, University, and many other peaks, named and unnamed in the Wrangells, Hesperus in the Revelation Range, Newton and St. Elias in the St. Elias Range and skiied 350 miles across the Bagley Icefield in the spring of 1981 (see *A.A.J.*, 1982, page 139).

Gunnar visited many of the world's other great mountain ranges. On his first visit to South America, he made ascents in the Central Andes of Bolivia and Peru. He also trekked and climbed in the Himalayas of Nepal and India. On his last visit to South America he climbed alone in the Cordillera Darwin of Tierra del Fuego after he missed shipping out to Antarctica by only one day. He next joined an Argentine expedition and with another climber made the fourth ascent of the beautiful Patagonian granite spire, Aguja Poincenot (see *A.A.J.*, 1982, page 195). On the day I learned of his death, I had just completed our joint application for a permit to climb a remote 24,000-foot peak in Nepal next year.

A self-effacing "snow cave philosopher", Gunnar spoke little of his mountaineering adventures and often made light of the attendant difficulties. His pack was never too full for one more item of group gear and he was always the first one out to shovel snow from the tent during a storm.

When I stood on the summit ridge of Needle Mountain the week following the accident and watched his brother, Eric, cut the rope and my friend's body slide into a crevasse on an unnamed glacier below as he had once requested, I found, at least for myself, the answer to the perennial question, "Why do you climb mountains?"—For the good company.

> Here's to you my Ramblin' Boy
> May all your ramblin' bring you joy
> He left me here to ramble on
> My ramblin' pal is dead and gone
> If when we die we go somewhere
> I bet you a dollar he's ramblin' there
>
> *Ramblin' Boy* by Tom Paxton

JOHN E. DUGGAN

ROGER G. WOLCOTT
1895-1982

The climbing fraternity lost one of the pioneers of Eastern rock climbing and the older climbers lost a long-time friend when Roger Wolcott died January 5, 1982. His climbing career spanned more years than that of all but a few of his contemporaries. He began climbing with the Appalachian Mountain Club around Boston in the early thirties. When he moved to New York late in that decade, he joined with climbers there to develop the Shawangunks as a climbing area. Teamed with Fritz Wiessner or Hans Kraus, he played a major part in establishing many of the classic routes such as the Three Pines and Fritz' Yellow Face. From then until the 1960s he climbed and hiked with the New York AMC. In 1944 he became a member of the American Alpine Club.

Roger's climbing career was by no means limited to technical rock climbing. He enjoyed as well the varied demands on endurance and technique, both on snow and on rock, made by the big mountains. With Hans Kraus he made trips to the Tetons and the Wind Rivers. At an age when many climbers would call it quits, he was doing major climbs in the Alps, particularly around Zermatt, a climbing center he dearly loved. In addition to the 4000-meter summits, he took delight in the great traverses like the Wellenkuppe-Obergabelhorn— a picture of the infamous gendarme on that ridge always hung on his wall. His relationship with the guides was one of mutual respect—you might say a throwback to the classic days of alpine mountaineering. Only eye trouble and, ultimately, a stroke could hold him back from the high places.

But a mere recitation of his climbing career hardly gives a picture of Roger the man. He had a wry, straight-faced kind of humor that often caught you by surprise. Under it lay a considerate, patient nature which made him an excellent companion. Whether it was a blown-down tent or struggles with the Soviet bureaucracy, Roger could handle the situation. Although a strong, steady climber who regularly led the more difficult routes of his day, he also gave unstintingly of his time to introduce beginners to the sport. He usually started off by telling them that the hard part was not getting up the rock but managing 120 feet of nylon rope! Regardless of how inept or frightened the novices were, Roger could calmly coach them up their first climb and give them a good introduction to a new sport.

Born in Canton, Illinois, in August 1895, he graduated from the University of Wisconsin and served as a lieutenant in the Coast Artillery during World War I. Early jobs included a stretch as a cub reporter and work as a consumer consultant with the American Standards Association. Then he founded his own advertising agency, a small, highly personal organization which emphasized educational advertising.

By his first wife, Roger had a son, Roger Jr., who lives in Florida. Much later he married Delphine Wilde, with whom he went on many camping, hiking and climbing trips. Her death was a hard blow for him. In 1976 he had a stroke which left him limited control of his left arm and leg. But Roger never gave up. He courageously and patiently continued physical therapy until the end. His wife, Charlotte (Carpenter), was his constant inspiration during those difficult years— encouraging, helping with therapy and sharing with him the kind of morale-boosting activities he needed.

Roger, we all miss you. You were a valued friend and a good companion.

PERCY T. OLTON, JR.

LEWIS S. SOUTHWICK
1888-1981

Lewis S. Southwick died on December 18, 1981 at the age of 93. An American Alpine Club member since 1944, he resided in Shelter Island, New York. He had made ascents in New Hampshire's White Mountains, the Canadian Rockies and the Alps.

WALTER L. WOLF

Walter L. Wolf died on December 9, 1981. A resident of Zürich in Switzerland for a number of years, he had joined the American Alpine Club in 1954 while still living in the United States. He was a life member. He had climbed extensively in the Alps.

PAUL VAN ANDA

Paul Van Anda, an American Alpine Club member since 1933, died on January 21, 1982 in Salt Lake City. He was an estate and corporation lawyer who lived in Upper Nyack, New York. He was educated at Phillips Exeter Academy, Harvard College and Harvard Law School. His climbs included ascents of Mont Blanc, the Matterhorn and numerous other peaks.

MARTY HOEY
1951-1982

On May 15 Marty Hoey died in a fall at 26,200 feet on the north face of Mount Everest. A day or two later, she would have stood a very good chance of becoming the first woman from this country to reach the summit of the world's highest mountain.

For over ten years, Marty actively climbed, principally as a professional guide on Mount Rainier and Mount McKinley, but also to further ranges. She climbed Pik Lenin during the 1974 International Climbers Exchange in the Pamirs and participated in the 1976 Nanda Devi expedition. On the latter, she was forced to withdraw before reaching the base of the mountain due to an intestinal disorder that nearly proved fatal. She was determined to perform well on Everest, spurred on, she freely admitted, by the acute disappointment that lingered from the Nanda Devi episode. The fact that she was selected to be in the first summit team on Everest confirms her exceptional performance prior to the accident.

Marty was a remarkably fast and strong climber, one who quickly dispelled any macho notions that women cannot meet the standards of their male counterparts. On a training climb to Aconcagua before we left for China, it was Marty's tremendous drive that mainly accounted for an ascent by a new route on the mountain's east side.

But for more than her sheer ability as a climber will Marty be remembered. She touched all those who knew her with a rare warmth and grace. As Lou Whittaker eloquently expressed at a memorial service we held for Marty at Base Camp:

> Marty will always be remembered as a beautiful young person. She left us that way and as long as we live, all of us will age and sicken, but she will remain healthy in our minds as she was on this climb. We'll always think of Everest and Marty.

JAMES WICKWIRE

Club Activities

Edited by FREDERICK O. JOHNSON

A.A.C., Blue Ridge Section. In 1982 this smallest section of the Club was undoubtedly the most active in proportion to its size. Section-sponsored outings were held in the Potomac Gorge and at Seneca Rocks, West Virginia. Members also climbed in the Alps, California, the Sawtooth Range of Idaho, the Cascades, the Wind Rivers of Wyoming, the Canadian Rockies, and British Columbia. Meetings featured a wide variety of speakers including Al Rubin's description of his experience on the Club's exchange with Poland; Gaston Rébuffat's film, *Les Horizons Gagnés,* (co-sponsored with the Union des Français à l'Étranger); and Doug Scott's slides of three Himalayan expeditions (co-sponsored with the Smithsonian Resident Associate Program).

Conservation was also a major Section effort. Together with the Potomac Appalachian Trail Club, the Section sponsored the Carderock Conservation Project, chaired by Janet Young, which has put hundreds of hours of work into halting and reversing erosion at Washington's nearest climbing area. Because of its location at the seat of government, the Section has assisted the Club's Conservation and Use Committee in pressing to prevent clearcutting in the Menagerie climbing area in Oregon.

With the loss of officers Will Davis to the Alaska Section and Vivian Mendenhall to Australia, Francis Soges was elected treasurer and Joe Wagner secretary for the remainder of the year.

GEORGE R. MERRIAM, *Chairman*

A.A.C., Cascade Section. During the year the Section sponsored several slide programs featuring local, national, and international climbers. In June Stephen Bezruchka described his 1981 ascent of Mustagh Ata in Western China. In the fall Doug Scott gave a program on climbing Kangchenjunga, Shivling, and Xixibangma. Later in the fall Jim Dockery presented a show that included slides of many major climbs in North America that he has done over the past years.

Our annual banquet was held in December. The program featured two local climbers who participated in the A.A.C.-sponsored climbing programs in Europe. Kjell Swedin showed slides of the men's rock climbing meet he attended in Britain at the invitation of the British Mountaineering Council. Matt Kerns described his trip to East Germany and Czechoslovakia on an A.A.C.-sponsored climbing exchange.

STEVE SWENSON, *Chairman*

A.A.C., New York Section. The highpoint of the year's events for the New York Section was the annual dinner, with Gaston Rébuffat as principal speaker. A capacity gathering of 150 attended the black-tie affair at the Union Club on October 1, attracted by the first visit to the United States in 15 years of famed French climber and author Gaston Rébuffat. The event marked the first showing in this country of Gaston's beautiful, prize-winning film, *Les Horizons Gagnés (To Touch The Sky)*, narrated in English by the author.

New features of this year's dinner were a special menu highlighted by salmon flown in from Alaska just for the occasion, courtesy of an anonymous benefactor; an art and photography exhibit featuring the works of local members Olaf Sööt, Louis Bergmann, and Anthony Horan; and various door prizes including a guided climb with Rébuffat himself, won by Garrett Bowden.

The dinner was held as a benefit for the Clubhouse Improvement Fund and netted a record $3300, which will be used to finance a number of much needed improvements to the facility.

PHILIP ERARD, *Chairman*

The Colorado Mountain Club. The C.M.C. experienced a healthy growth rate in 1982, adding a thirteenth Colorado Group and conducting more than 2000 trips. Present membership totals over 7300.

Our outings included a bicycle trip to Holland, a backpack trip to Cascade Pass in Washington, two canoe trips to Quetico Lakes, and trail building and maintenance work trips to Kenosha Pass, Chalk Creek, and Leadville in Colorado. The annual Colorado outing was held on the West Fork of the Cimarron area of the Uncompahgre National Forest.

We had an exceptional safety record in 1982. The Conservation Committee was active at the state and federal levels in the areas of clean air and visibility regulations, management plans for the national forests, and wild and scenic rivers legislation.

Next year trips are scheduled to Europe, Iceland, and many locations in Colorado. Our 1983 president, Glenn Porzak, will attempt a climb of Mount Everest.

GEORGE H. SAUM, *President*

Dartmouth Mountaineering Club. In 1982 the DMC continued to offer comprehensive rock-climbing classes to Dartmouth College students as well as other interested parties. In addition a new winter mountaineering/ice-climbing school was organized and activated. Various members climbed throughout the United States and in Europe. Besides new routes in the mountains of New Hampshire and Vermont, three new ones were put up in Texas at 5.9 and 5.10 difficulty. Work has started on a guidebook to the relatively unknown but high-quality crags in the Hanover, New Hampshire, area.

CARRICK M. EGGLESTON, *President*

Harvard Mountaineering Club. Each weekend in the fall and spring club members head for the rock climbing areas of New Hampshire, Connecticut, and New York, while the club continues to sponsor Friday afternoon beginners' trips to the nearby Quincy Quarries. Many of our current members are enthusiastic ice climbers, and the 1982-1983 ice climbing season promises to be an active one. Several alumni instructors have been recruited for the first winter trip to the H.M.C. cabin at Huntington's Ravine in the White Mountains. The club's annual January expedition up Mount Katahdin in Maine will include both skiers and climbers.

A reunion of four past club presidents—Bob Pelay, Nick Vanderbilt, Paul Milde, and Peter Sorger—took place in November for a week of climbing in Yosemite Valley. Plans for an H.M.C. summer climbing trip next year to Yosemite and Joshua Tree National Monument are being formulated.

The traditional fall dinner was a great success, attended by such A.A.C. notables as Henry Hall (our club's founding father), Ken Henderson, and Sam Streibert.

The 23rd volume of the *H.M.C. Journal* will be published in the spring of 1983 including articles by Dave Roberts on profiles of H.M.C. members in the '30s, by Will Silva and David Coombs on the Cassin Ridge of Mount McKinley, by Ken Andrasko on Yosemite's Half Dome, and by Clint Cummins and John Imbrie on a photographic description of Mount Katahdin's ice-climbing routes.

MADELEINE CARTER, *President*

Iowa Mountaineers. The club completed another active year in 1982, with membership growing to 1100. Nearly 450 members participated in one of the courses, the mountaineering camps, or the foreign expeditions that were one to four weeks in length. The courses and mountain camps were again offered for University of Iowa credit, if desired. Under the instruction of Jim and John Ebert, 85 members finished the concentrated one-week basic rock-climbing courses held at Devils Lake State Park, Wisconsin, and 75 completed the weekend rock-climbing courses. Three general weekend outings were held at Devils Lake with an average attendance of 60.

In January, 65 members joined a seven-day cross-country skiing and winter survival course near Leadville, Colorado. A winter and spring backpack trip to the Grand Canyon, led by Jim and Margie Ebert, brought out 75 members.

The club sponsored two foreign expeditions and a Canadian mountaineering camp. John and Jim Ebert led a group of 25 to New Zealand in January and February. Ascents were made of Mounts Ruepehu and Ngauruhoe on the North Island, and 18 members hiked the Milford Trek, with nine completing the Route-burn Trek. Inclement weather prevented the ascent of a number of the classic peaks in the Mount Cook region.

In July, John and Jim Ebert led a group of 42 to Tanzania to climb Mount Kilimanjaro (19,340 feet) and to visit the national parks and animal reserves.

This was the club's fifth trip to East Africa since 1967. Only six of the 126 members who attempted the peak on these trips have failed to reach the summit of this famous African mountain. This summer 35 of the 39 who started up the peak reached the summit. This five-day, 78-mile, 14,000-foot ascent and descent was an exhilarating adventure.

During August, Jim Ebert directed a basic snow-and-ice course and a general mountain camp in Alberta, Canada. Base Camp was located at the Castle Meadow Campsite, 18 miles north of Banff. This was the largest attended mountaineering camp in the club's history. With generally good weather, the group was very active and made over 272-manned ascents of 16 peaks during the 11-day camp. The major peaks ascended included Mounts Athabaska (Silverhorn Route)—16 members; Victoria—24 members; Aberdeen—20 members; Stanley—16 members; Hector—18 members.

In 1983 the club will climb in Peru, with Base Camp located in the Quebrada Rajucolta. Attempts will be made to climb Huantsán and Huascarán. The club will also sponsor a mountain camp in the Beartooth Range in Montana August 2-12.

JIM EBERT

Potomac Appalachian Trail Club. It has been an interesting and active year for the Mountaineering Section (MS). The membership has been extremely active in rock climbing, mountaineering, and conservation projects.

Last year, the club supported a trip to McKinley, the 1982 PATC Denali Expedition. A team of five MS members spent several weeks on the mountain in poor weather. A summit attempt reached 18,400 feet before being turned back by weather. MS members were also climbing throughout Europe. Former member, Gianni Battimelli, met with section members and other D.C. area climbers to climb in the Dolomites and on other crags in Italy. Other members did rock climbs in England and Germany and alpine routes in Switzerland, on the Mont Blanc Massif, and in the Austrian Alps. A few members went to the western U.S. and Canada climbing in the Canadian Rockies, North Cascades, Tetons, Colorado Rockies, Smith Rock, Oregon, Devils Tower, and Eldorado Canyon. Of course, our regular weekend climbing areas, Shawangunks, Seneca Rocks, and Stone Mountain, North Carolina, were visited. Local ice climbers continued to go to New Hampshire to climb.

The MS has also been involved in several projects that are beneficial to the climbing community. At Seneca Rocks, the MS, the Forest Service, and the Pittsburgh Explorers have relocated the trail leading to the west face of the rocks. The new trail should decrease erosion on the slope and provide climbers easier travel to the west face. At Carderock, the AAC, Park Service, PATC-MS, school groups, and concerned climbers have joined forces to repair river bank erosion near the rocks. In addition to participation in these projects, the MS has been reviewing management plans for Shenandoah National Park and the Monongahela National Forest to insure that interests of the climbing community are represented.

The Mountaineering Section has also continued its normal activities. At monthly business meetings, the MS provided entertainment in the form of a slide show or film. We also scheduled regular weekly climbing trips to local crags. The MS offered training courses, on a monthly basis, in Basic Rock Climbing, and Advanced Rock Climbing. We also offered special courses in Direct-Aid Climbing, Mountaineering Medicine, and First Aid. The MS newsletter, *Up Rope,* continued to be a forum for the club and the local climbing community.

The Mountaineering Section of the Potomac Appalachian Trail Club has maintained its objective of being an organization that is a positive influence toward the safe enjoyment of rock climbing and mountaineering, conservation, and good comradeship.

JAMES EAKIN, *Chairman*

The Mountaineers. The Climbing Committee experienced a lively and active season with reviews of climbing methods, policies, etc. The Committee was composed almost entirely of veteran climbers whose experience contributed significantly to the climbing program. Efforts towards improving the Basic Climbing Course included: the construction of a new belay practice tower at Camp Long; the installation of new beams in the skylight area of the Clubroom to provide prusik practice; revision of the seat harness tie-off to use the double fisherman (grapevine) knot; the adoption of the anchor wrap belay method based on a study begun in April 1981; replacement of the final exam with "Clint Kelley" quizzes at most lectures; addition of a new lecture in August on leading on rock; and the addition of an optional field trip, "Rock 3," for the introduction to leading on rock with about 35 basic students participating. About 125 graduated fom the Basic Course this year.

The Intermediate Climbing Course started with 70 students. The lectures included quizzes to stimulate thought, and lecture evaluation forms to provide rapid feedback on each lecture. Relevant films supplemented the lectures. A new lecture on snow climbing was added with focus on "criteria of when to be roped up" and "self-belay rationale and instruction." Some 18 climbers graduated from the Intermediate Course, which usually takes three to five years to complete.

In addition to its basic and intermediate experience climbs, The Mountaineers also schedule club climbs, which have been expanded to include more alpine-level climbs. These have been relatively successful, with no serious accidents occurring on these scheduled climbs.

The foregoing relates to the climbing programs of the club in Seattle. Branches of The Mountaineers in Everett, Tacoma, and Olympia also run separate courses.

MIKE PILAT, *Chairman, Climbing Committee*

AAC BOOKS

THE AMERICAN ALPINE JOURNAL, annually from 1929, illustrated. Many back issues still available, as well as indices for many volumes.

THE AMERICAN ALPINE JOURNAL INDEX 1929-1976, edited by Earlyn Church. A cumulative index covering the first fifty issues of The American Alpine Journal.

ACCIDENTS IN NORTH AMERICAN MOUNTAINEERING, published every June since 1948 by the AAC Safety Committee. Accounts of mountaineering accidents with an analysis of each. Many back issues available.

THE INTERIOR RANGES OF BRITISH COLUMBIA—SOUTH, by William L. Putnam and Robert Kruszyna. A complete revision of the portion of the 1971 edition covering the northern and southern Purcells. Index, appendix of passes, maps, photos. Sixth edition.

THE ROCKY MOUNTAINS OF CANADA—SOUTH, by Glen W. Boles with Robert Kruszyna and William L. Putnam. Covers the range from the International Boundary northward to Howse Pass. Completely revised from the earlier editions by J. Monroe Thorington. Seventh edition.

TAHQUITZ AND SUICIDE ROCKS, by Chuck Wilts. A new edition of this popular guide. Includes many revisions and new material. Sixth edition.

CLIMBING ICE, by Yvon Chouinard. The definitive work on the art and craft of ice climbing. 192 pages, 16 pages color, 175 black and white photographs.

CLIMBING IN NORTH AMERICA, by Chris Jones. The first comprehensive history of mountaineering in North America. 360 pages, 200 illustrations.

THE GREAT GLACIER AND ITS HOUSE, by William Lowell Putnam. The story of the first center of alpinism in North America from 1885 to 1925. The first climbers' original accounts in their own words as taken from the Glacier House register and other sources have been woven into a colorful vignette of the railroad that took them, the house that sheltered them, and the mountains that attracted them. Many historical photographs published for the first time. 224 pages, 9 x 12, 166 duotone illustrations, cloth.

GOING HIGH: THE STORY OF MAN AND ALTITUDE, by Charles S. Houston, M.D. A comprehensive history and analysis of the effects of high altitude. Written in non-technical language. 224 pages, 5½ x 8, illustrated, bibliography, appendix.

MOUNTAIN SICKNESS, by Peter H. Hackett, M.D. Prevention, recognition, and treatment of mountain sickness is discussed in this concise, handy guide. A must for high altitude climbers. Second printing 1983.

THE MOUNTAINS OF NORTH AMERICA, by Fred Beckey. A descriptive, historic and scenic odyssey among some of the greatest mountain regions on earth. Beautifully illustrated with 140 full-color photographs by 56 eminent photographers. 288 pages, 9 x 12, map, bibliography.

SHAWANGUNK ROCK CLIMBS, by Richard C. Williams. A new edition with many new route descriptions on The Trapps, Near Trapps, Sky Top and Millbrook Cliffs. 97 new photographs.

TOUCH THE SKY: THE NEEDLES IN THE BLACK HILLS OF SOUTH DAKOTA, by Paul Piana. An all-new work which includes a complete revision of the material in the 1971 guide by Bob Kamps. Descriptions of many routes. A great refresher for the veteran Needles climbers and a must for those making their first climbs in this unique area. 304 pages, 48 black and white photographs, maps, index, 8 area maps on 2 sheets. 1983.

TRAPROCK—ROCK CLIMBING IN CENTRAL CONNECTICUT, by Ken Nichols. More than 1300 route descriptions, many of them detailed in 129 pages of illustrations. Extensive history, geology, and other information on the area. 480 pages, 5 x 8, appendices, index, cloth.

A WALK IN THE SKY: Climbing Hidden Peak, by Nicholas Clinch. The account of the remarkable success of the small, casually organized expedition to Hidden Peak in 1958. This was the first American group to reach an 8000-meter summit. 208 pages, 6 x 9, 16 pages color photographs.

WHERE THE CLOUDS CAN GO, by Conrad Kain; edited with additional chapters by J. Monroe Thorington. Third edition of the classic autobiography of the internationally famous guide. 502 pages, 29 photographs. 1979.

YURAQ JANKA—THE CORDILLERAS BLANCA AND ROSKO, by John F. Ricker. An important book for anyone planning to climb in the areas covered. 224 pages, including 32 pages of black and white photographs, 2 folded maps. Second printing 1981.

In Production for 1983:

SURVIVING DENALI: A Study of Accidents on Mount McKinley, 1910–1982, by Jonathan Waterman. Discusses and analyzes the causes of the accidents with recommendations for prevention. Contains information on equipment, food and other essentials in planning an expedition to Mount McKinley.

THE RED ROCKS OF SOUTHERN NEVADA, by Joanne Urioste. A new guidebook to this popular area. Selected routes are well-illustrated with black and white photographs.

THE INTERIOR RANGES OF BRITISH COLUMBIA—NORTH, by Roger Laurilla and William L. Putnam. The first complete revision since 1971, with many new routes and all new photographs. Covers the Monashee and Cariboo ranges, and those portions of the Selkirk Range north of the Arrow Lakes. Illustrated. Seventh edition.

Prices and order forms upon request from The American Alpine Club, 113 East 90th Street, New York, N.Y. 10028.

SUPPORT THE AMERICAN ALPINE CLUB

Through its many programs in the public service, The American Alpine Club provides a national organization for the furtherance of American mountaineering. The Internal Revenue Service has classified The American Alpine Club as a nonprofit educational and scientific organization as defined in section 501(c)(3) of the Internal Revenue Code, and a public foundation as defined in section 509(a). All gifts to the Club are deductible to the limit of the law for Federal income tax purposes. Bequests are tax exempt without limitation. The Club is a registered charitable organization with the New York State Board of Social Welfare.

The Club represents the interests of climbers before United States and foreign governmental bodies to assist them in obtaining permission for both foreign and domestic climbing. It serves as a source of information on mountaineering activities in this country. It sponsors research and testing of climbing equipment and materials.

It maintains a large library for mountaineering research in New York, publishes climbing guidebooks and major mountaineering books. In addition, it publishes the annual *American Alpine Journal,* which is a major source of information on mountaineering activities in this country and throughout the world.

The Club also operates low-cost overnight facilities for climbers in the Grand Teton National Park to supplement those operated by the Park Service.

Gifts to the Club can be not only a source of personal satisfaction to the giver but also a lesser burden on the giver because of their tax deductibilty. All correspondence should be directed to the Treasurer, American Alpine Club, 113 East 90th Street, New York, New York 10028.

INDEX

Volume 25 ● Issue 57 ● 1983

Compiled by Patricia A. Fletcher

This issue comprises all of Volume 25

Mountains are listed by their official names and ranges; quotation marks indicate unofficial names. Ranges and geographic locations are also indexed. Unnamed peaks (e.g. Peak 2037) are listed following the range or country in which they are located.

All expedition members cited in major articles are included, whereas only the leaders and persons supplying information in the **Climbs and Expeditions** section are listed.

Titles of books reviewed in this issue are grouped as a single entry under **Book Reviews.**

Abbreviations used: Article: art.; Bibliography: bibl.; Obituary: obit.